PABLO ESCOBAR AND COLOMBIAN NARCOCULTURE

Reframing Media, Technology, and Culture in Latin/o America

PABLO ESCOBAR AND COLOMBIAN NARCOCULTURE

ALDONA BIALOWAS POBUTSKY

University of Florida Press

Gainesville

Production of this book was aided by a grant from the College of Arts and Sciences at Oakland University.

First cloth printing, 2020
First paperback printing, 2025

30   29   28   27   26   25   6   5   4   3   2   1

Library of Congress Cataloging-in-Publication Data
Names: Pobutsky, Aldona Bialowas, author.
Title: Pablo Escobar and Colombian narcoculture / Aldona Bialowas Pobutsky.
Other titles: Reframing Media, Technology, and Culture in Latin/o America. ·
Description: Gainesville : University of Florida Press, 2020. | Series:
   Reframing media, technology, and culture in Latin/o America | Includes
   bibliographical references and index.
Identifiers: LCCN 2019052093 (print) | LCCN 2019052094 (ebook) | ISBN
   9781683401513 (hardback) | ISBN 9781683401780 (pdf) | ISBN 9781683404866 (pbk.)
Subjects: LCSH: Escobar, Pablo. | Drug dealers—Colombia—Biography. | Drug
   traffic—Colombia—History—20th century.
Classification: LCC HV5805.E82 P63 2020 (print) | LCC HV5805.E82 (ebook)
   | DDC 364.1/3365092 [B]—dc23
LC record available at https://lccn.loc.gov/2019052093
LC ebook record available at https://lccn.loc.gov/2019052094

University of Florida Press
2046 NE Waldo Road
Suite 2100
Gainesville, FL 32609
http://upress.ufl.edu

UF PRESS

UNIVERSITY
OF FLORIDA

Contents

Figures

Acknowledgments

This project has been with me for almost a decade and has benefited from the insight and support of various people. Above all, I am indebted to my husband, John Eipper, who has graciously allowed my interest to take over our travel plans and, in many ways, our lives. His emotional support and willingness to listen and hash out many of the ideas that I had a hard time getting on paper have been a great help, and I cannot thank him enough. I am grateful for all the editing he has done on this book, his wide-ranging knowledge and intelligence, which made my project historically and factually grounded, and all the definite/indefinite articles he placed that I, growing up in the Polish language, still have a hard time mastering. I know that I would never have been able to complete this project in the way I did without his unwavering support and tireless work.

There are other people whose help and expertise have been invaluable. I am grateful to my sister Justyna Bialowas, whose expertise in marketing, acute intellect, and advice on the subject of branding gave a unique cohesion to my dispersed ideas. My colleague Daniel Lorca's knowledge of postmodernism, his enthusiasm and willingness to teach me theory through his grounding in philosophy, and his ability to make difficult points accessible made me very comfortable with my theoretical framework. Seth Howes, whose willingness to read parts of my project and reframe it to make it better, was of great help. I also would like to thank Óscar Osorio, who has cheered me on from Cali, Colombia, by sending me all the recent books published on the subject of Colombian narco (including his own incredibly valuable writings), by responding to all my inquiries regardless of his own time constraints, and by being a really good friend and mentor on things narco. I would like to thank Howard Campbell, who read my manuscript and gave me moral and intellectual support at a time when I felt my project would not move forward. Special thanks also go to Sabrina Laroussi, who invited me to give a talk at Virginia Military Institute on the subject of my book. This opportunity inspired me to synthesize my ideas and bring this project to fruition.

The people at the University of Florida Press have been a sheer delight. Héctor Fernández L'Hoeste, one of the editors of the series Reframing Media, Technology, and Culture in Latin/o America, is among the most careful and thoughtful readers I have ever encountered. My book has benefited greatly from his advice. I will be forever grateful for his enthusiasm and faith in my project. The other three readers, Juan Carlos Rodríguez (also editor of the series), Ryan Rashotte, and Juan Carlos Ramírez-Pimienta, provided excellent points and suggestions as to how to tighten and improve my argument. My editor, Stephanye Hunter, shepherded the book through the editorial process with sensitivity and grace. I am grateful for her belief in my project and for her guidance through the entire process. I also would like to extend my gratitude to the rest of the production and marketing staff at the University of Florida Press. Finally, I would like to thank the Research Office and the College of Arts and Sciences at Oakland University, my home institution, for their assistance with the production costs of this book.

Introduction

Escobar was a serious bandido. A bandido's bandido.
[Escobar era un bandido serio. Un bandido muy bandido.]

Germán Caycedo Castro, Operación Pablo Escobar, 75

He became a legend who controlled everything from the shadows. . . . At the height of his splendor, people put up altars with his picture and lit candles to him in the slums of Medellín. It was believed he could perform miracles. No Colombian in history ever possessed or exercised a talent like his for shaping public opinion. And none had a greater power to corrupt.

Gabriel García Márquez, News of a Kidnapping, 181

In June 2009, a photograph featuring a slain hippopotamus surrounded by a team of gloating hunters circulated in the Colombian press, stirring discontent and generating debates on animal rights and beyond. This indignation was triggered by the fate of the exotic beast, whose only transgression was to be out of place, a species foreign to yet thriving in Colombia. The hippo had committed the fatal error of leaving the relative safety of Hacienda Nápoles, his birthplace, following a clash with the herd's dominant male. Outrage was not the only emotion awakened by the event; nor was Pepe, the slain creature, just an ordinary hippo. The animal was part of an ostentatious project of Pablo Escobar, who in his heyday circumvented international regulations restricting the commerce of exotic animals to populate his ranch, Noah-like, with flora and fauna from the four corners of the globe.

Many creatures from Escobar's menagerie of zebras, giraffes, kangaroos, and rhinoceroses would not survive; the luckier few were transferred

2 · Pablo Escobar and Colombian Narcoculture

to zoos, but after the drug baron's death, the four original hippopotamuses remained at Hacienda Nápoles, where they flourished in the river Magdalena and the estate's artificial lakes. They also multiplied, setting off concerns about public safety at the national level, fears somewhat mitigated by the animals' attachment to the enormous estate and a lack of proof of their belligerence. By then Hacienda Nápoles, converted to a bizarre theme park, was attracting more than fifty thousand visitors a year. Yet unluckily for Pepe, once he and his mate, Matilda, moved away from their now touristy home and had offspring, thereby feeding fears of ecological imbalance and an infestation of Colombian waters with dangerous African behemoths, his fate played out with strange parallelisms to that of his notorious former master, grabbing the nation's attention and illustrating how engrained Pablo Escobar has remained in Colombia's consciousness years after his demise.[1]

When the kingpin of the Medellín Cartel died in a 1993 raid, Colombians sighed with relief. The last decade of his life was marked by bombings, kidnappings, and executions that brought the country almost to a standstill, causing the Colombian government, rival *narcotraficantes,* and the U.S. antidrug forces to unite in an effort to bring down the larger-than-life criminal. In the end, exploiting Escobar's attachment to his family, they traced the phone signal while he was talking with his son and found him almost unprotected in one of his multiple safe houses, in the middle-class neighborhood of Los Olivos, Medellín. He was gunned down in an operation immortalized by a series of unsettling photographs taken by a DEA agent, reminiscent of a hunting party, where the grinning executioners waved their guns in the background. Center stage is given to Escobar's bloated and undignified cadaver, with blood spilling onto the roof tiles, his paunchy stomach sticking out from a too-small shirt. In this photograph, Escobar, like the hippo, was a wild beast taken down by a team of jubilant huntsmen, who probably sensed that it would be the most important photograph of their lives.[2]

After all, by 1993, Escobar was already a legend. Dead or alive, he would reign in Colombia's dark folklore as an infamous antihero and international success story, recognized at one point by *Forbes* magazine as one of the ten richest men in the world. Escobar was the bandit of bandits in Germán Caycedo's assessment, and for Gabriel García Márquez, he was a magician or saint who could sway public opinion like no one before. The endless testimonies on his life, his ruthless cunning, and the audacity with which he defied the state while trumpeting his respect for religion and tradition make it hard to tell the story of Colombian drug trafficking, or the nation's history in general, without constantly referencing Escobar. What his killers could not imagine was that Escobar's legacy would change Colombian cultural production in print and on the screen for years to come, prompting the creation of a multimedial *narcocultura* and replicating the narco lifestyle in television, literature, music, architecture, language, fashion, the female beauty ideal, and social rituals, including those associated with death. *Narcocultura* came to represent a new way of life in the media-saturated world, a complex, hybrid social identity that embedded itself firmly through a slew of flamboyant characters.[3] Replete with drug lords, small-scale *traquetos* (*narcotraficantes* who move cocaine in tens of kilos rather than tons), *sicarios* (young assassins for hire), cocaine mules (individual transporters), *prepagos* (high-end prostitutes), and silicone-enhanced trophy women, it would become a defining feature of the nation's media landscape. Its discharges of violence, obsession with capital accumulation, and parvenu gaudiness—a mixture of Hollywood kitsch, Miami ostentation, Tex-Mex bravado, and local tastes—captured global audiences, tapping into present-day preoccupations with mass commodities, excess, and instant gratification.

Likewise, Escobar himself, albeit in every version imaginable, would sashay into the culture industry either to serve as a contextual backdrop or to occupy the center stage. His notoriety, adroit business acumen, rags-to-riches narrative, lawlessness, and terrorism against the Colombian state are an intriguing story that invited multiple interpretations and reproductions, leading to his instant recognition as an icon of bravado and evil. "Pablo Escobar-ness," as Colombia's prominent weekly *Semana* phrased it, has proven to be a particularly controversial subject to grapple with, divisive and still difficult to assess because "nobody agrees about the true breadth of his legacy—nor about the impact of his image—now mythicized because of a death that is increasingly distant and blurry" ("Pablo Escobar Refuses"). The Medellín capo has endured in the thug culture of ostentation, the exaggerated kitsch of narco fashion, the language of the *comunas*,[4] and in tales of antiheroes and good versus evil. Nowadays, narco stories in print and screen, fictitious or based on facts, unveil volatile worlds of drug lords who, through wealth and violence, get the flashiest women and properties only to lose them rapidly to another, even more brutal opponent.

The narco trend has spawned a wide variety of material for disparate tastes. While the bulk of these products underpin capitalist ideology, some also lay claim to a socially beneficial message, and others promise to reveal the long-hidden truth about the past by disclosing sensational information that would understandably elicit curiosity. As Alfredo Serrano, the man behind the 2012 documentary series *Las víctimas de Pablo Escobar*, assures, Escobar has never really died, for the tentacles of his corruption remain embedded in Congress, in the nation's justice system, and in how various presidencies were formed and sustained (Ángel). Serrano's production aims to undermine Escobar's social bandit reputation, by disclosing the suffering the capo inflicted on the nation as a whole. It goes to the core of the devastation caused by Escobar by foregrounding the reactions of husbands, wives, parents, and children of Escobar's countless victims, people who choke up in front of the camera, as if the tragedy that ravaged their lives two decades ago had just taken place.[5] Similarly, the 2016 RCN Televisión series *Bloque de Búsqueda* tells the story of General Hugo Martínez Poveda in the fictionalized character Colonel Hernán Martín (played by Rafael Novoa) and of Colonel Hugo Aguilar as Captain Antonio Gavilán (played by Sebastián Martínez), the men who headed the elite police corps charged with tracking down and killing the capo. Here, Escobar is but a shadowy figure looming over good citizens who want to free Colombia from narco corruption. The center stage is given at all times to the upstanding warriors for justice and to their innocent families who are ever threatened and subjected to Escobar's fury.[6] An online project titled Narcotour was created in 2017 by Mauricio Builes, former press director of the Colombian Center for Historical Memory, and his journalism students. The idea of a virtual exploration of Escobar's banditry through the eyes of his many victims came to life as a reaction to the growing popularity of the capo among tourists who flock to Medellín and Colombia in search of sensationalism. Understandably, the pain caused by Escobar persists. At the same time, the Colombian book market has witnessed an upsurge of narco-themed memoirs written by Escobar's family members and crime associates, by his celebrity lover who opens up about their affair, by other drug traffickers who offer from prison their versions of the Cali and the North Valley Cartels, by members of the police force who dealt with the criminals firsthand, or by a go-between, Madame Rochy, who claims to have procured the most desirable Colombian women for her wealthy criminal clients.

Treatments of the history of drug trafficking and its key players remain divided. While many pundits decry Escobar's recent popularity in
the media, others consider him such an elephant in the room that *not*
contextualizing national history within the trauma of the capo's legacy
delivers at best a half-truth. For Colombian film and media critic Omar
Rincón, Escobar became the national symbol, whether Colombians like
it or not. Fond of provocative opinions, Rincón argues that "it needs to
be accepted that he [Escobar] is one of our national heroes and that he
forms part of our history. Just as Germany had Hitler, our fate was to have
Escobar as an emblematic figure" (L. López) [es un aceptar que es uno
de nuestros héroes nacionales y que hace parte de nuestra historia. Así
como Alemania tuvo a Hitler, a nosotros nos tocó a Pablo Escobar como
la figura emblemática (my translation)]. Similarly, soon after the capo's
death, *Semana* pondered over his effect on Colombia, showing a passion
that merits quotation at length:

> [Escobar] essentially did not allow three consecutive presidents to
> govern . . . he transformed the language, culture, physiognomy and
> economy of Medellín and the country in general. Before Pablo Es-
> cobar, Colombians didn't know the meaning of the word *sicario*.
> Before Escobar, Medellín was thought of as a paradise. Before Pablo
> Escobar, the world knew Colombia as the land of coffee. And be-
> fore Pablo Escobar, no one would think that in Colombia a bomb
> could explode in a supermarket or an airplane in mid-air. Because
> of Pablo Escobar, there are armored cars in Colombia, and the se-
> curity demands have modified architecture. And because of him,
> the workings of the judicial system have changed, criminal justice
> has been reassessed to include prison design, and the Armed Forces
> have transformed. . . . Taking into account that the primary reason
> for creating someone like him—a colossal demand for cocaine in
> the world—is still there, the question remains: is it possible that the
> phenomenon of Pablo Escobar could repeat itself? One can say that
> undoubtedly other capos will emerge. But one can also say that no
> one will be like Pablo Escobar. ("Fin de una tragedia")

> [(Escobar) prácticamente no dejó gobernar a tres Presidentes segui-
> dos . . . transformó el lenguaje, la cultura, la fisonomía y la economía
> de Medellín y del país. Antes de Pablo Escobar, los colombianos
> desconocían la palabra *sicario*. Antes de Pablo Escobar Medellín

era considerada un paraíso. Antes de Pablo Escobar el mundo co-nocía a Colombia como la tierra del café. Y antes de Pablo Escobar nadie pensaba que en Colombia pudiera explotar una bomba en un supermercado o en un avión en vuelo. Por cuenta de Pablo Es-cobar hay hoy carros blindados en Colombia, y las necesidades de seguridad modificaron la arquitectura. Por cuenta de él, se cambió el tiempo de funcionamiento del sistema judicial, se replanteó la política penitenciaria y hasta el diseño de las prisiones, y se trans-formaron las Fuerzas Armadas . . . Teniendo en cuenta que la causa primero que permitió el surgimiento de alguien como él—la desco-munal demanda por cocaína en el mundo—sigue ahí, queda flo-tando un gran interrogante: ¿es posible que se repita el fenómeno de Pablo Escobar? Se puede decir que sin duda surgirán otros capos. Pero también se puede decir que no habrá otro como Pablo Escobar. (my translation)]

Singled out or lurking in the shadow, Escobar persists as the defining feature of Colombia's encounter with drugs. Adorning tourist souvenirs in Colombian outdoor markets and featured alongside Al Pacino's Tony Montana and *Breaking Bad's* Walter White on T-shirts available in Ameri-can beach resorts, he sells defiance and cojones to global consumers who like tough-guy aesthetics. A reflection of the cultural logic of late capital-ism, Escobar has grown to symbolize all the flashy Colombian traffick-ers put together, resistance and revolution, narco hedonism, as well as global and local tensions regarding vice, violence, and guilt.[7] Commodi-fied, mass-produced, and circulated in the infotainment society, Escobar has become a brand, transformed into his own image, much like Fredric Jameson's assessment of Marilyn Monroe and Elvis frozen in Andy War-hol's two-dimensional pop lens.

From Cocaine Flow to *Narcocultura*

Of course, Pablo Escobar as a household name did not occur in a cul-tural vacuum. Rather, he emerged within the larger context of *narco-cultura*, a multimedial, multigenre, indeed, multimodal discourse born out of concrete historical circumstances concerning the global cocaine economy. That cultural production on *narco* is a direct result of living

Left: Figure 1. T-shirts featuring Escobar's image (both real-life and Wagner Moura's television version), Rehoboth Beach, Delaware, 2018. Photo by author.

Below: Figure 2. Portraits of Escobar next to reproductions of Frida Kahlo, Bogotá, 2018. Photo by author.

and breathing the effects of cocaine trafficking is a common truth. Less known are the facts that coca/cocaine as a commodity circulated globally as early as the mid-1800s and that Colombians were not at all its leading entrepreneurs. As an illicit sphere—because Cold War politics after World War II criminalized the product—trafficking in cocaine sprang up across Chile, Cuba, Brazil, Bolivia, and Argentina from 1947 to the 1970s. Much earlier though, before cocaine's prohibition, it was Peruvians and Bolivians (mainly as producers), as well as the Swiss, Germans, Japanese, Americans, and the Dutch who developed the commodity, all the while raking in the profits.

Paul Gootenberg's 2008 *Andean Cocaine: The Making of a Global Drug* puts the discussion into a transnational perspective by tracing the historical links among the main stakeholders in the story of how cocaine, a commodity derived from the Andean coca leaf, the divine plant of the Incas, expanded and retracted on the global stage. Perhaps the most interesting aspect is the shifting trajectory of the coca/cocaine commodity and the way it readily adjusted to global shifts and popular tastes within a single century. Briefly put, it went from a party enhancer in Europe, to an acclaimed breakthrough in medicine (thanks to its anesthetic properties) and key ingredient in drinks, to a forbidden substance. Gootenberg points out that the demonized image of cocaine nowadays associated "with hyperviolent drug lords, atavistically clad in a veritably medieval (i.e. premarket) discourse about crusades of good against evil" (320) is a relatively new position on drugs, as is the so-called war on drugs that has complicated inter-American relations in a number of ways.

Originally, the coca leaf constituted an integral part of the Andean indigenous culture, who valued the plant as a hunger and stress suppressor, a mild stimulant, and a cure for the symptoms of altitude sickness (*soroche*). It was also applied in ritual acts (cleansing, fortune-telling) and commonly exchanged as a coveted good. Yet unlike other Latin American stimulants such as sugar, cocoa, and tobacco, coca for centuries did not enter the global circulation of commodities, being viewed instead as an indigenous vice associated with unsanitary mastication and witchcraft. Nor did it travel well, as the leaves would grow stale by the time ships reached Europe. Thus, while the Andean region had witnessed an upsurge of coca consumption by 1600, because the indigenous workers exploited in the mines used it to ward off hunger and exhaustion, the rest of the world knew next to nothing about its claimed properties. By the 1800s, however, coca had begun to attract curiosity among world botanists. A breakthrough in cocaine production was developed in Peru between 1884 and 1887 by the pharmacist Alfredo Bignon, who with the use of inexpensive and accessible materials (kerosene, soda ash, and lime) produced a "crude cocaine, or *cocaína bruta*" (Gootenberg 39). This product replaced the required tons of coca leaves and facilitated its export. The Bignon method attracted the attention of pharmaceutical companies across the globe, whose adoption of cocaine turned them into multinational corporations, and led to the development of a mass market for cocaine in Europe and the United States. For a while, cocaine was praised for its curative qualities and added to a variety of medicines and tonics. From the coveted world commodity between 1850 and 1900 (when the celebrated American health drink Coca-Cola depended on Peruvian imports), it grew into a prestigious national industry in Peru and the nation's dynamic export product.

Yet the social and legal acceptance of cocaine had declined sharply by 1910. By 1950, anti-cocaine laws and campaigns spread like wildfire across the world, largely due to U.S. politics, which turned 180 degrees from its initial excitement. The United States created new bureaucracies to combat illegal narcotics and coerced Peru into outlawing cocaine in 1949. Gootenberg applies the concept of commodity chains to connect metropoles with peripheries and to illustrate how actions in one domain affected other spheres. A prohibition regime emanating from the core—the United States—was "absorbed and accepted by actors and institutions on the political [read: Latin American] periphery" (189).

The encroaching world cocaine prohibitions brought to life a new breed of illicit Andean entrepreneurs, from cocaine clans in Chile (such as the Huasaff-Harb family) and Cuban middlemen with laboratories in Central America and markets in New York to Argentine and Brazilian mafiosos who trafficked across the Amazon. Colombia, in contrast, entered the illicit cocaine market relatively late—in the 1970s—but its incursion was precipitous and ripe with consequences for both its own people and the entire world. Gootenberg's perplexity over Colombia's sudden hegemony in cocaine trafficking is worth citing. While the author's research indicates that, contrary to some historians, it was anyone but Colombians participating in the illegal business until the 1970s, he suspects that the media coverage steered the popular opinion into permanently associating Colombia with cocaine and vice versa:

One of the great historical mysteries about modern cocaine trafficking is how it finally passed into the hands of the now-infamous
Colombian drug lords of the 1980s and changed, through their expansive business practices, into one of history's richest and most
volatile trades. Drugs in Colombia have attracted an endless stream
of journalism, sensationalism, and drug war mythology—producing, among other things, the misleadingly centralized and nonmar-
ket concept of "cartel" itself. (301)

Of course, there were plenty of reasons Colombians, and particularly
paisas, the inhabitants of the Antioquia/Medellín region, quickly took
up trafficking in cocaine: their well-known penchant for commerce, the
decline of the textile industry in Medellín, and the subsequent economic
recession, which increased interest in illicit economies and produced
waves of immigration to the United States. No less significant were the
preexisting "regional smuggling traditions that dated back to nineteenth-
century mining activities, and that continued through the smuggling of
cigarettes, liquor and stereos from the United States and Panama, as well
as marijuana trafficking" (Riaño-Alcalá 44). The ruthless Violencia period
of the 1950s weakened the Colombian state, thereby allowing a dynamic
growth of local enterprises across the nation's diverse regions. As early as
the 1950s, the elite Antioquian Herrán Olózaga family, owners of a chain
of pharmacies, would engage in drug trafficking right under the nose
of the Ministry of Health. By the 1970s, various cocaine traffickers, such as
Benjamin Herrera Zuleta, "El Papa Negro de la cocaína," worked together
with their prominent Chilean counterparts to strengthen production
and trafficking routes between Perú, Bolivia, and the United States
(Baquero 24). Chile's military coup of September 11, 1973, stalled the well-
established cocaine routing through that nation, because the military ex-
pelled the country's traffickers, suspecting them of financing the Leftist
opposition, and thus Colombians stepped into the vacuum.[8] The same
process occurred soon in Argentina, making Colombia the logical place to
pick up and amplify the preexisting Andean coca capitalism. Last but not
least, large numbers of *paisas* (and other Colombian nationals) were mi-
grating to the United States between 1965 and 1975, thereby supplying Escobar and other drug lords with a "ready-made international distribution
network for their increasingly lucrative commodity" (Roldán, "Colombia"
167). So, on the one hand, both economic and political circumstances in

the Southern Hemisphere were ripe for a Colombian takeover. On the other, it was also the ingenuity of the new figures of Colombian drug lore and their unprecedented brutality that pushed out established competitors, giving way to an "enforced sales oligopoly in the United States" (Gootenberg 306). A great part of the so-called Cocaine Wars of the 1970s and 1980s that took place in Colombia and the United States consolidated the control of Colombians over the South-North cocaine markets and routes, thereby replacing smugglers from other nations (Baquero 20). Colombian drug lords from Cali, Bogotá, and Medellín outrivaled other players by shoring up the existing Andean cocaine capitalism, refining *pasta básica*, and outgunning the Cuban competition, often in ways that would radically transform American cities. Miami quickly shed its image as a retiree haven to become a new Wild West. This Colombian diaspora soon became the foundation for future cocaine networking on the route between South and North. Certainly, cocaine activities threw Colombia into a turmoil of violence as well, affecting everyone, from the humblest peasants to the highest elites.

The rapid transformation of Colombian society under the narco economy has been amply addressed by the nation's cultural commentators—writers, journalists, sociologists, and film and telenovela producers. While the major television networks in Colombia today systematically promote narcocultural products, and both the small and the big screens feature Escobar transnationally with series and films such as Netflix's *Narcos* (2015–2016), *Escobar: Paradise Lost* (2014), *The Infiltrator* (2016), *American Made* (2017), or *Loving Pablo* (2017), the phenomenon did not go unnoticed much earlier. As Óscar Osorio documents in *La novela del narcotráfico en Colombia* (2014), both the stories that addressed narco reality directly and those that touched on it tangentially appeared as early as the 1970s. The 1978 novel *El cadáver de papá* by Jaime Manrique Ardila and the 1986 *El Divino* by Gustavo Álvarez Gardeazábal addressed the issue head-on, while Hernán Hoyos's 1977 *Coca: Novela de la mafia criolla* and Juan Gossaín's 1981 *La mala hierba* enticed their readers with the backdrop of new narco reality (Osorio, *La novela* 24–25).[9]

Yet it was the early 1990s when Víctor Gaviria, Alonso Salazar, and Fernando Vallejo drew attention both nationally and abroad to a new malady that was altering the social fabric of Colombia's lower classes and destroying its underprivileged youth. Their respective contributions, specifically the film *Rodrigo D: No futuro* (1990), and the books *No nacimos pa' semilla* (1990), translated as *Born to Die in Medellín*, and *Our Lady of the Assassins* (published in Spanish as *La virgen de los sicarios* in 1994, and translated into English by Paul Hammond), stirred interest and sparked academic discussions with their portrayal of an idiosyncratic world of young Medellín hitmen whose violent lives were molded and curtailed by the drug wars. Vallejo's *Our Lady* centered on fictional adolescent killers for hire, yet the occasional mention of a certain Don Pablo and a priest who participated in Don Pablo's surrender were clear references to Escobar's dealing with Father Rafael García Herreros, the founder of the television program *Minuto de Dios*. Salazar's *Born to Die in Medellín*, on the other hand, approached the *sicario* subculture from the ethnographic standpoint, as a local identity seeking definition against, but also in dialogue with, Western "hegemonic" cultures. Trapped in the peripheral and underdeveloped urban areas of developing states, Medellín's hitmen elevated their narco bosses to celebrity status because these individuals triumphed financially and thus could enjoy pleasures previously limited to the elites. Eager to follow this example, young toughs would trade their lives for a brief fling with a global consumerism that otherwise was out of reach—a pair of Nikes or a refrigerator as payment for a hit. Their hybrid subculture boasted a unique slang, peculiar death rites, and a whole set of bizarre values, where life—theirs and those of their victims—took the form of a commodity. Though written independently of Vallejo's novel, Salazar's work provided a rich sociocultural context to the fictional tale, proving that life affected by global drug trafficking can indeed be stranger than fiction. These were undoubtedly the most renowned early accounts devoted to the narco reality in Colombia.[10]

The following years saw a flurry of books, films, and academic research devoted to the narco world in general, while in the 2000s, narco-themed stories exploded in the sensationalist writing and outpouring of audiovisual production targeted to a broader public. Telenovelas, commonly understood as a showcase for bourgeois society that mitigates the unfulfilled material aspirations of its audience while endorsing extreme consumerism, found their perfect model in the narco nouveau riche, thereby taking the topic of drug trafficking into Latin America's prime time. Stories relating in some way to the drug trafficking world, the more intimate the better, have proven to be a sure-fire commercial success, often blossoming into a multifaceted merchandising campaign, where a feature film followed a book release and after that came a telenovela, as was the case with

Jorge Franco's 1999 *Rosario Tijeras*. There were also instances where a television series and its book version appeared simultaneously, as happened with the 2008 *El cartel de los sapos* and the 2009 *Las fantásticas* and *Las muñecas de la mafia*, all written by Andrés López López, an *ex-traficante* from the North Valley Cartel, whose photos by 2010 were appearing in the Miami society pages.

Television, the principal purveyor of popular culture, was hardly lagging in this rush to commercialize the trend. Narco telenovelas from *La viuda de la mafia* (2004), *Sin tetas no hay paraíso* (2006), *Cartel de los sapos* (2008), *El Capo* (2009), and *Las muñecas de la mafia* (2009 and 2018) to *Rosario Tijeras* (2010), *Correo de inocentes* (2012), *Escobar, el patrón del mal* (2012), *Alias el Mexicano* (2013), *La viuda negra* (2014), *Sin senos sí hay paraíso* (2016), *Bloque de Búsqueda* (2016), and *Alias J. J.* (2017) revisit the 1980s and 1990s to entertain with sex, violence, and an intense dramatization of the deterioration of Colombia's social fabric. Some argue that their purpose is to send a message to younger viewers on how crime never pays in the end. With the highest budget ever for a Colombian TV series, *Escobar, el patrón del mal* stood out from the rest of telenovelas. It weaved in documentary footage of the narco mayhem next to fictionalized encounters between real-life representatives of good and evil, thereby creating a national epic with Escobar as its main point of reference. With a script written by the descendants of two of Escobar's well-known victims, Guillermo Cano and Maruja Pachón, the series proposes to illustrate both sides of the conflict. Of course, writing about Escobar remains a risky endeavor; the very idea of a bandit appeals to the masses in how he defies the hierarchy of wealth and power, only to eventually exert influence and become part of the establishment (Hobsbawm 95). Another, even more obvious truth is that his cruel patrimony remains fresh in the minds of those who would rather erase him from the national memory altogether, thereby relegating the stigma of narco Colombia to oblivion.

Theorizing Narco

The sheer volume and variety of narco-themed products makes defining *narcocultura* a daunting task. Indeed, Hermann Herlinghaus notes that narco-narratives "stand for an array of interwoven phenomena whose increasing presence across the hemisphere seems to correspond to the difficulty in providing a general description of them" (51). The author points out the key changes in the imaginary and epistemological approaches in narco-narratives from the 1970s on, where the self-intoxication of the (privileged) literary/artistic subject of yesteryear (Thomas De Quincey or Charles Baudelaire) gave way to an overwhelming sense of skepticism and weariness when it comes to living the effects of the drug-fueled economy. Granted, earlier texts originated in the Hemispheric North, while the post-1970s narco-narratives emerged predominantly from the Global South. The vantage point of the latter is a bitter reaction to the widely held belief that the Global North has simultaneously been practicing: an orgiastic drug consumption and a puritanical rejection of the same, as evinced in how the "War on Drugs" is waged. After all, as Herlinghaus points out, "globalization has not only to do with the unequal distribution of wealth and poverty but also of these psychopathological stimuli and repressants that serve the 'achievements' of Western civilization" (52). The notorious drug trade adversely pervades the politics and the relationship between the North and some Latin American nations, which not only live day-to-day narco violence but also carry the stigma of narco contaminator.

In an attempt to define *narcocultura* as a whole, one could view it broadly as a complex negotiation of drug trafficking throughout the world's topography, history, and narrative possibilities in literature, television, music, architecture, language, fashion, and varied social practices. As such, it is open to wide-ranging interpretations, whether anthropological, ethnographic, sociological, literary, or in the media. Of course, Colombia was, and is, not the only country to have witnessed *narcocultura's* ascendance in the past thirty years; like the actual drug war and real trafficking networks that are its "raw material," *narcocultura* is fundamentally defined by transnationality: by the transgression of political, economic, linguistic, and cultural borders. Thus, when Herlinghaus writes that "narcotics . . . have moved to the center of ever accelerating consumerism and growing psychotropic saturation, without which contemporary lifestyles and cosmopolitan subject positions would be virtually unimaginable" (7) and aims to explain how the thematization of renunciation and excess necessarily links the West with its Other, the Global South, he turns not to Mexican or Colombian experiences, or even to American or German ones, but rather to "new, *transnational* epics of sobriety" (29, my emphasis).

Situated at the conjunction of crime and popular entertainment, *narcocultura* offers a highly variegated, stylized set of representations that permit Colombian cultural consumers, much like cultural consumers anywhere else, to recognize and mediate their own experience. Aside from its acclaimed literary and cinematic triumphs, *narcocultura* also comprises a host of pop-cultural encounters with drug trafficking's dark patrimony, stories that diverge sharply from the dry economic, political, and sociological debates of academics and political elites. Indeed, *narcocultura* is obsessed with affording popular audiences insights into the "real lives" of kingpins and queenpins—such as Escobar himself and his predecessor, Griselda Blanco—and of various hitmen or family members who insist on their version of the "truth." No less central a topic are the infamous narcos' and narcas' many erstwhile liaisons, such as trophy lover Virginia Vallejo or Griselda Blanco's African American employee and boy toy, Charles Cosby. By analyzing these figures' media presence, we can trace the impact that narco best-sellers and real-life drug traffickers have had on pop iconography and explore how *narcocultura*, in its turn, has both served hegemonic ideologies and questioned official narratives.

Be they mass-market memoirs of Escobar's friends and family, biographies of other drug traffickers, narco telenovelas, best-selling fiction, and both mainstream and yellow-press journalism—each text considered in this book contributes differently to the evolution of *narcocultura*, adding its own generic, thematic, and allusive qualities even as they all clearly resist the narratorial modes of performing objectivity and maintaining critical distance from their subject matter. Indeed, the bulk of the material emphasizes storytelling over facts, incorporates voices typically excluded from the "serious" news, and panders to emotions, voicing controversies and struggles over historicity.

Commonly classified as "middlebrow" or "lowbrow" material, many of these accounts trade in "popular" mythology as opposed to "official" history, inviting the dismissal or scorn of the cultural elites. Accordingly, the bulk of the material discussed here has received little to no scholarly consideration. But it is precisely here, in this material—by contrast with academic treatises, professional histories, and literary pieces—that we will gain access to Colombians' (and other Latin Americans') most common site(s) of encounter with the drug wars and their cultural legacies. Sales figures are not everything, but the record-setting, eye-popping viewership numbers associated with the *Sin tetas no hay paraíso* and *Rosario Tijeras* franchises say something very concrete about the pervasiveness, even the omnipresence, of *narcocultura* in the lives of ordinary Colombians. Farmer and urbanite, churchgoer and agnostic, day laborer and salaried professional—they inform themselves not with economists' white papers and historians' tomes but rather with popular fiction, true-crime monographs, newspapers, and portable electronic devices streaming the latest telenovela to thematize the narcos and their excesses. To exclude pulp fiction, gossip columns, narco autobiographies, telenovelas, or bio-documentaries from an analysis of this kind, or to present these as mutually unintelligible or discursively disconnected from one another, would be entirely to misunderstand the nature of narco-narrativity's self-constitution-in-progress. These nonacademic and nonliterary registers shed light on how drug trafficking altered the way many people live, think, behave, dress, and talk.

The preponderance of the "culture of consumption" within popular narco accounts—a factor that constitutes the core social fabric of neoliberal societies—invites a postmodern approach to the examination of the narco phenomenon. Likewise, the postmodern condition is reflected in the social and cultural pluralism of *narcocultura* and in how previously unheard voices of various participants or "visitors" of the drug world offer testimonies that then are picked up by the media and brought to life as "intimate" versions. Historically, the rise of mass-mediated consumerist popular culture in the 1960s and 1970s brought about societal and cultural transitions where the cultural hierarchies of the high and low, and the hegemonic and the local, were deemed artificially created and thus no longer operative. Instead, mixed cultural hybrids appeared in a networked, globally connected culture. Skepticism toward normative and authoritative official culture extended itself to metanarratives of history and national identity as accepted before World War II, where the idea of progress turned into a failed master narrative. Together with the loss of clear generic boundaries came fragmentation, intertextuality, pastiche, and nostalgic stylizations of the past, justified under the presumption that official history—the master narrative par excellence—was but one of many narratives, sanctioned by the powers of the day. Similarly, the accounts fleshed out in this book address the criminals' humanity, thus challenging the master narratives on Escobar and his ilk. They also explore the superficial *narcocultura* and its hyper reality, as it rejuvenates premodern myths and folklore in what appears to be the social need to feel a connection to a more meaningful and authentic past. They do away with the high/low categories, shoring up the subjective and the local while never detaching fully from global trends. As Fredric Jameson states, "At the cultural level, globalization threatens the final extinction of local cultures, resuscitatable only in Disneyfied form, through the construction of artificial simulacra and the mere images of fantasized traditions and beliefs" ("Globalization"). Likewise, the narco lifestyle as seen in telenovelas reconstructs a bizarre amalgam of the premodern and the postmodern, of celebrated social bandits who proudly flaunt traditional beliefs and behaviors, all the while engaging in the rapacious consumption of people and objects.

Drug trafficking per se epitomizes multinational consumer capitalism, the latest stage of capitalism, as it expands around the globe and thus needs "a global cognitive mapping, on a social as well as spatial scale" (Jameson, *Postmodernism* 54). Postmodernism is a consumerist culture, as is the narco subject. Yet rather than focus on the economic aspects delineated here by Jameson, I propose to employ the postmodern characteristics that emerged from history, sociology, and media studies. Three concepts of particular importance are Jean Baudrillard's emphasis on the image, Jean-François Lyotard's rejection of metanarratives, and Lyotard's concept of the commodification of knowledge, inasmuch as it is valued for its utility (Lyotard). The move toward *petit récits* in lieu of a single grand narrative legitimized the boom of narco memoirs. At the same time, Colombian narco telenovelas began to parade caricatures lost in hyperbolic consumption, thus bearing witness to how the relationship between individuals and their culture is increasingly shallow and artificial. Social relations in the narco milieu are mediated by a procession of simulacra that morphs into a daily series of commodity exchanges. This condition echoes Baudrillard's concept of hyperreality, of the reign of style over substance, and of the media's constant reproduction of symbols and images.

In the process of postmodern commodification, *narcocultura* blurs the distinctions between brutal drug lords and celebrity icons. It is therefore noteworthy to examine the texts through the prism of celebrity studies, particularly focusing on the "Criminal Celebrity" or the diffuse pseudo-fame of "notoriety" that ideally "concentrate[s] on the extratextual aspect of performance, all the 'surround' of the performer that sometimes is in vital response to whatever text is present but just as often is in tension with it, contradicts it, or ignores it" (Braudy 2). Since the greater part of the material examined here proclaims to give the readers an uncensored, "off the record" insider perspective on the narco milieu, I will also incorporate tabloid studies, as they explore the symptomatic traces of the role of "the people" and their discredited popular tastes. Its readers become voyeurs to the spectacle of sensationalism, implicitly accepting that the focus on melodrama and mayhem may come at the expense of actual facts. Its subject matter, much like the matter of the tabloids defined by John Fiske, is the one "produced at the intersection between public and private life," where "its modality fluidity denies any stylistic difference between fiction and documentary, between news and entertainment" (48). It is associated with "trash taste," as it resists objectivity and critical distancing, blurring public and private life, fiction, and documentary (Glynn 7–9).

Furthermore, my interdisciplinary theoretical framework will engage cultural criminology, which prioritizes the biographical accounts of everyday life with more expansive and intimate descriptions in order to address the complexity of the story beyond the merely statistical. To this end, I also found useful the attention that New Historicists have paid to the nonacademic and nonliterary registers, as they argue that even the most seemingly trivial anecdotes can reveal the codes and strategies that govern society as a whole, because they reflect how elements of lived experience enter in cultural production—and how these in turn shape literary forms. My aim here is not to demote art or aestheticize an entire culture but to capture flows of emotive energies that illuminate cultural occurrences and narratives of everyday life. With this I agree with Catherine Gallagher and Stephen Greenblatt, who champion a broader scope of material:

> To wall off for aesthetic appreciation only a tiny portion of the expressive range of a culture is to diminish its individuality and to limit one's understanding even of that tiny portion, since its significance can be fully grasped only in relation to the other expressive possibilities with which it interacts and from which it differentiates itself. (13)

Finally, the subject of Escobar as a global cultural commodity goes beyond the areas of history, crime, and popular culture. To many people's horror, Escobar, whose life and persona are by now firmly anchored in not just Colombian but also universal consumer culture, has become a performer of a myth that can be sold and purchased—in short, a thriving brand. The treatment of identity as a brand is symptomatic of the influence of

neoliberal dynamics, which makes viewing the popularization of Escobar's image through marketing theory both relevant and illuminating. It
sheds light on the contradictions and high emotional stakes embedded
in the reception and propagation of Escobar's stories by exploring concepts such as neoliberal ethics based on entrepreneurship, cultural flat-
tening across the globe, the monetization of culture, hip consumerism,
the popularity of brands that denote rebellion and individuality, and the
authenticity of brands firmly attached to locale, thus providing a "genuine" experience. Consumer culture production attaches and proliferates
meanings based on patterns grown from consumption, and the expansion
of free markets across the countries has broadened neoliberal influence in
both culture and politics. The neoliberal economics of global distribution,
flexible systems of production, and high competitiveness continuously
shapes and modifies culture and social behavior, where unfettered free
market forces provide a guide for how to live (Harvey 2). How this neoliberal economy has affected the popularity of Escobar's image across the
globe, what it has done to Medellín, and what that city is doing to erase it
can be elucidated by exploring the brand's coercive power to proliferate,
to discipline selfhoods, and to sow meaning.

Viewing narco material through the prism of Pablo Escobar-ness affords a panoramic and intimate insight into Colombia's cultural and
commercial encounter with drug trafficking, such as the construction of
formulaic Escobar-related products. While it unveils what we could call
"an ordinary life" and everyday practices within the narco milieu, it also
probes tendencies in the construction of formulaic Escobar-related products and formulaic *narcocultura*. It explores Escobar's notoriety sign and
the values it intersects, such as consumerism, the exacerbated masculinity
and femininity embedded in narco gender relations, the spectacle of greed
and excess, and the commercialization of violence. It bears emphasizing
that, unlike other academic studies that approach the story of *narcocultura* either by drawing from renowned sources and "high" literature or by
focusing on the ethical ramifications of drug wars on real-life people, this
book reads a variety of popular registers surrounding Escobar and *narcocultura* in general, because these are precisely the sources—verifiable or
contrived—that contribute to the construction, circulation, and instant
recognition of Escobar's brand and Colombia's narco mythology. As Luis
Alejandro Astorga Almaza notes, albeit on the subject of Mexican narcos,
"the distance between real traffickers and their world and the symbolic

production that talks about them is so big, that there seems to be no other way, current and factual, than to refer to the subject via the discourse of myth, whose antipodes could be represented by legal discourse and narcocorridos" (12) [La distancia entre los traficantes reales y su mundo y la producción simbólica que habla de ellos es tan grande, que no parece haber otra forma, actual y factible, de referirse al tema sino de manera mitológica, cuyas antípodas estarían representadas por la codificación jurídica y los corridos de traficantes (my translation)].

This study draws upon both biographical and fictional sources to discuss the shifts from initial descriptions of narco fixtures to today's deluge of micronarratives, enhancements, and parodies, and it grounds them in a broader social and political context by integrating both archival research and narco pop from the mass market. It explores why, given that Escobar's tale has been told over and over, the public remains interested in seeing and reading more. This, I believe, is the story of *narcocultura* yet to be told. Always present at the background of this book is the premise that the Escobar in question is a social construct and that *how* he and his milieu are presented may be more interesting than *what* is being said. We learn how the culture industry produces and consumes violence on the screen, how it envisions sameness and the other, how it addresses the complexities of gender and sexuality, and how it retells narco history and the Escobar brand to new generations of consumers.

Pop art exposes the role of the image in reproducing capitalist culture, reducing identity and style to a hyper simulacrum without a stable or real referent. Likewise, narco media culture has grown precipitously to reveal the triumph of the spectacle of consumer society, with Escobar's image—and that of other real or fictitious drug lords by extension—frequently reduced to a stereotype. In part by sheer overexposure, Escobar has achieved a transnational consumer awareness and brand equity in a society dominated by a glut of visual images and global symbols. Brand as such is separable from the product or service narrowly viewed, in that it is a psychological entity with associations far outside the context of consumption. And it can appreciate without strategic direction, which in part is what happened with the historical figure of Escobar. Due to the persistent curiosity of the public when it comes to anything related to the Medellín capo, many cultural models were built from his formulae (more or less consciously) and modified to attract attention, in the process increasing his brand equity while simultaneously stepping away from the complexity of the real-life figure. I thus choose to place my journey through Colombia's narco popular culture under the umbrella of what I call the Escobar brand. At times, the stories in question are separated from his historical persona and viewed as a commercial product, at times they delve into the history of Colombia's drug trafficking and Escobar's life, including its most private aspects. They appear to retrace history, attesting not to their authenticity but to the subjectivity of the histories retold and the power invested in each discourse.

From focusing on consumer products at first, branding came to engulf places (cities, nations), people, and knowledge itself. Brand is a repository not merely of functional characteristics but of meaning and value infused with symbolism that, when utilized strategically, increases the potential for the success of a given product. A brand, above all, is a good story told to the consumer and also by the consumer, involving a collective authorship of companies, sales agents, and cultural institutions. People remember stories better than facts because stories produce emotions, and emotions help sell "an experience" that takes us out of our ordinary lives. A brand story becomes perceived as truth when it is successfully incorporated into the everyday lives of consumers, when it taps into society's higher values, and when it becomes an important resource for social interaction (McEnally and de Chernatony; Bengtsson and Firat 375). In other words, while an effective brand relates to the individual consumer on a personal level, it also addresses collective needs, thereby connecting communities of individuals. Never wholly static, the brand also knows how to readapt to the rapidly evolving consumer base in order to regenerate and thus remain in circulation.

For many specialists in marketing, a thriving brand is a performer of a myth. Consistent with this theory, Margaret Mark and Carol Pearson's *The Hero and the Outlaw* offers a systematic approach to building brands through the power of archetypes. Destined as a manual for marketing professionals, the book aims at strengthening brand communication and the "understanding of the impact of brand meaning on consumer psychology and on the collective consciousness of our times" (46). I propose to use Mark and Pearson as a lens to view the resonance of Pablo Escobar and *narcocultura* in general, since the authors focus on the relationship between human passions (both good and bad), sales, and brand recognizability. The manual lays out how archetypes provide the intangible link between customer motivation and product sales because they speak "directly to the deep psychic imprint with the consumer, sparking a sense of recognition and of meaning" (Mark and Pearson 14). Archetypes are the "'software' of the psyche" (32), always present in our lived experience of the world, universal to the core, but having a "valance" that changes with culture.

Studies of branding techniques frequently point out a recent shift: While in the past consumers wanted to belong and keep up with the crowd, today they strive to stand out (Gronlund 173). Mark and Pearson describe this change in terms of what they call "postmodern marketing," wherein old rules no longer hold. The new breed of consumer, skeptical of advertising hype, forgoes brand loyalty for independence and authenticity. Few if any sacred stories remain, due to the collapse of prior narrative truths, and the meaning that formerly lay in the group now is left for the individual to find. In short, "people are thrown back on their own devices" (Mark and Pearson 36). For literary critics, this is a marketing parallel of Lyotard's rejection of one grand narrative and the postmodern move toward swirling galaxies of *petit récits*.

In marketing, consumer distrust enhances the appeal of the Explorer archetype, who finds its narco counterpart in the figure of the Outlaw. The general pathway is similar; both Explorer and Outlaw principally seek freedom, but the Outlaw goes further by defying the status quo. The Outlaw acts as a disruptive force, moving to action and in the process violating cultural norms and rules. He thus uses the energy to mobilize in order to destroy. In terms of its effect on the customer, the Outlaw brand enjoys a conflicting and often highly controversial reputation that can "reinforce soulless, cynical behaviors when values are absent. But they can also . . . help open and ease social restrictions or serve as a safety valve that allows people to let off steam, thus protecting the status quo" (Mark and Pearson 127). In other words, on the positive side of the spectrum, the Outlaw can release society's pent-up passions, act as a catharsis to vent frustration, or siphon off oppressive behavior, for it "speaks to consumer's underlying fear . . . of allowing life to just happen to you—of being a victim or a wimp" (103). On the negative side, it is blamed for abetting sexism, violence, and antisocial behaviors (125). While the Explorer qualities correspond to the customers' fears of inner emptiness and entrapment, people drawn to the Outlaw express fear of becoming powerless, trivialized, and inconsequential.

Instructions on successful branding emphasize the importance of focusing on just one archetype as the defining characteristic of the product in order to reinforce familiarity and trust. Yet the primary archetype can be nuanced by other archetypes to broaden the target groups or address other aspects previously less in vogue. This is where the Escobar brand reveals its adaptability, in that the newer voices address different and more nuanced aspects of his story. The capo himself has morphed into a fragmented entity that represents different things to different people. In the official grand narrative of yesteryear, Escobar stood for—and rightly so—criminality, terrorism, and overall monstrousness. The *petit récits* emerging in the last two decades address his other facets as a fun-loving man (the archetypal Jester), a Lover, a daredevil (Explorer), protector of the poor and of his family (Caregiver, Hero), and a charismatic leader (Ruler). These nuances redress Escobar's notoriety and open up his subject to a broader target group. The entertainment factor should not be overlooked. Criminality, adventure, drama, and (ill-fated) romances generate a broad spectrum of entertainment products for today's public. Thus, in marketing terms, Escobar's shifting symbolism today reflects the dynamic re-adaptability of his brand.

In this book, I adopt a two-pronged approach to the Escobar brand, with the first section, "Performing Pablo," exploring the social discourses that address the capo directly, and the second, "Beyond Escobar," delving into the larger cultural phenomena influenced by his figure. The first three chapters focus on cases where the figure of Escobar, the proverbial Outlaw, is deconstructed either to contest his legend or, more frequently, to replace it with a counter-myth of Escobar as the classic Lover, Warrior, Caregiver, or Hero. Particular attention will be given to Escobar's family members and acquaintances who rearticulate his story in the media—often in a competing fashion—all the while inserting themselves into the ongoing debate on his private life and political alliances. Each such account attempts to negotiate the individual subject position of the storyteller, thus offering readers a more voyeuristic entry into the multifaceted and often opportunistic social and cultural alliances surrounding the capo's memory. The intimate take on the capo does not always serve individual interests, however, for the 2012 telenovela *Escobar, el patrón del mal* blends archival material with melodrama in order to topple his myth. Whether these efforts are successful is another matter, but nuancing

Escobar's masculinity through the tabloid discourse of a wimp and mama's boy does chip away at the edifice of his legend.

The other equally important concern of "Performing Pablo" is how today's popular cultural production on Escobar—from artifacts like T-shirts and paintings to narco telenovelas and Escobar-themed tours—blends history with nostalgia and retro styles, altering the past by overplaying the more conspicuous *narcotraficantes* (*El Capo*, *Cartel*, *Alias*) for the sake of dramatization and better sales. Popular culture favors the most colorful drug lords at the expense of the more discreet players, thereby feeding the audience with a hyperreality that not only suppresses less visible figureheads of the past but also, more importantly, ignores the present-day diffusion of narco power.

If the second part, "Beyond Escobar," steps away from a direct take on the capo, it certainly does not lose sight of him. This is because, as the book argues, Escobar is an integral, if not sadly unavoidable, element of anything narco in Colombia. Thus "Beyond Escobar" explores how the brand has affected his surroundings, spatially and conceptually, rearticulating his predecessors and labeling the smaller players of the narco milieu to eventually pigeonhole them into caricatures. The chapter on Griselda Blanco, the cocaine queen who preceded Escobar and whose illicit activities tangentially coincided with those of the capo, examines Blanco's cultural comeback, enhanced and even legitimated by the celebrity power of Escobar himself. That Blanco returned to the limelight both in print and in a telenovela, invariably referencing Escobar, attests to the capo's hold over the Colombian cultural imaginary.

Part 2 also re-creates the world the capo arguably brought into existence, meaning *traquetos*, *sicarios*, and *prepagos*, not to mention the celebrities and beauty pageant contestants who positioned themselves as narco trophy women. That this cultural reflection of deviant social phenomena may be exaggerated, stylized, or rife with tawdry sentimentalism does not remove the imperative to acknowledge and examine it. Thus, the real-life epidemic of underage killers and teenage prostitutes whose heightened activity coincided with the explosion of the drug trade in Colombia attests to deep social inequalities within a society that pushed its unprotected and destitute youth toward vice. While the entertainment sector indulges in parodic or overtly sentimental takes on young narco delinquents, the-ever-more-distant historical referent is grim. From child killers who, on Escobar's orders, took the life of the Justice Minister Rodrigo Lara Bonilla and killed more than one hundred passengers of the Avianca Flight 203 in 1989 to countless female victims caught up in Escobar's war on the state through their role as "sexual entertainers," youngsters of both sexes contributed to and lost their lives in the narco mayhem. Their cultural counterparts in the likes of Rosario Tijeras and her male acolytes, the boys from *Sin tetas*, or high school dropout *prepagos* from the same telenovela titillate the viewer with their dysfunctional upbringings, reckless spontaneity, and total lack of remorse. Their media representation is a hyperreality run amok, a reign of illusion and appearance, where a cursory treatment of grave social ailments can come across as a celebration of delinquency. From commercial through social and historical sources, this book reads how the Escobar brand affected the way people perceive Colombia, how Colombia perceives itself, and how narco-themed cultural products describe and renegotiate Colombia's past and present. My final thoughts, included in the epilogue, extend beyond Colombia, observing the trajectory of the Escobar brand as a global commodity, much like the nefarious product he sold.

PERFORMING PABLO

1

Pablo Escobar and Narco Nostalgia

As far as the history of narcotics, there wasn't any narcotic trafficker ever
that came close to what Pablo Escobar was. There had been many probably
that had tried and some that are trying in Mexico at the present time, but
Pablo Escobar was one in a million.

Joseph Toft, former director of the DEA in Colombia, *Los tiempos*

I live with permanent suspicion. I was born guilty. . . . My personal slogan
is: I inherited a mountain of shit. So, what am I supposed to do with it?

Sebastián Marroquín, Escobar's son, in Anderson, "The Afterlife of Pablo Escobar"

Hegel's owl of Minerva, we recall, first took wing at dusk. This is how the
timing of the narco fad worked in Colombia. Curiously, narco-themed
cultural production in and about Colombia coincided with the rise of
uncontrollable drug violence in northern Mexico and on the U.S.-Mex-
ico border.[1] Mounting civilian casualties, gruesome assassinations of
high-level politicians, journalists, and police officers, kidnappings, the
corruption of Mexican government and law enforcement officials, and
other trappings of social collapse make the frequently applied term "Colombianization of Mexico" sadly applicable.[2] The expression connotes an
open warfare between the drug world and the state, echoing the havoc
unleashed by Escobar on his homeland beginning in 1984. Its application
to the Mexican context underwrites the common perception worldwide
that national disorder on such a scale is a thing of the past in Colombia
and that the drug-related pandemonium has moved north.[3] In the political arena, this belief was substantiated by the Mérida Initiative implemented in 2008 under President George W. Bush, a multi-billion-dollar
package echoing the 2000 Plan Colombia and designed purportedly to

fight drug-trafficking through the supply of military training and surveillance equipment to Mexico.[4]

That Mexico has become so violent does not mean, of course, that Colombia has seen the end of its internal strife. Nor does it mean that the country's cooperation with the United States under the aegis of Plan Colombia was indeed effective in decreasing drug production and consolidating democracy. Rather, it attests to the supremacy of mediated exposure as laid out by Guy Debord and Jean Baudrillard, where the topic receiving more attention is understood by the general public as the more compelling piece of news, and where the frequency of coverage determines its higher level of urgency in the real world. Tantamount to Baudrillard's theory of the perverse relation between images and their referent, the media's portrayal of the collapse of public safety in Mexico comes with a concomitant perception that the hold of Colombian drug trafficking over the world market is in the throes of a slow death—or that at least it does not pose the threat it used to, since very little is heard about it abroad. This is particularly true when it comes to the vox populi within the United States, influenced heavily by the proximity of drug-spurred disorder. Thomas E. McNamara, the U.S. ambassador to Colombia from 1988 to 1991, commented in his report published posthumously by the *New York Times* on August 12, 2009, that "Colombia's successful fight did not end drug trafficking. Narco Central moved to Mexico. Mexican mafias are today's 'kings of cocaine,' replacing the now-fractured Colombian mafias." Erroneously, his statement carries an implicit understanding of Colombia's successful eradication of the drug problem, even though McNamara hit home when, refraining from the common demonization of Latin America in U.S. public opinion, he pointed to "'the triple whammy' role the United States has played," serving as "the principal drug consumers, arms suppliers and money launderers"—in other words, both the instigator and the ideal market for international illicit dealings.

Indeed, Colombian traffickers remain strong despite years of efforts directed toward the suppression and eventual obliteration of the drug flow. Colombia remains the world's largest producer of cocaine, reaching by 2017 the highest coca production acreage ever recorded ("Colombia Coca Production"). Moreover, Colombian cocaine has branched out to the European markets, flooding them with its product. So, in reality, the only thing that can be said with certainty is that the war over the drug trafficking routes in northern Mexico has displaced Colombia on the media stage owing to the particularly aggressive and confrontational nature of Mexican cartels. Their no-holds-barred approach together with the colorful personalities of their leaders is reminiscent of the Colombian drug scene of the 1980s and 1990s.[5] And the perception that Colombia, despite many problems, is in some sense on the path to recovery persists in the mass media, both generating and politicizing a distinct aesthetic code for Colombian-themed production that borders on the nostalgic.

With Pablo Escobar's death and the subsequent capture of other Colombian drug lords, the era of a handful of powerful drug cartels led by charismatic caudillo types gave way to new, more fragmented, and more transnationalized narco operations, anonymous corporatism, and a militia model predicated on a bigger involvement of the paramilitaries and further atomization followed by the emergence of new gangs.[6] Their new smaller size ensured that they would not measure up to the state as their predecessors could, but it also made further state actions against them, including detection and intelligence-gathering, much harder. The demise of the highly visible cartels enabled the expansion of the paramilitaries, who muscled into the drug trade, creating powerful alliances with drug traffickers.

In other words, drug trafficking in Colombia has evolved, remaining out of sight and changing its operational techniques to adjust to enhanced transnational state surveillance. To use metaphors from the Latin American literary tradition, its trajectory shifted gears from Sarmiento to Angel Rama, in that it substituted caudillismo with the power structures of the *ciudad letrada*. The cartels that seized power after Escobar's demise used brains rather than physical force, by opting to bribe the State rather than wage war against it. In *Y refundaron la patria*, on the parapolitics of the Colombian government, Claudia López has documented the growing criminalization of the Colombian state. Starting with Escobar's brief career in Congress, López notes that while the drug lord's ilk principally sought protection from extradition via bribes, the far more powerful present-day nexus between illegal and legal forces has allowed the criminal element to modify the nation's key operations. Such was the case in the agrarian reforms, where the paranarco mafia sought to legalize land seizures. López's statistics are particularly telling: While under Escobar less than 1 percent of the members of Congress had confirmed ties to the mafia, this number grew to 12 percent in the infamous 8,000 Process of the 1990s and rose further to 35 percent in the Uribe era. Calling

Colombia a narco state is perhaps an exaggeration, but López points out that one in every three key posts in the Executive and Legislative branches has been taken over by the mafia, thereby showcasing the firm incursion of the criminal element into decision-making bodies ("La mafia"). Escobar's successors might have learned how to succeed in illegal business precisely by observing the infamous capo and doing the opposite, but it is the conspicuous figureheads who have enticed the popular imagination.

In fact, one could argue that the purveyors of cultural commodities have hardly noticed the transformation of the narco reality from flamboyant to low-profile, for it is Escobar and his charismatic contemporaries who remain the key fixture in the popular iconography, the object of a simultaneous fascination and almost microscopic scrutiny. They presently inspire more cultural production than ever before and prove, for the time being, that the consumer market remains insatiable when it comes to highly visible drug lords. The great majority of post-2000 narco-themed cultural production pits representations of authenticity against the stimuli of nostalgia and its concomitant consumerist *jouissance*. It has been noted that communal nostalgia rises within a given society "in the wake of epochal changes precipitated by wars, revolutions, invasions, economic dislocations" (Brown, Kozinets, and Sherry 20), and the relocation of the drug-fueled power dynamic constitutes a significant transformation in Colombian society—at both the conscious and the subconscious levels.

This fundamental narco nostalgia flourishes all the more because it reflects an era when criminals were distinguishable from the rest of society. Like the North American cowboys or the Argentine gauchos, Colombia's high-profile drug lords are beginning to occupy an important place in the cultural panorama. Much to the dismay of the political and intellectual elites and frustrating official Colombian discourse, the narco in telenovelas and popular culture is evolving into one of the country's national symbols: on the one hand, the embodiment of evil and, on the other, the epitome of social mobility in a hierarchical and paternalistic society plagued by injustice. Narcos were crass, unrepentant machos whose entrepreneurial dexterity combined with ruthless muscle, flashy cars, and sculpted women made them one of the cultural fixtures of Colombia's social fabric. Modern heroes to the poor and the harbingers of affluence, they not only challenged stuffy bourgeois hegemony but also transformed the political and social order, bringing in new cultural practices and beliefs. As Mary Roldán put it in the context of Escobar's Medellín, "Cocaine

Figure 3. Mural at the Faculty of Science, Universidad del Valle, Cali. Photo by author.

[and by extension its carriers] . . . ruptured tradition, transformed social mores, restructured morality, thought, and expectations. In the process, it also gradually emerged as the greatest threat yet to elite hegemony and the avenue for rethinking the city's structure of power and social relations" ("Colombia" 171). Power structures in Colombia and elsewhere can no longer be viewed without taking into account the illicit economy, a reality reflected wistfully in a graffiti at Cali's Universidad del Valle, where the proverbial power triad of church, state, and army is accompanied by a stereotypical narco—a relatively new yet already ingrained part of the nation's social reality.[7] As Ómar Rincón puts it, "The narco is our grand national story" [El narco es nuestro gran tema nacional] ("Amamos a Pablo" 95). Narco aesthetics is a way of life, a path out of poverty, and perhaps the only such path available to large swaths of a stratified society.

Though the link between Martín Fierro and Pablo Escobar may sound far-fetched, the Argentine gaucho and his Colombian drug lord counterparts have at least two points of contact that warrant attention. Cowboys and gauchos both came to the cultural spotlight precisely when they were on the brink of extinction. Barbed-wire fences, railroads, and refrigeration, in other words, modern technology, made them obsolete, while their unruly, indomitable spirit positioned them on the margins of growing societies whose goals at the time were to solidify urban expansion through centralization and adjustment to the rule of law. Yet it was the same period that witnessed their transformation into cultural icons as their manifestly romanticized portrayal began to channel and mitigate people's unfulfilled longing for the thrill of living outside of societal constraints. Look no further than Dahlmann in Borges's "El sur."

Likewise, the charismatic capos who concentrate the allure of the classic caudillo and defy state power in a showdown of will and resources are no longer part of the Colombian landscape, having been substituted by a faceless narcoparamilitarism and a new generation of college-educated drug scions who swapped ostentatiousness for elegance and discretion. In Escobar's day, when his conspicuous persona set him apart from the rest of society, he still managed to hide from the Medellín authorities, owing to the overwhelming support of the lower classes that embraced him as their hero. He was considered a Robin Hood among the underprivileged multitudes on account of numerous acts of charity that included new houses, soccer fields, and other tokens of largesse. His deeds and modest origins gained him local sympathies and often the near-religious devotion of the poor, as confirmed by the more than twenty thousand people who attended his funeral and by a lasting veneration in the *comunas*, where he is still remembered fondly (L. Saldarriaga).

This veneration leads to the second trait shared by the gauchos, cowboys, and narco leaders: an anti-establishment stance that was either attributed to them by their detractors or, in Escobar's case, fully embraced by the subject once his chances for a political career evaporated. Escobar was a classic social bandit who sought to make his own laws and refused to submit to the constraints of bourgeois globalization, despite the irony of serving as one of the central actors in developing multinational, multi-billion-dollar corporations.[8] He amassed a fortune beyond imagination, proving himself to be not only a fierce criminal but also a first-rate businessman. His entrepreneurial talent and his devotion to family (particularly to his mother) echoed qualities representative of the region of Antioquia, whose inhabitants, the *paisas*, according to Alma Guillermoprieto, characterize themselves as "the proud vanguard of enterprise and innovation," being inherently adventurous, family-loving, and "fond of wealth and risk" (*The Heart That Bleeds* 94, 114). Medellín stood out among cities in Colombia for its long history of smuggling and knack for risky business with the promise of fast money and social betterment. The ineffectiveness of many national industries in the 1970s only made the

drug business more acceptable among virtually all sectors of society, leading to an inversion of the value system where drug trafficking was viewed
as a form of enterprise rather than a criminal act (Salazar and Jaramillo
30–31). So, in a twisted way, Escobar was the embodiment of *paisa* pride:
a dedicated family man, a landowner, and a clever entrepreneur who suc-
cumbed to megalomania, eventually unleashing unspeakable terror on
his fellow countrymen through unprecedented acts of violence.

Escobar also substantiated the archetypal dream of the popular classes
by emerging from obscurity to fame and wealth and thereby proving that
upward mobility in a country known for its strict social stratification is in
fact possible. His capitalist rags-to-riches life story and his mannerisms—
a cross between classic caudillo and modern businessman—explain why
the nation might see itself in some of his traits and why these qualities
would entice the popular imagination and become part of the national
mythology. After all, because of the kingpin of Medellín, Colombia was
for a while the epicenter of world attention, even if for the wrong reasons.
Escobar was the world's official "bad boy," contemptuous of the Colombian state and elusive to the all-powerful United States. As DEA agent
Javier Peña fittingly assessed the capo in his conversation with Mollison,
"Pablo was the Wild West whereas Cali were more businessmen, more
suits" (136). The former director of the DEA in Colombia, Joseph Toft,
opined emphatically that no other drug trafficker, Colombian or Mexican,
has ever come close to Escobar's impact (*Los tiempos de Pablo Escobar*). A
flamboyant and unrepentant caudillo, he thumbed his nose at authority
and refused to play by the rules of the so-called First World, much to the
glee of the underprivileged masses. Interestingly, some of his cronies and
his opponents alike argue that it was exactly the other way around and
that Escobar's notoriety soared because it was fueled by outside influences. More specifically, the United States created a monster by naming
him the worst criminal ever, thus laying the foundation for the legend that
Pablo himself felt obliged to live up to.[9]

Like every social bandit, Escobar has engraved himself in the public
imaginary, signifying different things to different people but ultimately
becoming a compelling symbol of human potency fueled by ambition and
the evil that goes with it. He constitutes a permanent stain on the nation's
self-image, responsible for redefining the country to the outside world
through the prism of illegality, violence, and criminality. His continued
grasp on the nation's psyche is reflected in the Escobar-related news that

pops up with regularity in the national and regional (Antioquian) press. The 2013 visit of Escobar's only son from his self-imposed Argentine exile provoked a sentimental journey into the past, where newspapers recycled the same old photographs and Escobar-themed tales that have been part of the popular knowledge in Colombia for decades. A spate of articles has evoked Escobar's material legacy, featuring confiscated luxury objects that can now be viewed at the National Police Museum in Bogotá, such as his pimped-out Harley-Davidson with gold trim. The ten-year anniversary of the seizure of Escobar's self-styled jail, La Catedral, spurred a series of stories in Medellín's *El Colombiano* that harkened back to Escobar's reign and what remains of it (Yarce, "Pablo y otros"). The twenty-fifth anniversary of his death prompted an elaborate multimedia commemorative in *Semana*, with sections on Escobar's death, his savagery, witness testimonies, and a controversial upsurge of fiction about the capo. It includes reminiscences that are typically reserved for matters of world importance, such as: "where were *you* when Escobar was taken down?" ("25 años"). In other words, the legend of Escobar lives on, frustrating the sectors of the population who wish to redefine their nation through its signs of progress and potential rather than its heritage of banditry that appeals to a universal morbid fascination with the terrible "other."

Imagined or real, Escobar's feted qualities represent an essential ingredient in the continuous quest by Colombians to define the essence of their national character and to come to terms with their past. For the outside world, Escobar remains a curiosity, his horrific crimes watered down by distance and people's hazy historical awareness, leaving intact his rebel-like image enhanced by the exoticized framework of a volatile Latin America. New television productions and popular literature born of his legacy only underscore this selective and "abridged" version by offering a glimpse into a history cleansed of its sociopolitical complexities, of the true scope of the detrimental effect that narcotrafficking has had on all sectors of society, and of other obtrusive facts that could distract the present-day public from sensationalist entertainment. As such, they provide a stimulus for nostalgia, an all-powerful tool in the advertising-driven commercial arts. They reflect Baudrillard's claim about the postmodern approach to history, which is of "no value as conscious awareness but only as nostalgia for a lost referential" (*Simulacra and Simulation* 44). Rather, it is a process of simulation that retroactivates myths of origin while offering an anachronistic space that reenacts "desperate rehallucination of the past" (123). In other words, narcocultural production, particularly the telenovelas, approach "the past" through the stylistic connotations of the 1980s, blending history with nostalgia and fantasy with retro styles of pop culture and paying attention to signifiers without much regard for depth.

Nostalgia's ambiguity and poeticism factors in when it comes to the preference patterns of consumers worldwide, on account of nostalgia's quest for authenticity and a romanticized moment of yesteryear. Brought about by frustration with the present, it can lead to the subsequent idealization and filtering of the past, including the past's negative aspects—often for political and social purposes.[10] Originally viewed as symptoms of a serious malady that would attack the body and soul (Hofer in Davis 1–2), nostalgia today stands for an incurable modern state of mind exacerbated by late capitalism, globalization, and the successive deterritorialization of people and products. It is also related to worldwide immigration, a condition that brings about a sentiment of loss and alienation with the concomitant need to affirm one's belonging to certain localities and particular experiences, even if only in a vicarious fashion. As Svetlana Boym puts it, nostalgia is a curiously restless stance that looks toward the past without really wanting to be there, all the while enjoying the pain of yearning. It is "a romance with one's own fantasy" and "a longing for a home that no longer exists and or has never existed" (Boym xiii). In the context of the market demand for Escobar, nostalgia manifests itself in the nation's conflicting romance with its own turbulent history, a revisionist and simulated excursion through the past that in its pop-cultural manifestations unabashedly does away with the moral high ground and instead celebrates certain elements attributable to the narcos' superficial lifestyle, whitewashing factual references for the sake of attracting wider and younger audiences. One cannot conflate the mass media outpouring on the topic with the nation's attitude toward the commercial popularity of narco-inspired themes. Numerous blogs and newspaper articles confirm that much of the Colombian public is fed up with narco material, charging that its formulaic and trite representations only taint the image of their nation before the rest of the world. Yet high viewer ratings and lucrative sales tell a different story, confirming that nothing succeeds like controversy. As a result, one could say that the Colombian public has a love-hate relationship with narcocultural products.

Boym underscores the direct relationship between progress and society's need for history, where, ironically, the virtual global village has stimulated a "yearning for a community with a collective memory, a longing for continuity in a fragmented world" (xiv). From the Latin American perspective, Néstor García Canclini observes that although cultures have adapted to global realities by creating transnational productions founded on more comprehensive myths that can be deciphered by diverse audiences, there exists the opposite pull toward the regional and the specific. For Canclini, the deterritorialization of the arts has instigated concurrent movements toward a reterritorialization, because communities crave geographical attachment, particularly when the local and the global become so homogenous that they are hard to tell apart (*Consumidores*). What transpires from these commentaries is that settings exalting regional character and local specificities—and what is more idiosyncratic than the narco?—remain attractive to the public despite or perhaps because of the deluge of standardized commodities. Not only that, but since a distinctive locale is less and less common, it appeals more strongly to the public, becoming a self-reflecting cultural mirror but also a profitable source for the marketing of cultural otherness, thereby feeding into the world powers' investment in the exotic.

The concept of exoticism has raised red flags among scholars of postcolonial and postmodern studies concerned with cultures deemed "marginal," because it implies that some groups are branded by others with hierarchical encodings of cultural difference, where, conveniently, the latter represent cultural and economic hegemony. That is to say, difference is celebrated as an exotic festival and its actors are pigeonholed as curiosities whose portrayal comes filtered and negotiated through the gaze of the centers of cultural power.[11] Such mediation leads to the decontextualization of its objects of attention and to the subsequent "sanctioning [of] cultural ignorance" (Huggan 17). Thus, one could argue that nostalgia for the remote self or the exotic other reconstitutes meanings and cultivates a deliberate enhancement of the value of certain aspects of the past, because "collective memory is no longer grounded in history or social context, but also in the process of abstracting and rerouting meanings" (Goldman and Papson 40). Consequently, the massification of ethnic merchandise (artifacts and cultural production) implies a new generic form of exoticism not only devoid of historical content but also responsible for mystification and stereotyping that ultimately offends national sensibilities.

The Escobar Grand Tour

Alongside the slew of new narco television series is the high demand for knock-offs of Fernando Botero's Escobar paintings or T-shirts with likenesses of the Medellín drug lord, laid out in the tourist shops of Bocagrande, Cartagena, together with hammocks, tchotchkes, and bootleg DVDs. They attract multitudes of foreign visitors, many of them unable to speak Spanish, who triumphantly identify the king of cocaine by appropriate gestures to their nostrils before taking home an authentic piece of Colombia. International tourists have fetishized Escobar by his fascinating cultural otherness, equating in the process the whole nation with its criminal native son and, by extension, with cocaine.

Portrayals of Escobar stream spontaneously into the collective imagination via television, print, the Internet, tours, and items from pop culture, causing his legend to transform and grow in front of everyone's eyes. Escobar's prominence in bookstores, his ubiquity in the popular media, the ongoing commodification of his image and legacy by different people with conflicting agendas, and the disdain heaped upon narco-related material by high-brow critics and some members of the public make the drug lord a highly contested presence. Besides Gabriel García Márquez's 1996 *Noticias de secuestro* [*News of a Kidnapping*], Escobar is prominently featured in two post-2000 Colombian novels, José Libardo Porras's 2008 *Happy Birthday, Capo*, centered on the final days of his life,[12] and José Alejandro Castaño's 2012 *Cierra los ojos, princesa*, where he and his family are depicted from the perspective of his daughter, Manuela.[13] Escobar is no longer just the ringleader of the Medellín cartel but also the controversial cultural icon of his era reprocessed through the popular memory. If postmodernity entails an increasing reliance on media imagery for depicting and understanding historical events (Tomasulo 70), then the narco production deploys cultural sound-and-image history to create interpretive frames that constitute a popular alternative to the official discourses.[14]

Producers of mass culture, the intelligentsia, Escobar's cronies, his family members, and his victims all feel the urgency to recount their own version of Escobar. This process begs multiple interpretations. The polyphony of voices addressing various issues through the prism of Escobar's persona inadvertently contributes to Escobar-as-a-brand's continuous reinvigoration, because while his posthumous celebrity brings controversy, it also assures profits for the brand's stakeholders.[15] For one, Escobar's memory is manifestly in play, showcasing the preoccupation each author holds over how the Escobar brand will be interpreted by today's audience and readership, particularly in the face of generational disconnection with the actual events. In an era when, as Debord presciently observed half a century ago, one's worth is determined by the frequency of one's mediatic visibility (16), Escobar's triumphant return to the spotlight must be worrisome for those who suffered the effects of his terror.

Of course, it is not just a question of ideology. As cultural criminologist Mike Presdee says of the connections between violent acts, crime, and consumption, transgression (particularly exemplified by crime) has become a cultural necessity of everyday modern life: "Individualism, greed, destruction, dishonesty, fear and violence are woven, through the process of production and consumption, inevitably into all our everyday lives. Now crime, in the form of a commodity, enables us all to consume without cost as we enjoy the excitement, and the emotions of hate, rage and love that crime often contains" (58).[16]

The economic reasons that consign the drug lord to the world of popular entertainment thus come to mind here; after all, why kill the cash cow if it can be profitably milked? And milking indeed is in full force. Escobar has become a prime target of diverse market strategies. Many of his living contemporaries find receptive audiences, ever eager to share the morbid allure of the nation's biggest criminal. Escobar's brother Roberto, his sister, his hitman, his lover, his son, and his wife all wrote autobiographical books, some more than one, and participated in countless documentaries. While Escobar's son, Juan Pablo Escobar, who lives under the alias Sebastián Marroquín, claims to have dedicated his life to a campaign against violence and to making sure his father's story is retold accurately, the capo's brother Roberto is manifestly more motivated by profit. In a squabble registered on social media, Roberto lashed out at Netflix and the makers of the show *Narcos* over publicity rights. He demanded $1 billion for his company, Escobar Inc., or else he would "close their little show" (Abramovitch). By January 2018, *TMZ* reported that Roberto withdrew his demands for a huge payoff, but his presence in anything Escobar persists. Sebastián Marroquín also criticized both *Escobar, el patrón del mal* and *Narcos* for their allegedly glamorizing depiction of drug trafficking and for presenting a wishful-thinking government narrative of incorruptible Colombian cops in the former, and the gringo fantasy of equally honest DEA agents in the latter ("El hijo"). On social media, he published a list of *Narcos*'s supposed factual errors, as if the series had claimed to be a strictly historical account. Rumors circulate that various Escobar family members insisted in vain on offering their advice to Netflix for a hefty fee. Thus, possibly, criticisms of the media depiction have more to do with squabbles over the politics of heritage, over whether a criminal legacy can carry exclusivity rights, and over whether the profits of Escobar's legacy should be privatized at all. By interpreting their own story as a continuous Escobar saga, Escobar's intimates inspire the consumer to treat their product as part of one familiar brand. In marketing terms, "personal and historical nostalgic content can better, and with lower risks, be produced and continued or recycled, e.g. through prequels and sequels, because consumers are less likely to respond with boredom, negative effects, or psychological reactance" (Natterer 207).

Unsurprisingly, Escobar's family mediates its own role in the dynamic transformation of the Escobar myth by making sure that their unique relationship is immediately communicated to the consumer: Roberto's book features "my brother" in its title, Escobar's wife names her memoirs "my life . . . with," and the son not only includes "my father" in both of his book titles and the 2009 documentary but also publishes his books under his birth name. Meanwhile, he uses his alias everywhere else ("¿Cómo le podés?"). Thus, Marroquín's marketing moves make him appear intent on heralding a tight brand connection and the highest level of authenticity precisely as Escobar's one and only heir.

No discussion of the stakeholders of Escobar's heritage would be complete without addressing the present-day status of Medellín and the lingering effects of Escobar's mayhem. Medellín is an example of a "wounded city" (Wielde Heidelberg 75), and its wound is compounded by the continuous reinvigoration of the Escobar story—at times even by former victimizers (Roberto Escobar and the *sicario* Popeye). The ghost of Escobar has sustained public interest over decades, in great part because it has been reinforced by widespread media attention, which in turn heavily influenced the city's tourism. As result, Medellín is left with a distasteful stigma of death and tragedy, and it witnesses a renaissance of so-called dark tourism, a term that stands for exploring sites of death, tragedy, and the bizarre. Airbnb offers luxurious apartments that allegedly belonged to Escobar. For example, at $900 a night, guests can enjoy the capo's twelve-bedroom, ten-thousand-square-foot penthouse with first-rate amenities, a heated indoor pool, and dramatic views. More controversial perhaps are the ever more present Escobar-themed tours filled with visitors from all over the world who want to see more than the traditional city highlights, its museums, its rather unusual link to tango and Gardel,[17] or the legacy of South America's most successful living artist, Fernando Botero. And to be sure, much has changed since 2010, when I first explored Escobar's legacy in Medellín and Puerto Triunfo (with its Hacienda Nápoles) and saw no other tourists or businesses accommodating their curiosity.[18]

Sensing the high international demand for Escobar-themed attractions, some companies exhibit the true *paisa* entrepreneurial spirit by giving tourists an intimate Escobar experience. Primarily targeted at foreign visitors, the excursions culminate with an undeniably exciting perk: the chance to visit one of Escobar's later homes, sit in his chair, and try on his iconic Russian fur hat. If these show-and-tell moments were not enough, tourists also get to meet and greet Escobar's brother Roberto, who—depending on the day, as visitors comment on the TripAdvisor and Lonely Planet websites—will engage in conversation and even pose for pictures. Unluckier visitors are directed to a DVD presentation and rushed through the house "like sheep."[19] This is an example of the postmodern hyperreal for at least two reasons. First, it is an entirely simulated and an easily digestible experience of Escobar's legacy, enriched by snippets of "authenticity" that can be viewed and even safely touched in the span of a couple of hours. Second, by making a performance of Escobar's life—a narco Disneyland as it were—the tour offers a spectacle that has little to do with Escobar himself. Perhaps the strangest simulacrum of the tour occurs when Roberto puts on Escobar's Russian shapka, trying to pose the way his brother did in a famous photograph from La Catedral prison (De La Paz). Roberto appears quite consciously put-on, dressed up, and all simulation, as if he knew that any appropriation and replication of the original would do in the age of hype. Indeed, the audience is pleased: Relieved of the nuances of history, it is transported to the key places associated with the capo and offered a glimpse of his private life. Perhaps Roberto manages to unload a couple of his Escobar books conveniently available for purchase, and perhaps the visitors feel like they really experienced Pablo Escobar. For Baudrillard, everything in our world is taken over by the commodity logic, and as such "spectacularized . . . provoked and orchestrated into images, signs, consumable models" (*The Consumer Society* 208). A selfie with Roberto, a living breathing souvenir who authenticates the Escobar brand, puts tourists only one degree away from the infamous capo, making their fifty-dollar investment worthwhile.

Predictably, "Escobar tours" raise many an eyebrow in Colombia. Victims of the capo's violence protest his cultural appeal as demeaning, if not deeply insensitive and unethical. Marketing their trauma undermines the commemoration of the victims and opens old wounds. Other citizens also have their stake in not wanting to associate their beautiful city with drug trafficking. Studies of place branding repeatedly emphasize the importance of maximizing positive "place experience" both for visitors and for inhabitants, whereby an increased satisfaction derived from aligning expectations and actual experience assures the place's growth in the popular psyche. Place brands are built through promotional tactics and the collective construction of meaning, but they are also built through narratives or "place stories" (Ashworth, Kavaratzis, and Warnaby 5), which are hard to erase or even downplay, as is the case here. This is where conflict emerges between the presentation of history as heritage and its interaction with the commercial and marketing elements of tourism, between cultural memory and the commercialization of pain. Today, "sites, cultures, histories, and experiences are increasingly viewed as the commodified or objectified products for consumption—often for profit—by the marketplace" (Bird, Westcott, and Thiesen 646). While local authorities have no interest in celebrating Escobar's legacy, Escobar-themed tourism grows in popularity through media exposure and because, somehow, the capo became a staple of hip consumerism, as evidenced by the 2018 Netflix series *Dark Tourist*, with its very first episode unsurprisingly featuring Medellín.

The series' host, David Farrier, who trots the globe to places associated with death and destruction, finds himself on a taxi tour driven by a guide disguised as Escobar. Squeezed into a striped polo shirt, with the trademark hairstyle and moustache, this pseudo-Escobar comes off as endearing and comical. In an act reflective of Baudrillard's postmodern simulacrum, he conjures up the televised version of the capo performed by Andrés Parra in *Escobar, patron del mal*, both in mannerism and in the now-famous dialogue, as he threatens someone over a gigantic walkie-talkie: "And if he doesn't get it, he knows I'll kill his mother, his father and his grandma. If the grandma is already dead, I'll dig her up and kill her again. And I'll kill his dog. And if he doesn't have a dog, I'll get him one, and when he takes a liking to him, I'll kill him too" [Y si él no va a copiar bien las cosas, sabe que le mato a su mamá, a su papá y a su abuelita. Si su abuelita está muerta, yo se la desentierro y la vuelvo a matar. Y le mato el perro. Y si no tiene perro, yo le consigo uno y cuando se encariñe también se lo mato]. Another odd interview televised for the series is with a former policeman and a present-day Escobar tour guide who proudly shows David a photograph of a 1980s police squad, of whom only five survived the war against Escobar. Others were killed because they did not accept the capo's "silver or lead" (plata o plomo) bribe (Bellman). Rather than feel shame for what many would consider his moral debasement, the interviewee beams with pride over his survival skills. After all, Escobar is dead, while the corrupt ex-cop is still alive and profiting from the capo's legacy. If one can draw a message from this episode, it is that scruples lose out when there is a chance to make a quick buck. Medellín and its direct link to Escobar became the site of a prime commodity, which responds to the global market demands for horror and heightened sensationalism.

The situation in Medellín is rather unique because the official agencies involved in the city's development have been extremely hesitant to publicize or discuss Escobar. In fact, they'd rather obliterate the past, as if Escobar had never existed. Yet the media has popularized the capo, first for the Spanish-speaking world, with *Escobar, el patrón del mal,* and then, worldwide, through Netflix with the English-language *Narcos.* The dissonance between supply and demand provided ample business opportunities for private entrepreneurs and unofficial guides eager to cash in on the Escobar brand (Naef 486). Thus, the touristification of the narco past took off. The resulting tours are not sponsored by state institutions, and their content, together with their very existence, became a point of controversy among Medellín residents, city officials, and even the nation's president. At issue is who are the diverse stakeholders involved, what narratives do they produce, and what values are they reflecting? What stories and ideologies are being disseminated, and how are they affecting Medellín and the nation's image? More recent discussions focus on how the sites are or should be managed; what role, if any, local governments should play in their management; and what potential economic benefits, if any, such sites might offer. The touristification of Escobar mimics unfettered free market forces in which, ideally, state intervention is kept to a bare minimum (Harvey 2). Today's protests and specific steps taken by the city to do away with their popularity indicate a push for more civic engagement and state control, an overdue confrontation with the past that refuses to go away.

As TripAdvisor indicates, a wide range of tours run from a few hours to a couple of days, with prices increasing accordingly.[20] Scores of comments by satisfied customers attest to their popularity, with only some complaining of trite narratives and endless hours stuck in traffic. Some tours, such as the more-established Paisa Road, proudly claim undistorted historical accounts and the approval of local communities (Naef 493), thereby hinting at the faults of other excursions. Indeed, Escobar-themed tours are often criticized for falling into sensationalism, diffusing unverified myths, and going as far as depicting criminals as heroes. An NPR podcast Radio Ambulante from Colombia set out to investigate these excursions firsthand while expressing discomfort and disapproval of their very existence as a morbid and disrespectful means to profit from tragedy. Motivated by a public demand and alerted to its existence by a Canadian journalist eager to explore the subject, Radio Ambulante committed to experiencing it for themselves. The message is clear: It is foreigners who are interested in the tours, not Colombian nationals. Unsurprisingly, the journalists had nothing positive to report, other than numerous discrepancies between tall tales and facts. Objects of no historical significance donated recently by the local community were erroneously claimed to have belonged to Escobar, to heighten the sensationalism of the story. The guide repeatedly called Escobar "el Patrón," as if Colombia's worst criminal deserved veneration, and her dubious facts about more intimate narratives turned out to have been provided by none other than Popeye, Escobar's outspoken hitman (Alarcón).

How do you protect the positive brand of a city whose unruly locals promote its criminal past to the constant flow of the world's curious? In the early 2000s, Medellín sought to launch a brand identity based on its architectural marvels and physical beauty, but it continues to be plagued by notoriety. During the mayorship of Sergio Fajardo (2004–2008), Medellín began implementing projects to better integrate its inhabitants and improve the conditions of its poor (Arbeláez Tobón). These efforts culminated with such notable distinctions as winning the 2013 "City of the Year" competition organized by the nonprofit Urban Land Institute.[21] Thus when in 2012 the Madrid daily *El País* published a startling report about five thousand adolescent *sicarios* roaming the hills of Medellín and killing for as little as two euros, Colombians reacted with outrage. The response from Medellín was not long in coming: The city's then mayor, Aníbal Gaviria Correa (in office 2012–2015), accused the Spanish reporter, Pablo de Llano, of egregious exaggeration and of quoting outdated material, since Medellín had managed to bring order to the situation and the number of *sicarios* was some ten times smaller than those reported by Llano. When the mayor stated that "Medellín is no longer the world capital of drug trafficking nor is it the city of Pablo Escobar," ("Medellín ya no es la capital mundial del narcotráfico ni la ciudad de Pablo Escobar"), his comment touched the nerve of popular opinion in the country, but particularly in Antioquia.

Old tales die hard, despite systematic efforts and successes in transforming the city's image. Medellín's mayor since 2016, Federico Gutiérrez, became outraged over a 2017 article in Madrid's *El Mundo* that described the Pope's visit to Colombia as "Francisco in the narco patria" ("Federico Gutiérrez"). Elsewhere, Gutiérrez criticized Netflix for promoting series such as *Narcos* and *Escobar, el patrón del mal*, though he revised his criticism later on by hailing the Colombian production as far superior to *Narcos*. Gutiérrez also vehemently criticized the growing narco tourism industry, bluntly stating that tourists visiting Escobar sites are not welcome and that "the party is over" (se les acabó la fiesta), because these sites would be subject to demolition (see "El alcalde de Medellín" and "'Medellín no es'"). Having the Escobar brand reinforced from the outside must certainly frustrate attempts to promote a more positive place narrative, although, at the same time, protesting against narco tourism only adds fuel to the contradiction and the "hipness" of the Escobar brand.

Perhaps because of the nation's attempts to strip away the narco stigma, some architectural landmarks of Escobar's presence in Medellín (and elsewhere in Colombia) have been allowed to collapse, with buildings barely a few decades old turning into ruins through systematic pillage and neglect. Others were rebuilt and consciously repurposed to represent a present good versus a past evil. The Pablo Escobar neighborhood built by the capo himself holds on to its name, despite the official neglect suffered by its residents. Its community leader, Uber Zavala, told Arturo Wallace of the BBC that their neighborhood is systematically slighted by the city government, that it lacks schools, soccer fields, a community center, parks, and roads, and that the mayor promised better services on the condition that the barrio change its name, which it refused to do. Then, the Ovni building located in the posh Poblado neighborhood still haunts with its gutted interior, the result of a 1990 bomb attack by Escobar's Cali Cartel enemies. Of the parking structure that occupied the lower floors, only twisted pieces of metal remain. Escobar's flamboyant mansion on La Isla Grande (part of the Islas de Rosario, off the coast of Cartagena) is dilapidated, overrun by vegetation, wild pigs, and machete-wielding squatters. The ruins of La Catedral prison, which Escobar built for his own voluntary incarceration under the presidency of César Gaviria, were replaced by a Benedictine monastery. Presently, the compound contains a library for local children, a chapel, and an asylum for indigent senior citizens, although the ruins of a bunker that served as a torture and execution chamber remain in place.

During my visit in the summer of 2010, only the foundation of La Catedral remained, with tile floors of different patterns still showing through what looked like a construction site. A friendly engineer working on the site pointed to where the kitchen and some of the bathrooms used to be, but it required a great deal of imagination to conjure up any image of prior luxury. The engineer offered an impromptu tour of the premises, including the ominous bunker and the passage leading to it. Little rooms in ruin, with rusty tubs still in place, are all that is left. Perhaps most interesting was a bundle he produced at one point, a blanket filled with Escobar objets trouvés, including tools, a teacup, a spoon, fragments of ornamental tile and—the pièce de résistance—a tattered pair of Pablo's bikini briefs that could have been mine for $300. They allegedly belonged to Escobar himself. One other souvenir for the curious tourist was a fragment of human jaw with a couple of teeth still attached. The friendly engineer attributed the teeth to one of Escobar's victims.

Escobar's life has become fodder for numerous reminiscences. In Nicolas Entel's 2009 *Pecados de mi padre,* Sebastián Marroquín offered a somber and touchingly introspective journey into what it was like to be the son of the world's most notorious criminal. Loneliness, isolation, and relentless persecution hardly paint the narco lifestyle in a glamorous light. Marroquín recalled that when he lived with his father, they were surrounded by millions of dollars in cash and yet faced hunger and cold as the authorities closed in on them. Decades later, moved by a letter that Marroquín had written to the heirs of Escobar's most famous targets, the sons of the victims and victimizers came together in a televised meeting in the name of healing and reconciliation. Marroquín asked them for forgiveness, while the grown-up children of Justice Minister Rodrigo Lara

Above: Figure 4. Blanket with objects offered for sale from what was left of La Catedral, 2010. Photo by author.

Right: Figure 5. These tattered bikini briefs allegedly belonged to Escobar. Photo by author.

Bonilla and presidential candidate Luis Carlos Galán acknowledged that he too was a victim of the drug war. Their recorded union underscored the futility of cultivating animosities and the need to revisit and reflect upon the painful past. In a column for Spain's *El País* on May 30, 2000, Nobel laureate Mario Vargas Llosa applauded *Pecados de mi padre* as the most convincing and dramatic depiction of the narco phenomenon ever made ("¿Cómo le podés?"). Luis Carlos Galán's widow, Gloria Pachón, ambivalently assessed it as an important gesture of reconciliation but certainly not enough (H. Salazar). Others were far more cautious and critical, finding Marroquín's social presence excessive, his intentions disingenuous, and his ever-more frequent activism smacking of immodesty and opportunism.

Alfredo Serrano, the man behind a 2012 documentary series devoted to Escobar's victims, suspected Marroquín of whitewashing his own criminal past and fooling the sons of his victims (Ángel). Similarly, Ramiro Bejarano, former director of DAS (Departamento Administrativo de Seguridad), deemed the documentary a publicity stunt. After all, why contact the sons of most powerful political figures but ignore countless other victims of his father's wrath (H. Salazar)? Héctor Abad Faciolince, whose father, a defender of human rights, was murdered in 1988, was baffled by Marroquín's agenda, stating, "Guilt is ascribed to one person, I don't know why this man makes such a big deal of asking forgiveness for crimes he never committed. I don't enjoy this show of other people's shame. Some appropriate the guilt of another; others give pardons they can't give. It seems a little exhibitionist" [la culpa es individual, no sé por qué este muchacho hace tantos aspavientos para pedir perdón por actos que él no cometió. Este show de vergüenzas ajenas yo no lo disfruto. Unos se apropian de culpas que no tienen; otros dan perdones que no pueden dar. Todo me parece un poco exhibicionista] (H. Salazar). In the same vein, Alonso Salazar undermined Marroquín's statements in a 2018 interview with Jon Lee Anderson: "[Marroquín] is very clever, and clearly he's been pondering the opportunities offered by this resurrection. He's living off the image of his father but realizes that he needs to be critical." Marroquín paid Alonso Salazar back by publicly discrediting all biographies written about his father as "unauthorized"—including Salazar's *La parabola* ("¿Cómo le podés?"). In Marroquín's view, none of the authors knew his father well, implying that only he could be the true authority on the capo.

Marroquín's attitude appears to grow blunter with time: The legacy of his father is "shit," a permanent introspection into crime and culpability (Anderson). A video he posted on Instagram for the 25th anniversary of Escobar's death addresses that very guilt, yet, once again, the aftertaste is baffling. While the text challenges today's popularization of Escobar in the media and asks instead that we honor Escobar's victims, the images that accompany the words suggest otherwise, promoting the capo's iconization by showing Escobar's face in endless variations from historical photographs to tattoos on his followers' backs.[22] In the end, the video is no less than a hagiography strangely cloaked in a "never again" warning, emblematic of Escobar's son perennially seeking to have it both ways: to distance himself while capitalizing on his father's legacy.

Aside from Marroquín's various contributions to the subject, note-worthy too are the testimonies of Escobar's wife, his brother Roberto, of Virginia Vallejo (a 1980s television diva and Escobar's love interest), of Escobar's hitman, Jhon Jairo Velásquez, alias Popeye, who accompanied the drug lord almost to the very end, or of Juan José Hoyos Naranjo, a journalist invited to spend the weekend at Hacienda Nápoles in 1983. With the exception of Roberto, the other three pointed to Alberto Santofimio Botero, of Colombia's Liberal Party and a former minister of justice, as the mastermind behind the 1989 murder of presidential candidate Luis Carlos Galán. In fact, Popeye's detailed recollections of Escobar's inner circle of friends and allies served as testimony in a court trial against Santofimio, whereas Virginia Vallejo's offer to testify was reportedly ignored by the attorney general, with the case closed shortly thereafter. Hoyos's insightful two-decades-old report incriminated Santofimio as well, attesting to the politician's ubiquitous presence in Hacienda Nápoles.[23] In the end, in a surprising turn of events that only substantiates the allegations of Santofimio's close connections with the nation's elite and the fact that Colombia is striving to right past wrongs, the accused was sentenced to twenty-four years in prison, only to be released in 2008 and recaptured three years later to serve out the original sentence.

This, of course, is one example in which revisiting Escobar's heyday serves his victims in their attempt to come to terms with the tragedies that devastated the nation. In contrast, many other contemporary representations of Colombian narco bosses, particularly those originating from mass entertainment, tend to underpin the drug barons' capacities for conspicuous consumption and their subsequent power, thus tapping into an innate human desire for social climbing and success, exalted at the expense of cautionary teachings (Palaversich, "La seducción"). The ensuing glorification of drug lords created in the image of Escobar is what must prompt concerns in his victims, especially in light of his popularity among younger generations and foreign audiences who cannot remember the era of violent confrontations between the Colombian cartels and the state.

It is likely a truism that the commercial success of narco stories stems from the public's obsession worldwide with the dramatic vicissitudes of the rich—especially the criminal rich. Yet keeping in mind the effect that the mass media exerts on the public, Escobar's triumphant mediated presence—and this goes for any charismatic drug lord, real or fictional—together with the timing of the craze should be addressed. Acculturation in the twenty-first century automatically exposes one to the flow of mass media messages and spectacle, as well as to abstract social relations of consumption regardless of one's locale. It is understood that the reception and appropriation of media products is part of an extended process of self-formation, through which individuals develop a sense of their surroundings, of their history, and of the social group to which they belong. Logically, the market and the media's fascination with flashy narcos who channel Escobar's consumer power, together with the concurrent reduction of the sociohistorical context to a bare minimum, contribute to Escobar's mystification while also solidifying a number of social types found in the drug-trafficking milieu.

Redressing and abstracting Escobar's legacy has certainly taken place in Colombia. An impressive assortment of pirated films—wherein the most recent U.S. productions flood the Colombian market at nearly the same time as they hit U.S. theaters—did not fail to include and exhibit the 2009 Colombian series *El Capo*, which, as every vendor rushed to assure passersby, was the "real" and "the most authentic" rendition of Escobar's life at Hacienda Nápoles. Even though there is little truth to this asseveration, the telenovela and Escobar's famous estate have indeed coincided, allowing a physical and symbolic encounter between mass entertainment and the site of painful memory in what likely has been a good business deal for the private company in charge of Escobar's fiefdom. That *El Capo* was filmed partially at Hacienda Nápoles (where an entire faux mansion was built for the production) is not as unusual as the fact that the theme park commemorated the event with a number of placards that feature the show and its protagonists, thereby adding another stratum of referentiality to the Hacienda's already confused and convoluted self-image.

What struck me first about Hacienda Nápoles is that the place does not know exactly what it wants to be. During my 2010 visit, it was hard to tell whether the estate's most famous survivors, the hippos; its dinosaur sculptures, restored by the original artist after their years of neglect; or Escobar's notoriety as the evil "other" inspired the "exoticization" of a

Figure 6. Three African-themed folkloric masks, 2010. The center mask appears to represent Cartagena's monument to India Catalina (an indigenous woman who served as interpreter in Pedro de Heredia's conquest of Colombia) and the right mask depicts Escobar. The Escobar mask is also suggestive of an Easter egg, adding to its bizarre quality. Photo by author.

place that also, bizarrely, took on the guise of an African safari. A sculpture of three African folkloric masks, with one bearing an unmistakable resemblance to Escobar, bespoke a curious case of re-routing meanings and stepping away from history.

The iconic gate to the property featuring Escobar's Piper Cub (taken down in 2019, see the epilogue) was upstaged by another, more grandiose entryway, aping the style of Hollywood's Jurassic Park. Piped-in African drumbeats welcomed visitors at the beginning of the tour and deafening artificial roars emerged from hidden speakers placed farther along, near the miniature-golf dinosaurs; except for my husband and me, the vast estate was empty, instilling an overwhelming eeriness. In a curious turn of events, Hacienda Nápoles, together with Pepe, its now-deceased alpha hippo, have undergone a series of processes that reflect the fate of its original owner. The place became a bizarre hybrid of Jurassic Park, aquatic funland, driving safari, nature preserve, Holocaust museum, budding film studio, and family hangout. And although it attempts to bring together elements foreign to the area,[24] in a global sense it slowly does away with its historical uniqueness, instead emulating what the Colombian bourgeoisie could expect to see on a trip to Orlando. While Hacienda Nápoles attracts its (especially) foreign visitors by virtue of its original history, its current transformation into a family entertainment complex seeks to do away with its most unique element. Hacienda Nápoles, like the legend of Escobar himself, is on its way to becoming a profitable, globally appealing enterprise, its history diluted and kept to a bare minimum.

Aside from the lowbrow artifacts sold in the streets and the geographical spaces that bear the drug lord's mark, museums—the storehouses of traditional culture—also experience Escobar's selling power. Fernando Botero, who had already donated four hundred art works to different Colombian institutions, added another painting to the Museum of Antioquia in 2009, in reaction to the public's Escobar mania (J. Saldarriaga, "Obras donadas por Botero"). As it turns out, one of the earlier acquisitions that enjoyed the greatest popularity was "The Death of Pablo Escobar" (1999), featuring the criminal still alive and with a gun in his hand as he dodges the bullets that would finish him off. Botero followed up by donating his other painting of Escobar's demise, this time with the kingpin's lifeless body spread out on the terracotta roof. Drawing from Colombia's painful experiences, Botero painted a number of works depicting La Violencia period, as well as portraits of several individuals from Colombia's turbulent folklore, but it is Escobar who attracts the multitudes time and again.

A collection of pricey Escobar-inspired T-shirts also surfaced in 2004 on the European website deputamadre69.it, becoming an instant hit among Italian youth. Interestingly, the designer responsible for this clothing line is a Colombian citizen incarcerated in Spain on drug charges. Echoing Escobar's resourcefulness, the energetic entrepreneur sensed a demand for the exotic, and taking advantage of global neoliberalism, he manufactured and smuggled the merchandise from his Barcelona jail to Italian boutiques, drawing much attention and profits of more than nine million dollars (Janer). There are at least two lessons that can be drawn from this anecdote: first, that in global popular culture, the haze of time has stripped the Medellín drug baron's image of its incalculable evil and reinscribed it in the pantheon of dissident and nonconforming leaders, next to such hipster global icons as Che Guevara; and second, that in the process of the decontextualization of foreign material and the distribution of its strategic exoticism to Western audiences, moralistic judgments fade away, swept aside by the allure of scandal and controversy. Even the producers and writers of recent Colombian telenovelas, gathered at the 2009 Seventh World Summit of Industry of Telenovela and Fiction in Bogotá, acknowledged the urgency of changing the manner in which narco telenovelas depict the drug underworld: It is apparent that the transnational success of narco entertainment has inadvertently transformed narco telenovelas into a celebration of and an apology for the criminal ("Plantean ajustar temática").

Escobar Brand vis-à-vis Narco Aesthetic

Of course, keeping in mind the substantial profits drawn from the narco craze, the hardly unpredictable backlash has not measurably deterred narcocultural production. The TV industry justifies itself by claiming to portray Colombian reality for what it is, thus implying that drug trafficking has become one of its inseparable elements. Theirs is not an isolated verdict, for many voices from within Colombia insist that drug trafficking could not and did not spontaneously burst onto the social scene[25] but rather matured and expanded as a consequence of certain past circumstances, such as the tradition of contraband, the ineffectiveness of the state economy, and the inherent, if ineffable, "national character."[26] It gave birth to two types of narcos: the bourgeois model of a discreet entrepreneur remaining outside the public eye, such as the Rodríguez Orejuela brothers of the Cali Cartel, and the far more culturally resonant "Patrón," who sought out social protagonism, in short, the Escobar brand. And contrary to common assumptions that would bind consumerism with progress and modernity, it has been argued that drug trafficking has in fact left a reactionary imprint on Colombian culture. True, it has facilitated substantial demand for the most recent consumer products, yet it has also brought about a return to the rural, autochthonous lifestyle in conjunction with a certain conservatism exhibited by superficial religiosity and sexist, chauvinist attitudes predicated on the power of sheer muscle.[27] In the same vein, for Tom Feiling, both the Medellín and Cali Cartels "had one foot in the past and another in the future, oscillating between ancestral and consumerist in their ostentatious displays of power. They indulged in the landowners' traditional love of *paso fino* horses and stud farms, but they also employed *narquitectos* to design their homes" (Feiling 174).

This odd combination of commercial advancement and retrograde ideology brought about a bonanza of crass exhibitionism, prompted by an avalanche of luxury products previously out of reach for most Colombians. The lifestyle of the narcos became an expression of Lyotard's postmodern condition taken to the extreme, wherein the omnipotence of the free market economy spurred by the narco powerhouses sped up the mercantilization of knowledge and its exchange as commodity. Ceasing to be an end in itself, knowledge previously viewed through modern qualifications such as truth, goodness, or beauty no longer needed to be acquired through the training of one's mind but could be bought instantly for individual pleasure and shaped to one's liking in an environment where money was no object. Buildings and entire landscapes that reflected drug traffickers' ideas of comfort and luxury, female bodies artificially enhanced to compliment these men's power of acquisition and virility, weapons, and surveillance equipment better than that of the state were produced, consumed, and exchanged. In the long run, narco consumerism transformed Colombia's cultural and aesthetic landscape irrevocably.

Modeled on "virtues of frugality, thrift, and enterprise," the pre-Escobar Medellín worshipped money but not ostentatiousness, and it frowned upon conspicuous consumption (Roldán, "Colombia" 168–69). Through the 1980s, the city, from its entertainment sector to its religiosity, underwent a narco transformation whereby discotheques sprang up everywhere, fireworks began to shatter the silence of Saturday nights to celebrate a *mafioso's* success in smuggling cocaine to the United States, and inconspicuous chapels filled to the brim with the most extravagant cars imaginable, whose owners, no doubt drug traffickers, were thanking the Virgin Mary for keeping them alive. The cocaine bonanza shook social classes, uprooted hierarchies, and brought about new models of social advancement. Roldán writes:

> Upper-class women who had cultivated particular seamstresses, masseuses, and beauticians, and considered them practically part of their retinue suddenly found themselves jilted as it became far more profitable to cater to the needs of endless molls and would-be mistresses of the gangster underworld. Beauty queens who in the past might have expected to make a brilliant match with some up-and-coming businessman or politician were seen on the arms of

gold-chain-bearing individuals garbed in garish shirts unbuttoned to the navel, sporting cowboy hats and accompanied by hordes of pistol-toting youths. (169)

Cocaine wealth exposed the hypocrisy embedded in social divisions, where it was the rich who sold their properties to the narcos for exorbitant prices and eagerly offered their professional services as lawyers and accountants and yet refused to let the narcos into their social clubs and official circles and condemned them publicly once Escobar became a state enemy. But narcos and their armies of *sicarios* could buy what was previously off-limits, thereby contesting the historically exclusionary hierarchical social order. Since the formal education of the new consumer elite was in most cases questionable, formalized aesthetics rarely entered into play in their creations, giving way instead to culturally pluralistic, eclectic styles that resisted any uniformity. Narcos—Lyotard's "knowers as consumers" rather than traditionally trained knowers—created randomly as it were, drawing from the mediascape's hodgepodge of spectacle in their quest for the most performative exhibition of power. Swimming in money they did not know how to spend, the newly minted millionaires would proudly parade two gold watches at once, together with bulky bracelets and chains. Their multiple residences boasted gold faucets and shower fixtures, dining room sets of etched crystal and elephant tusks, and million-dollar art in their horse stables. As Simon Strong writes,

> Original paintings, usually in bright, lurid colors depicting voluptuous women or seaside sunsets, were snapped up in the belief that anything original was intrinsically valuable; artistic merit as a concept was a complete enigma. . . . One Medellín artist said: "Art prices went mad. The mafia were mostly ignorant people and liked to leave it up to their decorators to advise them. They wanted anything that was big and extravagant, which was the very opposite to the austerity typical of Antioquia." (69)

Robert Venturi, the postmodernist guru of architecture who famously proclaimed "less is a bore" in response to the previous dictum "less is more," would have marveled at the gaudy narco tastes as a vernacular art form worthy of examination. With no design too outlandish, these new styles created what many would consider an architectural aberration. As per Strong's description, "crystal tables gleamed beside huge, shiny, chromium-framed chairs that were dwarfed in turn by immense televisions; stuffed deer heads peered out of the walls. Everything possible shone" (69). Accompanying this overindulgence was the desire to replicate for the sake of replication. The Cali mogul José Santacruz Londoño built a replica of the White House and a faithful copy of Club Colombia in Cali since he was denied entry to the latter by the social elites. Spurred on by the rejection, Santacruz created a postmodernist hyperreality, blending the distinction between the actual place and its artificial simulation. José Gonzalo Rodríguez Gacha festooned his sports cars with gold steering wheels and trim (Escamilla 23). For his part, Escobar boasted of the latest technology in weapons, cell phones, and beepers that no one else in Latin America possessed. In fact, he was one of the world's first to avail himself of a mobile phone (Valasco). Escobar and Carlos Lehder also converted his luxurious vehicles into multifunction weapons that would spew tear gas, smoke, nails, or bullets, all controlled from the dashboard in the style of James Bond's tricked-out Aston-Martin.[28]

Abad Faciolince describes this emergent style as a local ranchero aesthetic influenced by the tackiness of the North American nouveau riche, a distinctive kitsch reflecting artificiality and gaudiness à la Disney World. Yet far from blaming outside influences for the deterioration of Colombian culture, Abad Faciolince traces this hybrid style to Colombia's national (bad) taste, which had been latent in the bourgeoisie for decades but unfulfilled due to a lack of resources ("Estética y narcotráfico" 513). Capitalizing on excess, exaggeration, and gigantism, which manifested itself in oversize SUVs, weapons, and outrageously garish mansions out of place in their environment, the narcos made the nation's subconscious dreams come true, flaunting their riches in everyone's face in the best Veblenian fashion. Rosso Serrano Cadena, former general de la Policía Nacional, traces the emergence of the "lobo" aesthetic (crass and ostentatious) back to the early capos from the Guajira region, who enriched themselves on the marijuana trade. They were the first to wear flashy gold jewelry and watches and drive Range Rovers (Serrano Cadena 105). Inhabiting the reality powered by capital, narcos, the new patrons of taste, popularized this lack of sophistication, thereby reflecting Lyotard's assertions about the condition of art when ruled by money:

By becoming kitsch, art panders to the confusion which reigns in the "taste" of the patrons. Artists, gallery owners, critics and public

wallow together in "anything goes" and the epoch is that of slacken-
ing. But this realism of the "anything goes" is in fact that of money;
in the absence of the aesthetic criteria, it remains possible and useful
to assess the value of works of art according to the profits they yield.
Such realism accommodates all tendencies, just as capital accommodates all "needs," providing that the tendencies and needs have
purchasing power. As for taste, there is no need to be delicate when
one speculates or entertains oneself. (76)

Such consumerist omnipotence and taste for the bigger, better, and
gaudier, preferably drawn from the North American ideal, has also evidenced itself in the women *narcotraficantes* sought for public display (if
not steady companionship). It goes without saying that a copious cash
flow has magical powers to lure top-notch beauties to men whose social
class and often less-than-average appearance would make such a union
otherwise unthinkable.[29] It is equally predictable that the high demand
for trophy women would create a whole hierarchy of expendable lovers,
whose very mothers would sometimes pimp them out to the highest bidder in exchange for college tuition and other monetary rewards (Serrano
Cadena). It was precisely in this circle of high demand and ample supply
that a class of *prepagos* emerged, a form of prostitution nonexistent before
the narco boom wherein well-off youth, models, and attractive celebrities
became escorts on the condition of a considerable fee paid up front.[30]

What was new, owing to scientific advances, is that narcos set out to
reshape nature by tapping into the "wow factor" drawn from their superficial take on the Western ideal and Hollywood fantasies. They targeted
the female body image by promoting and carrying out in the flesh their
standards of the idealized look calqued from the U.S. adult entertainment
industry.[31] Under the spell of unrealistically voluptuous females, whose
oversize buttocks and breasts contrasted with miniscule waists and willowy limbs, drug traffickers began to sculpt their trophy partners, thereby
stimulating the nation's plastic surgery industry. Breast and buttock augmentation, liposculpture, hair extensions, spas, and fitness centers have
thus become the modus operandi of the narco trophies, underpinning the
triumph of cultural shallowness.

Nowadays it is a cliché to associate silicone women with narco aesthetics, overdrawn Pamela Anderson clones popularized by telenovelas. *Sin
tetas no hay paraíso* (2006) and *Muñecas de la mafia* (2009) epitomize

the phenomenon of mafia dolls and wannabes whose bodies compete for attention and material gain. Of course, silicone beauty might be the patrimony of the narco aesthetic, but by now it has permeated Colombian society as a whole. As Michael Taussig writes in *Beauty and the Beast*, "Most everyone with whom I speak in Colombia now seems to be an expert on beautifying surgery. . . . What I thought was something private and best left unsaid, the state of a person's breasts and sexual appeal, was actually a public secret known to all" (49). Taussig muses at "500 cc breasts" in the Cali airport, noting with wonderment that "it seems that all the girls in Cali have been put to the knife, for it would be difficult to find in that city today young or middle-aged women without enlarged breasts, made all the more visible" (48). My visits to Cartagena have revealed how the transnational curvy beauty ideal has become a reality among women, who sashay around the touristy colonial city with oversize bosoms that require no bra for support. A wide assortment of clinics trumpeting affordable prices and tourist packages combining sight-seeing with multifaceted plastic surgery for foreigners only confirms Colombia's fascination with appearance and its growing reputation as a mecca for cosmetic surgery.

Other voices identify narco attitudes in the highest ranks of Colombian government, pointing to the former president, Álvaro Uribe, whose hot temper and frequent verbal attacks on his detractors—a behavior that, until the Trump era, was unusual for a head of state—earned him a reputation in Colombia and abroad.[32] His volatility and tantrums aside, Uribe exhibited other, more latent qualities that tie with the rebirth of traditionalist tendencies inspired by drug trafficking culture—namely, his showy piety that beguiled the conservative masses and his love for the ranchero lifestyle, complete with a passion for horseback riding. In fact, an argument has been made that Uribe's popularity resided precisely in his narco mannerisms, behaviors that generated, consciously or not, the identification of the nation's masses with their caudillo-like president who publicly favored a no-nonsense style of management and who scoffed at culture, declaring that literature and films are amusement fit only for the Bogotá bourgeoisie (Rincón, "Narco.estética" 147). Such commentary coming from Colombia's most prominent political figure makes a value judgment that rightly worried the nation's intellectual elites. It pits urban centers of culture against the myth of horsemanship and freedom, an image that only thinly veiled the classic attitudes of a regional strongman wary of metropolitan governance. In the same vein, Rincón equated Colombian democracy with the masses' adoration of the *patrón du jour*, be it Don Pedro, Don Mario, Don Álvaro, or Don Nobody ("Narco.estética" 162). Rincón's bitter if not cynical observation exposes Colombia's long-lasting romance with authoritative and populist figures and simultaneously sheds light on why the arresting persona of the drug baron would find such resonance in the nation's cultural consciousness.[33]

From fashion and architecture to television, literature, and the female body ideal, narco aesthetics encroached upon the Colombian cultural arena, changing it irreversibly. It transformed the underprivileged zones by spreading violence and disorder, and it spilled over into the opulent areas, through new alliances and conflicts between the criminal milieu and the traditional rich. From the poor to the nation's former president, from hyper machos to ultrafeminine silicone bombshells, in subjects as serious as politics and as frivolous as light entertainment, drug trafficking has become a thematic fixture whose grip remains strong despite the demise of the largest and most visible Colombian cartels. Better yet, *narcocultura* has tantalized not only the Colombian but also the transnational public, tapping into modern-day obsessions with scandal, violence, excess, satiety, and the drive toward instant gratification.

In the so-called developed world, where an abundance of food and resources leads to gluttony and squandering—thereby elevating restraint and self-discipline to a moral ideal—one could argue that narco opulence and eventual narco ruin serves as a fitting parable of the perils of modern-day overconsumption.[34] True, the vicarious experience of narco vicissitudes provides thrills for the scandal-seeking masses, yet the theme's greater force lies in the public's fascination with excess, normally restrained by the inner struggle against hedonism and by other, exterior circumstances. Yet one might ask, what if such debauched excess were within reach and rampant corruption guaranteed impunity? Exaggerated and yet strangely familiar, narco stories function as an overdeveloped photograph of common global obsessions, because they provide a guilt-free journey into the world of conspicuous expenditure, a self-reflection for societies deeply embroiled in a heady consumer binge. As such, despite or because of their fetishistic exoticism, they hit home on a number of levels.[35]

All these expressions of culture and their broader engagement with the troublesome commodification of narco identity propel the texts and the scope of this book—from the local to the global and from the unilateral to the international commercial dynamics—in which Colombian popular culture quite suddenly became centered on the narco aesthetic. They unearth Colombia's difficult process of coming to terms with the past via popular cultural outlets that increasingly represent sex and violence. This unrefined subject matter, targeted to a broader, less sophisticated population, has made the creation of any kind of female agenda particularly challenging. Though women's perspectives come out in the open through sporadic occasions of rebellion, frustration, and certain acts of courage, the conjunction of sex and narco violence, combined with the discourse of national identity, typically presupposes a male subject position.

In consequence, cultural production devoted to narco aesthetics favors male-driven story lines, reducing the great majority of female characters to the familiar archetypes of lovers, martyrs, and betrayers. It does not help that their depiction, usually sexually charged and enhanced by silicone augmentation, can be viewed as pandering to prurient interests. Yet there are those few female typecasts, real and fictional, who upset the prevailing myths and practices, showing that women's protagonism in the narco narrative has only just begun. Indeed, chauvinistic tales about the world of drug trafficking play a substantial role in the formation of conflictive gender images, as they reinstate damaging sexist stereotypes while instituting new representations of dynamic female subjectivity. Likewise, cultural renditions of the narco aesthetic exalt stereotypical machos who live to conquer, yet on the flip side, they almost always end up getting their just deserts—thus revealing their fragility and ultimate ineffectiveness in the unpredictable world of fleeting drug power.

Finally, the thematic and aesthetic predominance of violence would not sell to so many sectors of the public were it not filtered via humor, parody, kitsch, and melodrama, tools that mediate a brutal reality in a carnivalesque and often caricatural display. One could argue that their irreverence in conjunction with their constant references to the nation's narco reality validates the public's desires for more information, knowledge that has been concealed by corrupt official sources but can now surface precisely because mediatic forces propel the flow of information around statal censorship. Yet the opposite argument also merits reflection, for the outpouring of narco stories where, in the end, all bad traffickers (read: unruly citizens) end up incarcerated or dead imbues the viewing masses with optimism and faith in the present-day governmental institutions. All in all, in the narco tales, good wins over evil, and the transgressors reap their "reward" for flouting the established order. Such stories, replete with sex and outrageous violence, distract the public's attention from the issues troubling Colombian society today, by nostalgically underscoring the spellbinding era of narco caudillismo as a thing frozen in an unde-termined but definite past. What remains is the memory of a regional strongman, a figure, it would seem, vanquished by the largely ineffective yet ultimately triumphant modern law. The visibility of the narco aes-thetic is nothing more than a cultural mediation that stages cultural bod-ies and signs to tell us something about Colombian society and the global community in general. Regardless of Pablo Escobar's ultimate legacy, the narco craze bespeaks present-day anxieties, substantiating valid social preoccupations that rivet society today, from exorcising the ghosts of the past to reflecting upon—even celebrating—commodity fetishism.

2

From Man's Man to Mama's Boy

Escobar, el patrón del mal

Pablo sufría de mamitis—como le dicen los paisas al exagerado apego a
la mamá—y no importando las circunstancias ni los riesgos, mandaba a
buscarla con frecuencia.
[Pablo suffered from mommy-itis—as the *paisas* call the exaggerated attachment to a mother—and no matter the circumstances and risks, he
would consult with her all the time.]

Salazar, La parábola de Pablo, 216

don Pablito, ¿valiente para unas cosas y cobarde para otras?
[Don Pablito, tough for some things and a coward for others?]

Escobar's mother in Escobar, el patrón del mal

"It's not clear to me why Miss Yesenia is still alive, why this girl hasn't
died" [No entiendo por qué la señorita Yesenia sigue con vida, por qué
esta muchachita no se ha muerto]. The Escobar character makes this comment offhandedly to his *sicario* Yeison Taborda Marino (played by Carlos
Mariño) in the 2012 telenovela *Escobar, el patrón del mal*, based on Alonso
Salazar's biography *La parábola de Pablo* (2001).[1] The capo's polite tone and
his ostensible confusion over Yesenia's continued survival make the terrifying imminence of the girl's death even more spine-chilling. They also
reveal how the real-life Escobar, played by Andrés Parra, did not attach
emotionally to the women he bedded. Given that *narcocultura* bolsters
a particularly masculinized ideal of a *narcotraficante* who accumulates
wealth, power, and women only to consume indiscriminately and cast
them aside, Escobar's portrayal when it comes to his former lovers aligns
with cinematic conventions of the narco macho. In the series, Yesenia,
Escobar's young paramour from the *comunas*, dared to become pregnant

with the capo, proudly announced it to him, and insisted on keeping the baby. In response, Escobar tricked her into an abortion performed by his veterinarian at Hacienda Nápoles. He then sent Marino (the real-life Popeye) to nurse her back to health, in part out of a smidgeon of guilt, but mainly to keep her in check. Yet the insult to Yesenia did not stop there, because when Marino and the girl fell in love, Escobar made it clear that either his enamored triggerman would kill her or he would be eliminated himself. The budding romance was jeopardizing Marino's loyalty to his clique, and who could threaten their bond more than a woman previously scorned by the Patrón? The story is so melodramatic that it seems to be nothing more than a telenovela plot twist.

Yet the character of Yesenia (interpreted by Diana Neira) is based on the real-life Wendy Chavarriaga Gil, Escobar's former lover, sentenced to death for allegedly snitching on him. Like her cinematographic persona, Wendy had become pregnant with Escobar's child, and she was forced to have an abortion because the family-oriented capo adamantly refused to father children out of wedlock. Later on, she became Popeye's girlfriend, yet unlike the romance between Yesenia and Marino in the series, this relationship did not develop behind Escobar's back. In one of his many interviews, Popeye narrates how he felt obliged to consult with his boss on his private matters, in particular since the object of his affection "belonged" to the capo at one point: "Since you had to tell the Patrón everything, I asked him if I could go out with her. He agreed but told me to be careful" [Como al patrón había que informarlo de todo, le pedí permiso para ennoviarme con ella, me lo dio, pero me dijo que tuviera cuidado]. Later on, Escobar informed Popeye about Wendy's betrayal of the cartel and ordered his henchman to kill her. Because the *sicario* himself "loved her with all his heart," he instead sent five of his henchmen to do the job while she was waiting for him at a restaurant ("Popeye").[2] By volunteering to lure his lover into a mortal trap, Popeye once and for all subscribed to the "bros before hos" code of the mafia.

Fast-forward to 2014, with the gray-haired Popeye looking back on his life before his release from a maximum-security prison in Boyacá province. Wendy's death must have weighed on the *sicario*'s conscience more than his countless other crimes, for Popeye considers it one of the darkest moments in his life. Yet despite the irony of the situation, he echoes his boss's anxiety about strong women by equating his victim with female treachery: "Wendy taught me that broads in war are more dangerous than a bullet in the chest" [Wendy me enseñó que las hembras en la guerra son más peligrosas que un balazo en el pecho (Aranguren)]. Just as his boss ultimately feared Wendy's unruly spirit, bouts of jealousy, and hot temper, Popeye blames his victim for her own fate.

Aired in 2012, *Escobar, el patrón del mal* offers a sweeping portrait of Colombia's turbulent twentieth-century history while mourning its fallen heroes and tracing the drug lord's rise to power and his demise ("Personajes del año"). Created by Camilo Cano and Juana Uribe (interestingly, both direct descendants of Escobar victims), the series draws from archival data and life testimonies, all the while providing a gamut of melodramatic twists and turns, not just the ones inherent in Escobar's life story. With a star-studded cast and sparing no expense, Caracol Televisión describes the show as Colombia's most ambitious TV series to date. According to *El Espectador*, the first episode received the largest viewership of any debut in the nation's history. As typical with narco telenovelas, *Escobar, el patrón del mal* met with plenty of controversy in the press and social media, but the ratings and the awards it garnered attest to the quality of the series and its enthusiastic reception. In 2013, *Escobar, el patrón del mal* was nominated in fourteen categories for the *Premio India Catalina*, winning eleven and thereby becoming the most awarded series by that organization. For his portrayal as the adult Escobar, Andrés Parra received Best Actor of the Moment (Premio Momento Mejor Actor), Best Actor in a Series, Favorite Protagonist in the Series at the 22nd Premios TVyNovelas in 2013, Man of the Year by *Revista Elenco* 2012, and Distinguished Actor of the Year by *El Espectador*. In brief, the series had a significant effect on its viewers, and it turned the already famous Andrés Parra into Colombia's superstar.

Escobar, el patrón del mal brings to life the Medellín Cartel, even if most names are fictitious and some characters are combined into one. It also sheds light on narco masculinity, the subject of this chapter, exhibited principally by Parra's Escobar and his pack of trusted triggermen. The interactions between Escobar and his gun-toting enforcers disclose that the language of male heroism was instrumental in Escobar's ethos of banditry. In the same vein, their dismissive attitude toward women reinforces masculine hegemony. Yet, despite this misogyny, long institutionalized in the narco milieu, the treatment of gender reveals some cracks that ultimately subvert the formulaic depiction of Escobar as a tough macho. This is what makes the series particularly interesting, because its nuanced portrayal of Escobar's sexuality, with indications of pedophilia and deep insecurities in his relationship with his mother, undermine any celebratory, one-dimensional portrait of a gangster.

The Ubiquitous Popeye: Self-Proclaimed Narco Warrior (and Medellín's PR Disaster)

[*Popeye's career in social media turned out to be brief. As this book was going to print, he died of esophageal cancer on February 6, 2020. In May 2018 he had been put back behind bars on charges of extortion and criminal conspiracy, and soon afterward rumors began to circulate about his health problems. He died in custody.*] The telenovela portrays how a double standard reigned in Escobar's inner circle, since he was enjoying the company of his family at the same moment Yesenia met her end. Meanwhile, Escobar's henchmen were to be at his disposal night and day. They bonded and tested their manhood in a homosocial world almost bereft of women, where to become a member of Escobar's clique was the highest honor but was also synonymous with a peripheral, if any, personal life. Real-life accounts confirm that the double standard was indeed part of a strictly stratified hierarchy in which the boss's utmost manliness was already confirmed by his status and wealth, and thus was above the tests that his subordinates needed to take. Popeye remembers that joining the circle of the capo's closest bodyguards meant a steady salary of about $1,500 per month, where "it wasn't so much about the money—it was an honor to be on the payroll, but this also meant you had to be in the office every day" (Mollison, with Nelson, 118). With most of Escobar's henchmen deceased, Popeye's testimony is a rare glimpse into the capo's hold over his subordinates, where fierce, unconditional loyalty to the boss superseded all other bonds. In the first encounter between the capo and his future lieutenant, Escobar emerges larger than life, enigmatic and omniscient:

His eyes pierce through me. It's as if he was reading my entire past. His pupils, in a thousandth of a second, traverse each feature of my face . . . When I answer his question, he looks carefully at the movement of my lips, as if he had mastered a secret code to detect truth from lies . . . it is one of the best days of my life. *Pablo Emilio Escobar Gaviria, el Capo de Capos, el Señor, el Patrón, el Jefe*, the man most feared, most powerful, and the richest in Colombia, has taken note of me. (Legarda 17)

[Me mira a los ojos en forma penetrante. Es como si estuviera leyendo todo mi pasado. Su pupila, en milésimas de segundo, recorre cada rasgo de mi rostro . . . Cuando contesto su pregunta, mira fijamente el movimiento de mis labios, como si dominara un código secreto con el que detecta si se le dice la verdad o se le miente . . . es uno de los mejores días de mi vida. *Pablo Emilio Escobar Gaviria, el Capo de Capos, el Señor, el Patrón, el Jefe*, el hombre más temido, poderoso, y rico de Colombia, se ha fijado en mí. (my translation)]

Popeye's recollection to this day upholds the allure of Escobar's power. The henchman's unwavering affection for his former boss, proven by the fact that decades spent behind bars did not erase his feeling of wonder, befits his self-reconfiguration in the public eye. After all, to forsake his past with Escobar would deprive him of a celebrity thug status, an example of "an underworld exhibitionist" who actively seeks notoriety, as Ruth Penfold-Mounce puts it in her typology of criminal celebrities. Having given up criminality (usually because they end up in jail), these exhibitionists market themselves as sensationalist nostalgia for a public eager to "consume according to notions of newsworthiness" (Penfold-Mounce 87).

In the same vein, by proclaiming steadfast loyalty to Escobar—the "core" brand already infused with ample symbolism—Popeye obtains more social leverage among the market segments interested in the capo and all things narco. Very much like Roberto, Escobar's brother, Popeye has adopted the public persona of a former-thug-turned-storyteller and the guardian of the Patrón's legend. He has carte blanche to represent himself, for there are few people alive who could refute his standing in the capo's army. In fact, both Escobar's son and his sister, Alba Marina, whose relationship has been strained to say the least, insist that Popeye never enjoyed such a high status in the Escobar ranks, yet Popeye's ubiquity in the contemporary mediascape has drowned out their voices.

Regardless of its "truth," Popeye's identity performance offers a unique insight into the multifaceted narco discourse and the Escobar brand. The hitman appears candid and eager to share his story, even when claiming responsibility for hundreds of deaths. The most obvious ace up his sleeve is his close "professional" connection with Escobar and his having personally participated in numerous acts of violence perpetrated by the Medellín Cartel. With the immediacy of publicity afforded by social media, Popeye's avenues for promotion allow him instant technological gratification. After his release from prison in 2014, he built up a cult following as an avid YouTuber, posting hundreds of videos on the site POP-EYE_Arrepentido (Remorseful Popeye). With a subscriber base of more than one million by 2019, he never seems to run out of material, from presenting short videos on former hitmen friends and Escobar and commenting on the North Valley Cartel figureheads to discussing presidential candidates in Colombia, corruption, and Chilean and Venezuelan politics and hawking his line of merchandise. Aside from direct communication with his followers, Popeye collaborates with countless writers, journalists, and, seemingly whoever wants to listen. Featured in innumerable documentaries, television programs (the 2017 Discovery Series *Finding Escobar's Millions*, among others), and interviews—both televised and in print—Popeye incessantly constructs a celebrity status attached to the Escobar brand. If YouTube "has seized the periphery, providing access to the 'scene' far more actively than to the films (or television shows) themselves" (Grainge 34), then here, the periphery works on multiple levels, where a convicted assassin reached new participatory communities, new generations of digitally enabled viewers whose attention span favors audiovisual sources over print and clip culture over full-length films. Finally, Popeye is the main protagonist of Caracol's 2017 series *Alias J.J.*, with Juan Pablo Urrego in the leading role. Tireless and a virtuoso of various social platforms, Popeye markets himself nearly as efficiently as his Patrón marketed cocaine.

Part of stretching the Escobar brand—or linking one's reputation through umbrella branding, that is, selling several products under the same name—is assuring that the product is of a similar quality, that it is consistent "in all customer touch points" (Gronlund 143). Since weakening its familiarity automatically diminishes the emotional relationship the customer has developed with the brand, upholding a strong brand identity involves exalting its key qualities. It is here that Popeye appears particularly savvy in intertwining his agenda with Escobar's legend. His 2015 autobiography, awkwardly titled *Sobreviviendo a Pablo Escobar: "Popeye" el sicario, 23 años y 3 meses de la cárcel* (*Surviving Pablo Escobar: "Popeye" the sicario, 23 years and three months of jail*), reminisces about his years of incarceration, all the while framing them within the cult of the capo's personality. It suggests another insight into Escobar, both through its title and its cover page—though, in fact, Escobar is barely mentioned in the story. To live up to the archetype of the Outlaw, the essence of whatever

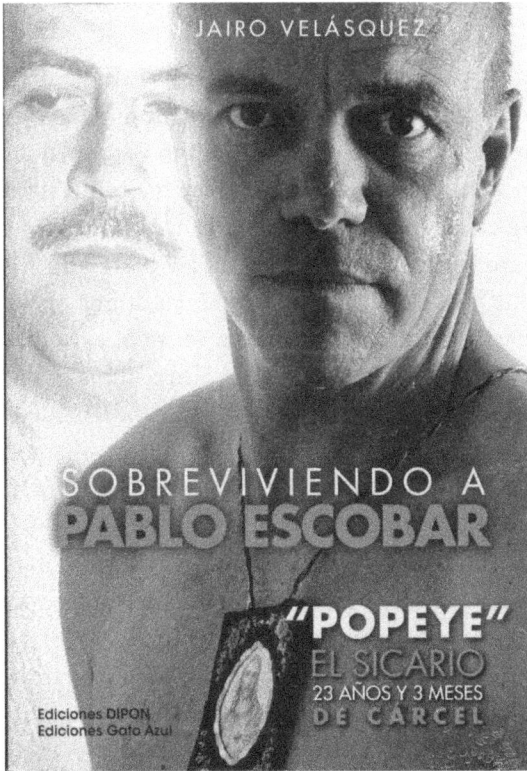

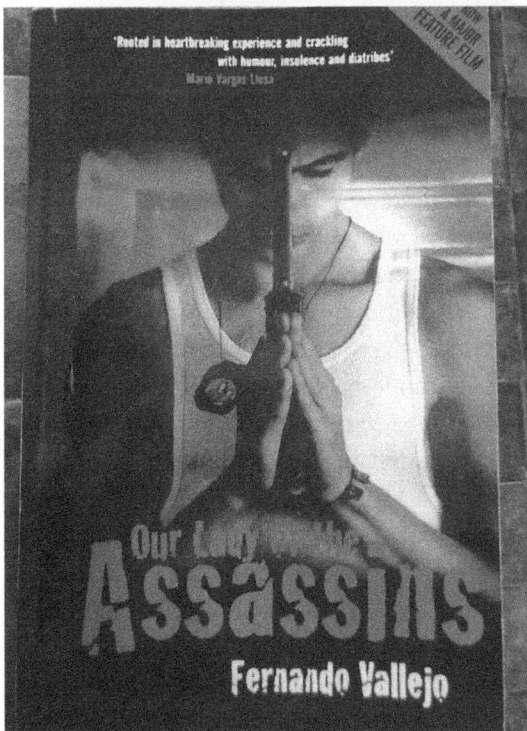

Above: Figure 7. The cover of Jhon Jairo Velásquez's 2015 *Sobreviviendo a Pablo Escobar: "Popeye" el sicario, 23 años y 3 meses de cárcel.*

Left: Figure 8. The iconic image from the 2000 film by Barbet Schroeder based on Vallejo's novel, and the 2001 English version of the book. Note the scapular in figures 7 and 8.

Popeye is selling needs to be congruent with the values of the desired brand. Here, the book cover provides well-defined visual points to cue the reader into the appropriate archetype. In the forefront, Popeye looks directly at his readers, with a scapular hanging on his bare torso. His stark appearance and direct gaze create discomfort in the reader, all the while providing two clues that are consistent with the Outlaw brand: an in-your-face image "with a bite," which suggests the inherent drama of the product sold under this particular archetype,[3] and a sense of exposure and toughness that creates an aura of authenticity. It is also reminiscent of the book cover of Fernando Vallejo's celebrated *Our Lady of the Assassins*, thereby connecting deeper with the cultural tradition of drug-themed stories and hitmen in general. A black-and-white picture of Escobar in the background gives historical depth, further underpinning an appearance of documentary truthfulness and the underlying thuggishness of its subject matter. Finally, the simple act of including Escobar on the cover positions the book under the brand umbrella.[4]

When all is said and done, the book itself disappoints with its monotone prose and uneventful accounts. One suspects that Popeye had already said it all in Astrid Legarda's 2005 biography and countless interviews, but as with today's celebrities, it is not so much the content as the continuous presence in the media that maintains his relevance.

Another example of Popeye's branding technique is his public reaction to conflict. An interview with Virginia Mayer shows him to be repentant and yet still toying with the idea of settling old scores. This menacing attitude, even if only acted out as a performance, aligns with Escobar's notoriety, thereby creating a deeper correlation between what Popeye represents and what the Escobar brand stands for. In reaction to Alba Marina's comment about his insignificant position in Escobar's ranks, Popeye retorts with a classic *sicario* solution: "I'm not a coward. I'm already retired from crime. For me it would be wonderful to go to Medellín to murder her. . . . I would be happy to seat Alba Marina down . . . and cut her into little pieces" (Mayer). [Yo no soy un cobarde. Yo ya estoy retirado del crimen. Para mí sería un sueño ir a Medellín a matarla . . . Yo sería feliz sentando a Alba Marina . . . y matarla descuartizadita (my translation)]. If in the same interview Popeye accuses Escobar's son of proclaiming a false innocence ("Juan Pablo now sells himself as Gandhi" [Juan Pablo ahora se vende como Gandhi]), he himself is not bereft of ideology. Time and time again, he adopts the stance of an Escobar wannabe, revealing his unfaltering admiration for the legendary macho ideal: "I could become the biggest bandit of Colombian Republic. . . . I have the experience I learned from Pablo Emilio Escobar Gaviria" [Yo estoy en la capacidad de ser el bandido más grande de la República de Colombia . . . tengo experiencia que me enseñó Pablo Emilio Escobar Gaviria (Mayer)].

In the 2018 *Dark Tourist*, Popeye pops up in the very first episode. He predictably serves not only as the usual self-proclaimed guide on anything related to Escobar but also as a shameless promoter of his own notoriety. For no apparent reason, and to the delight of foreigners touring La Catedral, Popeye re-enacts a murder for the cameras. Lost in self-aggrandizement, he makes the subject of Escobar secondary to his own self-fashioning in a scene more ludicrous than threatening. Yet tourists are thrilled with this unanticipated show-and-tell, and the host also appears tickled pink with his guide, calling the former *sicario* "literally a YouTube star . . . [and] one of the most charismatic, friendly people you've ever met. He's just such a different person from what you'd expect" (Bellman). As Medellín is trying to eradicate Escobar's legacy altogether, Popeye pops up all over social media and repeatedly rubs salt in old wounds. Within a particularly contested space in which the logic of pure profit, global mass media, and insurmountable local trauma meet face-to-face, the ex-murderer-turned-criminal celebrity cashes in on death. This conflict is not just over the profit-making enterprise associated with the memory market but also over history itself, over trivializing and modifying the past by sponsoring the memory of its victimizers. As Ksenija Bilbija and Leigh A. Payne comment on the marketing of trauma in Latin America, victims with post-traumatic stress disorder want to forget bygone atrocities, yet conflicts persist because the perpetrators of that violence and their supporters rewrite the violent past by whitewashing the criminals (7–8). While the authors focus on nations plagued by dictatorships, such as Argentina, Uruguay, and Chile, the tensions over memory-making hit the very nerve of what is happening in Medellín.

The telenovela *Escobar, el patrón del mal* draws to an extent from Popeye's tales, yet it does not uphold his overarching myth of Escobar's omnipotence. Rather, the series weakens this image through the relationship between the capo and his domineering mother. Popeye never commented on these nuances, invariably spinning tales of Escobar's infallible individualism. In a 2012 interview with Harold Abueta and María Elvira Arango, he lays out a classic mafia misogyny, in which belonging to Escobar's elite

Figure 9. David Farrier and Popeye look rather chummy in the photo, even though Popeye poses as if he has the show's host in a chokehold. Tattoos and a semiautomatic add to the gangster cachet. This is yet another contact Popeye made with Netflix (*Alias JJ* being the main one). Photo by permission of David Farrier and Netflix.

meant being chivalrous with the boss's wife and mother but treating all other women with indifference. He gleefully describes *sicarios* as devoted family men and loving spouses, all the while disregarding the setbacks his job caused in his own life:

> We used to respect the women of our associates. . . . The drug trafficker and the assassin are very good fathers and husbands. Since they live surrounded by so much hatred, upon their return home they have a lot of respect for their wives and children. Look at Pablo, he adored Manuelita. . . . And Doña María Victoria Henao, Doña Tata, his wife, she was a saint. (Abueta and Arango)

> [Respetábamos a las mujeres de nuestros compañeros . . . El narcotraficante y el asesino son muy buenos padres de la familia. Como viven rodeados de tanto odio, cuando llegan a la casa tienen mucho respeto por la mujer y por los niños. Mire a Pablo, adoraba a Manuelita . . . Y doña María Victoria Henao, doña Tata, su esposa, era una santa. (my translation)]

Yet Popeye's relationship with Wendy Chavarriaga Gil was not only disrespectful but fatal—as the episode "Yesenia's death" of the series *Escobar, el patrón del mal* reveals. Its central theme is male camaraderie solidified via the scapegoating of the female, not unlike Borges's "La intrusa," where a woman's demise restored the harmony between two confused and warring brothers. The sacrifice of Yesenia confirmed Marino's loyalty both to the Patrón and to his entire gang. If the real-life Popeye had his lover killed by his sidekicks, then the series unsurprisingly intensified the melodrama by having the henchman eliminate his girlfriend himself.

The story unravels as follows: A tormented Marino meets with the girl with the pretext of running away with her and shoots her dead as she trustingly embraces him. He is beyond despair while committing this crime, and the hopelessness and anguish of this scene make the audience mourn the destruction of something so pure in an environment so tainted. In the meantime, ready to seize him if he wavers in his mission, Escobar's other gunmen watch the fateful rendezvous from afar. Yesenia stands no chance next to the brutal cult of brotherhood. She is vulnerable and helpless like all the real-life "Escobar's virgins" described by Germán Caycedo, girls who were poor but beautiful—a staple in any Colombian city—who due to their life circumstances believed they had nothing to lose (160).

Of course, Popeye is not the only one of Escobar's henchman portrayed in the series. John Mario Ortiz, aka "Chili," played by Anderson Ballesteros (who won Best Actor in the 2013 Premio Talento Caracol for his performance), represents the real-life John Jairo Arias Tascón alias Pinina, fifth in rank in the cartel and the man overseeing two thousand of Escobar's assassins. Extremely efficient at recruiting shooters and bombers from the *comunas*, Pinina allegedly coauthored hundreds of attacks, including the assassination of Lara Bonilla and the DAS headquarters bombing.[5] A thief at twelve and gang member at fourteen, Pinina was considered very dangerous despite his short, slender frame and high-pitched voice.[6] Pinina's death on June 14, 1990, when he was ambushed at his apartment in the company of his wife and infant daughter, greatly weakened the cartel. In fact, General Miguel Maza Márquez assessed this *sicario*'s demise as a blow to the organization comparable to the killing of Pablo Escobar himself ("Golpe al sicariato").

In the series, the only woman in Chili's life is his sister, a tough prostitute and Escobar's occasional lover/confidante. Chili himself lives in a cramped room in her brothel, reminiscent of a jail cell, with its walls plastered with pictures from men's magazines. He is high-strung and ready to attack at the slightest hint of confrontation. He initially almost pounces at Gonzalo Gaviria (Escobar's cousin Gustavo, his closest partner in the Medellín Cartel, interpreted by Christian Tappan), only to relax upon receiving an order to carry out a hit on a local vendor who snitched on the young Escobar. The capo's attention seems to provide the *sicario* with a sense of purpose. At first a loose cannon, Chili becomes Escobar's most loyal and disciplined soldier. He embraces the gangsta ethos wholeheartedly, with serving Escobar as the highest honor.

Dagoberto Ruíz, "El Topo," the other key associate featured regularly in the series, is the real-life Mario Alberto Castaño Molina alias El Chopo,[7] the man in charge of Escobar's security following Tyson's death.[8] Ambushed by the elite Bloque de Búsqueda in his apartment in 1993, he died of forty-eight bullet wounds at the age of forty (Nullvalue). In the television series, El Topo breaks up with his young wife early on, viciously carving a smile on her face for allegedly snitching. Then he says goodbye to his male lover moments before the police storm into his apartment, thereby revealing a pervasive facet of masculinity in the Medellín Cartel. The capo's homosocial circles in *Escobar, el patrón del mal* do not openly display homosexuality, yet they do not refute it either. The real-life Escobar was heard to comment repeatedly that if he were to eliminate gay *sicarios* from his gang, he would have very few people working for him (J. Salazar, *La parábola de Pablo* 174). We can presume that nonheteronormative sexual practices were fairly common among Escobar's henchmen, yet little has been documented anywhere in this regard.

Mollison mentions Escobar's taste for lesbian sex shows and the variety of "adult" toys found in La Catedral prison after the army raid of 1992 (198–99). As for male homosexuality, Escobar's cousin Jaime speaks of the debauchery and excess of the capo's closest bodyguards, thereby attesting to the amply theorized thin line between hypermasculinity and queerness: "These people reached new extremes. They would sleep with whoever—beauty queens one day and beautiful 'queens' the next. There was an expression: *un culo al año no hace daño* [an asshole a year never hurt anyone]" (Mollison 200). Salazar, too, refers to the homoerotic desire among Escobar's thugs while taking note of the dialectic between homoeroticism and homophobia: "These warriors sometimes sought out young men, sometimes they focused on transvestites for unknown pleasures and later, with their machismo in full resurgence, they would kill them as 'crazy little bitches'" [Estos guerreros a veces buscaban jóvenes, a veces buscaban en los travestis placeres no conocidos y luego, con la hombría en plena resurrección, los mataban por "locas hijueputas" (J. Salazar, *La parábola de Pablo* 174)]. Intense homophobia among bonding alpha males as a symptom of their underlying anxieties about their sexual identity has been a leitmotif in literature and is frequently analyzed in gender theory. By scapegoating the object of their short-lived desire, Escobar's goons spurned and exorcised their own cravings for erotic contact with the same sex.

Popeye also had to deal with rumors casting doubt on his heterosexuality. Among the photos found in La Catedral after Escobar and his clique went into hiding were a couple depicting Popeye flirtatiously dressed as a female prostitute. Mollison, who includes these images in his book, writes that they prompted debates in Congress about the "gay mafia" (200–201). Popeye was less than happy with this turn of events: "This photo has been a real pain because it has gone around the world. When they had the debate in Congress about the escape, the senators said that we dressed up as women to have sex between ourselves. Stupid" (Mollison 200). Another picture in Mollison's book depicts Popeye sitting in the lap of an unidentified man, locked in an embrace and placing a smooch on the man's balding head (190). The police official commenting on the photograph seemed more intrigued by Popeye's affection toward the other man than the latter's identity, in that he pointed to the *sicario*'s behavior as an aberration: "One can observe Jhon Jairo Velásquez Vásquez in an embrace, exhibiting deviant behavior" [se observa a Jhon Jairo Velásquez Vásquez en un abrazo con actitudes desviadas], (Mollison 190). It is not difficult to follow the commentator's sense of wonderment over mafiosi who might be less than highly masculine. While it is difficult to discern what was really going on in La Catedral, one thing is certain: Popeye's anxiety over the rumors about his sexuality attests to the importance he ascribed to the desired image of an all-around masculine rogue. To this day, Popeye has the warrior hierarchy fully internalized, perhaps as a way to explain and accept his own infatuation with Escobar's charisma: "Pablo Escobar was a genius, maybe a genius of evil, but a genius regardless. . . . He inspired an infinite loyalty in all of us who believed in him. I ended up believing that he was immortal. The saddest day of my life was the day he was killed" ("¡Popeye sale de la cárcel!") [Pablo Escobar era un genio, tal vez un genio del mal, pero en todo caso un genio . . . Inspiraba una lealtad infinita en todos los que creíamos en él. Yo llegué a creer que era inmortal. El día más triste de mi vida fue el día que lo mataron (my translation)].

Escobar, Oedipus Rex

The overarching premise of Donald Moss's *Thirteen Ways of Looking at a Man*, itself drawn from Judith Butler's theory of gender performativity, is that just like femininity, masculinity is a continuous reaffirmation of a set of norms that secure for its male participant an image of what a "real" man should be. Even though the very myth of masculine self-making rejects such an explanation—endorsing instead a unified self that possesses a set of masculine traits utterly independent of their environment—masculinity, like femininity, is scripted and contingent on cultural rhetoric. For Moss, masculinity is tantamount to the feminine beauty ideal, in that it houses the unattainable (6).

It would be an understatement to say that the narco milieu is the ultimate playground for thugs, where alpha male attitudes and a readiness to unleash aggression are essential for survival and therefore conscientiously observed.[9] In the brief moments between "missions," Escobar's goons enjoyed binges of hyper consumerism, although they experienced narco power vicariously through their Patrón more than by their own account. True, their extravagant purchases set high lifestyle standards among the impressionable youth in the *comunas* who offered their lives in the hope of acquiring similar luxuries: "Sporting the latest fashions from Miami and driving Mitsubishi and Toyota four-wheel drives, the fast-living lifestyle of Escobar's combo influenced an entire generation" (Mollison 119). But in reality, violence, death, and betrayal were the daily fare of Escobar's banditos. In *La parábola de Pablo* (2001), Salazar describes how Chopo was involved in an internal conflict, which led to the deaths of *sicarios* loyal to Escobar's other right-hand man, El Mugre (The Dirty One). The bloodbath continued until Escobar discovered that the leaks to the police on Chopo's whereabouts had come from Chopo's ex-wife (296). Then Popeye admits to killing, on Escobar's orders, Gerardo "Quico" (also spelled "Kiko") Moncada, an important member of the Medellín Cartel and Popeye's close friend. Rather than ponder the absurdity of the situation, Popeye respects Moncada even more for his stoic resignation when faced with impending death:

In our world, one is always ready for such things. When you are a bandit, death can come at any moment. One has a different preparation for it than the rest of people. I handcuffed Quico and took him to the basement. He acted like a man and the only thing he asked was if I could read him some psalms from the Bible before shooting him dead. I got the Bible, and I read to him everything he asked me to read, and after that I shot him. ("Mató")

[En el mundo nuestro uno siempre está listo para esas cosas. Cuando uno es bandido, la muerte le puede llegar en cualquier momento. Uno tiene una preparación para eso diferente que el resto de la gente. Yo esposé a Quico y lo bajé al sótano. Él era muy varón y lo único que me dijo era que si podía leerle algunos salmos de la Biblia antes de disparar. Conseguí la Biblia y le leí todo lo que me pidió y después de eso le metí un tiro. (my translation)]

Thus romances, friendships, and loyalties take a back seat to an absolute submission to Escobar's governance and his code of vengeance, where "acting like a man" includes stoicism in the face of loss, even of one's life. Yet the cutthroat affiliative exigencies of Escobar's closest circle of goons should not overshadow their ideological and emotional power. A deep-rooted fantasy of military brotherhood emerges that facilitates the submission of self to a group identity and the inflation of self through daring, criminal deeds. As Mollison puts it, "Confronted daily with the death of friends and enemies, and armed with a seemingly endless supply of well-paid *vueltas* (errands), Escobar's men lived each day as if it were their last. 'Of course a lot of people died, but they wanted to live very intensely, even if it was just for a moment'" (119). Escobar makes selection into his inner circle appear highly competitive, where only the most daring can achieve the honor. For *sicarios*, such a role constitutes a compromise between self-sufficiency and responding to an idealized father figure, a leader of demigod status. This kind of relationship with patriarchal authority demands a submission to the father that is empowering rather than castrating.

Returning to *Escobar, el patrón del mal*, the ideal of warrior masculinity is observed by men who idolize their boss, but above all it is observed by the capo himself. Escobar upholds a masculinist culture that romanticizes hypervirility, homosocial camaraderie, prowess, and chase-and-kill practices. Hunting, the primordial occupation of humanity, takes on the symbolic qualities of a war or competition between Escobar's men and their enemies. It is a testament to their predatory nature, which in their logic elevates them above the common folk. For John Clum, masculinity is largely a homosocial enactment, where "most of the policing is done by other males" (xv). In other words, a support frame, a community of believers, is necessary for such a myth to perpetuate itself. Masculinity "lacks the capacity to legitimize itself. It always needs affirmation, and there, in that need, lies its delegitimizing 'weak point,' its confession to be less than—other than—it aspires to. No matter how complete, masculinity suspects itself of pretending" (Moss 7). In this vein, Escobar constantly perfected his image of a bona fide leader reflecting off acquiescent women and faithful associates who yielded to his aggressive politics.

The television Escobar is not immune from the ideological critique of anything that might deviate from male hegemony. In his pursuit of top-dog masculinity, he must repudiate weakness and maintain his image as a charismatic social bandit. Yet his post-Oedipal frame of achievement and power hides pre-Oedipal anxieties, which come to light most saliently through the capo's nuanced relationship with his mother. If, in psychoanalytic terms, masculinity is a progression toward masculine agency and away from the feminine, Escobar's growth is suspect from the outset, because he never establishes a willed separation from his domineering mother.

One of the stages of the traditional family narrative in a self-made man's rhetoric is "oedipal defeat by and accommodation to the father" (Catano 64). Thus, natural male development involves realizing one's father's superiority (read: threat), an ideal fought against and later emulated by the male subject. Yet Escobar's real-life progenitor, Abel de Jesús Escobar Echeverri, is no hero to compete with, much less imitate; his naiveté and cowardice point to a masculine failure. According to Escobar's brother, Roberto, while the sons quickly adapted to city life after their move from Rionegro to Medellín, their father always lagged behind. A rancher by trade and passion, he lost his business when his cattle caught a disease and died. This economic fiasco must have been a blow to Pablo's nascent ambition, when, as Roberto remembers, "eventually my father had to declare bankruptcy and we lost the farm, we lost everything we owned" (Escobar Gaviria, with Fisher, 6). Abel's regression only deepened with time because, as Roberto reminisces, "our mother and father eventually moved to Medellín to be with us, but my father was never comfortable there. He returned to the countryside and found work on other people's farms. We would visit him, but we no longer belonged to rural life" (Escobar Gaviria, with Fisher, 9).

It is not only that Abel fell in rank from rancher to farmhand; unable to confront the challenge of living in the bustling city, he retreated into his shell and became a ghostly presence in his own family. While the compassionate Roberto dresses his father's failure in a veil of excuses, Salazar put it more bluntly by describing a man who "nostalgically abandoned his farm duties and in the neighborhood of La Paz became a quiet neighborhood night guard dressed in a hat and a poncho, a mere shadow of his enterprising wife" [abandonó con nostalgia sus oficios del campo y en el barrio La Paz se convirtió en sereno—celador nocturno del barrio—y en una especie de sombra, de sombrero y ruana, de su emprendedora esposa (J. Salazar, *La parábola de Pablo* 43)]. This is when allegedly little Pablo verbalizes his desire to usurp the role of his father by making childlike promises to his mother. Roberto recalls how his brother made promises of success to his progenitor: "Wait until I grow up, Mommy. I'm going to give you everything. Just wait until I grow up" (Escobar Gaviria, with Fisher, 11). The young Escobar thus wishes to replace his demasculinized father with a masculinized new self. Shamed by Abel's defeat, Pablo quickly usurps his father's oedipal dominance, becoming more of a partner to his mother than her offspring, while she in turn begins to live vicariously through her enterprising son. In Marc de Beaufort's 2004 documentary *Los archivos privados de Pablo Escobar,* Luz María (Pablo's sister) identifies this role reversal between father and son, whereby Escobar "was perhaps replacing my father in a sense, because my father didn't live with us" [fue tal vez reemplazando en cierto modo a mi papá porque mi papá, él no vivía con nosotros]. In any case, Abel could have never measured up to his domineering wife, who "enjoyed better things in life. . . . She was a queen who should have been crowned" [era muy rebuscadora de la vida. . . . Ella era la reina que debía ser coronada" (Luz María in *Los archivos*)]. In this mismatched couple, the ambitious wife recognized her own social drive in one of her sons, and she cultivated it to the end, notwithstanding Escobar's notoriety. Unlike all the other women in Pablo's life, his mother Hermilda Gaviria Berrío (cast as Doña Enelia in the series, and interpreted by Vicky Hernández) was the only one whose opinions he ever valued.

The transfiguration of roles within the basic family unit, where the mother places her male offspring in the role of the absent father, is nothing new. A 1995 article in Bogotá's *El Tiempo,* "Madre santa, hijo perverso"

(Saintly Mother, Deviant Son), examines the unhealthy bonds between despondent single mothers and sons who become *sicarios*. With pop psychology and socio-anthropological insight, its author examines young males' initiation into the world of crime as part of their devotion to their suffering mothers, who, unable to act out their own frustration, silently foster aggression in their children as an expression of self-respect. The article quotes a common street joke in which Jesus Christ must have been from Antioquia because he lived with his mother until the age of thirty-three and died convinced of his mother's sanctity and she of her son's godlike status (Elkin Ramírez). Of course, oceans separate Escobar from the underprivileged *sicarios* who take up murder to experience moments of consumerist bliss, yet the case of what Salazar calls mommy-itis applies equally to Escobar, especially when it comes to instruction in the specific framework of masculinity that will not only bring financial benefit but also the respect of others.

A childhood scene in the first episode of *Escobar, el patrón del mal* foreshadows a path to masculinity shaped by maternal mentoring. Stuck in the middle of a rope bridge, little Pablo is being swayed back and forth by other kids as he desperately hangs on. Doña Enelia runs to the rescue, scaring off the pranksters, yet instead of comforting her traumatized son, she orders him to stand up and finish crossing the bridge like a man. This opening scene is no accident: It foregrounds Escobar's early toughness as his attempt to impress and satisfy the phallic mother. Later on, as an adult, the real-life Escobar, like his mediatic counterpart, never fails to emphasize that his actions are motivated by the gender imperative to resolve every issue "like a man."[10]

Little Pablo of the television series next stands up to his siblings, calling them out on their lack of courage and committing ever more daring mischief. He grows into a precocious prankster with little use for school (read: authority), who bores easily, and who thinks himself the cleverest. Likewise, in Beaufort's *Los archivos* documentary, Doña Hermilda proudly recalls how in grade school, Pablo "did politicking," "exhibited leadership," and was "bossy" [estaba tirando de líder, hacía política en la escuela, and era mandón]. Similarly, Escobar's cousin Jaime confirms Pablo's insistence on running the show: "From an early age, an unbridled ambition, dogged determination and sheer audacity made him stand out amongst his family and friends. . . . He always had these natural leadership qualities" (Mollison 43).

From this resourceful troublemaker, Escobar evolved into an ambitious and daring entrepreneur for whom traditional career paths held no appeal. He morphed into a paterfamilias and community benefactor, thereby completing the rags-to-riches cycle. Such a social ascent cannot be sabotaged by the impression that he was educated by a wimp or a woman, strong as she might be. Effectively, Escobar refashioned the past in his official discourse, by substituting familial intimacy with a national self-fantasy that forsakes the father altogether. Rather than Abel's child, Pablo considered himself a "son of war" (hijo de esa guerra), who together with his cousin Gustavo "grew up as banditos in the first war between clans, which were evolving from ordinary smuggling into drug trafficking. The capos would fight over money, honor, women, or just for the sake of fighting" [se terminaron de criar como bandidos en la primera guerra entre clanes que transitaban del contrabando al narcotráfico. Los capos se peleaban por cuentas, por honor, por hembras o porque sí (J. Salazar, *La parábola de Pablo* 52–53)].

The smuggling legacy aside, Escobar's early lessons came principally from his dominant mother. In the telenovela, when little Pablo got caught stealing exam questions in the first episode, Doña Enelia gave him a lesson on effective transgression: "I'm going to give you a piece of advice. The day you do something bad, do it well. Pablo Emilio, this world is for the clever, not for the dumb, it is for the quick-witted. And you need to learn who to pick fights with . . . you can't allow yourself to be caught" [Le voy a dar un consejo. El día que Ud. haga algo malo, hágalo bien. Pablo Emilio, este mundo es para los vivos, no es para los bobos, es para los avispados. Y uno tiene que aprender con quien cazar las peleas . . . uno no puede dejarse pillar]. She is sympathetic to her son's boundless drive to outwit the world, because she herself seems drawn to rugged masculinity and the outlaw mentality, which her husband ostensibly lacks. In consequence, the telenovela lays out that rather than eradicate Pablo's criminal inclinations early on, his mother gives him lessons on how to deceive and dodge trouble more successfully.[11]

Pablo Escobar, Mama's Boy

Salazar repeatedly emphasizes the mother's role in Escobar's criminal development. In one interview, he states that Doña Hermilda "justified all his actions. She blessed his atrocities. She was the protector of his evil deeds. That is why Escobar had an exacerbated Oedipus complex" [justificaba todos sus actos. Ella bendecía sus atrocidades. Ella era la protectora de sus maldades. 'Por eso Escobar tenía un Edipo exacerbado' (Páez)]. In another, Salazar underscores her greed and contempt for the law, qualities that manifested with much greater force in her favorite son: "The persona of his mother is the most important one, that is why I converted her into an icon. . . . She emerges as an ambitious woman, very content with material benefits. Their situation illustrates an immense devaluation of the law, an immense Oedipus complex, and a force where desire has no limit and can be fulfilled" [La figura de su mamá es la más importante, así que aproveché para convertirla en un ícono. . . . Aparece como una mujer ambiciosa y muy alegre con las consecuencias materiales. Allí se perfila una inmensa desvalorización de la ley, un Edipo inmenso y una carga donde el deseo no tiene límite y se puede cumplir (Rodríguez Dalvard)]. The series emphasizes the mother's mentoring role in Escobar's rise to power, all the while suggesting that Escobar's lifelong attachment to her chipped away at his macho persona. If we read the mediatic Escobar through the prism of Freudian theory, the capo remains in limbo, in that he does not renounce the mother to accept the authority of the father, the symbol of masculine autonomy. Although he clings to one side of the bargain by resisting wholehearted submission to his wife and numerous lovers—maternal surrogates—his strong connection to Doña Hermilda discloses unresolved attachments.

In *Escobar, el patrón del mal*, episode 1, the mother's use of the word "dumb" (bobo) on two separate occasions also reveals her philosophy on life and her attitude toward her spouse. First, it comes in her lesson to Pablo, separating losers from winners, while later on, using the same epithet, she scolds her spouse: "Are you really that dumb or do you just act dumb?" [Ud. es un bobo o se hace bobo?]. This is when Abel shows up with a shovel to look for a hidden treasure, which, as legend goes, forest spirits bring to the surface only one night a year. Doña Enelia has little patience for her spouse, who in accordance to her logic, fails to inhabit the circles of power. Escobar is too quick for his father, and Abel is no match for his son's creativity and nerve. With his pack of followers, little Pablo concocts a plan to dupe his naive progenitor into thinking he found the treasure, when in reality it's a lantern filled with cookies. Needless to say, the gullible father easily falls prey to the prank. Then, as Escobar moves up the ladder of success, Abel descends into masculine failure altogether, turning into a ghost of his former self. In the meantime, Doña Enelia rewards her most daring offspring with respect and blind adulation, since he succeeded where her husband had failed. An interviewer for the magazine *Cromos* describes in an article reprinted in *El Espectador* that the real-life Hermilda, in her final years, kept an altar to Pablo in her bedroom, and Abel's photo was conspicuously absent:

> Close to her bedroom, Doña Hermilda has an enormous painting of Pablo Escobar. He is harmoniously joined with nature, and from his generously open hands sprout houses and illuminated soccer fields. "It is the symbol of what he did for the poor," says Doña Hermilda. Her spacious room has a balcony facing a small park broken up by a ravine. On both sides of her bed, on the nightstands, she has his photographs, and religious images hang on the walls. It strikes me that I see no photo of her husband, Abelito, who died a few months earlier. ("La nueva vida")

> [Cerca de su habitación, doña Hermilda tiene un enorme cuadro de Pablo Escobar. Él está fundido con la naturaleza y de sus manos, abiertas de manera generosa, brotan viviendas y canchas iluminadas. "Es el símbolo de lo que hizo por los pobres," dice doña Hermilda. Su espaciosa habitación tiene un balcón sobre una zona verde que cruza una quebrada. A ambos lados de la cama, sobre los nocheros, tiene fotografías suyas y en las paredes imágenes religiosas. Me llama la atención que no veo ninguna fotografía de su marido, Abelito, fallecido hace algunos meses. (my translation)]

Photos of Doña Hermilda's house in Mollison's book corroborate these descriptions, from her bedside table overflowing with Escobar photographs (Mollison 333) to stuffed hippo heads from Hacienda Nápoles (332) and a painting of Escobar's face juxtaposed on a mountainous Medellín landscape (18). Her infamous son remains the apple of her eye. In the same vein, Salazar describes the reversal of gender roles in the Escobar family, where "'Abelito was never a meaningful figure in our lives,' said Osito, and I understand it as the way to say that in Pablo's family the surname which defined their character was not Escobar but Gaviria. Doña Hermilda, his mother, was for him an unconditional support and ever-present love, which marked his personality and his way of being" ["Abelito nunca fue una figura significativa en nuestras vidas," ha dicho el Osito, y lo entiendo como una manera de decir que en la familia de Pablo el apellido que marca el carácter no es el Escobar sino el Gaviria. Doña Hermilda, su madre, fue para él un apoyo incondicional y un amor omnipresente que le marcó lo esencial de su carácter y su manera de ser (J. Salazar, *La parábola de Pablo* 43)]. Yet the relationship between Escobar and his mother might have been a bit more complex, with her adoration for her most infamous son not so apparent or absolute. Escobar's wife's memoirs reveal a colder, more inflexible mother who denied her son time and affection when he needed it most. When the capo was in hiding, longing for family contact, particularly that of his mother, she ignored his pleas, imposing instead plans that did not include Pablo.[12]

Antioquian *sicarios* are known to worship their mothers, but they are usually placed on the pedestal, suffering and self-sacrificing, venerated by their offspring for virtues born out of passivity and not their agency. Abandoned by the father(s) of their children, they barely make ends meet, and in the long run, they are incapable of holding their children in check. In contrast, Doña Enelia from the television series remains in charge well beyond her sons' formative years. With Escobar already grown and married, she continues to instruct him on how to conduct his marriage and love affairs, as well as his criminal career. She is perceptive, calculating, and bossy, and unlike the rest of Escobar's entourage, she does not hesitate to call Pablo out on his actions. Her spirited attitude is shown in the series when Escobar interviews two Afro-Colombian brothers (Tyson and Kika) who become part of his gang later on. Doña Enelia causes a scene because he had made her wait unnecessarily: "If you can't, why do you promise, why don't you just say, it'll be ten minutes, I'll wait, and it's all good?" [Si Ud. no puede, por qué se compromete, por qué no me dice de una vez son 10 minutos, yo me espero y asunto arreglado]. Insignificant as this exchange may appear in the context of the story, it shows a contest of wills between two dominant personalities, performed for a trivial reason in front of two strangers who nonetheless buy into Escobar's myth of supreme banditry. In the next scene, Doña Enelia reprimands Escobar for spending too much time with thugs instead of catering to his wife, who has been feeling neglected. *Escobar, el patrón del mal* makes it clear that no one but his mother can safely rebuke Escobar.

Escobar brushes off his wife's recent moodiness by resorting to misogynistic clichés: "Because she is a woman. Women are like that. One day they bitch just because, and another just because it isn't" [Porque es mujer. Mujeres son así, un día joden porque sí, un día joden porque no]. When Doña Enelia reminds him that as his mother she is above his easily manipulated female admirers and male sycophants and therefore expects honesty, Escobar snaps back at her, disclosing his awareness of her authority and hers of his crimes, "Well, then you shouldn't be terrified by what I do or will do because this face, and this attitude, and this toughness come from you and not from my dad, and I shouldn't be named Pablo Emilio Escobar Gaviria but Pablo Emilio Gaviria, the son of Doña Enelia Gaviria. Period" [Pues no se debería aterrar de las cosas que yo hago y voy a hacer porque esta cara, y esta actitud y esta berraquera, se las deben a Ud. y no a mi papá, yo no debería llamarme Pablo Emilio Escobar Gaviria sino Pablo Emilio Gaviria hijo de doña Enelia Gaviria. Punto].

There is an inherent contradiction embedded in the basic rhetoric of masculinity, in that men must appear self-sufficient even though they already suffered a defeat that marked them as not-the-father. At the same time, both Freudian and Lacanian theory underscore men's desire (even if repeatedly denied) for the original wholeness of a union or reunion with the mother. Such drives manifest themselves through constant tension between masculine separation versus unity, personal victory over other men versus oedipal struggle and defeat. For James V. Catano, masculine anxieties over separation from the mother can reveal themselves by misrepresenting and devaluating the power carried by the maternal figure. Hence bossy female figures can be envisioned by their male offspring as sweet and suffering rather than in control of their children's lives (Catano 62–63), so as to preserve and buttress the man's image of his own authority. In contrast, Escobar does not even attempt to project a less domineering persona onto his mother. He calls her "berraca" (tough), and indeed, Escobar's mother is tenacious and forceful. Whereas Abel is crushed under his son's achievements, the mother is ever stronger, perfectly at home in her son's criminal world. The mediatic take on Doña Hermilda is close to the assessment by General Hugo Martínez of the Bloque de Búsqueda, when he insists that Doña Hermilda "knew about the income, about the distribution of goods, of the economic activities; without being a drug trafficker she was complicit in what her sons were doing . . . and in some cases eager to sic the dogs, she would scream bloody murder to get revenge" [(Ella) estaba pendiente de los ingresos, de la distribución de las cosas, de los intereses económicos; sin que fuera narcotraficante era complaciente con lo que hacían sus hijos . . . y en algunos momentos azuzadora, alcanzó a dar gritos de desespero para que se cobrara venganza (J. Salazar, *La parábola de Pablo* 328)]. She appears to be the silent ringleader behind some of Escobar's most violent moves. She, too, calms his homicidal tendencies when the situation gets overheated.

Following Escobar's failed attack on the Colombian Consul to Hungary, as presented in the television series, Doña Enelia confronts her son about his excessive use of violence in his campaign against the laws of extradition. When Escobar retorts that death is sometimes the best solution, she attempts to dissuade him from extreme measures, by quoting (on this very rare occasion) her peace-loving spouse: "The dead, what they do, is make the problems worse, complicate things" [Los muertos lo que hacen es enredar los problemas, complicar las situaciones]. Yet the series makes it clear that her judgment is governed not by empathy for Escobar's victims but to secure her son's well-being before the law. Whereas Escobar's wife (played by Cecilia Navia) is distraught by the ever-increasing levels of violence and appears sympathetic toward his victims' families (as in the case of the family of fallen patriarch Guillermo Cano), Doña Enelia does not exhibit such compassion. Instead, trusting Escobar's political savvy, she thinks of ways to make her son pass under the radar.

When she proposes less violent methods of doing away with Escobar's enemies, he takes her advice into account. In his discussion with Gonzalo on what to do with Marcos Herber (the real-life Carlos Lehder, interpreted by Alejandro Martínez), who harasses Pablo's favorite *sicarios* and whose reckless homosexual bacchanalias draw unwanted attention to their whereabouts, he proposes, inspired by mother's suggestion, handing him over to the police. This move will not only free them from the loose cannon Herber but will also provide the state with a trophy catch (per Pablo's account, "to me it seems a victory worthy of display" [a mí me parece que es un triunfo digno de mostrar]). Thus the series simultaneously shows Escobar's appreciation of his mother's professional advice and the workings of two similar minds: Doña Enelia does not have to say much for Pablo to catch her drift.

Another instance illustrating his mother's influence in the series emerges when the hapless Yesenia visits Hacienda Nápoles. Uninvited, unexpected, and with Escobar nowhere in sight, the young woman is received by the nosy Doña Enelia. Yesenia's apparent familiarity with her son, when she explains that she and her brother "are looking for Pablo," rubs the mother the wrong way, and Doña Enelia automatically puts the modest-looking girl in her place by bringing up hierarchy, "Ahhh you are looking for *Don* Pablo. Are you his friends?" [Estamos buscando a Pablo and ahhh están buscando a *don* Pablo. Uds. son amigos de él?]. Perhaps her reaction is motivated by her allegiance to Patico, Escobar's wife, yet it also attests to Doña Enelia's pride in the social status her son brings to the family. The satisfaction she draws from her newly acquired power resurfaces when Patico confides in her mother-in-law that associating with the elite has not come automatically, despite their wealth. When Escobar's son cannot play with a friend after school because the child's parents do not approve of the family, Patico feels helpless. To this, Doña Enelia suggests a solution worthy of her infamous son, namely, clever intimidation: "Why don't you take advantage of being the wife of a powerful man? Self-made, a poor guy with money, however you might put it, nouveau riche, but with power! That is your angle, take advantage of it!" [por qué no aprovecha que Ud. es la esposa de un hombre con poder? Levantado, pobre con plata, como lo quieran decirlo, venido a más, pero con poder. Eso es una ventaja, sáquele un provecho]. Patico, whose children's well-being is her primary concern, proves to be surprisingly adept at this threatening discourse. When she includes the figure of her husband in her final attempt to bring her son and his friend together with "Pablo and I understand that you do not want to be our friends. Therefore, from now on you're on our enemy list" [Pablo y yo entendimos que Uds. no quieren ser nuestros amigos. Por lo tanto, desde ahora forman parte de la lista de nuestros enemigos], her interlocutors quickly assess possible risks and allow their children to play.

Returning to Yesenia's confrontation with Doña Enelia, even though she tells the matriarch very little about herself and nothing about her pregnancy, Escobar's mother immediately understands that the young woman's connection with her son is sexual, and she senses the reason behind Yesenia's visit. In consequence, Doña Enelia gives Escobar a lecture on the sanctity of the institution of marriage, which while not excluding female lovers, relegates them to the realm of the hidden. This means that children out of wedlock are simply unacceptable: "One chooses one's children. Two. They are yours. They are no accident. . . . With the lovers you don't have children because they are not a blessing. One has one's children with one's own wife. . . . Don't you forget, Pablo, your cathedral is called Patricia" [Uno sí elige a sus hijos. Dos. Son suyos. No son un accidente. . . . Con las queridas, con las amantes, no se tiene hijos porque no son bendición. Los hijos se tienen con la mujer propia. . . . No se le olvide, Pablo, su catedral se llama Patricia]. As if it were a school lesson worthy of memorization, Doña Enelia has Escobar repeat the key point of her sermon: "What's the name of your cathedral?" [¿Cómo se llama su catedral?]. And her son, more a scolded schoolboy than a bloodthirsty criminal, sheepishly provides the name of his wife. The mother gets the last word, closing the discussion by cautioning him against foolish choices: "Well, then don't you forget it, young man" [Pues no se le olvide, joven].

Escobar's subsequent response to Yesenia's situation is reinforced by his dictatorial mother, when he almost pleads with the girl by laying out the rules he cannot violate ("I can't have children with women other than my wife" [Yo no puedo tener hijos con otra persona que no sea mi esposa]). For a moment, Yesenia forgets that her lover is a dangerous criminal and she insists on negotiating her choice with someone who does not bargain with the opposite gender: "All I want is that you take responsibility for your child" [Yo lo único que pido es que Ud. responda por su hijo]. When Escobar orders her to get an abortion, she rejects his money and leaves, failing to understand how vindictive and cruel mafia men can be.

Escobar's Performance of Masculinity

Like Doña Enelia, Escobar makes pronouncements instead of negotiating with his cronies. Proud of his banditry, he is unwilling to tell the truth even to his inner circle, let alone admit his faults. His associates are far from enthusiastic about the large-scale killing of civilians and political assassinations that only draw everyone's attention to the cartel, yet there is little they can do to stop it. Escobar's hot-blooded brother-in-law, Fabio Urrea (in real life, Mario Henao, played by Tommy Vásquez), takes his frustration out on Patico, Escobar's wife, accusing her of ignorance and blindness when it comes to Escobar's terrorist politics. This, as Fabio rightly foretells, is the beginning of the end of Pablo Escobar. Yet the fact that he has a hard time confronting Escobar and vents his anger with his own sister instead, shows how man-to-man rapport was not on equal terms, even though they were family and fellow cartel members.

Fabio's frustration over Pablo's bloody politicking would go unnoticed, but when Fabio tells Patico that her spouse is behind Luis Carlos Galán's assassination, the capo feels he must respond to Fabio's indiscretions. When the two meet, Fabio is drowning his sorrows in booze, crying over what he rightly senses to be the end of the narco bonanza. Escobar fakes interest in Fabio's opinion, and his embittered brother-in-law protests the uselessness of the gesture, knowing that Escobar does what he wants without consulting others. Fabio's verdict is harsh but prophetic when he accuses Escobar of wreaking havoc: "You screwed up my life, you screwed up the Medellín Cartel" [Te cagaste en mi vida, te cagaste en el Cartel de Medellín]. It is Escobar's reaction, however, that showcases the lack of communication between the two; the capo met with Fabio solely to rebuke him for breaking the unspoken code of their hermetic homosocial world. Thus, when Escobar retorts, "But this doesn't justify why you sold me out to Patico" [Pero esto no justifica por qué me vendiste a Patico], it becomes clear that Fabio's opinion had not even registered with the capo. The narcissistic Escobar also reveals himself to be a compulsive liar when he insists that he had nothing to do with Galán's murder. With the same false candor, he promises to Patico on his children's lives that the recent crime wave is not of his doing, even though, by now, no one believes him.

The hot-tempered Fabio was never a match for Escobar; from the series' first episode, when he disrupted a neighborhood party and physically attacked Pablo for making out with his adolescent sister, his outburst of anger attested more to his ineffectiveness than to his authority. In fact, soon after the confrontation between Patico and Fabio, and immediately after the bombing of the newspaper *El Espectador*, Pablo asked his brother-in-law to procure for him a teenage volleyball player ("I've never screwed a sports star" [Yo no he comido una deportista]), disregarding the inappropriateness of this request. The only thing Fabio could do was oblige. Similarly, when the news of Guillermo Cano's assassination reaches the media, the Motoa (in real life, Ochoa) brothers gather to assess the damage. Pedro Motoa (played by Joavany Álvarez and representing Jorge Luis Ochoa) questions Pablo's move from the standpoint of Cano's visibility in the media. Julio, the youngest of the brothers, suggests that Cano should have been "disappeared" discreetly, but "anyway, Pablo does things his way" [desparecido; pero igual Pablo hace las cosas a su manera]. The oldest of the clan sums it up, reflecting the popular opinion among the members of Medellín Cartel: "It's always like this, he does whatever he wants" [Siempre es así, él hace lo que quiere].

Thus, even with his closest cronies, Escobar exerted absolute authority at all times. When the Motoa brothers and Comandante Lucio Moreno (the real-life Carlos Castaño, interpreted by David Noreña) dispute his violent methods of trying to influence the state after he kills the attorney general and unsuccessfully kidnaps future president Andrés Pastrana, Escobar resorts to commands that accept no criticism or dialogue. His linguistic control is espoused through proclaiming, announcing, and brief, bald comments rather than negotiation founded on arbitration. Pablo's other discursive tool is his famous calmness, exercised even in the most chilling contexts, such as Yesenia's murder. He never admits uncertainty that would threaten his personal control. To be sure, his stoicism is not entirely innate; in real life, his brother Roberto reminisces that Pablo took lessons from his favorite Hollywood mafia saga, *The Godfather*:

> Pablo—the analyst, guarded, cold, calculating—acted according to the teachings of Don Vito Corleone. "Do not ever get mad. Do not utter any threats. Reason with people." The art of reasoning is based on ignoring insults and all threats; something like turning the other cheek. Be quiet and wait for revenge in silence is the proper behavior. The man who talks a lot does not say anything, the one who talks little is wise. The Mafiosi, men of respect, brood over things, meditate, and are able to keep inside what they know. . . . Pablo was a careful student of these lessons, he did not swear, he treated people well. "Even when ordering a killing he was calm," they say. (J. Salazar, *La parábola de Pablo* 162)

> [Pablo—analista, no reactivo, frío, calculador—actuaba según las enseñanzas de don Vito Corleone. "Nunca te enojes. No profieras amenaza alguna. Razona con la gente." El arte del razonamiento consistía en pasar por alto todos los insultos, todas las amenazas; algo así como poner otra mejilla. Callar y esperar en silencio la venganza es el comportamiento adecuado. El hombre que habla mucho no dice nada, el que habla poco es sabio. Los mafiosos, hombres de respeto, rumian, meditan y son capaces de guardarse para sí mismos lo que saben . . . Pablo, juicioso aprendiz de esas lecciones, no pronunciaba malas palabras, trataba bien a la gente. "Hasta para mandar matar era tranquilo," dicen.]

Roberto's recollections illustrate that no mythic rhetoric operates in a cultural and historical vacuum. Escobar's carefully studied hypermasculinity attests to his preoccupation with self-image, revealing the specific steps he took to solidify his own criminal legend, where one of his tools was a cinematic blockbuster. On one occasion, in the company of his teenage son and 250 men who gathered in the discotheque El Conde, he went on a rampage to avenge the death of one of his lieutenants, Tyson. A menacing caravan of sixty cars, equipped with weapons and dynamite, slaughtered several policemen (including Captain Posada, a prominent character in the television series) and destroyed the house in which Tyson had been murdered (J. Salazar, *La parábola de Pablo* 309). Another instance of conscious self-promotion occurred when the megalomaniac Escobar posed in a Russian fur hat (the same one in which Roberto poses nowadays for tourists), hoping this image would achieve the iconic status of Che Guevara's beret (J. Salazar, *La parábola de Pablo* 293).

With the exception of his mother and his wife (whose role is perfunctory, in that she solidifies his image as a good family man), Escobar's attitude toward women as presented in the television series is strictly utilitarian. When Marino asks Escobar if he is going to get killed on account of his romance with Yesenia—a reasonable reaction since Marino was bound in a chair by his former buddies, as his boss appeared in the room—Escobar lays out the code of "bros before hos": "Look, Marino, I want you to be fully aware of the fact that, for me, your life is much more important and valuable than this young lady. And you should be aware of how uncomfortable this situation is for me, that because you run around in heat, I must consider killing one of the best men I have ever had" [Vea Marino, Yo necesito de que Ud. sea completamente consciente de que para mí es muchísimo más importante y valiosa la vida suya que la de esa señorita. Y Ud. es consciente de la situación tan incómoda en que me pone por Ud. andar de arrecho, que ahora me toca tomar la decisión de asesinar a uno de los mejores hombres que yo he tenido]. As Marino justifies courting a woman previously involved with Escobar on the grounds that the capo clearly no longer cared about her, Escobar nips such sentimental talk in the bud. In Escobar's worldview, Yesenia is too insignificant to be addressed in terms of feelings, which, to be sure, are expressed exclusively in the context of Escobar's family: "And what's with you and these conjugal jealousy issues? Get over your romanticism because this is much more serious and much more consequential, Marino" [Y Ud. para que me vuelve con estos problemas conyugales de celos? Quítele el romanticismo a esto porque esto es muchísimo más serio y muchísimo más grave Marino]. The capo suspects that Yesenia's hatred for him and having a killer by her side puts Escobar's safety at risk. Thus Escobar gives Marino an order that transforms Marino's romantic dilemma into a matter of security: "I kill her or I kill you. . . . You must do your job" [O la mato a ella o lo mato a Ud. . . . Le toca].

There are sporadic situations where Andrés Parra's Escobar is not entirely in control of the discourse, yet in the end he always manages to assert his position. When in the television series he summons Regina Parejo (the real-life Virginia Vallejo, discussed in the following chapter) after their relationship had gone sour—and the dismayed ex-lover complies only to avoid his wrath—Escobar attempts to woo her back by appealing to her singular role of "my girlfriend, my consultant." By now tired and disheartened, Regina (interpreted by Angie Cepeda) rejects his plea and distances herself from commitments, all the while affirming her independence: "I'm not your girlfriend, I'm not your consultant, I'm not your anything" [yo no soy su novia, yo no soy su asesora, yo no soy nada suyo]. Her refusal to bend to his will no doubt angers the narcissistic capo. To make matters worse, there is a witness to his apparent ineffectiveness, Marino, who at that point was still Regina's bodyguard.

Hurt in his ego but outwardly calm, Escobar proceeds to win this confrontation on a different front, by asking Regina's bodyguard to work for him. As he redirects his attention to Marino, Escobar employs the macho talk as bait, simultaneously relegating Regina (read: women in general) to an inferior category: "Let's talk like two men. . . . Marino, you want to work with me? Or are you gonna remain a lapdog . . . you want to work like a man with other men, the way it should be, or you will stay with this Hollywood diva?" [Hablemos como varones. . . . Marino, ¿Ud. no quiere trabajar conmigo? O va a ser el perrito faldero . . . ¿quiere trabajar como un varón con varones como tiene que ser o va a seguir con esta diva de Hollywood?]. This is an invitation to a romanticized virile community, where homosocial camaraderie is tantamount to "freedom, autonomy, and heightened masculinist power" (Pettergrew 57)—in short, the hallmarks of mythical manhood. Escobar indulges in the male fantasy, which posits a feminized, "soft man" against an ethos of masculine honor. He buttresses his argument with the standard arsenal of male metaphors: the language of war. To strengthen his own role as a leader, he provides himself with yet another loyal soldier. An incensed Regina cannot believe her ears, as she unsuccessfully pleas with her employee not to succumb to the offer.

Escobar had lost Regina's support much earlier, yet he renegotiates his dominance in this very moment through a call for brotherhood, which renders her no longer worthy of his attention. It will not be Regina who rejects his half-felt advances but Escobar who ostensibly downplays her role by repudiating her gender. His persistent appeals to male companionship, aggression, and competition are symptomatic of underlying apprehensions of dependency and feminization, of long-standing fears of being not masculine enough. Therefore Escobar's constant preoccupation with virility may be read as a compensatory response. To expel vulnerability, he devalues women, whose barely decorative function underpins male potency. In other words, women are a canvas on which mafiosi play out their rituals of virile agency. The fear of feminization is therefore combated by outbrutalizing other males and pigeonholing women as the despicably weak other.

Escobar's tough facade gradually crumbles in *Escobar, el patrón del mal* as he begins to lose his cronies in his war against the state. Distraught yet calm after Chili's death, he allows Topo to grieve, with an understanding that his warriors (*guerreros*) must mourn their companions to the full in order to take their subsequent cold revenge. Yet he loses his composure when his cousin, close childhood friend, and business associate Gonzalo Gaviria dies in a confrontation with the police. Disheveled and wide-eyed, Escobar suffers a panic attack, wheezing and gasping for air in front of his terrified family, who are unaccustomed to seeing his insecurities. Curiously, it is his mother, not his wife, who rushes to console her adult son. She presses his head to her colossal bosom and tells him to control his breathing and drink some water. This image transports the viewers in time: It is as if Escobar had never grown up, as if he were playing cops and robbers with his childhood friends under his mother's protective tutelage and only now realized that his game had deadly consequences. This bizarre regression in time, which attests to an unresolved Oedipus complex, surfaces again when Escobar organizes a wild bacchanalia with *prepago* prostitutes, in the presence of his family. Feeling helpless and deeply offended, his wife, Patico, retires to bed. The next day she attempts to reproach Escobar, yet he will have none of it. Instead, haughty and impatient, he brushes off both his wife's jealousy and his mother's outrage, raising his voice and announcing that they will talk only when *he* feels like listening. To restore order, Doña Enelia resorts to the same method she might have used when her adolescent son was overly rambunctious: She smacks him across the face in Patico's presence and forces him to look her in the eye. Her misbehaving son must learn his place, and like a scolded little boy, Escobar immediately regains his composure. Always the mama's boy, Escobar will cower only to his mother, the one person who knew how to keep him in line from day one.

Escobar, el patrón del mal carefully unveils the ideological scripting of the macho man and how it went hand in hand with a warrior ethos both for Escobar and for his ilk. They lived life as if it were warfare, viewing everyone exclusively as winners or losers. Yet notwithstanding the hypermasculine enculturation and socialization that Escobar consciously reenacted and celebrated, his dependency on the domineering mother hampered his development, frustrating any attempts to achieve a mythical virility. Despite his unparalleled violence, his Machiavellian mind, and a life of debauchery, Escobar remained attached to his mother's purse strings until his final day, crying in her bosom as his empire crumbled. Thus, in the end, the series offered a more nuanced version of Escobar, allowing for the edifice of his mythic masculinity to collapse not just owing to the actual historical circumstances but also via a careful deconstruction of his macho persona.

3

Romancing Pablo Escobar
The Allure of the Narco Caudillo

The modern version of the self-confident macho who shows no scruples as he works his way up is the shrewd businessman, or someone like Pablo Escobar who came from humble beginnings . . . and became popular with the general public not least on account of his generous donations.

Waldmann, "Is There a Culture of Violence in Colombia?" 67

What was Virginia Vallejo thinking—a woman so desired and envied for her beauty, wealth, intelligence and fame—to end up cozying up to Pablo Escobar?
[¿Qué pudo pasar en la cabeza de Virginia Vallejo, una mujer tan deseada y envidiada por su belleza, riqueza, inteligencia y fama para terminar intimando con Pablo Escobar?]

Mastrodoménico, "¿Qué le vio la diva al criminal?"

When Virginia Vallejo, the television reporter, actress, and Colombian diva of the 1980s, published her 2007 memoirs *Amando a Pablo, odiando a Escobar*, the subject of the heyday of Colombian drug trafficking yet again came to the forefront of the national public debate. Vallejo had spent the last two decades in obscurity, following her scandalous romance with the Medellín kingpin and the subsequent ostracism that put an end to her media career. In 2006, the DEA flew her to Miami as part of an arrangement that would offer her protection in exchange for testimony on drug-related cases. Vallejo's book became a best seller, and various television stations rushed to interview her not only because she finally admitted to her romantic involvement with Pablo Escobar but also because the diva accused prominent Colombian politicians of ties with Escobar, notably pointing the finger at the former president Álvaro Uribe.

These allegations were nothing novel, for Uribe had long been parrying attacks about his political past, both from within Colombia and from abroad, striking back at Supreme Court judges and reporters whose relationship with the president could be described as at best turbulent.[1] In fact, a 2007 survey conducted among two hundred journalists from thirty different Colombian cities painted a grim picture that was vastly different from the optimistic state-sanctioned reports prepared for the international public: A staggering 90 percent claimed that the official data on the armed conflict had been manipulated, while 88 percent expressed that freedom of the press in Colombia was endangered. What was new, however, was that Vallejo's book prompted Uribe to fend off accusations made on the public stage by Escobar's former lover, thus evidencing the effect of one woman on national and international drug politics.[2]

In an interview with the Colombian radio station Caracol, Uribe categorically distanced himself from Vallejo, pledging that he had never been her friend—to be sure, the diva never claimed that either—and that they had spoken only once, during a flight from Bogotá to Medellín. Elsewhere, Uribe attacked the journalist Gonzalo Guillén, charging him with ghostwriting Vallejo's memoirs and dedicating his entire career to defaming Uribe. Indeed, Guillén's 2007 *Los confidentes de Pablo Escobar* describes Colombia as a narco state and alleges close ties between Uribe's father, Alberto Uribe Sierra, and a number of infamous cocaine kingpins. It denounces some of Uribe's closest associates as either Escobar's family members or people associated with the criminal underworld. In the end, Uribe's heated commentaries achieved the opposite of his intent. His outbursts drew more attention to Vallejo's book in the Colombian press, while the *New York Times* ran a story on their conflict, dusting off a 1991 declassified American intelligence report that had named Uribe as one of Colombia's important drug traffickers and a close friend of Escobar. Even though both the U.S. and Colombian governments disavowed the report's findings, rumors and uncertainty have persisted, giving Vallejo and her allegations more credibility in the eyes of the general public and leaving the story on Uribe's links to the narco world open to discussion.

Virginia Vallejo was born into the sociopolitical aristocracy, attended a prestigious English-language school in Bogotá, learned a number of languages, and built her career in the media. She became a news anchor for

Noticiero 24 Horas, Telediario and the cohost of various shows, including beauty pageants, *El Show de las Estrellas*, or *¡Cuidado con las mujeres!* Erudite and at ease with the camera, she could talk with the same authority about politics, economics, and fashion. Her face and body became an object of veneration in the early 1980s, and Vallejo's image adorned countless magazine covers and TV commercials. Not only that, but in her memoirs she revels in recounting her contacts and relationships with cultural royalty on an international level, presenting herself as a cosmopolitan socialite at home and in jet-set destinations around the world. It is precisely this aspect of her narrative that has drawn criticism from reviewers, who disparage the combination of catchy melodrama and half-told truths, but above all they decry her frequent manifestations of megalomania and vanity.

Perhaps to historians of the subject of drug trafficking, her romance with the capo seems a triviality of daily life and, as such, methodologically unimportant. Nor is her position—the confidante of a criminal—conceived as conducive to the protocol of objectivity.

Yet with the boomlet of books on Colombian drug cartels and their key players, Vallejo's memoirs offer an unusual approach to Escobar, humanizing the criminal through the sentimental discourse of a love affair. Her romantic angle aims for a different target group of consumers who are less interested in the politics perhaps and more in the intimate side of Escobar's story.[3] In marketing terms, Vallejo thus nuances the hegemon Outlaw with secondary characteristics of the Lover, a man worthy of infatuation, and thereby fleshes out other, less traveled aspects of his brand. Her insight into his private life and the many anecdotes she recalls constitute a previously unheeded voice, struggling to be heard against the historical establishment—in short, a counterhistory that for new historicists is precisely the window to epochal truths.[4] Vallejo stages her story of Colombia's cocaine pandemonium through the rhetoric of female corporality while drawing on the parable of the nation's infatuation with Escobar's billions and her own rocky romance with the charismatic outlaw. The effects of this approach are twofold. First, it creates a public of voyeurs peeking into Escobar's private and intimate space. Second, it draws attention to Escobar's machismo by tying his *modus vivendi* with the legacy of the classic Latin American strongman, a born leader capable of amassing unfathomed wealth and power through violence and a womanizer whose sexual prowess is as extraordinary as his awe-inspiring audacity.

Vallejo's sentimental investment in Escobar leads to another important factor that determines the storyline; his acquisition of someone like the diva, a woman of superior social status and a publicly admired television personality, is a crucial trope for constructing his symbolic power. Simultaneously, the class-conscious Vallejo must palliate Escobar's delinquency and legitimate his worth to justify her own surrender to the man whom she believed, if only for a while, to be a breath of fresh air on the stage of Colombian politics.

The balancing between Escobar's historically proven acts of villainy and Vallejo's personal fascination with a titillating criminal requires her to marshal an array of legitimizing narrative strategies.[5] Primarily, Vallejo reconciles divergent forces by drawing upon universal myths, such as fairy tales, Hispanic cultural tradition (i.e., polarizing gender paradigms, and machismo in particular), some formulaic pop-cultural devices characteristic of celebrity writings, and her identity as a woman. Owing to the relative scarcity of women's accounts of the Latin American drug trafficking scene,[6] Vallejo's construction of gendered selfhood and how she fashions female presence in the misogynistic criminal milieu are of particular relevance. After all, Vallejo fits well in the paradigm of a popular celebrity who has attracted tabloid attention for straying and falling out of favor with the elite. She grew accustomed to a public profile in the 1980s, only to vanish from the spotlight for two decades following the demise of the Medellín Cartel. She returned fearlessly to the front pages in 2007, this time reinscribing her dissident self into the national discourse. Whether Vallejo's account is entirely accurate is perhaps not as important as how she presents herself and her lover or how she reconstructs her relationship with Escobar.

The wealth of literary tropes that Vallejo weaves into her recollections unveils a particular case of self-fashioning. Virginia Vallejo is like no other, and she knows it: a member of the elite who confessed to intimate ties with the drug baron at a time when its other members worked hard at obscuring their own connections with the narco world, a bridge between the establishment and the nouveau riche, a noncriminal in the criminal demimonde, and an outspoken woman where feminine presence has been predicated on good looks and serviceability but never on opinions. Vallejo carefully situates her self-portrait between opposite ends of the spectrum, framing her subjectivity from the double perspective of Escobar's equal and mentor during his assent in politics, on the one hand, and victim of

Escobar's malevolence and rage. Nonetheless, she confesses to owing her life to him.

Virginia Steps into an Enchanted Narco World

Her first meeting with Escobar takes place at the Hacienda Nápoles, where Virginia nearly drowns in the treacherous currents of the river. It is Pablo who, despite having his eyes set on another woman at the party, rushes to rescue her while the rest of the group—Virginia's boyfriend at the time included—remains unaware of what is happening. Pablo's heroic act sets the stage for their tacit bond and budding attraction, distinguishing the drug baron from the rest of the party retinue as an all-seeing, fearless, and gallant savior. The description of that first visit to Pablo's estate is vibrant with color, as if everything had preternaturally enhanced hues; a venturesome man whose fortune and personality make up for his unsophisticated physique, exotic wildlife roaming freely on the extensive ranch, and a lush nature with crystal clear rivers and lakes fixate this first visit in Vallejo's memory as a near-nirvana experience.

Fittingly, Virginia describes herself as "a pardoned Eve" (una Eva perdonada) rescued from the watery clutches to enjoy "the second vision of paradise" (su segunda visión del paraíso; V. Vallejo 37). She thus implicitly imbues Escobar with the superior power of a newfound benefactor, a role she reconfirms shortly after, in the context of a domestic dispute between Vallejo and her estranged husband. In the diva's own words, Escobar is a "fox" who will silence "the ogre" of her uncooperative spouse by threatening him into signing their divorce papers to "set free the princess trapped in a tower" (la princesa enterrada en la torre; 2007, 61) of a failed marriage. Virginia, the proverbial damsel in distress, allows her undaunted protector to obliterate the forces of evil in a chivalric act that predetermines their eventual union and maybe even the happily ever after. Pablo's power, reinforced by his cohorts of trigger-happy hitmen, sets him in stark contrast to the types Vallejo had dated before—beau monde dandies blessed with money and pedigree, but small-minded and often stingy, plagued by addictions and somehow sissified next to the drug lord's raw energy, the quintessential man's man.

Vallejo's description of Escobar leaves no doubt that beneath the veneer of his unimpressive stature lay a spirit that commanded everyone's attention, a locus of prestige and power. In Vallejo's memories, Pablo channels the classic strongman in that he possesses a "certain air of a respected elder, with words carefully thought out that come from firm and upright lips, because he speaks in a serene manner . . . with the absolute certainty that his desires are his orders and that his grasp of the topics that interest him is absolute" [un cierto aire de respetable señor mayor, a las palabras cuidadosamente medidas que salen de su boca recta y firme, porque habla en una voz serena . . . con la absoluta certeza de que sus deseos son órdenes y su dominio de los temas que le conciernen total (31)]. Young and physically unassuming, Escobar occupies the very center of the social gaze: He appears calm and composed, yet commanding and perfectly in control. He reincarnates the mythic paragon of masculinity, for he has transcended his origins to accumulate the accoutrements of status—women, riches, and power over others. Driven by a combination of will and guts, he has grown to embody the quintessential caudillo, the lord of an ostentatious country estate, surrounded by a coterie of confidants, bodyguards, and beautiful half-naked women.

Escobar first takes Virginia and her group of friends on a tour of his private zoo. He jokes that his elephants and some endangered species are happy at Hacienda Nápoles because they enjoy two or more females for their peace of mind. Escobar's comment insinuates his own sexual prowess, a sense of entitlement natural to real machos who deserve different (read: more lax) sexual arrangements by virtue of their extreme potency. Nonetheless, in Vallejo's eyes, Escobar's maleness best evidences itself in his actions. He loves speed, risk-taking, and taming danger, as he masters a number of "manly" toys that attest to his daring and venturesome spirit. First, he takes his guests on a ride in one of his powerboats. Effortlessly breezing through the river's treacherous curves, he is in control at all times while his entourage of spectators remains huddled in the back, transfixed by Escobar's bravado. Vallejo describes this moment in the conventions of an action film, where the irresistible host—the James Bond of Hacienda Nápoles[7]—thrusts himself into the untamed nature with the same ease and determination that he has used to conquer society (and will soon use to conquer her heart): "We took off like a blast of air, with Escobar at the helm of our boat. Hypnotized by the pleasure, he flies above that river, dodging obstacles as if he knew every twist and every rock, every whirlpool big and small, every fallen tree or a floating trunk, as if he wanted to impress us with his ability to rescue us from the dangers that we only perceived" [Arrancamos cual exhalación con Escobar al volante de nuestro bote. Hipnotizado de placer, vuela sobre aquel río esquivando los obstáculos como si conociera cada recodo y cada piedra, cada remolino grande o pequeño, cada árbol caído o tronco flotante, y quisiera impresionarnos con su habilidad para salvarnos de peligros que sólo avizoramos al pasar por su lado cual flechas y que desaparecen en instantes como productos de nuestra imaginación (V. Vallejo 34–35)]. Mesmerized by this display of virile audacity, Vallejo exalts Escobar's almost superhuman capacities, thereby building onto the myth of the drug lord's exacerbated maleness: "Fascinated, I realize that in each second of the last hour our lives depended on the millimetric sense of calculation that this man seems to have been born with to defy the limits of his survival or to rescue others" [Fascinada, me doy cuenta de que en cada segundo de la pasada hora nuestras vidas pendieron del sentido milimétrico del cálculo de este hombre que parece nacido para desafiar los límites de su supervivencia o para rescatar a los demás (V. Vallejo 35)].

This spectacle of blood rush and acceleration is replayed when they join Escobar for a midnight ride through the hills of Medellín in his sports cars. Vallejo ends up in a different vehicle, since at this point Escobar's affections are still focused on a different woman. Even though Vallejo's car departs earlier than his, Escobar quickly takes the lead and grabs the spotlight once again: "After some time we see him coming like a bat out of hell; we don't know if he flies over us, but seconds later he is ahead of us; time and time again we try to pass him but as soon as it seems possible, he takes off vanishing on the curves of the deserted streets" [al cabo de varios minutos lo vemos venir como alma que lleva el diablo; no sabemos si nos pasa volando por encima, pero segundos después está delante de nosotros. Una y otra vez intentamos sobrepasarlo pero, cuando estamos a punto de conseguirlo, emprende la huida y se esfuma entre las curvas de las calles desiertas (V. Vallejo 43)]. The absolute man's man, Escobar seems to defy the laws of physics, zipping through the steep streets of Medellín as if the city were his personal playground. His fearlessness and voracious appetite for life are unparalleled, so it seems, and Vallejo marvels at how the world is Pablo's oyster. The drug lord goes after what he wants with the same boldness he exhibited in his brief demonstrations of athletic bravado, proving himself irresistible and superior to all the other men she has dated. Once they begin their affair, Escobar confesses to the all-consuming drive that has propelled him to become who he is, a self-made man who has risen above the rest of humanity by the sheer power of his will: "I only wanted to be rich . . . richer than the richest man of Colombia, at whatever price and using the resources and each and every tool that life has placed at my disposal. I promised myself that if I didn't have a million dollars by the age of thirty, I would commit suicide" [Yo sólo quería ser rico . . . más rico que cualquiera de los ricos de Colombia, al precio que fuera y utilizando todos los recursos y cada una de las herramientas que la vida fuera poniendo a mi disposición. Me juré a mí mismo que, si a los treinta años no tenía un millón de dólares, me suicidaría (V. Vallejo 81)].

A digression is called for here, since this particular confession is a constant in Escobar's numerous biographies, according to which narco leaders put their reputation at stake by making hazardous public promises in order to live up to them through a continuous assertion of will. That Escobar would make them repeatedly points to his need to "perform" the role of a go-getter, all the while revealing his anxieties before the spectacle of masculinity that he himself consciously adopted. Similarly, the first episode in the series *Escobar, el patrón del mal* features an important scene of Escobar's self-fashioning through an entrepreneurial oath. The still very young capo (played by Mauricio Mejía) shares his plans with his faithful entourage as they sit on a hill reflecting on things to come and enthusiastic about their goals. Pablo looks into the horizon as he proclaims that he would rather die than continue as a common man, thereby declaring his awe-inspiring drive. This public pledge is the leitmotif of the narco bildungsroman, an element so common that it very well might be nothing more than an urban legend or a formulaic device in the cultural construction of narco barons' identity.

In fact, that very claim appears in the story of Gonzalo Rodríguez Gacha alias El Mexicano (Escobar's most important crony from the cartel), as presented by Fernando Cortés in his 2009 *La cacería de El Mexicano*: "In the municipality of Pacho . . . they say that at one point, in a frenzy of a narco celebration in the Castillo de Marroquín in Bogotá, Gonzalo Rodríguez Gacha swore that soon he would run the nation's affairs or else end up dead. 'Either I become president or I get killed'" [En el municipio de Pacho . . . se cuenta que en una oportunidad, en un arranque de delirio y mientras se celebraba una concurrida fiesta de narcos en el Castillo de Marroquín de Bogotá, Gonzalo Rodríguez Gacha juró que un día no muy lejano dirigía los destinos del país, porque de lo contrario terminaría en la tumba. "O soy presidente o me matan" (158), all translations of Cortés's book are mine].

As history has proven, Gacha fulfilled his self-prophecy, though maybe not in the way he wished, when he died in a shoot-out with government forces on December 15, 1989. But going back to the quote, this oath solidifies the birth of the narco caudillo, whose superior position among his cohort stems precisely from his inflated ego and willingness to take the biggest risks to fulfill his wish for ultimate power. It articulates confidence in his ability to shape the world. According to Catano, such pronouncements are a key component in negotiating the mythical rhetoric of masculinity vis-à-vis other rhetorical arguments that serve to naturalize gender practices. The myth of the self-made man "argues masculine success and successful masculinity" (Catano 3), thereby corroborating the importance of gender rhetoric in the construction of a figure with particular accomplishments. Paeans to open self-making privilege a singular aggression that resonates with the social construct of the caudillo, whether he emerges from legitimate or illegitimate loci of control.

There is another leitmotif present in Escobar's and El Mexicano's respective narco bildungsromans, this one aimed at the construction of a self-making patriarch. Both capos provide patronage where the state has failed the general population, by engaging in public acts of social work predicated on gift-giving and the subsequent expectation of loyalty if not codependence. Altruistic motifs aside, such gestures also cement their own position in the network of influences, confirming their leverage through relationships based on servility and the exertion of individual power. At the same time, they point to adopting more acceptable tropes of behavior that sometimes diverge from the traditional image of a crude narco who indulges in banditry, returning instead to a more palatable authority as it is understood in broader circles. Escobar, for instance, did not engage in drug or alcohol consumption, nor did he publicly use vulgar language or raise his voice. General Maza Márquez described El Mexicano, his archenemy, in a similar convention: "El Mexicano was disciplined and moderate, he would wake up early, drink little. . . . He was elegant and always dressed for the occasion. He spoke gently and did not use vulgar language. He had expressed his satisfaction with the money he had, announcing his interest in dedicating future profits to ambitious plans that would benefit the community" [El Mexicano era disciplinado y moderado, se levantaba temprano, bebía muy poco . . . Era elegante y lucía ropa apropiada para cada ocasión. Hablaba reposadamente y no utilizaba palabras soeces. Había manifestado sentirse satisfecho de la cantidad de dinero que poseía, anunciando su interés por dedicar los nuevos dividendos económicos a planes ambiciosos de beneficio para la comunidad (Cortés 155)].

Cortés describes El Mexicano as a man who performed charitable efforts in his community. Following the 1983 earthquake in Popayán, the capo distributed four million pesos among the affected population. In his hometown, El Mexicano reconstructed the church, built roads, and set up an office to supply food and medicine for those in need. He even served as a judge in local disputes. In return, like the classic caudillo he was, El Mexicano expected utter loyalty and submission to his will, for he "was vengeful and intolerant. He did not forgive mistakes or put up with dissenting ideas" [era vengativo e intolerante. No perdonaba los errores ni soportaba las ideas contrarias (Cortés 156)].

As the history of the Medellín Cartel teaches, the concept of a self-made entrepreneur who overinvests in individual domination ultimately fails, because it rejects mutuality, solidarity, and commitment, behaviors symptomized as feminine and thus not practiced. When Escobar pronounced a death sentence on his most faithful partners of the Medellín Cartel, Gerardo Moncada and Fernando Galeano, his situation deteriorated precipitously. This time, he became the public enemy number one for all—criminal elements included—because he proved himself capable of betraying his own ilk. That the Perseguidos por Pablo Escobar (Persecuted by Pablo Escobar) or Pepes, his enemies, were able to gain such momentum and successfully destroy Escobar's remaining networks of loyalties speaks to the capo's own inflated ego and failure to honor coalitions that had heretofore bolstered his authority.

Yet perhaps owing to the irresolvable contradictions of behaviors understood as gender-bound, narco narratives insist on extolling the virtues of masculinist self-making, short-lived as they might be. Their effectiveness rests on their ability to trigger a deep set of cultural beliefs that enact initiative, aggression, and competition—all part and parcel of individual and social masculine development. Aggression is keenly honed in this myth, be it directly, through acts of violence, or more subtly, for example, in Escobar's attitude toward women.

Even Escobar's early seduction of Virginia showcases his inability to relate on any terms other than power dynamics, whereby the capo displays his threatening and risk-taking disposition for no logical reason. As the couple play fights, he whispers in her ear: "I'm a depraved sadist, a thousand times worse than those people from horror films, haven't you heard?" [Soy un sádico depravado mil veces peor que los del cine de terror, ¿o no te habían contado? (V. Vallejo 82)]. Then he takes her on a joyride full speed into oncoming traffic, thereby showcasing his daredevil bravado. When a trembling Virginia steps out of the car, "in a threatening tone and with a frozen expression," he goes straight to the point: "So now you see . . . who's got a bigger set of balls, right?" [En tono amenazador y con una expresión helada en la mirada, me dice:—Pues ya vas viendo . . . quién es el dueño de los cojones, ¿no? (V. Vallejo 83)]. Escobar's flirtation techniques speak volumes about his obsession with the phallus and his need to reenact the cultural practices associated traditionally with masculine leaders. He mythologizes his masculinity at all times, overinvesting in his own image at the expense of building real relationships based on communication and intimacy. Perhaps because Vallejo comes from the elite, which Escobar envisions as his principal opponent, the capo engages in a game that displays and confirms his power of will rather than resorting to his customary ways of "using" women like objects and discarding them as such.

Drawn to a behavior uncommon among her own milieu, Vallejo buys into Escobar's unrepentant individualism. Astute and ruthless, the Escobar of Vallejo's recollections is a born leader who never takes no for an answer. Having amassed riches beyond his earlier dreams, his insatiable appetite moves to his next goal of subjugating the haute bourgeoisie and entering their ranks. He wants to transition from criminal to legitimate power, not only to secure his own safety via influencing the nation's laws on extradition but also to establish himself where authority carries far greater benefits, that is, within the very epicenter of the law-making state. Vallejo calls it an absolute delirium of grandeur and an example of his outrageous cult of personality (91), yet she is irreversibly infatuated with his proclivity for danger. The defiant hero-rogue who has money galore and no authority other than his own excites Vallejo by resurrecting the bad-boy aura. Naturally, Vallejo is not the only celebrity beauty to give in to the excitement of the emergent class of the criminal nouveau riche, so much wealthier and so much more exciting than the usual milquetoast suitors. Next to these gangster dynamos, traditional choices for romantic relationships strike her as boring, ultraconservative, and unjustifiably cocky (185). Vallejo comments that her glamorous girlfriends begin to date a variety of new "big men," including the bosses of M-19, but nonetheless keep their romances secret.

Machismo and Politics in Latin America

There are as many versions of Pablo Escobar as there are narratives about him, although his outrageous criminal acts ultimately frustrate attempts at humanization. Likewise, he dons many faces in Vallejo's memoirs, where the initial portrayal of a gallant savior quickly morphs into a far more complex rendition that harkens back to the classic Latin American strongman, a *narcotraficante*-turned-caudillo with aspirations for statesmanship—a sum of qualities that have historically been unified under the umbrella of machismo. A glimpse at the twelve major marketing archetypes shows that Virginia fleshed out a number of them, aside from the obvious Outlaw and her perspective of choice, the Lover. In her account, Escobar also represents the Magician who makes her visit to the Hacienda Nápoles almost unreal and the Hero who saves her from drowning just as he saves thousands of the poor by caring for them when the state does not.[8]

Virility and machismo have long been the bane of Latin American statesmanship, marking national and international politics with frequent manifestations of aggravated masculine individualism. The heated exchange between Álvaro Uribe and Hugo Chávez at the 2010 Cancún summit of Latin American presidents only highlighted the holding power of an image that equates authority with *hombría*, that is, manfulness founded on aggression. Incensed by Chávez's insinuations of an alleged assassination plot on his life originating in Colombia, Uribe scolded his Venezuelan counterpart by telling him to "act like a man." The *comandante* responded in an even more direct way, by telling Uribe to go to hell. Guillermoprieto attributed this exchange to "the hemisphere's two leaders most obsessed with their virility" and branded their spat as either "a last hurrah for embarrassing machismo" and a backlash on the rise of influential women in politics or, much worse, the return of the strongman, whose rule drained Latin America's resources through brutal dictatorships for two centuries ("The Return"). Alas, time has proven it was the latter.

Of course, Escobar was never acclaimed politically, nor did he manage to enter the establishment. Nonetheless, his violent incursion into national and transnational politics via acts of terrorism and bought-off politicians placed him in the middle of state affairs, thereby, as Peter Waldmann points out, equating his symbolic power with that of a strong-arm leader—the classic caudillo (67). Vallejo thus does not have to look far to channel the age-old tropes of a charismatic chieftain who disobeys the law because he himself is the law. Her melodramatic take on Escobar reveals a plethora of conflicting emotions—albeit via the application of pop-cultural narrative tropes—with frequent references to key moments in Colombia's volatile 1980s and 1990s. She does not shy away from disclosing Escobar's good and bad qualities, his generosity and his cruelty, his logic and his arbitrariness, his independence of spirit and his reliance on faulty advisers such as Senator Santofimio, for example. Her personal insight into Escobar's mind evidences his megalomania combined with a subsequent disrespect for others, his utter lack of fear tied with blind self-confidence, his ruthlessness, and his unquenchable thirst for control. In Vallejo's recollections, these are manly qualities to the core—and she finds them hard to resist.

The legacies of machismo have a strong holding power over Latin American culture, and history sheds light on the rise of the caudillo figure and on the prevalence of political caudillismo through the twentieth and twenty-first centuries. One of the explanations for its origin is that from colonial times, different groups in the Americas were forced to forge alliances because alone they could not monopolize wealth and power, nor could they protect their interests against the colonizing hand of Spain and rivals at home. Hence the tiny but powerful planter class of *criollos*, pure-blooded Spaniards born on the Continent, and the numerous yet socially underprivileged *mestizos* built patron-client relationships, predicated on ties of dominance and submission as well as the common aim of achieving wealth. Its chieftains boasted the muscle power of the strongest man in the pack and exhibited a proclivity for violence to secure their leadership position. They possessed business acumen, strategic talents, and an ability to build a circle of devoted lieutenants through gift-giving that cemented their loyalty even further. These personality traits were indispensable, because the line of succession of caudillos was not institutionalized nor was the position secured. Through the present day, it is commonly agreed that the caudillo's "leadership resides in his person, not in his office" (Wolf and Hansen 175), thereby making charisma and exacerbated virility in-eluctable prerequisites for the role.

Interpersonal dynamics contingent on an aggravated masculinity have been commonly described as hallmarks of machismo, an attitude and life-style inscribed by Octavio Paz into the cultural matrixes of Mexican/Latin American identity in his canonical 1950 *The Labyrinth of Solitude*. The model of a macho has affected Colombian society as well, even though po-litical caudillismo did not enter into the nation's history the way it affected many other Latin American countries. As Roldán affirms, "In contrast to many of its neighbors, Colombia has rarely suffered from dictatorship, boasted no powerful military. . . . Moreover, except for the brief appeal of a Liberal populist leader, Jorge Eliécer Gaitán in the 1940s and the military government of General Gustavo Rojas Pinilla in the mid-fifties, Colombia rarely fell victim to the sway of populist or authoritarian politics" (Roldán, *Blood and Fire* 11). Nonetheless, the roughly one hundred and fifty years of civil wars and violence have affected the system of order in Colombia, where volatile coalitions and short-lived pacts brought about destabili-zation and weakened the nation's legal system. This, in turn, gave room to the rise of many illegal as well as institutionalized agents of violence and to power relationships based on intimidation—another articulation of machismo. Critics point out the cultivation of enmities in Colombia, where antiquated behavioral patterns such as kidnappings, informant net-working, or circulating lists of victims prior to the actual acts of violence have remained strong despite the nation's transition from rural to urban and from religious to secular (Sánchez [38] quoted in Waldmann 66). Its most emblematic example is the era of La Violencia, the twentieth-cen-tury conflict that was fought "in terms of mid-nineteenth-century politi-cal partisanship not modern political or social objectives" (Roldán, *Blood and Fire* 12). The culture of violence was ingrained deeply into the na-tional psyche and to "the tolerance of a ruthless individualism that shirks no means of enforcement," demonstrated by reverence for imperious, brutal individuals. Cruel butchers and inhuman monsters were revered during their lifetimes, so it was hard to distinguish between the villain and the hero.[9] In the particularly bleak era of La Violencia, the worst per-petrators who committed the most heinous massacres induced not only terror among the threatened peasant population but, curiously, also awe and admiration.[10] This focus on the victimizer at the expense of exposing injustice or attending to the victims has also characterized how the mass media tends to present social and political conflicts to the general public, a practice that not only desensitizes a public accustomed to a continuous flow of tales of aggression but also, more importantly, condones brutal acts of criminals who can turn their life around, sign peace agreements, and enjoy political careers notwithstanding previously committed crimes.

In other words, the image of a bellicose and at times ruthless leader has established itself in the national psyche, and to this day popular opinion holds that a forceful approach in the world of politics can be positive, perhaps owing precisely to the decades-long internal conflicts that have exhausted the country's resources and patience. One essay inspired by the phenomenon of former president Uribe's overwhelming popularity during his 2002–2010 mandate laid bare that while a direct, head-on take reminiscent of the caudillo style is valued, negotiating is deemed to be the realm of sissies. Focusing on the postings that emerge spontaneously in the online feedback forums of *El Tiempo*, Claudia Delgado unveiled that readers' unfiltered observations bespeak age-old gender dichotomies. They exalt traditionally masculine qualities by perpetuating the marriage of violence and authority, with the concomitant denigration of what has been deemed largely characteristic of women. Uribe, for example, was often described in hyperbolic "manly" terminology as a heavy-handed leader and exterminator, well fitted for unleashing destruction upon the guerrilla opposition. In contrast, César Gaviria's (in office 1990–1994) soft-handed, *ancien régime* politics of negotiation with the state's enemies placed him in a wimpish category suggestive of females, as evidenced by pejorative descriptors such as "crazy girl" (nena loca) or "plush-toy candidate" (candidato de peluche). Likewise, critical commentaries that tie mental illness and hysteria to the female gender were reserved for Gaviria, noting his "pathological envy" or "jealousy and inferiority complex." In short, the word on the street repeatedly feminized the guerrillas and Uribe's opponent, César Gaviria, while Uribe emerged as a hard-line and take-charge leader (*berraco*) capable of taming and controlling insubordinate elements (Delgado 9).

Uribe built his career—especially through the media—on being direct and confrontational (*frentero*), on not mincing words, and on taking the bull by the horns, yet his numerous critics charge that the same rules have never applied to scandals and conflicts that involved his inner circle.[11] Cultivating the aura of a haughty macho, Uribe constructed a persona aimed at convincing the nation that his character was congruent with po- litical demands.[12] Caballero substantiates this stance by accusing Uribe of staging a not-so-spontaneous mishap, whereby the ex-president allowed the now-famous recording of his vulgar outburst against his former of- ficial, Luis Hernando Herrera,[13] to be leaked precisely to reinforce his ma- cho mystique ("Fonda paisa").

After all, as everywhere else nowadays, politics in Latin America is a media-conscious form of performance where leaders, who are celeb- rities in their own right, have manipulated the image of themselves on television with a created mythology predicated on populist tendencies. A curious dichotomy has taken place when it comes to mass media venues and the political propaganda played out by the heads of state. Colombian media critic Jesús Martín-Barbero makes a note of this, as he draws a sharp contrast between how Latin American presidents approach jour- nalists and how they employ television for their benefit. While the press tends to be treated with great suspicion for making efforts to get to the truth, television is the presidents' most successful tool of propaganda and their stage par excellence, from which they can safely project convenient self-images (Martín-Barbero, "Cómo se comunican" 16). This brings to mind that the socialist Chávez and conservative Uribe had more in com- mon than it might seem at first glance; as passionate, charismatic speakers who prided themselves on direct language, both were adept at manipulat- ing social media to popularize and control their image. Authoritarian and bent on ruling beyond the prescribed law, they knew how to appeal to the masses while attacking journalists who shed light on their notoriety. Chávez shut down thirty-four radio stations, allegedly for their bourgeois tendencies, and instituted a law permitting imprisonment for journalists acting against the so-called peace and stability. In the meantime, Uribe's government fended off accusations of tapping phones and spying on jour- nalists critical of his government. Some press members, both Colombian nationals and others, were famously accused of terrorism, of lying, and of cooperating with the guerrillas, or worse, received kidnapping and death threats. The *Los Angeles Times* reported the case of a Colombian newsman who, following his investigation of ties between the Medellín Cartel and Uribe family, was threatened by none other than a former senator and a friend of Uribe, Carlos Nader Simmonds, a man who served prison time in the United States for drug trafficking (Romney).

A Criminal among Criminals: Vallejo's Take on the Elite

Part of Virginia Vallejo's deftness at renegotiating her position is how she simultaneously frames her subjectivity from the perspectives of the highest social class and of the oppressed. Unlike corrupt and hypocritical politicians joined at the hip through decades of dirty deals that have allowed them to amass capital and prestige, she—and Escobar by extension—are somehow more truthful and more direct and faithful to themselves, in short, more authentic and closer to the "real" people. Her self-exposure constitutes an act of public service: Although he was killed like an animal and she was shunned by society, corrupt politicians who benefited from the narco bonanza profit to this day. Thus she presents herself as an advocate for truth, as one who is risking humiliation to speak up about what really happened when Escobar was in control. If "being ordinary, authentic or 'real' is a dominant rhetorical device of fame" that allows celebrities to achieve a closer connection with the public through identification (Redmond 28), Vallejo similarly moves between extraordinary personage (worldly, beautiful, crème de la crème) and common folk familiar with failure and despair.

As a public figure, Vallejo proves to be very self-aware of how identities are created, performed, and disseminated and how her own visible status is a double-edged sword, where she can be vilified with the same ease as she was previously admired. Jacqueline Rose suggests that celebrity worship "is often a ritual of public humiliation," for feeling ultimately inferior to the stars' glamour and achievements, the general public wallows in their foibles and loves to knock them down when their weaknesses come to light (Rose, *On Not* 203). Facing this potential for humiliation—since Vallejo had already paid with her career for having romanced the most hated criminal in Colombia—the diva treads carefully when confessing her faults and disclosing an affair hidden from the world for twenty years. Principally, she attempts to justify her errors by emphasizing the trope of a woman in love and by reconstructing her experience as a recovery story: She loved a mysterious visionary but ran away from the criminal he became. She saw herself as an equal partner of a would-be statesman, a graceful mentor who shaped his public persona and steered him—albeit unsuccessfully—toward negotiations rather than armed confrontation and toward a legitimate career that had the potential of benefiting the nation. She reenacts the trope so familiar to female readers and so pervasive in self-help narratives and popular psychotherapy that it ultimately becomes believable: of a good girl who falls for a bad boy and naively plans to tame his personality and convert him into something he is not. This wishful thinking becomes evident when she muses early on that Escobar "is the biggest macho I have ever met, a diamond in the rough and I believe he has never had a woman like me; I'm going to try to polish him up, to teach him everything I have learnt, and I'm going to make sure that he needs me like one needs water in the desert" [Tiene la personalidad más masculina que yo haya conocido. Es un diamante en bruto y creo que nunca ha tenido una mujer como yo; voy a intentar pulirlo y a tratar de enseñarle todo lo que yo he aprendido y voy a hacer que me necesite como al agua en el desierto (V. Vallejo 72)].

Since Vallejo's reputation depends in part on how she presents Escobar, she weaves his portrait carefully. To legitimize his position, she disrupts the criminal/noncriminal dichotomy by demonstrating that criminality has been in fact the defining quality of most members of the ruling class: "As you get to know them, it is clear that some of them are so small-minded and so cruel that next to them, you, Pablo, are a decent human being" [Cuando uno los conoce, sabe que algunos de ellos son tan mezquinos y tan crueles que a su lado tú eres un ser humano decente (V. Vallejo 222)]. Many leading politicians enriched themselves on contraband and bribes or from the turmoil of La Violencia, which enabled them to dispossess peasants of their land: "All of them, absolutely each and every one, is guilty of crimes and death: at their own hands, at the hands of their parents during La Violencia period, at the hands of their landowning grandparents, slave-owning great-grandparents or of Inquisitor and *encomendero* great-great grandparents" [Todos ellos, absolutamente todos, cargan con crímenes y muertos: los suyos, los de sus padres durante la Violencia, los de abuelos terratenientes, los de bisabuelos esclavistas o los de tatarabuelos inquisidores o encomenderos (V. Vallejo 223)]. In other words, Vallejo lays out a long tradition of pillage, injustice, and illegality that, instead of the usual practice of demonizing and singling out Escobar, frames him within a tradition of publicly sanctioned delinquency. From this angle, the drug lord's principal transgression is not his illicit activity or his ruthlessness but his audacity to engage in moneymaking on such a grand scale while being an outsider to the otherwise closed circle of Colombia's typical beneficiaries. Salazar, too, paints a larger picture of corruption and narco bonanza, pointing to other factors and groups that have enabled the capo's ascent: "[Escobar] was a product of its society, and of its incoherent authorities, he did not fall out of the sky" [fue producto de la sociedad y de autoridades incoherentes y . . . no cayó del cielo (J. Salazar, Interview; my translation)].

Vallejo's examples of the marriage between the narcos and the ruling politicians include the already famous accusations of Escobar's business deals with the Uribe family, such as permission to land his planes in exchange for a cut of the profits (48, 112). She also holds in contempt Santofimio, insisting that the slick politician who publicly claimed to have no special ties with the drug lord visited him on a regular basis not only to mooch exorbitant sums of money but also to have Escobar do the dirty work of eliminating Santofimio's political opponents. Many other members of the elite that claimed to have stayed away from the cocaine king showered him with offers of property for outrageous prices, knowing that such seemingly disadvantageous deals would benefit both parties: The narco class could launder its money and the rich could become even richer. Vallejo goes further in her whitewashing campaign by claiming that Escobar in fact possessed a "rigorous ethical code" (riguroso código ético; 228), as he identified with the oppressed and refused to cooperate with individuals whose families had committed injustices toward the *campesinos*. That is why he never bought the extensive Hacienda Bellacruz from Minister Carlos Arturo Marulanda, whose father, as Escobar presumably explained to Virginia, had brutally dispossessed its former inhabitants with the help of *chulavitas*, mercenaries who enforced their employer's unlawful appropriation through burning, raping, and murder during La Violencia (228–29). In Vallejo's account, Escobar is even magnanimous, not stooping to the level of pretension and duplicity that characterizes many representatives of Colombia's ruling class: "Pablo never talks about little things nor does he lose his guard with anyone. . . . Pablo always sends the very next day 100% of [the money] he has promised and never expects a receipt. Pablo does not talk about little things" [Pablo no habla de cosas pequeñas y jamás baja la guardia con nadie . . . Pablo siempre manda al día siguiente el ciento por ciento de lo que promete y nunca pide recibo. Pablo no habla de cosas pequeñas (V. Vallejo 164)].

From Sexual Object to Sexual Subject: Vallejo's Role in the Romance

Despite Vallejo's praises for Escobar's integrity, perhaps no other element contributes to Escobar's status in Vallejo's book as much as Virginia herself. Since the symbolic power of a strongman is also reflected in his consumption of all the women he craves, conquering a national celebrity, a notable member of the elite, and one of its most desired beauties asserts Escobar's worth and attests to his social mobility. Virginia seems quite aware of her role in the drug lord's process of public self-aggrandizement, in serving as the crucial trope for the advancement of his social status. Early in the book, she highlights her role in Pablo's transformation, quoting a friend who lays out the benefits Escobar will reap through associating with the diva: "He's got big political aspirations and needs a real woman by his side, elegant, who knows how to speak in public; not a model or a girl from his same class, like his last one . . . 'you are this country's professional beauty, pure blood, something Pablo has never had!'" [Él tiene aspiraciones políticas muy grandes y necesita a su lado a una mujer de verdad, elegante que sepa hablar en público; no una modelo ni una chica de su misma clase, como la última novia . . . 'tú eres la *professional beauty* de este país, un purasangre, algo que Pablo jamás ha tenido!' (V. Vallejo 53)].

Virginia suspects that her romance with Pablo is in some way his means of subjugating the bourgeoisie and joining their ranks. It also serves to affirm his rising stature with other machos he holds in high respect. Here is where Salazar confirms Virginia's declarations by commenting on Escobar's excitement in presenting her to his bigwig associates in 1983: "He felt proud to be accompanied by this woman who, no doubt, was at that time the symbol of beauty and fame in the national spotlight" [Él se sentía orgulloso de estar acompañado de esta mujer que era sin duda en aquel entonces el símbolo de la belleza y de la fama en la farándula nacional (Salazar, *La parábola de Pablo* 109)]. Virginia herself describes in great detail one such episode, where her looks and eloquence bolster Escobar's status in the eyes of one of M-19's founders and "toughest *comandantes*," Iván Marino Ospina (Salazar, *La parábola de Pablo* 232–34). The effect is as expected. Vallejo plays the part of a charming seductress who excites the tough macho with her pampered sensuality, seemingly effortless graciousness, and blue-blooded etiquette. Unaccustomed to women of her caliber, Ospina becomes immediately transfixed by her style. Ospina's bravado shows a stunning disregard for Escobar's reaction, as the guest does not even try to hide his fascination with Vallejo. She writes: "I realize that this legendary guerrilla leader does not fear Pablo or anyone else, because from the moment he lays his eyes on me, he does not turn his inflamed gaze away from my face, my body, my legs" [Me doy cuenta de que aquel legendario jefe guerrillero en verdad no le tiene miedo a Pablo ni a nadie, porque desde que me pone los ojos encima no despega de mi rostro, ni de mi cuerpo, ni de mis piernas una mirada inflamada (V. Vallejo 234)].

Then Vallejo describes a conversation the men believed to be carrying out in private, as she excuses herself and overhears through the semi-closed doors. The exchange is a manifestation of Latin American virility that goes hand in hand with the men's brazen attitude toward politics. The leaders of two rogue organizations emerge hot-blooded, lascivious, responsive to women's physical charms, and set on possessing them as part of their (self)-confirmed prowess. Pleased with what he sees, Ospina requests from his host not one but two women identical to Vallejo, thereby emphasizing his exacerbated virility. In this transaction, Virginia, and all the other women by extension, stands for a fungible commodity devoid of agency, available and replaceable on a whim. In response, Escobar politely informs his guest that Virginia is a Colombian celebrity, a star, and his own treasure (V. Vallejo 236). He even proudly exhibits various magazines whose covers are adorned with his lover's face. Only then does the guest retreat, understanding that he has crossed the line. Virginia is far above the faceless one-night stands they are accustomed to bedding. Resigned, the guest requests two lovers resembling Sofia Loren, preferably deaf and mute. (Aside from the objectification, the allusion is to Loren's darker looks, sometimes equated with the Mezzogiorno, thus hinting at race and ethnicity, and, ultimately, class.) With a sigh of relief—for Escobar holds Ospina in high esteem and does not wish to disappoint him—the host relaxes, knowing that supplying his guest with beautiful female companions without pedigree is much easier than conjuring up another Virginia Vallejo.

While this dialogue substantiates women's objectification in the narco world, it simultaneously validates Vallejo's specific agenda. Sure, she is ultrafeminine and aware of her sexual allure, but throughout the narrative, Vallejo insists she is not just another pretty face (V. Vallejo 236). In the scene with Ospina, Vallejo turns the tables on Escobar and ignores her boyfriend's gesture to sit quietly by his side. She instead chooses to sit between the two men and engage in a discussion on the La Violencia period. This scene is indicative of her self-exposé throughout the book, for Vallejo repeatedly presents herself as men's equal whose numerous merits make her a bridge between the criminal world and her world—"a leader of the guerrilla . . . another of drug trafficking, . . . and a woman with no possessions but related to half of the country's oligarchy and friends with the other half" [jefe de la guerrilla . . . jefe del narcotráfico, . . . y una mujer sin un metro de tierra pero emparentada con la mitad de la oligarquía del país y amiga de la otra mitad (238)].

Escobar's display of Vallejo as a manifestation of his symbolic capital is not just about her fame and beauty, for the drug lord could delight in a bevy of belles every night. Rather, his display is about her social status. Class-conscious at all times, Vallejo emphasizes her superiority when, later into their rocky relationship, Escobar purposefully humiliates her by presenting her to his new girlfriend. Virginia does not hesitate to put down the girl as attractive and sweet but cheaply dressed (wearing a sweater made from domestic wool) and looking like a clerk at the cosmetics counter (304). By highlighting the other woman's lack of worldliness, Virginia makes it evident to the readers that this new companion is no competition for her, nor can she be her rival. Dressed in designer clothes from head to toe (red Thierry Mugler for this occasion), Virginia will remain Escobar's only lover with an enviable pedigree.

Beauty and designer clothes are not the only aces up Virginia's sleeve. It is above all her own self-confidence that matches Escobar's inflated ego. Even her description of the couple's initial encounter foretells a dynamic uncharacteristic of the narco milieu, where men dominate all the possible venues of power. While the capo's scantily clad female entourage serves only an aesthetic purpose, Virginia engages in flirtatious banter barely a day after meeting Escobar at Hacienda Nápoles. The ease with which she carries herself in front of the man whose riches overwhelm even his most renowned guests showcases that the diva is not starstruck. She shares with Escobar an unparalleled arrogance (82), suggesting that theirs is the union of a "power couple" whose strengths might be different but whose charisma is alike.

Once Escobar's celebrity status is confirmed by frequent press coverage, Virginia jokes that they will begin to compete for magazine covers. Recognizing her expertise, Escobar also shares with her various aspects of his business, such as his trafficking routes, contacts, and strategies. To prepare him for indiscreet questions from the press, Virginia tackles his past life of petty crime, knowing that men of his ego are unaccustomed to challenges from women. She thereby oversteps certain unspoken boundaries that trophy women cannot cross at the risk of angering their volatile lovers. When Virginia mentions his youthful business of stealing tombstones for resale, Escobar grows silent: "I know that I took him by surprise and have crossed the line, and I wonder if I had touched his Achilles's heel all too soon. But I know that he has never been in love with a woman of his age or my class and . . . if we are to love each other as two equals, I must teach him from day one where the immature amusement ends and the relation between adult woman and man begins" [Sé que lo he tomado por sorpresa y que he traspasado un límite, y me pregunto si habré tocado su talón de Aquiles demasiado pronto. Pero sé que Pablo nunca ha estado enamorado de una mujer de su edad o de mi clase y que, si vamos a amarnos en términos de completa igualdad, deberé enseñarle desde el primer día dónde termina la diversión de dos niños grandes y dónde comienza la relación entre un hombre y una mujer adultos (V. Vallejo 68)].

This observation might be the key to reading Virginia's rendition of their romance, in that she lays out her worth next to the capo by converting her disadvantage, that is, her age, into a plus. Escobar was known for his penchant for pubescent virgins from the Medellín slums, girls who offered no intellectual or emotional challenge and who were swiftly vanquished with cash.[14] The melodramatic mode sets the stage for an intimate and passionate portrayal of their relationship, where their shared ambition makes them equal, despite all the other factors that so evidently set them apart. Vallejo emphasizes that Escobar is unaccustomed to true partnerships in his romantic relations and that all his prior relationships have been predicated on his complete dominance.

It should come as no surprise that Vallejo's assertions meet with criticism from Escobar's circle of friends and family members. After all, each of them has some stake in the capo's dark legacy, and Vallejo's portrayal undermines *their* version of a self-reliant leader who did not need any "crutch" to climb the ladder of success. Popeye dismissed the importance of his boss's romance with Virginia by commenting with an outright misogyny that Escobar quickly tired of what he considered a woman past her prime.[15] Escobar's sister, Alba Marina, questioned Virginia's romance with her brother in even stronger terms, when she accused the diva of staging her first meeting with Escobar. For Alba Marina, the diva's desperate attempts to keep the relationship going only made the capo concoct different schemes to keep her away.[16] Escobar's son considers Virginia's memoir an unreliable source of information, and Victoria Henao, Escobar's wife, explains that Virginia was but one of at least three lovers the capo dated simultaneously, including Wendy Chavarriaga Gil (later killed by Popeye on Escobar's orders) and the blond and blue-eyed Elsy Sofia Escobar Muriel, whose two-year relationship ended the moment she insisted on marriage (*Mi vida*, chapter 4). But Virginia exalts in the uniqueness of their relationship, and she does so precisely through the prism of equality, both in age and in celebrity power. She is aware that the kingpin, too, gains in the eyes of the world by associating with her; after all, despite his wealth, Escobar was shunned by the same elites who profited from dealing with him, a fact that created even deeper resentment in the capo.[17]

She repeatedly highlights her role as Escobar's mentor/teacher and as an experienced television personality whose highly successful career in the spotlight will be of great use for the attention-hungry Escobar. In a reversal of gender roles, she becomes Escobar's Pygmalion, teaching the political neophyte how to talk properly and how to act in front of the cameras so that he can be the equal of other acclaimed demagogues: "When he has to take into account other people's possible reaction to his political discourse, he uses me detachedly as his spokesperson—a cross between defense lawyer, prosecutor, witness, judge, and audience—aware that, while he seduces a trophy-woman, the woman-camera is analyzing, questioning, cataloguing, and almost certainly comparing him with others of the same rank" [Cuando necesita medir la posible reacción de otros a su discurso político, me utiliza fríamente como interlocutor—mezcla de abogado defensor, fiscal, testigo, juez y público—, consciente de que, mientras él seduce a la mujer-trofeo, la mujer-cámara lo está analizando, cuestionando, catalogando y casi seguramente comparando con otros de su misma talla (V. Vallejo 227–28)].

Escobar was well aware of the power of the media. In an era when Colombian television was state-owned and centralized from Bogotá, he founded a news program called *Antioquia al día,* thus pioneering regional television in the country. Pressured to give public appearances and well aware of his plebeian mannerisms, Escobar turned to Virginia for help, for she was renowned nationwide for her impeccable delivery and supreme onscreen sophistication. Salazar confirms Vallejo's influence on the capo in *La parábola de Pablo*, noting that their televised training sessions had the twofold purpose of perfecting Escobar's responses to the most predictable questions and eliminating the embarrassing tics that revealed his lack of refinement (100). This was one of very rare instances when Escobar treated a woman like his equal, even if only briefly. More of a teacher than a student, Virginia coached Escobar's public persona and also spearheaded the media infatuation with Escobar's philanthropy, a fleeting trend that ended when cozying up to him was no longer in vogue.[18]

Vallejo goes even further by claiming to have instructed him on successful politicking and on strategies of fruitful negotiation that her philistine lover had never had to master before (94). Her musings lay bare Vallejo's self-exposé as a woman who graciously offers to share the fruit of her pedigree and talents with the epitome of barbarism, as per Sarmiento's famous dichotomy: "Will he play his cards well? Will he one day learn public speaking with a less discernible accent and in a more educated tone? Will my diamond in the rough be able to perfect a powerful message in order to reach beyond the provinces? Will he manage to find a more controlled form of passion to achieve what he proposes and a better one to keep it?" [¿Sabrá jugar bien sus cartas? ¿Aprenderá algún día a hablar en público con un acento menos marcado y un tono más educado? ¿Podrá mi diamante en bruto pulir aquel discurso elemental para transmitir un mensaje potente que trascienda la provincial? ¿Logrará hallar alguna forma de pasión más controlada para obtener lo que se propone, y una aún más inteligente para conservarlo? (V. Vallejo 93)].

Virginia is the light of civilization brought into Escobar's world of barbarism, his Malinche in that she embraces the role of lover/interpreter who speeds up her man's conquest of the New World via her language skills. She offers to teach Escobar some smatterings of foreign languages and pronunciation when the capo proudly shows her his numerous passports that could one day allow him to escape Colombia. She is eager to help him make the leap to the status of a bona fide statesman so that he can seduce and permanently conquer the elites.

History has shown that this transition never occurred, because Escobar gave up on his negotiating skills once he felt threatened and betrayed by the establishment. Notably, a discouraged Virginia describes his later war against the state no longer from the insider's perspective but as a person distanced from Escobar by her conflicting emotions and by subsequent events that bring other men into her life. Her sporadic contacts with Escobar oscillate between her asseverations of the ended affair and of threatening encounters and fleeting moments of passion, where she still professes her love for Pablo, proving to be attached emotionally to him long after they go their separate ways (V. Vallejo 211, 285). Such positioning as a mere spectator of his wrath strategically places her again with the rest of the world; no longer his true confidante, she relinquishes her mentorship, hence exerting no power over him and becoming little more than a witness to his crimes. As it stands, their intimacy came almost to an end, and Virginia can now reveal very few secrets that the public does not know.

But even when Escobar plunges into paranoia and begins to take revenge on anyone and everyone he deems suspicious, Virginia claims to still provide a voice of reason in his life. She assures her readers that Escobar recognized how she had vanquished his temper and hotheaded politicking: "You are my only true friend . . . the only one I can relate to about things I cannot talk about with my mother nor with my wife, but just with other guys. . . . You have saved me from committing many errors and I can't let you go away" [Tú eres mi única amiga del alma . . . la única con la que se puede hablar de cosas de las que uno no habla con la mamá ni la esposa, sino con otros hombres . . . Me has salvado de cometer muchos errores y no puedo permitir que te me vuelvas a ir (V. Vallejo 290)]. Similarly, Virginia cites Gustavo Gaviria, Escobar's cousin and closest associate, who allegedly considered her the only candid voice in Escobar's close circle of thugs and flatterers: "Thank God, each time you come back Pablo becomes reasonable for a while, but then you guys separate again and there is no one who can put brakes on him, smoking pot in that world of *sicarios* and *prepagos* . . . surrounded by a family who treats him like an omnipotent God" [A Dios gracias, cada vez que tú vuelves Pablo entra en razón por un tiempo, pero luego ustedes se separan otra vez y él queda sin nadie que le pegue riendazos, fumando yerba en ese mundo de sicarios y niñas . . . rodeado de una familia que lo mira como si fuera un Dios omnipotente (V. Vallejo 293)]. Such quotes—truthfulness aside, for no one can confirm what really transpired among the now deceased actors of this drama—assuage Virginia's possible culpability by creating a distance between the Pablo she supported in his efforts to rule out extradition and the Escobar she only tried to appease, even if these efforts proved ineffective.

Framing their falling-out as an escape from a destructive love affair allows Virginia to reconstruct her experience according to the conventional master plot of recovery narratives, the myth of life as a journey where she recounts first her infatuation, the blinding power of love, and then the descent into hell that makes her see the true horror of Escobar's personality. She then moves on to a new, difficult post-Pablo stage of her life, marked by unemployment, public shunning, looming poverty, social scapegoating, and the most basic fear for her safety. The great losses and disappointments Vallejo has suffered redeem her prior involvement with the criminal to an extent, diminishing her possible relationship to Escobar's war on Colombia and converting her narrative into a formulaic trope of the celebrity autobiography, which becomes "one more chronicle of personal failure, personal triumph" (Avrahami 167). As is well evidenced in the high sales of scandalous materials around the globe, "the failures of celebrities are as profitable as their successes" (Harper 312), making Vallejo's confessions a good business move not only on account of Escobar's notoriety but also by virtue of her own fluctuating reputation.

Indeed, Vallejo remains faithful to her melodramatic focus to the very end, for even the falling-out between the two lovers is portrayed less as a consequence of Escobar's escalating tug-of-war with the state and more as a personal crisis born out of his inability to have a healthy partnership with a woman. She is aware that as a classic macho, Pablo does not hold much esteem for the fairer sex, treating the great majority of women with indifference, condescension, and utilitarianism (186). He loves his family (although they also bore him silly, as per Virginia's account) and greatly enjoys paid one-night stands with anonymous beauties, but the rest of the female world could cease to exist for him. Vallejo feels that she escapes all these categories by virtue of her extensive experience in the world of politics, skills that Escobar associates exclusively with a masculine domain of knowledge. His understanding of gender roles goes hand in hand with the misogynistic attitudes upheld by the criminal world, where women are currency in the hands of the transaction-making men and where the worst offense is to disrupt this tacit code by appropriating someone else's female partner.[19]

In contrast, the breach between Vallejo and Escobar was almost civil. She was disappointed that he never really outgrew his environment or its trademark macho attitude toward women and that he remained the most comfortable surrounded by people from his social background or lower, thus evidencing the quondam lovers' incompatibility. Once again, Virginia puts her most revealing commentaries about Escobar in the mouth of another acquaintance, this time a certain Clara, who sold him jewelry on a regular basis and thus knew how much the drug lord invested in his sexual conquests. Clara's criticism reflects a strong class sensibility. Escobar, Virginia's "ex-lover with the face of a truck driver" and a "miserable assassin," has just spent a quarter million dollars on a "little whore with a tin-can crown," who "under economic pressure will sell it for a mere five thousand bucks" [ex-amante tuyo con cara de chofer, ese asesino miserable, and una putica con corona de lata . . . que en una necesidad ¡lo venderá por cinco mil dólares! (V. Vallejo 296)]. This, of course, implies that only Virginia would know how to rightly exhibit her luxurious jewels, thereby in her mind legitimizing her complaint about the lack of remuneration for the social shunning she suffered. In the end, what Escobar likes "are expensive whores from his own social class" [putas caras de su misma clase social" (V. Vallejo 296)], whose utilitarian function does not force the classic macho to confront his own prejudices against women. Thus their longtime romance proves impossible to sustain, despite a mutual attraction that originally awakened so many hopes. At some point early in their affair, Vallejo remarked that what they would never admit but deep down was obvious to them both was that, when all was said and done, she was still "a bourgeoisie diva and he, a bandit multimillionaire" [una diva burguesa y él sólo un bandido millonario (118)].

Jean Franco argues that rather than confront a dominant patriarchy with a new feminine position, Latin American women writers often unsettle "the stance that supports gender power/knowledge as masculine. This 'unsettling' is accomplished in a variety of ways, through parody and pastiche, by mixing genres, and by constituting subversive mythologies" ("Going Public" 74–75). Admittedly, Vallejo is no writer, but her voice has been heard through her tell-all memoir. In it, she places herself somewhere in between, with her literary debut as a diva of yesteryear and present-day sensationalist who assesses Escobar and the political environment during his rise to power. On the one hand, she epitomizes defiance with her bold political accusations that have become known in the press as the "virginazo," suggesting a "Virginiagate" in the Colombian context.[20] On the other, her narrative repeatedly exalts her beauty, her seductive body, and her luxurious clothes and perfume, in short, the type of embodied female subjectivity that places her in the role of a trophy woman who has consciously used her sex appeal to manipulate the men in her life, professing an attraction for rough machos and a desire to "soften" them under her loving tutelage. In other words, she replays a number of conventional gender tropes characteristic of Harlequin productions that in many ways undermine her otherwise independent stance.

Conflicting tendencies aside, Vallejo's unique life experiences and, above all, her dexterity at negotiating each and every situation make her a forceful presence and a maverick among women in the popular narco iconography. In the end, even though Jean Franco had a very different type of female agenda in mind, it is fitting to say that Vallejo, too, created her own mythology of Pablo Escobar, one predicated above all on the intimate sphere of feelings and sentiments. A powerful marketable commodity in her own right, she legitimized a sentimental approach to *narcocultura*, conferring on women a certain visibility in Escobar's and, by extension, the general narco milieu. She broadened "the terms of political debate by redefining sovereignty and by using privilege to destroy privilege" (Franco, "Going Public" 80), in that she made female agency a phenomenon Pablo Escobar had to reckon with, even if only partially and for a period of time. It is ironic that, accustomed to the chauvinistic attitudes that relegated women to the private sphere, Escobar, the classic macho, took lessons on how to inhabit the mediated (read: public) space precisely from a woman.[21] Vastly different from the classic narco *muñeca*, Vallejo was never a guileless appendage to her infamous man, a protégé, a minion, or a tiring tagalong. In fact, quite the contrary, one could credit Vallejo with inaugurating the kingpin before the society at large, for the diva dedicated her program to Escobar's charity works in the shantytowns of Medellín, thus catapulting an unknown humanitarian of shady resources into the spotlight. She also lent her trademark face to Santofimio's campaign, a movement that was supposed to protect Escobar from the threats of extradition. Thus, it is no surprise that years later, on María Elvira's talk show in Miami, Vallejo expressed her discontent at being grouped together with other women with a recognized connection to the drug world. And though she quotes monetary benefits as the principal point of contrast, above all, one could argue that it is her voice and her consistently unclassifiable stance that sets her apart and allows her to negotiate her own category of a maverick.

Virginia Vallejo in the Spotlight

Of course, her memoirs met with a variety of opinions, many of them highly critical. Roberto Escobar accused her of dishonesty and an intent to profit from denigrating the man who had lavished her with endless favors. Edgardo José Maya Villazón, procurador general (attorney general) of Colombia, characterized her as Escobar's silent accomplice who should be prosecuted for obscuring the truth for so long. Some were not as critical or dismissive; Juan Carlos Galán, son of the assassinated presidential candidate, deemed her testimony a valid historical source worthy of the attention of the Colombian courts.[22] Similarly Salazar, whose meticulous study of the subject grants his voice an indisputable legitimacy, contended that Vallejo's position as Escobar's romantic partner who moved in the highest political circles makes her reminiscences particularly valuable. He also defended her long silence, arguing that fear for one's safety is a valid and understandable reaction and has kept many witnesses unwilling to come forward even to this day (Rueda).

Yet Salazar's vote of confidence for Vallejo's testimony was more the exception than the rule among the Colombian intellectual elite. Though many deemed her book well written, the great majority discredited her confessions as a calculated attempt to draw attention to herself without providing any new facts. They cast doubt on Vallejo's timing and economic motives while expressing reservations regarding her over-the-top presentation of a story targeted to elicit sympathy for what should be considered a criminal, or at least a contemptible, act. Yet predictably, criticism and scandal generate excellent publicity, since, as *Semana* commented on July 29, 2006, Vallejo's interview on RCN, as part of the book launch, drew reportedly 56 percent of the nation's audience—numbers rivaling only those of World Cup Soccer. This made the $20,000 honorarium for her appearance a true bargain for the network.

Of course, one cannot attribute Vallejo's popularity solely to the well-publicized bickering between the diva and former president Uribe. Vallejo's mystique remained etched in the nation's memory despite, or maybe due to, her disappearance from the spotlight two decades earlier. The continuous public display of her personal life and image throughout the 1970s and 1980s—characteristic of mass performance culture and a star system that coincided with the era of expansion in the communications industry (Martín-Barbero, *Communication, Culture and Hegemony*

82)—both made her intimately familiar to the masses and elevated her to an object of emulation. She grew to fulfill the role of a celebrity, a figure who, as it is commonly perceived, stands for "every consumer's dream of what it would be like if money were no object" (Ewen 99). For Ewen, who focused on U.S. culture and its celebrity system, "in a society where everyday life was increasingly defined by feelings of insignificance and institutions of standardization, the 'star' provided an accessible icon to the significance of the personal and the individual" (93). Likewise, Vallejo became a household name with whom audiences grew to sympathize and subsequently identify.

Vallejo's return to the limelight brought about a debate on *Noticias RCN*, where a panel of four prominent public figures, moderated by Clara Elvira Ospina, offered a critical assessment of her book and, in a wider sweep, of other publications written by Escobar's confidants. Jorge Amando Otálora, acting attorney general, and Alfonso Gómez Méndez, attorney general of Colombia between 1997 and 2001, expressed concern with how Vallejo's questionable and distorted take on history misrepresents Colombia's image to the rest of the world. Journalists Edgar Téllez and Poncho Rentería covered more personal grounds, as they called her writing the kitschy musings of a mythomaniac who perfumed the proverbial pig to justify her own past. In fact, the latter comment relating to the rationalization of Vallejo's romance epitomizes the general consternation and perplexity among the Colombian public. To this day, people relish the memory of her elegant presence in the media, oceans apart from the déclassé lifestyle of the drug lords she cozied up to.

In other words, Vallejo's paeans to the blinding power of love convinced few commentators. Public opinion, exemplified by Hugo Mastrodoménico's quote in this chapter's epigraph, reexamined one question to no end: Why would a woman like Virginia Vallejo fall for a man like Pablo Escobar? Óscar G. Domínguez's comment, "We had no idea she had such a bad taste" [Ignorábamos que tuviera tan mal gusto], exemplifies the general trend; most critics simply reprimand Vallejo's relationship preferences, in a sense marking the class difference as the most "natural" barrier that Vallejo seems to have disregarded. Vallejo's critics mark a disconnect between the quintessence of class and grace, "the beauty in the beasts' pigsty," as Collazos once said ("La diva"), and the primitive brute who, like Poncho Rentería quipped, used to gobble down two portions of *bandeja paisa* at a sitting. It is unclear whether Rentería wanted to rebuke

Escobar's taste for the unpretentious Antioquian cuisine or to scoff at the kingpin's gluttony. What is certain, however, is that the examples contrasting Escobar's inferior social status with Vallejo's unquestionable pedigree are both hilarious and telling: They disclose more about the prejudices of her detractors than about Vallejo herself.

Others scapegoat Vallejo as a spoiled socialite who cracked under the pressure of her own hunger for power, betting on a wrong horse and failing miserably. Some hypotheses acquire rather asinine pseudo-scientific dimensions, putting the blame for Vallejo's romance on human instinct born of primates' need to follow the alpha male for the preservation of the species. Others psychoanalyze the diva, attributing her scandalous affair to craving strong emotions or, better yet, to her need for the love and admiration of individuals who actually could care less about her. Fernando Londoño Hoyos and María Paulina Ortiz opine that it was Vallejo's unbridled desire for power that eventually brought her to her knees. Mastrodoménico psychoanalyzes the diva, and another article combines the pop science of instincts with a cursory glance at the behavioral patterns of women involved with the narcos ("¿Cuál?"). Other forms of speculation become even more personal, digging into Vallejo's private life and objectifying the star of yesteryear in a way that no public male figure would ever have to endure.

Commentaries return to her looks, scrutinizing and taking apart her life and her body, musing, for example, about her low-cut neckline from a well-known cookie commercial or her legs popularized by a famous TV spot for pantyhose. Caballero, for instance, states semi-jokingly that Virginia's seemingly naked photo from an old magazine cover conceals her chest in the same way her 2007 book obscured the details of her past. The title of Caballero's essay says it all: "Virginia's Boobs" (Las tetas de Virginia). There are also cruel anecdotes about her multiple plastic surgeries, her histrionic tendencies, her arrogance, and her absurd vanity whereby no one, not even her husband, could catch a glimpse of Virginia sans make-up. Then, not without satisfaction, they trace her eventual downfall, marked by the loss of her earlier lucidity and dazzling looks (Ortiz). One thing is clear: Colombians, like everyone else, love to hate their celebrities, dissecting them through the lens of schadenfreude. Virginia Vallejo shares the fate of other women who have suffered from the onslaught of public curiosity and media pursuit; as Jacqueline Rose wrote of Lady Di, the Colombian diva came to embody "so dramatically the paradox and the perversion—the passion and the loathing—of celebrity" (*On Not* 211).

Theories and speculations abound. Some consider Vallejo's case of infatuation with Escobar to be a national parable of society's romance with drug trafficking, thereby, in a rather grandiose and melodramatic fashion, equating the fate of the television icon with the decline of Colombian morality. Collazos also compares Vallejo's downfall with the collapse of Colombian morality ("La vida"), while Salazar draws a similar parallel, notwithstanding his more measured approach: "Virginia Vallejo is a tragic reflection of many people in this country who having it all, allow themselves to be seduced by gold and power and fall into an abyss. It's a national image that to a degree showcases our disgrace" [Virginia Vallejo es una imagen trágica de mucha gente en este país que aun teniéndolo todo, se deja seducir por el oro y el poder y va al precipicio. Es una imagen muy nacional, que marca un poco nuestra desgracia (Rueda)]. Similarly, in her autobiography, Virginia Vallejo herself equates her own infatuation with Escobar with the nation's craze over the capo's wealth and the power it gave him: "I am his permanent challenge and that is why he tries out with me on an individual level the same seduction that he has put in practice in the country as a collective; the country that he sees, treats, and intends to utilize as if it were an extension of Hacienda Nápoles" [Soy para él un desafío permanente y, por ello, ensaya conmigo a nivel individual esa misma seducción que a nivel colectivo ha comenzado a poner en práctica con un país que él ve, trata y pretende utilizar como si fuese sólo una extensión de la Hacienda Nápoles (V. Vallejo 227)]. Thus, not just in her eyes her romance becomes a national allegory, a foundational fiction of modern Colombia with a romance more fit for the tabloids and crime chronicles than literary registers.

As for writers' commentaries, in addition to Collazos, Jorge Franco, whose *Rosario Tijeras* took Colombia by storm and gave the young author immediate fame, assessed Vallejo's memoirs as a book suitable for scandal-seekers and gossip-followers, suggesting that a traditional reader would ignore it due to its manifest shoddiness. Understandably, Alfonso Carvajal, editor of Random House Mondadori, the publisher of Vallejo's book, defends her and other popular narratives, arguing that if such acclaimed intellectuals as [Franco], Caballero, and Collazos spend so much time discussing Vallejo's memoirs—even if only to unearth their inconsistencies and irritating trends—clearly there must be some cultural value to her message (Baldoví Giraldo).

This argument echoes the centuries-old debate between apologists for mass culture and elites who argue that the institutions of democracy have eroded the so-called high culture, degrading its standards and subsuming its value to a consumer product. From Max Horkheimer and Theodor Adorno to José Ortega y Gasset and T. S. Eliot, various representatives of cultural institutions have been dismissive of the producers of low and mass entertainment, all the while appealing for strengthened cultural aesthetics and tastes. Yet as sales are the principal barometer of popular taste, and there is a continuous demand for eyewitness testimony to the dark moments in Colombia's history, Vallejo's memoirs have found an audience among the fans of the *narcocultura* boom.

The Colombian public devours personal accounts of witnesses and accomplices to these criminal activities, precisely because they find the "official" version of events incomplete and unsatisfactory and because, in contemporary postmodern culture, the private has become very public. Memoirs and their celebration of the ordinary, as well as the display of celebrity private lives, have forged a dialogic relationship within the mass culture of capitalism, where more people can participate in the exchange of knowledge (Rak 328), thereby circumventing the sanctioned institutions of information and literacy. In other words, popular culture can be seen by its supporters not only as a homogenous product fed to passive consumers but also as a cultural battleground where "the definition and representation of the people are fought over and determined" (Marshall 45). While the dominant culture invariably strives to project the cultural text that obviates the reforming of cultural meanings, the popular view "celebrates the potential and possibility of audience reconstruction or play with dominant symbols and signs of a culture."[23] In other words, there is an element of resistance that can be found in tabloid-like mass production; it is a site of tension between domination and subordination, where the collective is never utterly manipulable.

But returning to Virginia, such an outpouring of opinions and criticism would silence many lesser souls, who would allow the public witch hunt and decades-old fascination erase their agency. Yet Vallejo refused to be pigeonholed as a passive woman with a shameful narco stigma, resorting instead to an impressive toolbox of strategies to return the gaze and debunk the hypocrisies of her detractors. She lashed out at her critics and politicians, bringing back to the fore some unsavory anecdotes and connections whose protagonists would prefer to stay forgotten. She also made full use of social media, granting interviews, blogging, and finding creative ways to interact with the general public from her official website.[24] She does not hesitate to call out companies that in her mind take advantage of her image without consulting with her.

This goes for the series *Narco*, which portrayed Virginia in the semi-fictitious character of journalist Valeria Vélez (played by Stephanie Sigman), allegedly without consulting her on her life story. Vallejo sued Netflix for what she deemed to be misappropriation of her memoir and benefiting from her celebrity status. Likewise, she repeatedly expressed discontent with the 2017 *Loving Pablo*, based on her memoir, even though Javier Bardem had purchased the rights to her manuscript. Upset that they ignored her offer to coach the two main characters (played by Penélope Cruz and Bardem), Vallejo thought them too old by at least a decade, and Cruz not elegant enough and not convincing with her accent.

In other words, the diva of yesteryear is a feisty opponent who refuses to have her image impugned without a fight. Vallejo's reaction to this nation's nitpicking is reminiscent of guerrilla warfare in its application of often aggressive, but more importantly, democratized, user-driven platforms that surpass any press coverage (of her persona) delivered through traditional print. She thus defies the historically upheld notion that the public space belongs to men and is where women tend to be objectified under the scrutinizing male gaze. In that, she distances herself from the majority of female figures who are related in some way to drug trafficking, women who cringe at their association with the narco underworld, since such exposure brings shame and humiliation, the perp walk, or, worse, a postmortem photograph in the press.

II

BEYOND ESCOBAR

4

Who's the Real Boss?

Griselda Blanco Refashioned

Griselda wore violence like a bloody boa.

Smitten, *The Godmother*, 87

Before El Chapo, before Pablo Escobar, there was Griselda. Queen of all kingpins.

Cocaine Godmother trailer, 2017

In his iconic "Kafka and His Precursors," Borges states that contrary to the conventional logic regarding the succession of time, writers create their predecessors, not vice versa. The impact of latter cultural contributions alters our perception of the past, bringing to light a causality that otherwise would not be there. This seems to be the case with Griselda Blanco, ominously known as the Black Widow or Cocaine Godmother, whose recent return to the cultural spotlight has been woven into the legend of Pablo Escobar, her successor in drug trafficking. Would RTI Producciones for Colombia's Caracol and the U.S.-based Univision have created the 2014 telenovela *La viuda negra* had the 2012 *Escobar, el patrón del mal* not become an international blockbuster? Would the 2012 biography of Griselda Blanco by José Guarnizo have been published almost immediately after her death and picked up promptly by the film industry for yet another narco series, if not for the same reason? (Another biography, by Martha Soto, would appear a year later.) Would Guarnizo make such a clear connection between the infamous queenpin and the capo by titling his book *La Patrona de Pablo Escobar. Vida y muerte de Griselda Blanco*?

Would the above-cited trailer to the 2017 Lifetime full-length biopic *Cocaine Godmother* stand on its own without trumpeting Blanco's relationship to Escobar? Finally, would Catherine Zeta-Jones play Griselda if the series *Narcos* had not proven such a bankable success for Netflix?

These are, of course, rhetorical questions, but the connection between Griselda Blanco and Escobar is unavoidable. As for Guarnizo's title, one can make a couple of assumptions, beginning with the fact that Griselda's name appears subordinated to that of Escobar. And it is worth emphasizing that titles, like brand names, are the most palpable shortcuts in communication between a product and its potential consumers. That the author and the publishers bet on the brand awareness of the capo implies that perhaps Griselda alone would not have attracted as much attention. And then by establishing a hierarchy wherein Griselda surpasses Escobar, the title suggests that the book's content will at least match up to Escobar's well-known criminal hype. Yet that Griselda's criminal notoriety must refer to the latter kingpin takes us back to Borges's premise: Her life is revised through the prism of her more famous disciple. In marketing terms, Griselda thus becomes a copycat brand, the new positioning of an old tale—a female version of Pablo Escobar so to speak, "a killer with boobs" (Smitten 180)—backed up by advertising that mimics the themes and slogans of the Escobar brand.

Of course, one could say that likening the two drug traffickers is to be expected, since they both came from Medellín, both waged total wars against their enemies and even former friends, and both flooded the United States with cocaine. They employed armies of *sicarios* from the *comunas* and were each outlived by one hitman (Escobar's Popeye and Griselda's Rivi) who happened to be quite the raconteurs of their bosses' lives. As if these similarities were not enough, both Escobar and Blanco were murdered in Medellín and buried in the same cemetery. Yet tracing Griselda Blanco's reemergence in the public eye, one can see how her image has shifted over time, recently (and particularly after her death) appearing through the Escobar lens.

Blanco came into the U.S. entertainment spotlight with Billy Corben's dynamic 2006 documentary *Cocaine Cowboys*, which depicts the blood-drenched drug culture in South Florida during the late 1970s and early 1980s. Escobar, whose heyday comes later, does not really make it into the story; it is Griselda who takes the main stage once the ties between the original Colombian cocaine suppliers and the American dealers are established. The documentary's fast-paced narration accompanied by the *Miami Vice* theme song is delivered through talking-head interviews with smugglers, snitches, reporters, cops, and coroners. It taps into the perverse thrill of experiencing the confidential ins and outs of drug trafficking through numerous anecdotes revealed by the criminals themselves. Punctured by archival film, crime scene photographs, graphic overlays, and fast-paced edits, it refrains from moralizing and instead represents both sides of the law and the outside perspective of a journalist. The primary guides for the first half of the film are former traffickers for the Medellín Cartel, Jon Roberts and Mickey Munday, who reminisce about their reckless criminality with astounding openness and narrative panache. The second half draws heaviest from the former *sicario* Jorge Ayala, aka Rivi, Griselda's right-hand executioner. He delivers chilling tales of assassinations with a pronouncedly unrepentant attitude; bragging about killing eleven people in one day on Griselda's orders brings a smirk of pride.

This is when Griselda Blanco finally takes the stage, about an hour into the documentary. If the previous anecdotes recounted by Roberts had some innocence of "new rich kids on the block" who, undeterred by the police (at least at the very beginning), ran relatively little risk and enjoyed lavish lifestyles with a murder rate still somewhat under control, Griselda transformed this cocaine funland into a rollercoaster of wanton violence. Before Rivi (a Colombian-born export from Chicago) was introduced to Griselda and her operation in Miami, he went through a series of encounters with local gangsters who eventually recommended him to their boss. Rivi points out that crossing paths with her was not easy, for she was occupying the very top of the criminal ranks, while he was just a punk dabbling in petty crime. He was allowed to meet Griselda in a taxicab, where her husband seemed to be little more than a prop: "She's the one calling the shots"; "She's the one with the power" (*Cocaine Cowboys* 55:30). One could draw parallels between Rivi's admiration for Griselda's cachet and Popeye's allegiance to the Escobar myth. It appears that in front of the cameras, Rivi relives his days of notoriety by upholding the queenpin's famed viciousness—the brutality that perhaps needed to exceed that of her male counterparts to justify the effect she had on the men from both sides of the law. Yet whereas Popeye seemingly never suffered Escobar's wrath—even when he abandoned his boss to surrender to the police—Rivi, who ratted out Griselda to avoid the death penalty, was viciously attacked in jail the day Griselda was released from prison.

Returning to Rivi's recollections on Griselda in *Cocaine Cowboys*, a barrage of similar opinions ensues, although this time coming from criminals and law enforcers alike. According to Raul Diaz, former commander of CENTAC 26, "In that very very Latino culture it is not usual that a woman would be the head of her own organization, so I figured that she had to have been one mean lady" (*Cocaine Cowboys* 1:05:03). Former homicide detective Sgt. Nelson Andreu agrees that due to her notoriety, "people were so afraid of her that her reputation preceded her wherever she went." Eventually other descriptors touch on bold sensationalism: Griselda "was pretty decadent," "she gave me a brand-new Ferrari for Christmas," she was "a free base cocaine user," "a lesbian," "paranoid," "I don't even think Miami Vice would be this flamboyant," and "her crew was almost like you see in the movies." In short, the documentary asserts that she was the biggest, toughest "badass" among the Miami criminals of the day. Repetitive still photographs of Griselda and the bloodied cadavers of her many victims add to the gripping account of her villainy.

The audience and some critics speak highly of Corben's documentary, praising its wealth of fresh anecdotes, forceful imagery, and compelling delivery. Others admonish the director for the subject matter and for appearing too impressed with his interviewees. The implication seems to be that the documentary is too entertaining and too violent to be truly useful and that the director should have adopted a moralizing stance to offset its exaltation of vice. Some indeed express remorse for having enjoyed *Cocaine Cowboys*, comparing watching its fast-paced delivery to getting high on cocaine (Schager). Others feel there should have been more focus on the enforcers of the law, to deliver a morally positive message. Instead, there are plenty of recollections of the good old days of the cocaine bonanza. Hence, we see critical epithets such as a "bottom-feeding documentary" with a story "as oppressive and inarticulate as the lives it represents" (Catsoulis). Rather than appreciate the documentary at face value—a trove of never-before-heard tales—the detractors pillory the entire project, when, in reality, they are put off by its sensationalistic style and narrative objectivity. The "stupefying, only-in-Scarface anecdotes" (Schager) in fact echo Gallagher and Greenblatt's "undisciplined anecdotes," stories that emerge from "previously disregarded historical subjects, who could give access to a multiplicity of pasts" (51, 55). In other words, they deliver a new perspective or "counterhistory." Perhaps for this reason, *Cocaine Cowboys* earned a cult following. Viewers praise its broad range of interviewees, the perceived genuineness of the stories, the gripping delivery, and the absence of the moralistic framework that tends to accompany documentaries about drug trafficking. Above all, they commend Corben for delivering the historical account behind such blockbusters as *Scarface* and *Miami Vice*.

Griselda's Demise

On September 3, 2012, an execution-style murder in Medellín brought Griselda back into the spotlight. No one suspected—least of all the employees of a butcher shop in the Belén district—that the unassuming elderly victim was the infamous Cocaine Godmother, whose reign of terror spread from Medellín to Miami and New York. The employees knew her as one of their best customers; every three weeks she would buy a huge quantity of meat for unknown purposes, and one of those market days would prove fatal (Soto 229). Although the media has attempted to reconstruct Blanco's final years following her release from prison in the United States and subsequent deportation to Colombia, only a few details are known with certainty. During her brief time of freedom, Griselda lived quietly and comfortably in a high-rise in Medellín's posh El Poblado, supporting herself from real estate. She did not have to fear the law, for despite the notoriety surrounding her name, there had never been any criminal case against her in Colombia.[1] She was also negotiating deals with Colombian and U.S. television, regarding documentaries and feature films.

Cuervo, a close relative of the Blanco family, remembers Griselda's funeral as unusually brief, with everyone flocking outside the viewing room, as if they still feared an impromptu attack. He was struck by how "normal" Griselda appeared in the coffin, silenced and defenseless: "She was dressed simply. With an ordinary dress, white, with a rosary wrapped around her hands, dude. Lots of flowers. Man, she ended up in this box as if she were nobody. You get me? As if she were nobody" [Estaba con un vestido sencillo. Un vestido común y corriente, blanquito, con la camándula entrelazada en sus manos, parcero. Mucha flor. Ella terminó en esa cajita como si no fuera nadie, hermano, ¿Sí me entiende?, como si no fuera nadie (Guarnizo Álvarez, *La Patrona* 35)].[2] Griselda's burial only added to her legend, since the press and photos were prohibited. The question on everyone's mind was who were the attendees, which would perhaps shed light on Griselda's mysterious final years.

Two busloads of youths showed up at the cemetery; unidentified young men carried her coffin, and the burial included a vodka-fueled party, fifteen mariachi songs, and occasional cries of despair. Some speculate that she had close ties with the gangs from the Belén neighborhood, where her charisma and notoriety elevated her to iconic status. Others think the youths were from the Barrio Antioquia, whom she had generously sponsored over the years. Then there was a rumor that a middle-aged man with a daughter on his arm was her son Uber, thought to be already dead or in hiding. The weeping girl was invoking her "*abuelita*" (grandma), while the mystery man, too, was sniveling (Soto 125). Perhaps most symbolic is that Griselda Blanco was laid to rest in the Jardines Montesacro cemetery, barely a hundred and twenty steps away from her infamous frenemy, Pablo Escobar. (One of the journalists measured the distance, probably since he had little else to report.) To be sure, this coincidence will be especially accommodating for morbid pilgrimages.[3]

The coroner's report of her autopsy, reproduced in Soto's 2013 biography *La viuda negra*, eviscerates the queenpin, quite literally. Only now, it seems, when her hapless, bullet-ridden cadaver is laid out and exposed to the world, can she be approached. We learn that she wore a white linen shirt and white Capri pants on the day of the fatal attack. Her clothes were soaked in blood from two wounds, one near her right eye (it destroyed the upper part of her face), and the other passing through her shoulder. Griselda recently had her hair dyed, and her sixty-nine-year-old body had two large moles on the left breast and four scars: one from an older bullet wound, a souvenir from a shoot-out with her second husband, Alberto Bravo, and others from plastic surgeries, including liposuction and a facelift. Perhaps the strangest piece of information was the breakfast her body had no time to digest: one *arepa* with cheese, all two hundred grams of it. Beyond the facts that her killers were skilled professionals and that Blanco attempted to hold on to her youth, the autopsy reveals very little. Similar are Griselda's statistics upon her release from prison in the United States: on June 6, 2004, at the age of sixty-one, she weighed 193 pounds, and her last jail photo showed a white-haired woman with harsh wrinkles, giving her a severe, masculine appearance (Guarnizo Álvarez, *La Patrona* 192–93). Again, in all probability, Griselda disliked both her weight—rotund for a woman of 5'1"—and the unflattering headshot since she always tried to make herself presentable to the world.[4]

L'éducation criminelle

Soto described the very young Griselda as "clever, a leader, pretty, very intelligent, and extremely aggressive" [hábil, líder, linda, muy inteligente y extremadamente agresiva (31)][5] due to her rough upbringing. Her education in toughness began early on, as a necessary armor and a basic survival tactic against extreme poverty and dysfunction. Her prostitute mother was violent and unpredictable (systematically beating and stomping on her child), while one of her stepfathers abused her sexually. Corben's rendition of this story, as presented in his 2008 *Cocaine Cowboys 2: Hustlin' with the Godmother*, is narrated by Charles Cosby, Griselda's African American lover and business partner. In cartoon images, we see a young and curvaceous Griselda knocked about by her mother like a rag doll. With tears welling up in her eyes, the comic strip Griselda tears away from her tormentor, leaving her shirt in her mother's powerful grip. Half-naked, she runs out of the house and into the night, never to return home. A far cry from the evil stocky queenpin she became, Griselda appears defenseless and beautiful in this version of events, thereby evoking sympathy in an audience that cannot help but feel sorry for a classic damsel in distress. Griselda's initially endearing portrayal in the Corben film constructs a romanticized criminality from the start, one founded on an exaggerated physical attractiveness and on the wounded body in pursuit of vengeance.[6] It contributes to the creation of a popular rogue heroine, because Griselda's path seems to derive from protest and rebellion against injustice rather than from an innate viciousness that spurred collective horror among her enemies and *sicarios* alike.

Soto's and Guarnizo's biographical accounts depict Griselda in a less romanticized manner, but their findings at times clash with those of other commentaries, which raises questions about the truth behind each interpretation. According to Guarnizo, the future Black Widow confessed to Robertico, her hairdresser, that she met her first husband, Darío Pestañas Trujillo, in a brothel, where, alongside the prostitutes selling themselves under the red light, she danced for tips while still a preteen (62). She married Darío and joined his gang, allegedly participating in all types of crimes, including the murder of a kidnapped child whose family had hesitated to pay the ransom. She quickly learned to equal the ruthlessness of her male counterparts, most likely in an attempt to gain the respect and street cred reserved typically for men. In the course of this passionate yet volatile marriage filled with drug-infused bacchanalias and heated arguments, Griselda gave birth to three sons: Dixon, Uber, and Osvaldo. Although some sources blame her for Darío's death, those who knew her argue that he was in fact the love of her life. It is telling that despite two subsequent marriages, she kept his surname (Trujillo) and the house in which they spent their brief years together (Soto 178).

When Darío's liver suddenly gave out, a desperate Griselda took him to United States for treatment, which proved ineffective. The aftermath of her first husband's demise allegedly spawned a new cultural phenomenon for Medellín. He returned in a coffin, and his extravagant funeral inaugurated the tradition of parading around recently deceased narcos before burial. As a former employee of the funeral home describes it:

> From that moment on, the services we began to offer in Barrio Antioquia were with big caskets and a minimum of fifteen to twenty buses to transport the mourners. We had to take the casket all around the neighborhood and stop on those street corners which the recently deceased used to frequent . . . [There was] sound equipment with corridos blasting from one end of the street to the other, *mariachis*, shooting into the air, *aguardiente,* and marijuana. It was like a street party in which, instead of euphoric shouts, one would hear cries of despair. (Guarnizo Álvarez, *La Patrona* 69)
>
> [Desde aquella ocasión, los servicios que empezamos a prestar en Barrio Antioquia eran con féretros grandes y con quince o veinte buses como mínimo para transportar a los deudos. Había que darle al ataúd la vuelta al barrio y parar en las esquinas donde la persona normalmente, antes de muerta, se hacía . . . equipos de sonido con corridos que resonaban de calle a calle, mariachis, tiros al aire, aguardiente y marihuana. Era como una fiesta callejera en la que en vez de gritos eufóricos se escuchaban vagidos descarnados de despecho.]

Here is another example of a construction of a criminal myth, showcasing not only Griselda's deep love for her first husband but also how she initiated unprecedented post-mortem practices that would become a fixture of narco stories, both real and novelized. Unsurprisingly, there are different accounts of Darío's death, some more mundane and less applicable to flamboyant criminal romance. According to Salazar, Darío Pestañas Trujillo was killed in Colombia by his own associates who, envious of his increasing power, ambushed him at a gas station. To confirm this version, Salazar quotes from *El Colombiano*, July 16, 1973: "While he was listening to music and shuffling through some papers, they shot him point blank. Pestañas, an old-school gunman, didn't have time to pull out his Beretta pistol loaded with full metal jacket rounds. In his pockets, they found some IOUs, signed by the city law enforcement officials to whom he used to lend money" [Mientras escuchaba música y revisaba documentos le dispararon a quemarropa. Pestañas, pistolero de vieja guardia, no alcanzó a desenfundar la pistola Beretta, cargada con proyectiles blindados. En los bolsillos de su ropa se encontraron unas letras de cambio firmadas por agentes del cuerpo de seguridad de la ciudad a quienes acostumbraba prestarles dinero (J. Salazar, *La parábola de Pablo* 52)].

If Griselda's initial schooling in criminality involved stealing, robbing, kidnapping, and perhaps killing, these activities only intensified with her second partner, a gangster in his own right and a wealthy bad boy from El Poblado, Alberto Bravo. He initially told Griselda he was dealing in electronics, perfume, brand-name clothing, and liquor, but he soon revealed that his most lucrative product was drugs. Bravo would buy legal cocaine from a clinic in Medellín and sell it in New York. Ever the risk-taker, Bravo also initiated Griselda in high-end robberies. Twice a month, the couple would travel to the United States, with cocaine hidden in false-bottom suitcases, and return with luxury goods to sell to the Colombian elite. As one renowned district attorney remembers, "Much of Medellín's upper class bought clothes from Griselda" [Buena parte de la clase alta de Medellín le compró ropa a Griselda (Soto 29)].

Sentimental Detachments

Even though Alberto Bravo was a dangerous criminal in his own right, Griselda's increasing taste for violence, her cocaine addiction, their mutual infidelity, and business irregularities—where she would pull off cocaine deals behind his back and drain their accounts to shower her sons with luxuries—put an end to their romance. While Bravo was losing romantic interest in her, Griselda was outpacing him in violence, a transformation that also brought unwelcome visibility to what he had attempted to run clandestinely: "Crimes with her stamp—victims shot, beheaded, and dismembered—were drawing attention to the underground network of drug distribution that Alberto had weaved silently for years. And the high-rolling playboy was not willing to put himself at risk for a woman who, no longer the same *costeña* with a firm body, had conducted a lucrative business in the era of the Lovaina brothels" [Los crímenes con su sello—baleados, degollados y descuartizados—estaban visibilizando a la red subterránea de distribución de droga, que Alberto Bravo tejió silenciosamente por años. Y el señorito de clase alta no estaba dispuesto a ponerse en riesgo por una mujer que ya no era la costeña vigorosa y de carnes firmes, que impulsó el jugoso negocio en los tiempos de los burdeles de Lovaina (Soto 47)].

Direct competitors rather than sentimental partners at this point, the couple agreed to meet, albeit protected by their respective cadres of bodyguards. And again, the fateful encounter of former lovers has become part of the mythical annals of crime. Brought to life by Rivi's testimony, it has differed according to the style and imagination of each storyteller. For example, a 2008 article in the racy men's magazine *Maxim* exalted Blanco's belligerence. The narrative erupts with an action-packed anecdote, where a diminutive thirty-two-year-old woman lands in Bogotá in 1975 and is whisked away in a convoy of black limousines to meet Alberto Bravo, whose financial shenanigans in her mind required first-person resolution. The showdown takes place in a nightclub parking lot, between two teams of bloodthirsty *sicarios*.

In a scene straight from a gangster flick, Griselda draws her gun from an ostrich-skin boot (note the admirable attention to detail) and fires repeatedly point-blank at her unremorseful and defiant spouse. Bravo in turn brandishes an Uzi, but in the end, he succumbs to an avalanche of bullets ("Searching"). Wounded in the stomach but triumphant, Griselda lives up to her "Black Widow" nickname. Again, this ultraviolent scene might be a figment of someone's imagination. Richard Smitten maintains that it is unclear whether Griselda killed Bravo herself or ordered her spouse's death and later bragged about doing him in (84). He quotes Griselda's version, which she boasts to her next partner, Darío Sepúlveda:

Griselda said, "Alberto was sitting in the car, and I was standing next to the car. We were talking through the open window, fighting.

I don't even remember what it was we were fighting about. He said some very nasty things to me. I said to him, 'Those words will never come out of your mouth again,' and then I stuck the barrel of my gun in his mouth and just pulled the trigger. It wasn't really my fault; it was just a reflex." (Smitten 104)

This spousal reunion, unrealistic and resplendent in imagery reminiscent of Quentin Tarantino's cinematographic style, immortalized Griselda Blanco as a quick, cold-blooded, and unsentimental aggressor, a woman uninhibited by gender norms. It also speaks to a contemporary imagination trained on video game culture that draws heavily on the militaristic aesthetics of violence. Thus, not surprisingly perhaps, *Cocaine Cowboys 2* takes advantage of the story's blood rush as it delivers its most vivid action scenes in black-and-white comic-book imagery. When referring to the Griselda-Bravo showdown, the comics medium celebrates the gore factor and a preternatural cache of weapons. This simulated territory, with its kitschy, gratuitous violence, where a slick Griselda dons 1920s gangster attire on a much-enhanced silhouette, taps into the rich legacy of the U.S. action genre and the predictable tropes of car chases, gunplay, and bravado.

Sources reveal that in her own barrio, Griselda became known as "a successful *berraca* [tough, fearless woman], and internationally as a feared criminal" (Riaño-Alcalá 43). One of her former "mules" remembers Griselda's language as direct, forceful, and sprinkled with vulgarities (Soto 81). She savored bluntness and a taste for coercion and violence—staples of hegemonic criminal masculinity. Max Mermelstein, one of the key cocaine traffickers of the 1980s, described her in his autobiography *The Man Who Made it Snow* (1990) as unpredictable, manipulative, bloodthirsty, and boorish (she could barely read and write and never learned how to drive, 159–68). She was "possessive to the point of insanity" (159) and "incredibly paranoid" (160). When he met her, she was already rotund and far less attractive than her gallant husband Darío Sepúlveda, though traces of her former attractiveness lingered. Accustomed to making deals with the Colombian and U.S. underworlds, Mermelstein nonetheless felt apprehensive in her presence: "Griselda was the most vicious person I have ever met in my life. Others killed because they had to, Griselda killed because she enjoyed it. You could see the bloodlust in her eyes. Death lived in those eyes" (168).

When on one occasion Mermelstein's wife bad-mouthed him to Griselda, the queenpin lightheartedly suggested offing the spouse as the most natural solution to her predicament. This, despite being his friend and his work associate. Well aware of her reputation as a black widow, Mermelstein took this incident to heart and changed his ways with his wife. This is how feared the narca was among her own cronies. Similarly, Salazar paints a portrait of a terrifying, trigger-happy queenpin who used *sicarios* and her own sons to spread terror, who silenced journalists and bribed the army and police, who killed many of her sex partners, and who slaughtered best friends and entire families and then went to their funerals, shedding crocodile tears and picking up the tab (J. Salazar, *La parábola de Pablo* 52). Attending the wakes of her victims was a ritual she performed to dissipate suspicion and to be sure that her targets were in fact deceased. This is how she "dispatched" Myriam Luengas de Arango, her best friend, aka La Pájara, and the important drug trafficker "El Negro Duqueiro"; she sentenced them to death and mourned them after. She even paid for the man's funeral and delivered wreaths of flowers.

Her proclivity for dismemberment and habit of canceling debts by eliminating her creditors intimidated all from testifying against her for sixteen years. In the 2009 book *Miami Babylon*, Gerald Posner describes her personal army of *sicarios*, "Los Pistoleros," whose savage practices only added weight to her notoriety: "Membership in *Los Pistoleros* required killing someone and slicing off an ear or finger as proof of the murder. . . . Another *Pistolero* was renowned for duct-taping the mouths and eyes of his victims, draining their blood into a bathtub, then folding the corpses into large cardboard boxes and delivering them to rival gang leaders or the dead men's families" (84). Soto claims that in total, 230 hitmen worked for Griselda, in both Colombia and the United States (172). Everyone who has written about her states that she was capable of violence worthy of mafia films. At one of her lavish parties, she ordered the assassination of four guests she suspected of treason. With the bodies still warm though out of sight and the dance floor freshly hosed down, she told the orchestra to resume playing and her guests to party on. On a different occasion, when a man called her "fat"—an epithet she particularly disliked—Blanco had him executed, dismembered, and scattered along a highway. In the mid-1980s she buried alive, in his plane, one of Escobar's pilots who had lost in transport a kilogram of her cocaine. A *sicario* called El Mono, who worked for both Escobar and Griselda Blanco, considers her the cruelest of them all because of how quickly she would resort to murder without even attempting to verify a person's guilt:

> Of the capos from the Medellín Cartel, or Cali Cartel, whatever cartel you choose, no other boss could have killed more innocent people than Griselda Blanco. Because here's the problem: Griselda would first kill and then investigate. That's what was so fearless about her. She would say for example, "I think this whatshisname did it, go and kill the son of a bitch." So they would go and kill him. And if there was still doubt lingering or even later they would find out that the victim had not been guilty, Griselda would write it off with one sentence and a sigh: "Oh well, he's dead anyway." (Guarnizo Álvarez, *La Patrona* 29)

> [De los Capos del Cartel de Medellín, del Cartel de Cali, del cartel que me coloqués, ningún jefe pudo haber matado más gente inocente que la que mató Griselda Blanco. Porque el problema era este: Griselda primero mataba y luego investigaba. Eso era lo berraco de ella. Decía, por ejemplo, 'yo creo que fulano de tal hizo esto, vayan y maten a ese hijueputa.' Entonces iban y lo mataban. Y si quedaba todavía la duda e incluso luego encontraban que la víctima no había sido el verdadero responsable, Griselda se dejaba venir con una frase y un jadeo: 'Ah, bueno, ese ya se murió.']

Griselda's third significant other, and the father of her youngest son, Michael Corleone (named after Griselda's favorite film, *The Godfather*), was the already mentioned Darío Sepúlveda, a trafficker and bank robber-turned-*sicario* in the United States. Soto writes that in 1983 Sepúlveda was murdered in Colombia by assassins disguised as policemen, in the presence of his son. This occurred on the orders of Griselda, in what could be described as an unofficial custody battle, since Sepúlveda wanted to take their son back to Colombia while Griselda remained in the United States. In *Cocaine Cowboys 2*, Rivi gives a more graphic version of the couple's falling out, by which Sepúlveda admitted to Griselda that he no longer wanted to be with her and planned instead to return to Colombia with his new American lover, Cindy (34:37). Rivi then quotes a harsh exchange, wherein Griselda's jealousy and outrage transform her love into hatred, the same reaction she seemed to display with every man who in her mind had done her wrong: "'If you leave, you'd better disappear,' she said, to which he asked if that was a threat, and Griselda retorted that it was simply her advice" (35:00). Griselda thought it unthinkable that her youngest and favorite son would have a stepmother, and when Sepúlveda blindsided her by flying off to Colombia with Michael Corleone, Griselda had the Colombian cops gun him down. The documentary insinuates that this assassination turned everyone against her, prompting many of her former triggermen to defect.[7]

However, because Griselda promoted and reinforced her own legend of a tough, gun-toting dame, it is not clear exactly what transpired. According to Griselda's acquaintances from Medellín, the narca confessed that she had personally killed Sepúlveda after a nasty fight in which he questioned her toughness: "C'mon, you think you're so tough? Come and hunt me down then!" [—Venga, ¿se cree muy verraquita? Entonces, ¡cáceme si puede!" (Guarnizo Álvarez, *La Patrona* 55)].

In response, Blanco caught up with him in Medellín, at the entrance to the Olaya Herrera airport. Before firing at him, she got in the last word: "What did you think? That you could take my kid from me, the one I carried in my tummy, the one I gave birth to? It's you or me, asshole" [¿Usted qué pensó? ¿Que me iba a dejar quitar a mi hijo, al que tuve en la barriga, al que yo parí? Es usted o yo, no sea hijueputa (55)]. In this story, again, the surprised lover succumbs as Griselda empties her clip into his face.

In *Killer Woman Blues*, Benjamin DeMott examines the social transformation of female movers and shakers in the corporate world and of women who become vicious killers. The first and foremost characteristic in their hardening process—the one that elevates them to the status of the top male players—is shedding attachments and arming oneself against sentimentality about sex (DeMott 150). Since "commitments to others inevitably mean subservience to others" (25), power-hungry women treat their partners as useful "sex objects," thereby replicating the classic Don Juan, whose desire for conquest is an end in itself. Only by "refusing commitments, whether to people or manners or codes" (25) can tough women maintain their credo. A similarly predatory Griselda makes her own well-being and that of her children her exclusive prerogatives. No one can accuse her of sentimentality: She couples with men, enjoys them, but when they fail her, she disposes of them without a second thought. Where ordinary women regret such angry outbursts, and apologize, compromise, or fret over conflicting emotions, Griselda relishes her pugnacity.

To be sure, her own version of the showdown with Sepúlveda (husband #3) and Smitten's version of her finale with Bravo (husband #2) sound suspiciously similar, as if the same denouement were attributed erroneously to each of Griselda's partners. Thus, it is conceivable that Griselda so cherished this imagined script of bloody vengeance that in the end she grew to believe it herself. Smitten claims that Griselda was proud of her notoriety and that she bragged at parties about her murders (104). To her acquaintances, Griselda was "one hell of a vicious bitch" (298), reminiscent of "a damn gangster out of the 1930s who just gets pissed off and shoots the shit out of anything and anybody who gets in her way" (110). Charles Cosby, whose romantic/business relationship with Griselda is described below, also showcases the narca's infatuation with her own *leyenda negra*: "Griselda told me on a couple of occasions that 'she's the baddest bitch to ever take a breath of life'" (*Cocaine Cowboys 2* 34:15), and Rivi confirms that Griselda simply liked violence for its own sake (34:00). In other words, Griselda learned how to re-create showdowns for her audiences, where her sentimental partners inevitably came out on the losing side. She seemed thrilled with her own bravado, building it by pillaging her gender identity with the ultimate purpose of shock and intimidation. Only Escobar could lay claim to such a bloodthirsty, ruthless brand.

Griselda contra Pablo Escobar

Inevitably, Griselda Blanco and Pablo Escobar would end up in the same criminal myth, wherein Escobar began as her apprentice and admirer only to turn into an inconvenient rival and finally her nemesis. With lives as hyperbolically lawless as theirs, sooner or later both would be featured in television series during the narcocultural bonanza.[8] In the first episode of *Escobar, el patrón del mal*, the very young Escobar, a gangster in the making,[9] has the opportunity to meet with the legendary Griselda (interpreted by Luces Velásquez, who also played the role of Escobar's mother in the 2016 *Bloque de búsqueda*) at a cockfight in her barrio Santísima Trinidad. Proud of the criminal reputation that preceded her, Griselda introduced herself as "hija de perra" (loosely translated as "one tough bitch"). Despite her markedly feminine attire, she exuded a strong dose of gangster swagger. While Escobar and his boss seemed less secure on Griselda's turf, she looked menacing and in control. This was her most memorable appearance in the Escobar series, and two years later Griselda Blanco reemerged in *La viuda negra*. In the opening scene of the first episode, audiences see the elegant beauty Ana Serradilla looking like an uptight lady from a posh cocktail party. Further images highlight her U.S. incarceration and the New York skyline, thereby establishing the transnational setting of her story. These pictures are accompanied by Griselda's voiceover, wherein she asserts her authority over just about anything narco: "I'm the queen of cocaine, the one who invented the cocaine business, the one who set this country on fire . . . and I also invented motorcycle assassinations . . . and I came up with a thousand ways to transport drugs and mock the law" [Soy la reina de la coca, la que inventó el negocio de la cocaína, la que incendió este país . . . y también inventé el asesinato desde motocicletas . . . y me ingenié mil formas para transportar la droga y burlar la ley].

As one blogger bluntly puts it, Griselda seems to be able to give birth to just about anything, short of Escobar himself ("Lo bueno"). The first episode makes it barely one minute before mentioning Escobar: "While I was making a fortune, and had taken over the streets of New York, Miami, and Los Angeles, Pablo Escobar was stealing tombstones in Medellín" [Mientras ganaba una fortuna y me había tomado calles de Nueva York, Miami, Los Angeles, Pablo Escobar estaba robando lápidas en los cementerios de Medellín]. Then the show wastes no time in piggybacking on the Escobar brand as it shows the capo's trademark grinning mug shot in the opening credits.

In truth though, while Escobar would surpass her in banditry, it cannot be denied that Griselda had reached the heights of her criminality long before Escobar became notorious, and the contextualization of her cred seems to be the hallmark of most present-day configurations of her story. When Soto refers to Escobar and his cousin Gustavo Gaviria during Griselda's reign of terror, she describes them as "ordinary thieves and smugglers, mafioso wannabes" [En este momento, ambos eran vulgares ladrones y contrabandistas, aspirantes a mafiosos (52)], establishing that the Medellín queenpin was a cocaine pioneer. Indeed, many claim that Griselda's various contributions to drug trafficking attest to her business acumen, which was unhindered by her illiteracy (Smitten 34). Even though Blanco's cocaine distribution enterprise took off when she worked with Alberto Bravo, it was Blanco's suggestion that they smuggle cocaine to the United States. She came up with the idea of the brassiere and girdle factory, where cocaine could be sewn into the clothes during production so that the garment seams would look perfect—each "padded" bra, for example, concealed a kilo of cocaine. She employed inconspicuous female mules who traveled in factory-made undergarments and wigs that no one in the 1970s suspected to be heavily laced with drugs. Griselda also set up a birdcage factory, with each cage containing a false bottom that was impossible to detect or open without a welder's torch, as well as similar trick cages for dogs. Her other inventions included hollowed-out coat hangers; a double-bottomed suitcase, with one Samsonite hard-shell piece attached to another and a layer of cocaine sandwiched between; and, later on, shipping containers with false walls for concealing much larger quantities of drugs (Posner 84). Her drug empire included ranches in Colombia with hundreds of employees, where cocaine base was processed into powdered cocaine, as well as a fake visa agency that supplied her with the necessary documents for her numerous mules. Griselda is credited with smuggling more than three hundred people from Barrio Antioquia to the United States. A former friend who eventually cooperated with the DEA confessed that she had expedited enough false visas to rival a full-blown embassy (Guarnizo Álvarez, *La Patrona* 127). Last but not least, Griselda was popularly credited with inventing the idea of the two-person motorcycle hit, with the shooter riding behind. El Mono, her former *sicario*, told Guarnizo that it all began one day in Medellín, when her gunmen failed to carry out an assignment because their car was stuck in traffic. Allegedly Griselda forbade them from using cars from that day on, insisting on motorcycles as more efficient vehicles for targeting her victims (28). Guarnizo recalls that when Griselda was "the Queen of Cocaine, Escobar barely rode his Lambretta scooter, trying to score a kilogram of cocaine to send up north" [cuando Griselda ya era la Reina de la Coca, Escobar apenas andaba montando sobre el lomo de una motico Lambretta, tratando de conseguir un kilo de coca para mandarlo hacia el norte (66–67)]. *Maxim* emphasizes that at the time Griselda controlled a vast international empire, Escobar was nothing but a petty car thief with big dreams ("Searching"). In brief, each source exalts her clout by emphasizing Escobar's onetime amateurishness.

One person who had a lot to say regarding the Escobar/Blanco relationship was the ever-loquacious Popeye, interviewed for Guarnizo's biography on Blanco. He sheds light on the two capos' power struggle and—inadvertently perhaps—on his own anxiety regarding notoriety and gender. According to Robertico, Griselda at first appreciated Escobar, only to bluntly conclude that "he was a jerk" (era un güevón; Guarnizo Álvarez, *La Patrona* 67). For Robertico, Griselda perhaps "believed that she was more exceptional, more intelligent than Escobar, and . . . thought he was easy to manipulate" [creía que era más aventajada, más inteligente que Escobar y porque consideraba que él era una persona fácil de manipular (67)]. Popeye, who begins by saying that he believed himself to be God when living in the shadow of one of the most important men in the world (94), obviously sees things differently.

Escobar is known to have talked a lot about Griselda, assessing her as a crazy broad hell-bent on killing him sometime between 1976 and 1977, just as his business was beginning to pick up (95). She wanted the entire cocaine enterprise for herself and thought that her *berraca* aura from that legendary cradle of criminals, Barrio Antioquia, would secure her supremacy forever. According to Popeye, Escobar enjoyed talking about Griselda, because their violent confrontation was his first successful battle against a weighty opponent. One time she summoned him to a meeting, yet when Escobar saw her *sicarios* emerge from a car with a blacked-out license plate, he immediately sniffed out the trap. After an exchange of gunfire, he managed to retreat, yet Griselda's failed attempt on his life marked the beginning of their war. Together with his *sicario* El Negro Pabón, Escobar began to systematically eliminate Griselda's people, and she of course reciprocated. In Popeye's version of events, by 1981, "Pablo had made her leave Colombia. Because Griselda was taken out by Pablo, by Jorge González, Gustavo Gaviria Rivero, el Negro Pabón, and Tata's (Escobar's wife's) brother-in-law, Mario Henao" [Es que a Griselda la sacó Pablo, la sacó Jorge González, la sacó Gustavo Gaviria Rivero, la sacó el Negro Pabón y el cuñado de doña Tata (María Victoria Henao, esposa de Escobar), Mario Henao (Guarnizo Álvarez, *La Patrona* 95)].[10] Thus Popeye enhances Escobar's image—and by extension his own cachet—all the while making Griselda look like a defeated has-been.

Comparing Griselda to Escobar, Popeye criticizes her lack of entrepreneurial acumen and for cowering before the State. Rather than tax the other narcos (as Escobar did), and thereby maintain control over illicit activity while drawing extra revenue, Griselda preferred simply to kill off her competition. In her shortsightedness, she wanted to be the only trafficker in all Antioquia, and she never managed to organize an infrastructure on Escobar's scale. Thus, for Popeye, "you can never compare

Griselda with Pablo Escobar. Never" [usted no puede comparar nunca a Griselda con Pablo Escobar. Nunca" (Guarnizo Álvarez, *La Patrona* 101)]. Surely, she was a pioneer but not a visionary. She may have been extraordinarily aggressive, but she was not a good businesswoman. Ambitious to a fault, in the end she remained a little fish compared to Escobar: "We forgot about Griselda because for us she was a nobody. This old hag had no more power. But yeah, she was a crazy predator. And she was fierce, so fierce that look now how her past has caught up with her" [Nosotros nos olvidamos de Griselda porque para nosotros no era nadie. Esa vieja ya no tenía fuerza. Eso sí, fue una asesina loca. Y la vieja era brava, tan brava que vea cómo la alcanzó su pasado (104)]. Popeye's sexism is evident in his damning criticism. He has no qualms about disqualifying Griselda because of her age, while Escobar's weaknesses, physical or other, are never addressed.

Then Popeye builds another contrast founded on male coolness versus Griselda's excessive emotionality. Of course, no one would suspect the former *sicario* of reading Hippocrates or Aristotle, yet it is hard not to evoke the example of the wandering womb in his distinction between rational men and female hysteria, which makes women unfit for the public sphere. The capo was sly and fearless, but above all, he never revealed his emotions, be they good or negative: "When receiving the news that he just earned twenty million dollars, the patrón wouldn't begin to hug people and jump up and down like someone who won the lottery. No. He would say okay and remain quiet. If they told him his mother had just been killed, he would respond, 'ah, okay'" [Si al patrón llegaban y le decían que se acababa de ganar veinte millones de dólares, él no empezaba a abrazar a la gente ni a brincar como el que se gana el Baloto. No. Decía "listo" y se quedaba quieto. Si le decían que le acababan de matar a su mamá, podía responder, "ah, listo" (94)].

Next to the gun-crazed Griselda, Escobar emerges in Popeye's tales as far more stoic and in control. And to be sure, the fact that he never took drugs or drank much, while Griselda was frequently strung out on cocaine, makes him look like a sedate Godfather next to a coked-up Scarface. Yet other interpretations of Escobar's life story do not fully agree with Popeye's assessment; the series *Escobar, el patrón del mal* suggests that the true businessman behind the Medellín Cartel was Pablo's cousin Gustavo Gaviria, whereas Escobar was primarily obsessed with power and his war with the State. Nor was Escobar so level-headed; over and over again the telenovela shows that most of the violent acts committed by the Medellín Cartel were instigated by him and forced on his less-than-enthusiastic associates. In other words, the telenovela suggests that his stoicism and reserve were merely a front for Escobar's otherwise volatile and vindictive nature, which, as mentioned earlier, Roberto credits to the capo's favorite film, Francis Ford Coppola's *The Godfather*.

It is unnerving to follow Popeye's logic regarding Griselda's inferiority as a bandit, because of the nonchalant way the former *sicario* describes the most horrific crimes. If his dispassionate reasoning is to be followed, slaughtering one's enemies is not that big a deal, as anybody can do it. The real courage involves standing up to the State. This way, Popeye once again puts Escobar on a pedestal, relegating all other drug traffickers to the level of amateur:

> Griselda next to Pablo meant nothing. She waged a teeny little war, twenty or thirty dead in Medellín, then she stirred up some shit for eight or ten years in Miami and that's it. Griselda never went beyond that, though she was fierce, it's true. Griselda could jump out of her barrio to Envigado to pick some good fights. And let's say, she could kill and dismember somebody, true, but nothing beyond that. But to wage the war against the State . . . she couldn't do it. (Guarnizo Álvarez, *La Patrona* 111–12)

> [Griselda al lado de Pablo no fue nada. Griselda hizo una guerrita ahí chiquita, veinte o treinta muertos en Medellín, después pataleaba por ocho o diez en Miami y ya. Griselda no pasó de ahí, aunque era muy brava, para qué. Griselda podía saltar del barrio de ella a Envigado a cazar unas peleítas chimbas. Y ella misma, digamos que podía matar a alguien y descuartizarlo, sí, pero de ahí no pasaba. Pero ya de enfrentar a un Estado . . . ella no era capaz.]

His use of the diminutive ("guerrita chiquita") in matters of war and violence discloses his partiality when it comes to the Medellín Cartel and, even more so, a criminal mindset where human life holds little value. But no one, including Popeye, would accuse Griselda Blanco of cowardice or sentimentality, for she left behind a trail of corpses stretching from Medellín all the way to the United States. Measured by the masculinist standard, Griselda's achievements were substantial; she aimed and successfully reached for power in a male-dominated business par excellence.

Her infatuation with cruelty, her lack of sentimentality, and her hardball interaction with men all worked to cement a legend that will only grow.

Vice in Miami

That Popeye brushes off Griselda's criminal doings in Miami is more a case of partiality than a fair assessment of the facts. It seems that in his frame of mind, nothing should eclipse Escobar's notoriety, yet the Miami Cocaine Wars of the 1970s and 1980s attest to Griselda's adaptability to new circumstances and her criminal clout in the United States. One statistic suggests her effect on Miami. According to Robert Palombo, the DEA agent who captured the queenpin after a decade of investigation, the homicide rate went down drastically in that city after Blanco's incarceration in 1985 (Sutta). As Soto confirms, there "is no doubt that, aside from techniques to introduce cocaine to the US, a good part of the mafia manual of crimes was of Griselda Blanco's authorship" [No hay duda de que, además de las técnicas para introducir coca a los Estados Unidos, buena parte del manual de crímenes de la mafia fueron autoría de Griselda Blanco (Soto 159)].

Indeed, in the late 1970s and early 1980s, Miami underwent a dramatic metamorphosis, where the previously serene tourist town became home to more than a hundred thousand Cuban *marielitos*, undocumented Haitian immigrants, and Colombian traffickers who turned the city into a gateway for Latin American cocaine. By 1980, 70 percent of all the cocaine and marijuana entering the United States was passing through South Florida. Charlie Seraydar, then a Miami Beach homicide detective, confirms that in 1980 alone, the crime rate went up 600 percent (Posner 5). In November 1981, a nine-page cover story published in *Time* called South Florida the epicenter of an epidemic of drugs, violent crime, and illegals. Posner writes: "Every year starting in 1979, murders in Miami set a record (349 in 1979; 569 in 1980, 621 in 1981). Fifty percent were drug-related; 25 percent died from machine-gun fire; 15 percent were public executions. The Dade County Medical Examiner's Office rented a refrigerated trailer from Burger King to handle the overflow of corpses" (87). Handgun sales doubled in just one year; by 1981, there were seven registered guns per Miami-Dade household. If in New York Colombians took over the drug trafficking business nonviolently, through deals cut with the Italian Mafia, in Miami the transition was far more violent because pre-*marielito* Cuban traffickers refused to step aside until they learned that, in retaliation, Colombians were killing not just the narcos but also their entire families (87).

With drugs came wealth, and Miami established itself as a money-laundering mecca. Small banks, many Latin American–owned, had mind-boggling deposits of billions in cash, and in the depths of a recession that engulfed the entire nation after 1975, the Miami drug trade provided tens of thousands of jobs in construction, banking, and services. By 1984, South Florida cocaine seizures exceeded twenty-five tons, and the skyscrapers gracing the Miami horizon were erected largely with the narco money. In a 2012 episode of *Gangsters: America's Most Evil*, in which Blanco ranked eighth, her role in Miami's transformation was duly acknowledged with comments such as "in many ways Griselda Blanco built this town" and "[Miami is] a city she painted blood red." According to the show, her organization made between $8 and $10 million per week.

Griselda felt at home in Miami. Surrounded by trusted gunmen (such as the aforementioned Jorge "Rivi" Ayala, Colombian-born and Chicago-raised, and Miguel Pérez alias Miguelito, a *marielito* Cuban), she began going after her enemies using methods so outrageous that she landed squarely on the police radar. Juan Miguel Álvarez writes that there were three narcos who transformed Miami: Rafael Cardona Salazar (a *paisa*), the New Yorker Max Mermelstein, and Griselda Blanco. The first two worked together, collaborating with the Ochoa family of the Medellín Cartel. In contrast, Griselda was a lone wolf, with her own network of clients and distributors and her personal hitmen from Pereira and Medellín. In fact, she even owned a Colombian restaurant in Southwest Miami, allegedly for the sole purpose of spying on customers to fish out possible competition. Pastor Restrepo, who worked for another narco, tells how it was dangerous even to talk about business or show wealth, because Griselda's vigilant gunmen were targeting anyone who seemed successful: "You know how fond we are of buying an arepa or Colombian cheese, of sitting down to chat with someone and tell him, 'don't speak English to me, talk *paisa* to me.' But now you couldn't even go to the restaurants" [Usted sabe que uno es apegado a eso, a ir a comprar que la arepa, que el quesito, que a sentarse a conversar con alguien y poder decirle, 'no me hablés en inglés, a mí hablame en paisa.' Pero ya ni a los restaurantes se podía ir (Soto 142)]. With Griselda's army of thugs, the murder rate in Miami skyrocketed, going from 35 killings per one hundred thousand in 1976 to 175 in 1981, thus making the city the deadliest in the United States.

Griselda's international notoriety emerged principally from her involvement in the Dadeland Mall shooting, a massacre that occurred in broad daylight, on July 11, 1979. Griselda's gunmen attacked her rival, Jiménez Panesso, when he showed up at Crown's Liquor store for his habitual supply. (Griselda owed Jiménez money and resented his growing power.) After killing Panesso and his bodyguard, the *sicarios* fired indiscriminately into the parking lot and at shop windows, throwing terrified shoppers into a panic. About this event Surovell writes: "Her hitmen assassinated the two targets, and then chased two liquor store employees, who had been witnesses, throughout the mall, pushing aside shrieking little old blue-haired Jewish ladies and spraying bullets, 'Miami Vice' style." Police found Panesso with his head literally blown off and his body so ridden with bullets that there was hardly anything left. The cache of weapons left behind in the attackers' van proved that criminals were better armed than the police. This brazen midday hit put the city's cocaine power struggle on the national map. Miami's police began to fear that "the Colombians were turning Miami into Medellín" and, overnight, the shooting gave Miami a "Wild West" reputation, with the Colombian traffickers now called Cocaine Cowboys (Posner 81–82).

In an exhaustive confession that helped the police clear up a number of unresolved homicide cases, Rivi described how he targeted Jesús "Chucho" Castro, Griselda's former enforcer. There are at least two versions as to why Griselda Blanco sentenced him to death. In an interview with Billy Corben, Rivi claims that a mysterious attack on a stash house, which yielded a booty of millions of dollars in cash and weapons, was possibly Chucho's doing, thus infuriating the narca. Guarnizo provides a different account, which involved Griselda's fifteen-year-old son, Osvaldo. Drunk and rowdy, Osvaldo ended up banging on Chucho's door in the middle of the night on his way from a discotheque. When he insisted on crashing for the night in the *sicario*'s house and Chucho refused to take him in, Osvaldo threatened to tell his mother. To that, Chucho came out, grabbed the youth by the neck, and kicked him in the butt, allegedly saying that he didn't "give a shit" about Osvaldo's mother [¡Me importa una mierda su mamá! (Guarnizo Álvarez, *La Patrona* 137)].

This display of bravado cost Chucho his son's life. The very next day, Griselda offered Rivi $250,000 to kill her former triggerman. Chucho survived a barrage of bullets as he drove in South Miami-Dade, but his two-year-old son, Johnny Castro, who unbeknownst to the attackers was in the passenger seat, was slain. In other words, "To be Griselda's enemy in the Miami of the 1980s meant to belong in the cemetery" [Ser enemigo de Griselda en Miami de los ochenta, era saberse dueño de una membresía en el cementerio (140)]. Rivi told the police that, at first, Griselda was furious they had missed Chucho, but when she heard they had killed the toddler by accident, she felt satisfied, that they were now even. This comment reappeared in numerous sources, emphasizing Griselda's lack of "traditional female values." As a woman, she is supposed to be a nurturer by nature, yet instead, Griselda had no protective instinct or qualms about killing children. Riaño-Alcalá quotes one U.S. federal judge whose commentary on Griselda's mothering skills reflects the common gender assumptions held by the general public: "If there ever was a case, other than the 'Ma' Barker case, that truly has demonstrated what a mother's influence ought not to be, it's the one" (43).

But in *Cocaine Cowboys*, Rivi recounts the story of Chucho's son differently, where neither the gunman nor Griselda could brush off the uneasy feeling that they would pay for their crime against an innocent. In other words, Griselda's nonchalant attitude toward this tragedy is nothing more than an urban legend, buttressing the image of a woman whose monstrosity lay in not being womanly enough. Thus, the headline grabber in Griselda's case goes against the common assumptions about femininity, be they emotional attachments to her sexual partners or the maternal instinct she reserved for her offspring. In the aforementioned episode of *Gangsters*, numerous similes and metaphors denaturalize the narca by questioning all the common assumptions regarding the fairer sex. Griselda is alternately compared to a black widow spider and a praying mantis, in that she "mated and then she killed" because "she didn't have the DNA for sympathy."

Another simile from the *Gangsters* episode was that Griselda ordered "murders as readily as other businesses order stationery," and indeed, her take-no-prisoners ferocity was literal. In 1982, Blanco tasked Rivi and Miguelito with liquidating a drug dealer couple, Alfredo and Grizel Lorenzo, for failing to pay for five kilos of cocaine. They were executed in their South Miami home, as their three children watched television in another room. Griselda wanted the entire family killed, but when Miguelito attempted to follow her orders, Rivi claims to have put a gun to his head and thus saved the children's lives. Rivi also described the murder of Edgar Restrepo Botero, who was assassinated in plain view one Sunday while playing soccer in a tranquil Miami neighborhood. Restrepo Botero owed Griselda money, a debt that only grew during a ten-year jail sentence he received and completed, without repaying the debt. Griselda also ordered Miguel to murder her former business partner Papo Mejía as he got off a flight at Miami International Airport on September 15, 1982. She chose to carry out this hit with a bayonet, which Miguel plunged into the victim's body seven times. This brazen attack occurred in the presence of airport authorities and travelers at midday. Because Papo survived the attack, Griselda ordered his Miami house bombed, a chilling precursor to Escobar's later terror campaigns, which heavily relied on bombs made with the help of Israeli and Basque ETA explosives experts (Soto 148).

These tales of blood and gore, of outlandish viciousness and thirst for revenge, did not make it into *La viuda negra* or *Cocaine Godmother* for Lifetime Television. Somehow, the ferocious Griselda—heavy-set in middle age, suspicious of everyone, and strung out on cocaine—became a stoic, sophisticated, and well-bred beauty in the soap and an equally stunning, melancholic codependent in the feature film. Serradilla's Griselda evokes Audrey Hepburn with her pronouncedly waif figure and impeccable manners, rather than the manic, tough-looking, Roseanne Barr doppelgänger observable in Griselda's notorious mug shot. Likewise, while Griselda was known for her feisty attitude and foul language, Serradilla would feel more at home among the proverbial Stepford wives. Thus, while Serradilla was awarded with the 2014 Premios Talento Caracol, comments in the media unsurprisingly find the show "unconvincing and over-stretching its material," with the main protagonist failing to portray the genuine "physical threat" she was known to be (Morin). Rincón sees her as false and silly (*se ve falsa, boba*) and forgettable, even bland (*olvidable por neutral*) ("El narco"). Perhaps the most scathing critique is the use of an "objectionable victim/revenge paradigm" on the show, which contributed to a "deeply dishonest and immoral storytelling" (Morin). A blogger on welovesoaps.net bemoans Griselda's representation as "the 'good' drug trafficker" whose motivations "are almost exclusively framed in a way to justify them as either retribution of a betrayal or a defensive act. The Griselda character (or her mother or son) are continuously victimized" (Morin).

Similar is the 2017 *Cocaine Godmother* with Catherine Zeta-Jones. The actress's cringeworthy, vaguely central European accent, inept "schlocky lines," and "superficially crass dialogue" result in a "movie [that] is no

Narcos, no matter how hard it tries" (Nguyen). Ciara Lavelle likewise condemns the "salacious, soapy plot lines . . . [and] lingering sexual innuendos," bluntly assessing the film as "a series of wasted opportunities." Again, the strongest criticism centers on its manipulated gender representation, as was the case with Serradilla's soap. Lavelle points out that Blanco was known for her intelligence and the ruthlessness with which she executed her crimes, yet *Cocaine Godmother* is "obsessed with traditionally feminine roles she also played: lover, wife, and mother. . . . The result is boring." Why, we might ask, was Griselda whitewashed?

While violent female figures proliferate in media accounts, film, and literature, their motivations and *modus operandi* tend to be presented formulaically, owing, perhaps, to what Josephine G. Hendin describes as persistent beliefs in nonviolence and cooperation as female values, or else the fear of stripping women of their nascent political power.[11] Patricia Pearson goes further, arguing that since the 1990s, it is no longer permissible to depict women in the mass media as fallible human beings capable of gratuitous rage and aggression. Following the shield-the-victim principle, this strategy has transformed itself into a kind of whitewash campaign that, in turn, has distorted the perception of genders, presenting women as inherently blameless and thus beyond criticism (Pearson 126). Female critics who find female aggression far more widespread than what official accounts and common perceptions purport them to be warn that the disadvantage of the protectionism of an entire gender distorts reality and renders its members permanently dependent on the good will of those who *can* be labeled as aggressors. To say the least, the perpetuation of the rhetoric of gender difference, where women are somehow beyond violence, upholds the old sexist gender divisions, preventing women from becoming full-fledged, multidimensional individuals equal to, and no different from, men.

Similarly, *La viuda negra* and *Cocaine Godmother* return to these same disarming gender-based cultural conventions that in the end make Griselda look less dangerous than she really was and, simply put, vapid. Slimmed-down, beautified, and no longer foul-mouthed, Serradilla's and Zeta-Jones's Griseldas are denied agency in representation. Pearson writes, "We respond to female predators with curiosity rather than dread: 'We can be fascinated without being afraid,'" because "sexual monikers like the 'Beautiful Blonde' and 'Black Widow' hook almost jocularly into men's sexual fear of women. The monster is tamed in her feminine guise"

(Pearson 153). Surely, this is the case with Agent Palombo, Griselda's long-time pursuer, who admits to kissing the narca on the cheek when he finally caught up with her in Irvine, California, where she hid following her reign of terror in Miami. His unexpected reaction to the decade-long chase bespeaks the common fascination the world holds for lethal women and their almost automatic sexualization, which, in Griselda's case, transformed her into a model onscreen for no apparent reason. The absurdity of such a move would be evident if *Escobar, el patrón del mal,* featured a muscular Adonis-like protagonist, blatantly doing away with facts, or if Escobar's real-life chasers expressed a desire to kiss him upon capture.

Griselda's Turn of Fortune

One of Griselda's most infamous murders was that of Martha Ochoa Saldarriaga, a first cousin of Medellín's Ochoa Vásquez clan, as well as a close friend of "Rafa," Rafael Cardona Salazar, one of the three top dogs of Miami cocaine. Martha was also a good friend of Griselda, with whom she enjoyed lavish shopping sprees in Miami. Because Griselda owed her some two million dollars, Martha, who felt protected by her powerful ties, did not hesitate to meet up with Rivi, hoping to resolve the debt issue. Instead, Martha was subjected to torture, burnt with cigarettes and beaten, her nails ripped out, and eventually shot to death and dumped in a roadside ditch. This killing marked the end of Griselda's network of power in the same way that Escobar's 1992 murder of the Moncada brothers led to his isolation, as the capo's former associates turned against him, sensing they might be next on his ever-growing death list. At this point, Griselda was growing paranoid and feeling isolated; she either owed money to people, and thus tried to avoid them or kill them to cancel her debt, or she herself was becoming their target (Guarnizo Álvarez, *La Patrona* 158). In *Cocaine Cowboys 2,* Rivi describes how at the height of Griselda's and Darío Sepúlveda's quarrel, he quit his job as a triggerman, intending to go back to Chicago to start a new life. Yet her pleas to defend and avenge her made him return to Miami and resume his old job. Barely in the first week, he says, he liquidated three of her enemies. Perhaps the most interesting anecdote pertinent to these times is when Rivi was caught off guard in a Miami shopping mall and was confronted by Cardona and Bravo's *sicarios,* who were after Griselda, just as she was attempting to hunt them down. Rather than kill Rivi, they offered him a million-dollar bribe to hand her over. Rivi refused, remaining loyal to his boss and thereby illustrating Griselda's charismatic hold over her toughest thugs.

Soto's description of the Griselda/Escobar relationship differs from Popeye's tale recounted earlier, in that Martha's murder was the event that drastically changed their uneasy peace. According to Soto, after Griselda ended up in jail, she pleaded to Escobar to help her hold on to her distribution routes, something he complied with initially. Yet when the news of Martha's murder reached Colombia, Escobar took over Griselda's business and had her son "Oswaldito" gunned down in 1992 as the youth returned to Colombia with the intent of recovering his mother's Medellín business. As expected, the impulsive and grief-stricken Blanco ordered a brutal revenge on her son's immediate killers. Her *sicarios* not only killed the culprits, cut their tongues out, and chopped up their bodies but also did the same with their entire families a week later, once Griselda decided that her initial killing spree did not satisfy her thirst for revenge ("La historia negra"). Her plans for retaliation were announced at Osvaldo's funeral, where Griselda's letter from jail was read to the grieving crowd.

With her Miami contacts weakening and the police on her tail, Griselda escaped to Irvine, California, where she pretended to be an ordinary citizen, living with her mother and her youngest son in a middle-class neighborhood. She was caught by Palombo on a ten-year-old indictment and put behind bars for the crimes she committed in New York. Her luck worsened when Rivi, her triggerman, began to implicate her in crimes that in Florida would certainly put her on death row. Yet Rivi's sexual shenanigans with certain secretaries in the prosecutor's office discredited him as the key witness and enabled Griselda to cut a deal. In 1998, Blanco plea bargained to three second-degree murder charges and received a twenty-year sentence. It was then that she met her fourth partner, Charles Cosby.

Griselda's Boy Toy

Cosby, the African American narrator of Corben's second installment of *Cocaine Cowboys*, was a small-time hustler from California who hooked up with the already incarcerated Griselda by writing her letters full of admiration, to which the narca responded by initiating a phone relationship from jail. Their face-to-face meeting led to a sexual relationship and criminal collaboration, making Cosby her boy toy, her business partner, and an instant millionaire. The description of their first meeting attests to

Cosby's infatuation with Griselda's criminal cachet and her forceful personality when it came to sex: Griselda embraced him and French-kissed him instantly. Undeterred by his mentor's advanced age, Cosby found the narca confident, feminine, and tantalizing, with high heels and red fingernails that sharply contrasted with her white clothes. His recollection of Griselda's entrée into the visiting room reveals his admiration: "Everybody stopped talking and stared. She was like a queen walking through the room."

According to Cosby, who was ever eager to emulate his idol's larger-than-life persona, Griselda was taking in 50 million dollars a year while incarcerated. His intent was to do whatever it took to profit from her influence: "I was basically looking to upgrade my status and Griselda Blanco was my passport" (*Cocaine Cowboys* 2 44:12). His business instinct was spot-on, because barely a week after meeting Griselda, an unidentified Latin American woman delivered fifty kilos of cocaine to his home. This is how his new fortune began, punctuated by frequent business trips and the unconditional obligation to be available for the moody and ever-suspicious narca.

For a decade, Cosby watched over Blanco's drug empire, reporting to her during their "conjugal visits" arranged through the generous bribery of jail personnel—each sexual encounter cost them $1,500. He befriended her son, Michael Corleone, and even participated, albeit unwillingly, in a half-baked plot to kidnap John F. Kennedy Jr. a scheme concocted in an attempt to secure her release from jail. Yet their arrangement was not free from strife. Cosby, who met a young attractive blond during one of his jail visits, began secretly to see her, all the while carrying on his relationship with Griselda. Cosby's fate could have been that of Griselda's second and third husbands, because one day he almost died in an ambush from armed gunmen. A subsequent phone call from Griselda confirmed his suspicions: She had found out about the lover and demanded to see him the next day if he wanted to stay alive.

This time, instead of a seductive narca, he encountered an enraged woman scorned. She said, "You black son of a bitch, how dare you cheat on me?" (1:08), after which, as Cosby narrates vividly, "she reached across the table and grabbed me around my neck, she had a hell of a grip, her hands were very strong" (1:08). No one attempted to stop the attack, and their heated exchange of words became a gender power game, where Cosby allegedly stood up to Griselda by warning her not to attack him ever again. To this, a surprised Griselda commented crudely that he was growing some balls, when in fact he was nothing bigger than a fly to her. Cosby's way out of this predicament was to sugarcoat his betrayal: He cheated on Griselda because she was not available to him as often as he wished. Thus, in the twisted logic of an insatiable macho, she "made him" cheat. In many ways, Cosby argued, he was faithful because he was looking after her business, her son Michael Corleone, and even her mother. In the end, as Cosby relates it, Griselda calmed down and accepted his explanation. It is doubtful that the seasoned Griselda would buy into Cosby's questionable excuse, yet her weakened position must have taken some of the edge off her usually volatile and unforgiving temper. By then, Cosby was already eager to cut off the relationship to protect his own life. Money did not bring him freedom, and he barely escaped her wrath.

Cosby's new mediatic fame following the Corben documentary seemed to sit well with him, for he proudly bared all on his personal website, responding to numerous interviews that invariably led back to Griselda Blanco. Charles's homepage, filled with press articles, videos, private photographs with Griselda and her surviving son, Michael Corleone, and their correspondence (the originals of which Cosby had already sold) made his relationship with Griselda Blanco a credible tale of love and opportunism. The centerpiece of the website is an in-depth interview that opens with a pimped-out photograph of Cosby smoking a cigar in a fine white suit with strategically exhibited gangster bling. Cosby was well aware of the power of presentation, for in his characteristically colorful and engaging narrative style, he elaborated in an interview with Jason Lavezzari on the importance of dressing to the standards of his chosen hustler lifestyle.[12]

Cosby's slick reconstruction of his marginalized selfhood (poor, African American, and criminal) responds to a mainstream demand for ethnic (minority) autobiography "precipitated by voyeurism on the part of dominant culture" (Hawthorne 623). His narrative is a curious case of mise en abyme—the U.S. audience, largely white and noncriminal, can look at Cosby looking at Griselda. Cosby's double-layered vehicle of cultural interpretation is reflected in the U.S. fascination with the volatile Colombian "other." Griselda concretized the exotic aura on at least three levels, any one of which suffices to disrupt the homogeneous comfort zone: She was a foreigner, a criminal, and a woman who made a mockery of traditional gender roles. While Cosby and his mentor belonged to different cultures and races, they overlapped through their marginality, living on society's fringes and profiting from its prohibitions. Their eventual transformation, befitting the autobiographical trope of a repentant criminal who "outgrew" his criminal lifestyle—not unlike the classic *pícaro* of the Spanish Golden Age—was another unifying if not altogether convincing device. Cosby assimilated Griselda's "exoticism" to his own formative cultural modes, transforming her into a female Scarface, a device that justified his own submission to his volatile partner-in-crime. That she was a woman problematized the relationship, yet Cosby navigated the power dynamic skillfully, at times showing how he would fool around behind her back or how his loyalty to the matriarch went no further than business.

While Cosby reminisced in public about his decade-long romance, his former boss, somewhere from her hideout, reportedly gave tacit approval for his filmic portrayal. In the meantime, Blanco's son joined other descendants of infamous drug traffickers on the Univisión show *Cristina* to reveal his mother's gentler side. From a bloodthirsty predator Griselda morphed into a desperate mother who was obligated to feed her offspring and who, upon leaving jail, rejected her previous bad ways and became a born-again Christian. Cosby, too, apotheosized her image, almost sanctifying the myth that allowed him to step into the world of U.S. gangster culture. In the previously mentioned interview with Lavezzari, he went on to proclaim that Griselda's detractors "see her as a murderer, but she is far from that. She's a very loving mother and grandmother. She's respected in Colombia, and is a mother to thousands of young misguided men who don't have mothers of their own. She believes in helping those who are unable to help themselves but quite often she's labeled an evil woman by the media."

Fast-forward to the post-*Narcos* era, where Michael Corleone's presence in the media is frequent, as are his mercurial shifts in attitude. In "The Last Blanco" (El útimo Blanco), a 2018 episode of the Investigation Discovery documentary series *Evil Lives Here*, he chokes up in front of the camera, remembering his frightening and lonely childhood with bodyguards as his only playmates. They were temporary at best, because Griselda would make them disappear at a slightest suspicion of insult or betrayal. This somber portrayal of his early years notwithstanding, Michael Corleone has been cashing in on his mother's notoriety by running a clothing brand called "Puro Blanco" (Pure White, predictably for co-caine). Then, in 2019, he bears his private life in a VH1 docuseries *Cartel Crew*, which follows the descendants of drug lords. On the one hand, he somberly recalls burying twenty-two members of his family, including his mother. This final loss, he says, made him turn his life around and leave crime behind. On the other hand—and more befitting the series' unabashedly celebratory thug lifestyle—he brags about his narco pedigree (growing up as "part of cartel royalty") and his criminal past ("At the age of 12 I actually was running the family business while my mother and my brothers were incarcerated. I was a child doing boy things").[13] He admits to loving "that lifestyle" and "that rush" back then. His wife, too, praises Griselda as a "historic badass" who hopefully would be fond of her son's present bride.

But even on this show, the moment Michael Corleone introduces himself against the hip-hop beat, "I'm the youngest son of the queen of co-caine," a voice in the background clarifies that Griselda was "the woman known as the female Pablo Escobar." It appears that, yet again, Griselda's cachet requires that of Escobar and, yet again, the narco-descendants cash in on their families' criminal past. Unsurprisingly, Michael Corleone an-nounces to Fox News his soon-to-be-published memoirs. Publicly at least, he is happy to participate in the cultural narco bonanza, just as many of Escobar's former acquaintances and family members are: "Anything that I can lend consultation on my life. As long as it's a lucrative project. . . . As long as the story is told correctly from the horse's mouth. Meaning from myself and other family members" (Nolasco).

That Griselda would become a television celebrity was only a matter of time. *Cocaine Cowboys 2* elevated Griselda to the ranks of pop-cultural celebrities, a living mystery hidden at the time somewhere in Latin Amer-ica. Her tough exterior and close relationship with an African American crack dealer, Charles Cosby, were the inspiration for a number of U.S. rap songs paying tribute to the deadly queenpin.[14] The vogue of narco-themed stories and the particular interest in its still enigmatic female sector have been fertile ground for the revival of the Griselda Blanco legend.

The final message of a 2012 episode of *Gangsters* was the general be-wilderment over Griselda's survival after her 2004 deportation to Colom-bia. After all, she had accumulated so many enemies that just remaining alive was nothing short of a miracle. Thus, the reaction to her death in 2012 was univocal: No one knew who did it, but everyone agreed that she had it coming, hence substituting the expected *why* for *when*, as if a prompt and violent death was the only possible denouement to her story. Palombo was in fact surprised that she was not gunned down the moment she stepped off the plane in Medellín. He called Griselda's death a case of poetic justice that happens only in fiction. It was not just because she died by the method she popularized but also because, being a butcher herself, she was finished off in front of her favorite "carnicería" (Sutta). In the end, it is to be determined how Griselda's mythicizing will fare next to that of Escobar, since both figures are still evolving in the cultural imaginary, appearing in the media with ever greater frequency. One could surmise that it is perhaps more difficult to bring back the essence of a female predator, because Hollywood standards impose physical attractiveness when it comes to the portrayal of women, destroying authenticity in the process. This is perhaps how narca myths are mobilized on the screen, while those of men flourish on a combination of bravado, brutality, and humanizing techniques, leaving more room for envisioning the appearance. Will Blanco's notoriety stand on its own without having to refer to Escobar? Time will tell.

5

Mad about Boobs

Sin tetas no hay paraíso

The truth is that in Colombia there is no television without breasts. Television has brought home the narco taste, silicone, and the money ethic.
[La verdad es que, en Colombia, sin tetas no hay televisión. La TV ha socializado el gusto mafioso, la verdad de silicona y la ética del billete.]

Rincón, "Sin tetas no hay televisión"

We the bandits would fall for tits and ass, we used to marry mafia dolls.
[Nosotros los bandidos nos enamoramos de la cola y los senos, nos casábamos con muñecas de la mafia.]

Popeye interviewed by Mayer, "Soy una rata: Popeye"

The iconography of the Escobar brand, of exacerbated virility and an unlimited power of consumption, presupposes a constant influx of female groupies whose sheer number and anonymity only shore up the narco's cachet. The epithets attached to these girls—CDT ("carne de traqueto," loosely translated as narco meat [Colorado Grisales 103]), *muñecas* (dolls), and *prepagos*—underscore their objectification and the transactional nature of such encounters. In *Operación Pablo Escobar*, Caycedo Castro mentions how *los señuelos*, go-betweens responsible for a steady supply of adolescent virgins for the patrón, would store "fresh meat" for his entourage in different houses across Medellín. These were predominantly high school students, volleyball players, and models, with the common denominator of youth and sexual innocence. Money usually sufficed to win them over, whereas the more resistant types walked away with an inexpensive new car (41, 74). Likewise, the widow of Escobar's last bodyguard lays out the procedure: "Pablo would tell the *muchachos* what he wanted—the most beautiful girls from the colleges of Medellín,[1] and how many he needed and Limón [the bodyguard] would be in charge of sorting it out. Pablo loved 'sardines,' 15 or 16-year-olds . . . a lot of girls went up there" (196). In Popeye's account, "through his bed crawled naked beauty queens, models, TV presenters, high school girls and more" [Por su cama gatearon desnudas reinas de belleza, modelos, presentadoras de televi-sion, colegialas y más ("Ellas fueron")]. Mollison's generously illustrated book includes a page layout of an unnamed young woman whose photo-graphs were found by the police in La Catedral after Escobar's escape in July 1992 (197). In some pictures, she dressed demurely, in others, as if she were ready to go to a nightclub. Throughout, the girl appears youthful and innocent, thereby stirring discomfort in the observer, who is aware of her transactional sexual function.

Bluntly put, Escobar and his entourage had the buying power to pick and choose virtually any girl they wanted. In the code of consumer values, narco wealth represented distinction and social status, thereby prompting the underprivileged (but not only the underprivileged) to sell themselves to the highest bidder regardless of the consequences. On various occa-sions Popeye commented on how woman's physical attractiveness was di-rectly proportional to the narco cachet and how perfectly sculpted mafia dolls were their sought-after partners (Mayer): "Women always were the warrior's trophy" [La mujer siempre fue el trofeo del guerrero] and "the more guerrero, the hotter the woman" [entre más guerrero, más bella la mujer] ("#ElOtroPatrón"). In a Baudrillardian diagnosis of the social con-dition of late capitalism laid out in *For a Critique of the Political Economy of the Sign*, the object that is being consumed—here, attractive young women—becomes the subject inasmuch as it determines the consumer's status in (narco) society. For drug traffickers, the function of surrounding themselves with available beauties transcended mere sexual services; the girls also brought what the postmodernists would call a sign exchange value. Drug lords craved the image that "ownership" conferred on them in the eyes of the world. Thus the narcos' capitalist world of unlimited consumption was regulated by a spectacle of the image: While they could afford to buy almost anything, underprivileged (and privileged) youth could join in the fun only if their attractiveness stimulated the narcos' desire and sense of self-worth. And since the power of acquisition among successful narcos was limitless, there was no reason to stop at natural beauty if enhancements were available.

The idealized look included hyperbolic voluptuousness with an exaggerated bosom, which, in accordance with the notions of the postmodern instability of "truth" and "reality," did not need to be authentic. Narcos customarily bankrolled plastic surgeries to create an experience straight from *Baywatch*, whose richly endowed women were epitomized by Pamela Anderson.[2] Soon enough, as Roldán puts it, the narco taste for excess and artificial enhancement spilled over to society as a whole: "Pert models with bursting décolletages and reinforced rear ends touting everything from beer to lingerie intrude as constant reminders of the feminine ideal the cocaine trade fashioned into a societal norm from plastic surgery" ("Colombia" 179).

A 2014 article from *Colombia Reports* credits the linkage of trophy women and narcos to none other than Pablo Escobar: "The fact that he has that much infamy, that much notoriety, that's how [the drug trade] shaped things. . . . He was the super rock star of the day. Anything he did became that big and lavish." But beyond simply associating beauties with cocaine drug barons, the article claims that the very narco aesthetic, which has spilled beyond the drug trafficking milieu, had its origins in the capo: "Escobar liked his ladies, and he often liked them 'operadas,' or '[aesthetically] operated.' In a sense, the biggest drug baron in history set an example to follow for those who had the means to do so. Pablo Escobar made [aesthetic surgery] more socially and culturally acceptable. . . . He almost made it unacceptable to not change" (Yagoub). Whether Escobar can take all the credit for this trend is debatable. Cetina's *Jaque a la reina* convincingly exposes how countless drug lords dedicated themselves to the pursuit of the newest *belle de jour*, underwriting surgeries and beauty pageants. Other sources insist that Escobar preferred simple high school girls, innocent and inexperienced.[3] Since none of his one-night stands have come forward or have "gone public," we are left with mere speculation when it comes to the truth behind the origin of the trend. However, it is not the historical accuracy that speaks volumes here; it is the very potency of the capo's legend: Decades after his death, his name is recalled in association with an entire aesthetic phenomenon still growing in force.[4] If we look at this story from the marketing standpoint, a new association (plastic surgery) only enhances the Escobar brand by rerouting its meaning to the evolving consumer base. Now he is relevant in the realm of plastic surgeries, morphing into the archetype of the Magician, the emblem

Figures 10 and 11. Well-endowed store mannequins in Cartagena attest to a cultural shift in
beauty standards in Colombia. In earlier times,
the mannequins were more demure. Photos by
author.

of a wondrous transformation via (aesthetic) miracles (Mark and Pearson
146).

The 2005 novel *Sin tetas no hay paraíso* and the 2006 telenovela of the
same title are not specifically about Pablo Escobar, but they reflect the capo's alleged practices followed by countless drug traffickers. Asked about
the story behind his novel, Gustavo Bolívar Moreno recalled his encounter with the fourteen-year-old Catalina, who approached him while he
was working in the city of Pereira. She wanted to know how to become an
actress so she could afford breast implants from a competent plastic surgeon, which would in turn secure for her a powerful sugar daddy. Bolívar
was struck by the perverse logic of her adolescent dream to become the

girlfriend of a "third-rate narco with airs of Pablo Escobar" [la novia de un narco de tercera con ínfulas de Pablo Escobar (Intxausti)]. Motivated by an anecdote that revealed to him an entirely new social phenomenon, Bolívar thus dedicated *Sin tetas* to the subject of anonymous masses of young Colombian girls who aspire to narco glitz—even if only as prostitutes with fake breasts. For Greenblatt and other New Historicists, anecdotes are "mediators between the undifferentiated succession of local moments and a larger strategy toward which they can only gesture. They are seized in passing from the swirl of experiences and given some shape, a shape whose provisionality still marks them as contingent" (Greenblatt 3). Likewise, Bolívar's random encounter with a stranger revealed to him unfamiliar local practices that are far from isolated instances. At times, he imposes his own lens, observing his protagonists from the vantage point of the intellectual elite; at others, he seems to identify with his young subjects and their distorted approach to success.

Tackling in a single story the subjects of underage prostitution, obsession with beauty, and loose morals opened up a can of worms for *Sin tetas*, earning the book enormous popularity and criticism at the same time. Its "trashy" topic, populist tone, and heavy use of campy irony, parody, and broad humor firmly situated it in the tabloid mode, which is often accused of "'cheapening' public life" by lacking taste, decorum, and seriousness while encouraging voyeurism that produces subject matter somewhere at the intersection between public life and private life (Glynn 7 and 10). Though in the media industry "tabloidization" connotes a dumbing down of media content, critics also recognize its potential in that it opens spaces "where some progressive forces can develop and even gain social momentum" (10). Since its rhetoric, attitude, and posture speak to the majority of ordinary people and hold many people's attention, the tabloid mode has become an alternative arena for public discourse. Indeed, *Sin tetas* sparked many debates, bringing success together with scandal. As for its triumph, just between 2005 and 2007 Bolívar's book, published by Oveja Negra and Quintero Ediciones, went through twelve editions, becoming one of Colombia's top ten books in 2006.[5] Likewise, the finale of its 2006 televised adaptation (with Bolívar's script) set a telenovela ratings record in Colombia, attracting almost seven million viewers[6] and surpassing that of the worldwide smash hit, *Ugly Betty*. In 2007, the original telenovela won seven Premio India Catalina awards and two TVyNovelas prizes for

Figure 12. A telling image of Escobar's relevance to the Colombian romance with the voluptuous, surgically enhanced female body. Note the play on words associating Escobar with the social phenomenon of *prepago* call girls. The graffiti appears on the ruined Ovni building (previously owned by Escobar), Medellín. Photo by author.

the Best National Series and Best Theme Song, while the European version received the 2008 Premio TP de Oro for the best series in Spain.

Concurrent with the story's commercial triumph came vehement criticism that echoes the typical disparagers of tabloid writing. Detractors lamented its dismal literary quality, questioned its lopsided moralistic premise, and accused Bolívar of selling out to the scandal-seeking masses. One such representative criticism charged *Sin tetas* with "the vulgarization of a literary product," because it failed to transcend a "unilateral interpretation of reality," aiming instead at high sales in global markets. Compared to novels by Laura Restrepo and Jorge Franco, Bolívar's debut exemplified bad prose and a superficial analysis of a topic deemed frivolous to begin with (R. Bermúdez 78–79). In other words, Bolívar presumably failed on all accounts in that neither his subject matter, nor his prose, nor even the ideological position he adopted could satisfy the audience.

No one would defend the work's literary merits, yet the resonance of its subject matter proved this critic wrong, because *Sin tetas* inspired many a debate. For starters, it surfaced as a pretext to delineate between *belles-lettres* and kiosk literature in a public exchange among four Colombian authors, namely, Sergio Álvarez, who defended Bolívar's success, and Collazos, Abad Faciolince, and Santiago Gamboa, all of whom bemoaned the deplorable state of Colombia's present-day culture.[7] Abad Faciolince decried the overwhelming success of sensationalist texts written by criminals and of "editorial trash" that included Bolívar's "lumpen novel," while Collazos criticized Bolívar's financial success, placing it in stark opposition to the pittance generated by real literature, with the predictable exception of Gabriel García Márquez. Standing in defense of Bolívar's best seller, Álvarez pointed to the growing democratization of the book market in Latin America, where books are no longer a cult object but an item of consumption whose popularity is determined by the response of the reading masses.

In a nutshell, the conflict among the writers is an argument about literature as the realm of the masses and no longer of the intellectual elite, where oceans separate the elite's preferences from popular tastes and consumption patterns. It is also an insistence on the value of art over that of the cutthroat consumer market, an attitude that implicitly questions the integrity of a writer whose work too easily satisfies the popular palate. While some thought that Bolívar was breaking new social ground by stepping into the sticky mire of exploitative adolescent sex in the narco underworld, others saw a sordid story placed in a sordid environment: a social problem aptly packaged, marketed, and sold for profit. Finally, the writers' aversion to lucrative best sellers is indicative of a frustration with the thirst for narco literature in the Colombian market after 2000.

These, of course, are not the only voices that take sides in the discussion on high versus low culture in Colombia. In fact, a lot has been said about the easy-to-read narratives branded "instant books," because they sell well only at first, proving to have a brief shelf life and little effect on the nation's collective memory. To a degree easily confused with journalistic reports, they focus on trendy topics such as drug trafficking, *prepago* prostitution, political corruption or kidnappings, and the guerrilla. For Moisés Melo of the Colombian Cámara del Libro, and Gabriel Iriarte, Director of Norma Publishing, the popularity of instant books came at a time when a broader selection of news items in the national press displaced in-depth investigative journalism and analysis. In turn, this shift in focus left the reading public hungry for more substance. Sensing increasing market demand for more exhaustive accounts, some publishing houses such as Oveja Negra branched into the instant book market, enhancing its profits even further by turning successful books into multimedia franchises. José Vicente Kataraín, Oveja Negra's editor, boasts of having invented the genre of "audiovisual books," that is, texts designed to be converted easily into television series. Bolívar's *Sin tetas* happens to be the inaugural audiovisual book ("El libro de occasion" 108), whose model was repeated with *Las muñecas de la mafia* by Andrés López López.

These arguments are of importance in the era of rapidly changing and evolving hybrid genres that draw on discourses and practices that were once confined to tabloid journalism but are now spreading into media culture, particularly into television and, as the Colombian book market shows, print as well. If nothing else, Colombian writers' criticism of the present-day populist cultural practices and controversial content makes note of a changing media landscape. They show concern for the nation's cultural capital and pure taste, which, as Pierre Bourdieu points out, are tied to social power. The growing importance of market research in print and television greatly increases the pressures on classic enlightenment ideals in these fields, because what is being produced is what sells and what sells is sensationalism, personalization, and the superficial treatment of a given subject.

Catalina's *Prepago* World

The provocative title of Bolívar's story proved to be a catchy gimmick, garnering praise and criticism.[8] The venerable Spanish proverb "Tiran más dos tetas que dos carretas" (loosely translated as "A pair of breasts pulls harder than two wagons") does not fall far from Bolívar's assertion of woman's sexual power, particularly when and if she happens to be well-endowed. While female sexuality is not the only item on the telenovela's menu, it certainly constitutes its main course. Small-time *traquetos* come into the picture tangentially, yet the true protagonists are neighborhood girls, *peladas* convinced that their only ticket to happiness is to sell their bodies to the highest bidder and to become a *traqueto*'s pampered plaything. Although the girls' aspirations subscribe to the traditionally acquiescent position that women occupy in criminal organizations, their cunning and manipulations are the motor behind the story. Yes, they forever remain enclosed in the lustful gaze of the hypermasculine drug trafficker, but, ultimately, they are the ones who lead men to ruin.

Sin tetas treats the topic of prostitution with an ambivalent if not disingenuous moral compass, even though its final message to the audience, delivered as a coda by its heroine Catalina (played by María Adelaida Puerta) and her brother Byron (Andrés Toro), endorses honest work while condemning the narco lifestyle.[9] Such discursive fluidity goes back to the tabloid genre, with its "sensational, sometimes skeptical, sometimes moralistically earnest" style that rejects the pretense of "objectivity," engaging instead in different ranges of melodrama and humor (Fiske 48). It can be progressive and regressive at the same time, producing conflicting discourses of, for instance, sexism and female liberation in one single story (Glynn 87). The telenovela itself constitutes a campy portrait of money-hungry youth brought up in the shadow of narco consumer excess. It does not preach or attempt to instruct by providing uplifting examples. Nor does it wallow in sadness in the face of social disintegration or the inexorable plight of youth. In fact, *Sin tetas* pokes fun at absolutely everyone, constructing a world free of heroes or truly likeable characters. Even the heroine's deliberate homicide/suicide at the end elicits little pathos. Such a nihilistic perspective can predictably stir outrage among readers/viewers. Possibly to counter accusations of corrupting the audience, Caracol and the producers of the series added an educational angle. Judging from what the telenovela's producer revealed in an interview with Norbey H. Quevedo—namely, that it took her six months to convince the television station to keep Bolívar's original title, not to mention producing the series in the first place—such an assumption could hold true. Even though Bolívar pledges to have written the story as a lesson on what *not* to do—thereby following the autochthonous Hispanic literary genre, *la picaresca*—his intentions to educate future Catalinas remain debatable.[10]

Sin tetas lays bare present-day obsessions with superficial beauty, sexuality (as opposed to love), and hard-core partying—all in the context of dysfunctional households and moral relativism. Its indiscriminate rejection of traditional values presents a new everyday norm for teenagers who aspire to be hookers and hitmen. It probes serious social ailing, albeit in a detachedly humorous fashion, leaving viewers to question how to react. Should we enjoy its brazen exuberance, or should we look for a didactic end, hidden somewhere in the interstices of endless pleasure-seeking?

The camp aesthetic does not resolve the conflict between the earnest and the irreverent, leaving moral premises delightfully ambiguous and imposing upon good taste "a daring and witty hedonism" (Sontag). The youth of *Sin tetas* are governed by money and sex, while scruples are rejected as a thing of the past. *Peladas* of the likes of Catalina, Yésica, and Paola appear sexually skilled, uneducated, and untroubled by moral codes. None possesses the insight or positive personality traits to ingratiate themselves with the audience. Extraordinarily shallow and naive, Catalina, the protagonist, whines to no end about needing breast implants, as she oscillates between self-pity and megalomania. A contemporary *pícara*—today's version of Lazarillo de Tormes—she wants to live like a queen without doing actual work. Her street-smart sidekick, Yésica, is mature beyond her years in matters of organized prostitution but otherwise inscrutable. Similarly, the other three friends, Paola, Ximena, and Vanessa, are barely explored, as they strut their stuff around Pereira, seemingly bereft of moral dilemmas when it comes to their life choices. Proud of having what it takes to attract men—artificially enhanced breasts, that is—their only complaint is that working in a whorehouse when the narcos are unavailable is not as fun or profitable.

As for narcos—by no account Adonises—their worth is measured proportionally to the size of their bank account. Thus, even *traquetos* of lesser importance, such as the repulsive Mariño, claim to own garish mansions, when in fact they rent them for parties to bolster the illusion of wealth— the postmodern hyperreal in full display. Honest work and courting the opposite sex are unthinkable for either gender. Always lusting after fresh meat, *narcotraficantes* take possession of the girls by flashing wads of cash, while *prepagos* make it clear that their affection is proportional to their remuneration. Yésica's description of her *traqueto* female stable constitutes a paean to consumerism and an utter devaluation of romance. Sex is but a transaction, served exclusively on men's terms: "One, or two, or three women are not enough for them. Many of these guys could have as many women as there are days in a month, and the girls would all get paid proportionally to the guy's wealth, his sexual needs, and his availability" [Ellos nunca se conformaban con una ni con dos ni con tres mujeres. Que muchos de ellos podían tener tantas mujeres como días tiene un mes y que a todas les correspondían de acuerdo con su capacidad económica, sus arrestos sexuales y su disponibilidad de tiempo (22)]. Thus the story's characters possess few redeeming features; no one boasts stringent moral principles, let alone self-reflection. Corrupted to the core by drug trafficking culture, the youth of *Sin tetas* respond to immediate needs and opt for the shortest path to success.

Sin tetas is a hyperbole of commodity-driven consumerism, where the few *traquetos'* right to appropriate people and their lives goes beyond gender, claiming hordes of despondent youth who sell their souls for the mirage of consumerist bliss. While the girls hope for the status of steady trophy lovers, the boys yearn to become assassins, with the hope of an eventual rise to a seasoned *narcotraficante. Sin tetas* not only confirms the cynical lesson that everyone has a price but also underscores how the drive to acquire becomes the prime motivator of the young. The very few who refuse to buy into the narco dream remain poor and hence unappealing, even if they profess true love, as in the case of Catalina's boyfriend, Albeiro. His gifts of stuffed animals or the ironing board he buys hoping that Catalina will accept his offer of domesticity simply have no appeal for girls of his generation.

One of the principal allures of a telenovela in general is its relation to the enveloping reality and how such representation facilitates the audience's voyeurism. Telenovelas allow the exploration of the sites of collective memory "complicit with the imaginative universe of the masses" (Martín-Barbero 231). While Mexican telenovelas exalt suffering as a pathway to morality, and Chilean series fixate on national identity in the context of industrial modernity, Colombian telenovelas highlight social ascent achieved through crime and an instrumentalization of the body (Rincón, "Nuevas narrativas televisivas" 47). In the same vein, *Sin tetas* recreates narco reality with its violence, corruption, and rapidly gained and lost fortunes. It exposes the ubiquity of *prepago* girls, scandals involving national beauty pageants financed and manipulated by the criminal underworld, and an epidemic of slipshod plastic surgeries that enriches unscrupulous practioners and endangers the lives of their ignorant patients. These phenomena stem from the crisis of the contemporary subject as a consumer who partakes in the surrounding circumstances through the acquisition of goods and the commercialization of her own body, thereby turning it into another product. Catalina feels that she *must* acquire big breasts to become more marketable. In other words, her drive for acquisition has no other purpose than a continuous reaction to market stimuli in search of a consumerist *jouissance.*

Narcotrafficking and the Society of Enjoyment

For Todd McGowan, whose Lacanian interpretation dovetails with a Marxist reading of the world, contemporary culture has shifted from the society of prohibition to that of enjoyment, where fulfilling individual pleasures has become almost a social duty, thus producing subjects unconcerned with society or productivity but endlessly lusting after individual satisfaction. Partaking in the full-fledged culture of commodification, consumers are urged to maximize their own enjoyment to achieve happiness, but since desire cannot be fulfilled, this goal is never attainable (McGowan 123). Although McGowan presents this apocalyptic vision in the context of U.S. society, his take on capitalist hypercommodification can be applied anywhere within the transnational market of dynamic globalization. As for the Colombian context, Jean Franco links manliness, globalization, and consumer culture when she comments on the Colombian *sicarios*, whose careless attitude to human life bespeaks the collapse of patriarchal governance. Franco highlights the code of masculinity, "in which the idea of social success no longer has connection with work. Removed from any loyalty to a national or family structures, or from any system of ethos, individualism is turned into indiscriminate violence" (Franco, *The Decline* 224). In other words, Colombian narco subculture, as described by Franco, mirrors McGowan's society of hedonistic drives, where the chaos and permissiveness of contemporary social order teach that there is no need to compromise one's own enjoyment. Work ethic and conventional aspirations to marriage and career are substituted by shortcuts; it is a society where money and instant gratification objectify and eventually bring about everyone's demise. The narco lifestyle characterizes itself by the very low value attributed to human life in general, which in turn underwrites the worthlessness of the human body. Notorious drug lords and *sicarios* live fast and dangerously, compressing the normal human life span into a brief but intense encounter with pleasure, before someone else takes their place. As a narco friend from Sinaloa explains to Arturo Pérez-Reverte, the author of *Reina del sur*: "Better to live like a king for five years than like a chump for fifty" (Pérez-Reverte) [Más vale vivir cinco años como rey que cincuenta como buey (my translation)].

While the feminine world in *Sin tetas* is dichotomized into women who have big breasts and those who do not, men fall into the category of either those who can afford the buxom trophies or those who cannot. Breasts, possibly the biggest fetish of Western culture, become the most desired attribute in sundry subplots throughout Bolívar's story: Everyone, regardless of gender, wants to possess the breasts, assuming that having them will satisfy their needs and secure their social position. In other words, capitalist consumerism merges neatly with psychoanalysis in this tale of tainted social aspirations, because it is founded upon the impossibility of satisfying one's desire, which, as Lacanian thought teaches, always slides from one signifier to another, leaving the subject incomplete and craving more.

Catalina, a naive fourteen-year-old, who as a sop to the audience's sensitivity is portrayed as three years older in the telenovela, wants an easier life than that of her single mother, Doña Hilda, who has struggled as a seamstress to support her two children in a hardscrabble existence. At the start of the series, the girl is confronted with the Other's enjoyment in its most unbearable dimension: Everywhere she turns, she sees her high school dropout girlfriends happily stepping out of limousines. Though their appearance is disheveled from a weekend-long "date" with the local *traquetos*, their faces beam with satisfaction, and countless shopping bags filled to the brim attest to the girls' consumer triumph. The mesmerized Catalina wishes to partake in the pleasure, yet Yésica, a seasoned go-between for the narcos and a connoisseur of their taste in women, makes the heroine aware of her physical lack, which henceforth becomes Cata's obsession. In this caricature of teenage peer pressure, the willowy Cata is moved by the desire to be desirable, and what the consumer culture around her dictates as the ideal is to possess unnaturally big breasts.

In the course of the story, Catalina gets duped, raped, used, and cast aside by a number of lascivious men. A modern-day Lazarillo in search of the perfect "protector," she is deceived by each and every candidate. Her journey through an abjectly corrupt society brings her into contact with drug traffickers, *sicarios,* doctors, and politicians, all equally fraudulent and devoid of scruples. Some goons refuse to sleep with her on the grounds of her flat-chestedness while another one takes away her virginity, promising money for surgery only to disappear afterward. The owner of a sketchy modeling agency tells her to come back when she gets implants, and even the gullible Albeiro confesses that she would be the beauty queen of Pereira were she better endowed. To add insult to injury, all other women in the telenovela, Catalina's attractive mother included, possess pronouncedly curvaceous figures, making her lack ever so obvious. Thus it is no surprise that, in Cata's eyes, breasts are the signifier of economic opulence, the only enabler of the idyllic now and the successful forever after. In this sense, Bolívar's story strays from the classic fairy tale, because it strips the prince of his semiotic powers. It is not he who will provide the heroine with happiness but rather Catalina's enhanced physique, which will supply her with many princes who, in turn, will secure her financial well-being. Within the economy of hyper consumption, both men and women unashamedly use each other to catch a fleeting pleasure, given that rapid turnover and an almost immediate obsolescence constitute the hallmarks of narco society.

In psychoanalytic terms, Catalina sees that neither her humble mother nor she herself possesses the phallus, the symbol of power, and that her physique is incomplete, henceforth needing "masquerading" to compensate for the lack. Lacan's famous assertion that man's sexual relation comes down to fantasy finds resonance in Catalina's story, in that she must alter her appearance and behavior accordingly to approach what narcos crave the most.[11] Catalina aspires to "become a woman" in a performative, superficial fashion, simultaneously resurrecting every stereotype of female sexuality that feminism has endeavored to banish. Bolívar's novel is even more explicit about the required measures than the telenovela, in that it gives an absurdly exaggerated list of corporeal alterations Cata must follow to approach the feminine ideal. She must "thin down her waist, enlarge her hips, tone her muscles, lift her butt, straighten her hair with all types of treatments, care for her face with sundry recommended unguents, bleach her body hair, shave her legs and bikini area every three days, and toast her skin" [adelgazar la cintura, agrandar sus caderas, reafirmar sus músculos, levantar la cola, alisar su cabello con tratamientos de toda índole, cuidar su bello rostro con mascarillas de cuanto menjunje le recomendaran, desteñir con agua oxigenada todos los vellos de su humanidad, depilarse cada tercer día las piernas y el pubis y tostar su piel (Bolívar Moreno, *Sin tetas* 9)].

In other words, the teenager's imperative is to become part European runway model, part Playboy bunny. Its first component would make Retamar's Caliban cringe, as it asks for the impossible fair-skinned, straight-haired idealized beauty standard from the North, which has become the hegemonic look around the globe. Some go as far as to call this trend an informal system of apartheid, which continues to influence Colombia not only in beauty pageants but also in the exposure of certain sports celebrities, whose blue eyes and fair complexion assure them greater dissemination in the media simply because they reflect the Colombian social elite and satisfy international tastes.[12] Likewise, despite the premise of reflecting the nation to its own citizens and to the outside world, Colombian beauty queens lose what could be considered a "Colombian look" in favor of the internationally craved model-like height, European chiseled features, and measurements of 90–60–90 centimeters (36–23–36 inches).[13]

Commodity fetishism plays one of the key roles in the culture of consumption because it "triumphs as spectacle": "As spectacle, the object becomes image and belief, and it is secured by an erotic . . . aura." Since fetishism involves the attribution of self-sufficiency and autonomous powers to a man-derived object, it relies on "the ability to disavow what is known and replace it with belief and the suspension of disbelief" (Mulvey 4 and 7). Likewise, the artificiality of a voluptuous chest does not undermine the call girl's worth. When Catalina complains to Yésica that Paola's popularity among the narcos stems from the girl's artificial physique while at least Catalina is the "real deal," the all-knowing procuress sets her straight. Her response points to an increasing reliance on mediated rather than real experience, where it is not just a reverted relation between sign and signifier but instead the erasure of the signifier in the reign of postmodern hyperreality. In the very first episode of the telenovela, Yésica lays out the parameters of the narco aesthetic: No one cares what lies beneath the surface of the skin. Breasts "can be made out of rubber, wood, rock, whatever, as long as they are visible. What matters is that they are big, get it?" [pueden ser de caucho, de madera, de piedra, de lo que sea con tal que se vean pues. Ay, lo importante es que sean grandes. ¿Entendiste? (Bolívar Moreno, *Sin tetas* 8)]. With the reference each time less apparent, it is the process of derealization of the real. Authentic beauty no longer takes precedence over the artificial remodeling of the body; what matters is the final effect. This new aesthetic is blatantly superficial, where everything desirable, from sex to social status, can be instantaneously improved on and transformed into commodities as fetishes-on-display.

Life after (Dis)Satisfaction: Colombia Bought and Sold

Predictably, Catalina's "quest" for big breasts is filled with setbacks. First, Cardona, her first powerful protector, runs from the police before he can finance the girl's surgery. Next, an unscrupulous plastic surgeon taunts her with the promise of an operation in exchange for sex, only to install previously used silicone implants. But, for a while, before the complications come, Catalina experiences the *jouissance* of a narco *muñeca*. It is an orgy of consumption and excess, in villas each time more extravagant than the one before, with ever more luxurious amenities. Catalina not only attracts a steady stream of clients drawn by her now-impressive bosom, but she also enamors a sexagenarian narco, Marcial, who marries her and showers her with money in exchange for her exclusive services.

This would be the culminating scene both in traditional fairy tales and in makeover shows, for it attests to the power of image without probing into what happens next. True, Catalina's new breasts ensure her luxurious future, but, in satisfying her adolescent dream, she simply transfers her voracious consumer appetite to the next signifier. Unashamedly self-absorbed, Cata sets new goals for herself by pestering her narco husband to secure her first place in a national beauty pageant. Marcial's efforts notwithstanding, Catalina only achieves the position of a dissatisfied first runner-up. Having grown accustomed to believing that her enhanced body will guarantee her success, the heroine becomes detached from reality and certainly from her roots, alienating her childhood friends and even Marcial with her ever-growing demands. Her drama is that she just does not enjoy herself as much as she thought she would.

This addiction to the pursuit of enjoyment is not exclusive to Catalina, but she takes it to a level disproportionate to her modest milieu by attesting to the impossibility of satisfying one's desire. After all, unlike the other *peladas* of her barrio, for a while Cata does manage to leave poverty behind. Meanwhile, her girlfriends, her brother Byron, her boyfriend, Albeiro, and even her mother all succumb to the imperative of enjoyment that goes against communal restrictions and creates the sense that the social order has run amok. Perhaps because Bolívar's telenovela lacks paternal figures who could take up the position of the symbolic father and impose prohibitions, the young measure success in terms of instant gains while rejecting delayed gratification. Cata and her brother are convinced that the long-term benefits of education pale in comparison to the instant financial gratification of partaking in the narco economy: "Yésica was right that girls from her class didn't need to study, and the reasons were beyond obvious: a pretty girl willing to whore herself could immediately get the same as a lawyer, a doctor, a scientist, or a CEO, that is, if they studied for 20 years and worked another 20" [Yésica tenía razón en afirmar que las niñas de su clase no se veían obligadas a estudiar y las razones saltaban a la vista: una niña linda y dispuesta a putearse podía conseguir en un instante lo mismo o más que un abogado, un médico, un científico o un administrador de empresas, luego de estudiar 20 años y trabajar otros 20 (Bolívar Moreno, *Sin tetas* 27)]. In a picaresque fashion, these adolescents yearn to achieve comfort with the least work possible.

Speaking of male authority, the youth of *Sin tetas*'s contact with adult males is limited to *traquetos*, brothel owners in Pereira, or crooked plastic surgeons or politicians in Bogotá. Not one single father inhabits the Pereiran households, thereby pointing to a gender imbalance; the younger generation experiences no good—or even bad—paternal model or discipline. Similarly, McGowan's society of enjoyment substitutes for the traditional father figure who stood for law and prohibition. No longer positioned at the top of the social structure, he is less visible yet more omnipotent. Whereas previous authority founded on prohibition had to maintain at least the pretense of infallibility and integrity to hold on to power, the father who commands pleasure is openly on the side of enjoyment, thus not striving for flawlessness (McGowan 46). In other words, he can be corrupt and criminal, just as the narcos who command pleasure and dominate Pereira, while converting school, police, and traditional family into ineffective institutional relics.

Kept under the sway of narco glitz, impressionable youth want to emulate the kingpins by either accompanying or becoming them. At one point in the telenovela, when Catalina and Byron have a heart-to-heart in which they reveal to each other the source of their sudden cash influx, Cata muses how their poor mother would be horrified to know she had a whore (*puta*) and a thug (*matón*) for children. Byron's matter-of-fact answer replaces individual agency with an imperative of adaptability, thereby attesting to the fatalistic determinism of their milieu: "This is the reality that was given to us, right? You can't change it, I can't change it" [Esta es la realidad que nos tocó vivir, ¿sí o no? No la puede cambiar Ud., no la puedo cambiar yo (*Sin tetas* television series)]. In other words, hegemonic masculinity[14] in *Sin tetas* is that of crime, violence, and unbridled promiscuity.

Consistent with the centrality of law-breaking to hegemonic masculinity, men in the series are taught that asserting manliness through legal activities is hardly plausible (due to unemployment) and inferior to illegal enterprise in terms of gains.[15] The narco milieu glorifies and culturally idealizes primitive virility, aggression, prowess, and male camaraderie. It rejects domesticity, the idea of the family man, and, of course, monogamy. Byron is not exactly perfect material for a hegemon, but he surely does his best to fit in. His first kill makes him physically sick, and he vomits as he hides his gun in the bathroom, all the while trying to gather his composure before he can face the world. Yet the wads of banknotes he receives for his first important victim dispel whatever misgivings he had; Byron returns home overjoyed, and he showers everyone with money, including Cata's boyfriend, Albeiro. Heartfelt as his conduct may be, his generosity is an instinctive display of his new masculine capacity. Having joined the ranks of Pereiran *sicarios*, now Cata's brother can dream of becoming a *duro* (high-ranking trafficker) someday. In other words, his own anxiety over his masculinity is put to rest via the spectacle of criminal masculinity. What is more, the realist Byron takes up killing in the hope that his girlfriend, Ximena, will stop prostituting herself, because he will provide her with consumer bliss; it is telling that only now does he propose that they begin a steady relationship. This means that her pursuit of enjoyment pushed him onto the same path, causing a chain reaction that ultimately engulfed the entire community. If parental authority prevented the quintessential teenage lovers Romeo and Juliet from happiness, the new pleasure imperative denies Byron and Ximena the chance of a successful relationship because they are simply too busy chasing the narco ideal to take notice of the demise of their love.

The only traditionally successful romantic couple in the series is that of doña Hilda, the quintessential cougar, and Catalina's boyfriend-cum-stepfather, Albeiro. Of all the characters, these two are the most credulous and least impressed by the narco blitz, but they also succumb to the economy of instant (sexual) gratification by initiating an affair behind Cata's back. Their tender romance is laced with problems however, because Albeiro also sleeps with Catalina, thereby complicating the familial relations. If the traditional society of prohibition was defined through strict laws against incest to maintain social structures (McGowan 12), *Sin tetas* goes in the opposite direction. Sharing a bed with both mother and daughter (albeit not simultaneously) corroborates the reign of sexual indulgence, a side product of narco bonanza and its exaltation of pleasure-seeking. Yet, ultimately, Albeiro impregnates doña Hilda and assumes the role of the head of the family. If we adopt Doris Sommer's famous claim about how romance and politics go hand in hand in Latin America, with modern nations and their projected ideal histories implemented via novels, the romance in question sends a rather bittersweet message regarding narco hyperreality. Through her own shortsightedness and naiveté, doña Hilda, symbolic of the nation, is caught off guard by the deadly tentacles of drug trafficking. Her two teenage children rush headlong to their perdition and die tragically young, thereby underscoring the loss of an entire generation to narco violence. It does not help that Hilda, too, is blinded by her own romance, reflecting Colombia's temporary infatuation with narco wealth. But because she couples with the only man who is not infected with narco bonanza, they may restore order by sheltering their offspring from Pereira's depravity.[16] Poor but honest seems to be the only way out. Its somewhat incestuous nature goes hand in hand with Colombia's canonical national romances, such as Jorge Isaacs's *María* or Gabriel García Márquez's *One Hundred Years of Solitude*, both of which feature romantic couplings involving cousins.

Cata's temporary bliss ends when her enormous implants become infected, transforming her most praised possession into a grotesque wound. The cartilage covering her sternum collapses, and the artificial breasts become one gigantic protrusion covered with oozing blisters. Since in *Sin tetas* the implants symbolize the power of image, their collapse proves the superficial bliss to be temporary and the underlying reality to be a site of contention. Catalina's accident is a symptom of a bigger disenchantment pervading the series: It is not only her masqueraded body that refuses to play along with her demands but her very being that begins to experience the illusiveness of enjoyment.

In the end, no one emerges unscathed from the narco environment, and certainly no one holds on to the *jouissance*. Devastated and devoid of hope, Cata intentionally allows herself to be murdered by *sicarios*, her girlfriends resign themselves to a dreadful routine at the local whorehouse, her brother is killed by the police after carrying out a hit, and her mother ends up losing both of her teenage children. Law-abiding policemen die after being snitched on by the criminals infiltrating in their forces, and tarnished plastic surgeons and pageant organizers end up in body bags for disobeying the wishes of their mafia benefactors. Even the all-powerful narcos are extradited to U.S. jails, compliments of Cata and Yésica, who have no qualms about revealing their whereabouts for a hefty reward. The only remaining couple is doña Hilda and Albeiro—the Adam and Eve of this questionable paradise. In a city now populated by ghosts, they are reminiscent of Juan Rulfo's incestuous siblings, whose shame of inbreeding kept them sheltered from Pedro Páramo's destructive power and, ultimately, protected.

The final episode drives home the unfeasibility of the society of enjoyment, when the newly flat-chested Catalina returns to Pereira in her last desperate effort to find solace. By now she has lost her implants and her husband, Marcial, to Yésica. As the heroine encounters her mother in an advanced stage of pregnancy with Albeiro, she realizes that this new familial arrangement does not take her into account. Cata then accompanies her girlfriends to the bordello, where, as in old times, she is told that a set of big breasts could become her ticket to fame. What they do not know is that Catalina has already made this journey to hell and back. This is where the circle closes and the heroine's flight comes to an end; slightly wiser but alienated and out of place in her hometown, Catalina decides to die, thus stepping aside for another naive girl in the rat race for illusory *jouissance*.

Sin tetas blatantly sexualizes female imagery, going against the less objectifying attitude promoted and struggled for by feminism. Both the title and the opening credits reject the pretense of inconspicuous manipulation in exchange for an objectification so deliberate that it simply cannot be read in any other way than caricaturesque and cartoonish. This reading of Bolívar's show ties with Martín-Barbero's view on the telenovela and its protagonists, the common people, whose weapon is "their capacity for parody and caricature" (*Communication* 238). The opening credits take the audience to an underground meeting where two thugs in business suits and narco bling exchange suitcases as if sealing a deal. Next, one of them opens his case, and the spectators, trained in the conventional cinematographic imagery of the gangster genre, expect to see stacks of cash or perhaps a cache of weapons. Instead, the suitcase holds Barbie-like doll parts with long limbs, microscopic waists, and unnaturally large breasts, which the man begins to assemble to his liking, choosing the biggest bosom for his creation. Next, the dolls on the screen transform into real-life women, stiffly spread out on chaise lounges, smiling at the viewer with glossy, unseeing eyes. A cord wrapped around one woman's neck for a moment suggests sexual subjection, only to be replaced with the patently capitalist imagery of store packaging: The woman transforms back into a doll, held tightly by the same cords inside her cardboard box, as she is placed on a shelf full of other, identical-looking *muñecas*. In the background, a catchy tune proclaims the desire for social improvement, and thus joins the slew of other telenovelas, where dreaming of riches and striving to exceed one's social class are the driving forces behind the plot.[17]

The opening scene underwrites the literal objectification of the female body through its fragmentation and reconstruction. It presents the female body as castrated and femininity as fragmented and then reassembled according to men's whims. In the most elemental reading, the man stands for the drug trafficker, wealthy enough to collect women as luxury objects. The scene presupposes gender subordination, where women are placed at the root of male fantasies, all the while echoing Claude Lévi-Strauss's notion of kinship in which females are objects of exchange. Yet judging from the outcome of the telenovela, where male characters lose as much as their female counterparts, Bolívar's *Sin tetas* is more about the national body in crisis, damaged in the rapacious economy rather than in the melee of gender wars. To be sure, human trafficking, not unlike the show's rampant prostitution, involves a disproportionate number of women and children, making men the profiteers and women a product whose acquisition and exchange confirms men's holding power to acquire and accrue. But Bolívar's story renders his subjects defeated regardless of gender, instead pointing to the menace of the late capitalist, commodity-driven global market and its devastating fusion with Colombia's narco business. In a society whose members are willing to die for the ephemeral chance to become the haves rather than the have-nots, everybody is forced metaphorically into prostitution.

Sin tetas thus constitutes a prostitution narrative with an added nationalist twist, where Cata is the female embodiment of a debased and commercialized Colombia.[18] Her entire generation pimps herself to the highest bidder, converting Colombia into a depot for human spare parts. Catalina's melodramatic story thus becomes an allegory of Colombia's relationship with transnational drug trafficking—the epitome of aggressive capitalism. Rich in natural beauty, Catalina/Colombia sell themselves for the narco illusion, only to suffer heartbreaking defeat and nostalgia for their lost innocence.

Airing Dirty Laundry: Sex Scandals Revisited

It is safe to say that *Sin tetas* has been received enthusiastically outside of Colombia because the story ties into the global obsession with excess and because the topic of teenage prostitution feeds into universal fascination with the morbid. Yet the story is also pronouncedly national and local in that the telenovela (and the book) alludes repeatedly to issues pertaining to Colombian reality. An expression of oral culture that blends with a hodgepodge of images drawn from television, advertising, and all other media (Martín-Barbero, "Memory and Form" 276), *Sin tetas* holds a mirror to the sordid narco corruption that permeates society, "a televisual 'national' in which the imagined community rallies around specific images of itself" (A. López 262). As Rincón observes, the small screen brought into Colombian households *narcocultura* with its questionable money ethics, its gaudiness, and its excess imprinted on objects and female bodies alike ("Sin tetas"). Whereas many Latin American countries produced telenovelas that obviate historical complexity, neutralizing temporal and special references for the sake of primordial passions that have proven to unite audiences worldwide, Colombians followed the Brazilian model built alongside specific references to national history and culture.[19]

In the same vein, *Sin tetas* revisits the sites of collective national memory, referring not only to the ills of the narcotrafficking tackled by the intellectual elites but also to those complicit with the imaginative universe of popular mass media entertainment. It shifts its focus away from the key male players, unearthing the link between the narcos and their women, whose relationship to the drug industry has been the topic of rumors for years in Colombia, thus in a sense becoming the pulse of the nation.[20] In the most general terms, this relationship involves different forms of prostitution, in which Colombia places second only after the Dominican Republic for the internal and international trafficking of women in Latin America (García Suárez 324).

Nevertheless, the underworld of *prepago* girls highlighted in *Sin tetas* differs from traditionally understood prostitution spurred by economic hardship and domestic violence, even though Bolívar's telenovela focuses on the social margins that in reality are not the most representative of this trend. *Prepagos* often come from nonviolent, middle-class backgrounds and frequently hold university degrees, thereby defying presumptions about prostitution stemming from economic need.[21] As the

2013 telenovela *La prepago* unveils, they are college students—much like sugar babies in the United States—who turn tricks on the side to finance their education or help with the family budget.[22] The thirst for adventure, money, and power are quoted as the primary reasons for the proliferation of the *prepago* girls. This change in circumstances alters their appearance, where prostitutes standing on a street corner are substituted by inconspicuous high school and university students, or celebrities, thus making their identification so much more difficult and their disclosure so much more exciting for the general public.

Sin tetas makes numerous references to the phenomenon of luxurious women for sale. At one point in the telenovela, a *duro* hires Yésica to procure for him a celebrity who has repeatedly refused his advances. With the right bait, a new Mercedes, the star eventually agrees to a weekend with her admirer, yet her haughty attitude inspires him to fool her by "repossessing" the car the moment she returns home. This episode echoes the connection between real-life Colombian celebrities and the mafia, a link exposed in lowbrow publications dismissed by Abad Faciolince as "editorial trash" and heretofore mentioned in relation to the legal wrangling between Colombian model Natalia París and the scandalmonger Madame Rochy. The trashy and contentious *¿Las prepago?* divulges anecdotes about the bacchanalian narco parties frequented by posh call girls, features a chapter mockingly titled "Honor Roll" devoted to celebrities who allegedly sold themselves to narcos, and—as if this were not sufficiently scandalous—contains photos of famous *prepagos* with inscriptions detailing their sexual services for *narcotraficantes*, such as Alfredo Tascón, Luis Fernando Rebellón, or Víctor Patiño Fómeque. In the same vein, Escamilla alleges the existence of albums of naked models and otherwise famous beauties who offered, for a price, weekends in the Caribbean. These same albums supposedly circulated among incarcerated narcos who, from behind bars, could order women for delivery to their jail cells, just like one would order pizza (Escamilla 44–45).

That such rumors are recycled in *Sin tetas* attests to the connection Martín-Barbero made between telenovelas and the oral culture of a given community. It also shapes popular urban culture through theatricalization and degradation, with topics like "filial love, laziness, sentimentality, [or] the programmed humiliation of women" ("Memory and Form" 279). Their scandal-seeking spurred some elites to pigeonhole these popular forms as "entertainment with no cultural or redeeming value for the increasingly visible, primarily urban masses" (A. López 260). Yet it is precisely lower body humor, as Mikhail Bakhtin famously argued, that provided the masses with a self-image they enjoyed, owing partly to its irreverence and partly to its subversive message, which defied hegemonic representations. Centuries ago, picaresque novels (*Lazarillo* and Francisco de Quevedo's *El Buscón*) re-created society through scatology and parody, if not via sex. Likewise, *Sin tetas* taps into the national rumor narrative, by re-creating the gossip and mocking women and narcos alike. No one is off limits: *Sin tetas* pokes fun at underprivileged families who turn a blind eye to their children's ruin in exchange for material benefits, and it scorns privileged beauties selling themselves for frivolous luxuries.

The latter group surfaces in *Sin tetas* in the episode mentioned earlier, when Catalina, now wealthy and hungry for more power, pressures her narco husband, Marcial, to secure her a win in a beauty pageant. The show does not even attempt to maintain the appearances of a fair competition, making it obvious that the girl with the highest-bidding narco supporter will take the crown. With Marcial's generous sponsorship, Catalina is certain to succeed in her plan: Through dishonest manipulation, she becomes the representative of a Colombian department she has never even visited, and she stumbles in an interview, not knowing the capital of her alleged home province. Notwithstanding her blunder, Catalina moves on to the finals, only to lose to the girl whose benefactor had upped the bid. The final verdict devastates her and provokes a shoot-out between the two shady sponsors. Later on, much to Cata's bewilderment, Marcial exacts revenge on the pageant's organizer, by having him killed and dumped on the side of the road.

Again, this subplot allows the audience to reminisce about scandals that swept the nation when beauty pageants, one of Colombia's most popular institutions, became tarnished with narco money. Historically, the National Beauty Pageant, held in Cartagena, would captivate Colombia every November, overshadowing even national tragedies, such as the Supreme Court bombing of November 6, 1985, or the assassination of presidential candidates (1989, 1990). The nation diverted its attention from pressing political matters to evaluate each candidate's body measurements and runway walk (Juanita Darling). Likewise, in the Colombia of the 1980s, pageant beauties became a form of commodity, delivered to the wealthy *narcotraficantes* through an elaborate web of videos and catalogs organized by the event's hairdressers, stylists, and fashionistas. Cetina mentions one such stylist from Bogotá, Elías Bustos, who was rumored to have set up a net of women for the mafia and who did not confirm or dissipate the hearsay, up until he was murdered before his scheduled interview with the author in 1994.

Cetina's book goes into detail about the weekend-long parties with beauty queens. El Mexicano hosted a number of such events, and Hugo Hernán Valencia (a narco from Cali, killed on Escobar's orders in 1987) sponsored pageant contestants from 1984 until 1987. Just like Marcial, the fictional character from *Sin tetas*, Valencia generously tipped the waiters at Cartagena's Club Naval to sit closer to the jury, so as to have more influence over their final decision. Valencia was photographed with Sandra Borda Caldas, Señorita Colombia 1984, and next to Deborah Carthy Dew, the Puerto Rican Miss Universe of 1985, to whom he presented a compromisingly expensive gift of jewelry. Valencia's death effected the pageant community in many ways. First, the festive alliance of beauty competitions and narco fortunes toned down, as it became overshadowed by violence, and second, beauty pageant organizers felt pressured to send a formal declaration to the media, denying the presence of dirty money in their decision-making. Such public exculpation on the part of the event's organizers only added fuel to the rumors that had been circulating throughout society.

The list of scandals goes on and on, tainting countless pageants. The corruption not only involved bribing judges, hiring stylists, or financing candidates' wardrobes but also, as in *Sin tetas*, making their participation possible by manipulating their region of origin. Cetina writes that designers would put regional beauty titles up for bid, disregarding the official selection process. Just as Bolívar's Catalina, who joined the competition illegally, many real-life competitors stood in for the wrong departments; in some, *narcotraficantes* would buy the titles for their protégées, and their intermediaries would in turn "persuade" the governor to issue a decree naming the girl the department's representative. For example, in 1993, Marcela Serrano, Yamile Plata, Milena Giraldo, and Sandra Soraya Giraldo, all candidates from Bogotá, represented the departments of Guainía, Guaviare, Arauca, and Vaupés, respectively (Cetina 33–34).

Rampant corruption did not spare the beauty aesthetic either. In *Sin tetas* there are plastic surgeons who refuse to perform a risky procedure on Catalina's adolescent body even when offered substantial remuneration, but others, far more unscrupulous and common, jump at the chance to partake in the narco bonanza, disregarding the risks. The corrupt doctor who agrees to operate in exchange for sex installs used implants that soon cause infection. Similarly, in real life, the boom of plastic surgery attracted unethical doctors and sundry unqualified "practitioners" who prey on people's ignorance and on their dream to conform to the new beauty standards popularized by the narco aesthetic.

Of course, the desire to enhance one's appearance should not be attributed solely to *narcocultura*, since breast implants and liposuction have been the two most popular procedures across the globe. The upsurge in plastic surgeries is a global phenomenon, tainted by scandals of unscrupulous surgeons who deform or kill their patients. In 2006, the year *Sin tetas* aired, there were reports of more than 250 requests per week for every clinic in Cali, the city known as Colombia's mecca of plastic surgery. At the same time, Cali specialists were warning that close to half of the reported procedures were performed by unauthorized individuals ("Las cirugías plásticas"). As a result, Edna Patricia Espinosa, Miss Tanga 2009 from Colombia, who had already undergone rhinoplasty and breast augmentation on prior occasions, died during a liposuction procedure. Another case involved Ina Andrea Ontiveros and Katherine Torrado, winners of the North Santander beauty pageant in 2008 and 2009, respectively. Even though plastic surgery was part and parcel of winning the pageant, Andrea Ontiveros claims she was not eager to alter her body. Yet pressured by a plastic surgeon, fittingly a member of the jury, she authorized a small laser liposuction, only to find out upon completion that she had been equipped with bigger breasts instead. To add insult to injury, the filler turned out to be toxic, and the beauty queen had to undergo painful corrective surgeries. Katherine Torrado had an identical experience ("Exreinas destapan"). In other words, botched plastic surgeries, which often result in irreversible damage or death, are a widespread phenomenon. *Sin tetas* tapped into this preoccupation, thus making the telenovela a reflection of a larger problem.

The nonchalance with which narcos undertook to enhance their trophy partners, habitually sending them to plastic surgeons kept "on staff," corroborates the dangerous fad that locked the Latin American female body in the impossible image of a svelte figure with exaggerated curves. This is an issue brought up by Lucrecia Ramírez, a psychiatrist and the coordinator of the Academic Group for Women's Mental Health in Medellín [Grupo Académico de Salud Mental de las Mujeres en Medellín], who argues that *narcocultura* has generated a disregard for the common Colombian female biotype. In its place, it promoted an impossible physiological utopia that has not only devastated women's psyche but also made surgical intervention indispensable, herewith perpetuating the artificial look (Jiménez Leal).

In the same vein, Baruch Vega described an encounter of narcos and top-notch models whom he had invited to Colombia for a fake calendar shooting, with the sole purpose of satisfying the narcos' whim of meeting world-class beauties.[23] On the María Elvira talk show (in an episode also featuring Virginia Vallejo), Vega recounted how the hosts, who were accustomed to artificially enhanced models, could not fathom why the internationally acclaimed beauties from abroad were so thin and how their flat-chested look could be considered appealing. Their sincere bewilderment over the models' willowy appearance untouched by the scalpel exemplifies the imposition of a utopian standard in Colombia, which naturalized the necessity for medical intervention.

Pereira and Female Stereotyping

Returning to Bolívar's best-selling book, one cannot ignore the distancing between the viewer and the fictional drug-fueled world and the lack of earnestness in favor of playful sarcasm. The narrator clearly moves away from his protagonists, poking fun at the girls' shallowness and the drug-traffickers' nouveau riche gaudiness. In other words, no one, not even the protagonist, Catalina, escapes ridicule, as all seem to be motivated solely by greed. This stinging mockery throughout the novel loses some of its bite in the telenovela, which, in lamenting the effects of misguided aspirations, converts Pereira's youth into more sympathetic characters. The city's real-life inhabitants protested against Caracol's *Sin tetas*, blaming it for promoting a negative image, wherein most Pereira women are portrayed as prostitutes and most men as criminals. In the same vein, the show was criticized for its chauvinistic approach to women and the shameless exploitation of the female body, which has no function other than the decorative, teasing the spectators with nudity and female curves. Several sponsors spoke of withdrawing their ads, and the mayor of Pereira, Juan Manuel Arango Vélez, threatened to sue the network, thus adding to the notoriety of the telenovela.

In his rather unconvincing defense, Bolívar argued that the series could have easily represented any other region of Colombia and that he chose Pereira simply because this is where he met the two adolescent girls who inspired the story. Yet the issue is more complex, for this public outrage touches on a sensitive nerve not necessarily limited to *Sin tetas* but related to deeper-rooted stereotyping that has affected Pereira's citizens, arousing speculation that there was more to the choice of their city than mere coincidence. Pereira, a relatively new city (founded in 1863) known for its mixture of races, was first settled by radical liberals, mostly single men and other groups who did not feel comfortable in the white, conservative, and very Catholic towns nearby, such as Manizales. From this background emerged women known nationally for their exuberance and outspokenness. Somewhere along the way, this image transformed into a stereotype, whereby Pereiran women became stigmatized as the "easiest" and most sensual in Colombia. Historian José Danilo Trujillo Arcila ties this damaging myth to the history of the city, in that men left in search of jobs in the nascent industries a century earlier, leaving women to their own devices. This in turn gave Pereiran women an independent character, born out of historical necessity that many misrepresented as loose morals and promiscuity. Also, Pereira has long held a reputation as an epicenter of the sex trade, going back to the early days of the coffee boom, when, given rampant gender and economic inequality, sex workers would flock to the city seeking some of the profits of coffee growers in a rigidly patriarchal society.

Of course, the negative image would have not prevailed with such intensity had it not been reinforced in popular expressions and the mass media. A popular joke that Pereiran women when invited to take a seat readily lie down attests to their sexual availability and only affirms the harmful myth. In the 2015 *La fama de las pereiranas* (an assertive defense of Pereiran women), Aldemar Solano Peña offers a literal explanation of this confused interpretation: Namely, when visiting, Pereiran women lie down on sofas to chat with one another rather than sit like more formal people from colder climates (177–78). In the pornography industry, a number of films refer specifically to women from Pereira, while no other city in Colombia (with the possible exception of Cartagena) has such a wide representation. This means that putting the Pereira label on a given production sells by virtue of its promise of beauty and sensuality, all the while adding to the stigma attached to the city. In a similar fashion, Richard Smitten inadvertently stereotyped the city while describing one of Griselda Blanco's partners: "He was not from Medellín; he was from the town of Pereira. Colombians have an expression: Nothing comes from Pereira except whores and hitmen. Most of the heavy-duty hitmen in the drug business came from Pereira" (102).[24] Solano Peña quotes another popular saying, "Pereira produces only soccer players and whores" [Pereira solo da futbolistas y putas (209)]. The Pereiran stereotype, though in this case denoting the positive example of a tough woman, emerges once again in the context of Griselda Blanco, whom one of her former *sicarios,* El Escritor, describes as "an awesome broad, like a Pereiran woman" [una vieja espectacular, parecía pereirana (Guarnizo Álvarez, *La Patrona* 24)]. Then too came a defamatory incident on the program *El Poder del 10,* a remake of the short-lived U.S. game show *Power of 10,* which launched in 2008 on RCN. The show asks contestants to guess how a cross section of Colombians responded to a variety of polls, and one of the questions was precisely about the looseness of Pereiran women.

Thus it should be no surprise that Pereira's citizens grew tired of their stigmatization on national television. In reaction to Bolívar's telenovela, the city organized a "Pereira Pride Parade" to decry the stigma imposed on its women and, in the mayor's own words, as a "gesture of collective self-esteem" ("Los pereiranos"). Local artists led by Rafael Ortiz organized a powerful if controversial exhibition titled "Easy" in the city center. Eighteen signs featuring offensive expressions used by Colombians to refer to Pereiran women, such as "I'm from Pereira but I don't perform," "They say I carry my own mat around with me," or "I am a Pereiran woman with a cotton mattress," were intended to stimulate a national dialogue and thus affirm the dignity of Pereira's female population.[25] This artistic happening was particularly timely in the era of globalization, where the local can easily transform into the transnational through mass-media dissemination and the migration of populations.

A 2002 report from Spain on the topic of human trafficking goes back to Pereira as well. Salud Hernández describes the plight of underprivileged Latin American girls who, caught in a web of lies and poverty, end up in Europe working in international prostitution rings. A staggering fifty thousand Colombian women work as prostitutes abroad, with half coming from Pereira and neighboring areas. Hernández points to Spain as the second largest importer of Colombian prostitutes, exceeded only by

Japan. Her victimized subjects either returned from this hellish life penniless and addicted to pain-numbing substances or disappeared altogether.
The report unearths how the global human trafficking mafia could not
move about freely within Colombia, since small numbers of international
tourists made suspicious foreigners stand out. The traffickers thus relied
on local women procuresses, themselves exploited previously, who sought
out new victims in their own neighborhoods. This is how Hernández explains the high concentration of Pereiran prostitutes abroad, yet her sympathetic intentions are somewhat undermined by the sensationalist title
of the report, which, again, brands Pereiran women as easy by character-
izing their city as a cradle of prostitution, only this time for European
readers.

The association between Pereira and international prostitution networks comes up again in 2009, with the arrival of another "instant" book
edited by Marcela Loaiza, *Atrapada por la mafia yakuza*. It purports to be
the true testimony of a Pereiran girl who ended up in the sordid underworld of the Japanese sex industry, a milieu replete with unscrupulous
madams, sadistic *mafiosi*, and an international crazy quilt of criminals.
The protagonist's first words attest to the typecasting Pereiran women
experience in transnational crime circles and to the harmful effects of
globalization that thrust the underprivileged into the Asian meat markets:

> Now I'm working the street Ikebukuro, in Tokyo, Japan. I'm sur-
> rounded by about twenty-five to thirty women . . . and the rest are
> Colombians from around the country, but many of them claim to
> be Pereiran because men consider Pereiran chicks hotter in bed.
> So, to get more clients and cash that's where they say they're from.
> (Loaiza 7)

> [Ahora me encuentro parada en la calle Ikebukuro, en Tokio, Japón.
> Estoy rodeada de unas veinticinco o treinta mujeres . . . y el resto
> colombianas de diferentes ciudades de país, pero muchas dicen que
> son de Pereira sin serlo, porque a los hombres les parecen más cali-
> entes en la cama, y para ganar más clientes y más dinero dicen que
> son de allá. (my translation)]

Hence, considering the long history of stigmatization of Pereiran women,
it is logical to assume that the city's outrage is not so much about the racy
title or the breast-centered plot of the telenovela, as many oversimplified

the conflict. Rather, the Pereirans' indignation over Bolívar's *Sin tetas* stems from having witnessed a phenomenon of objectification and stereo-typification of their women, a local joke that in time grew into a nationally recognizable cliché, now reaching other countries. The critics of Bolívar's story charge that his invention only consolidates the harmful rumor among its global audience, exploiting and disseminating a facile com-monplace—regardless of what the author's intentions might have been.

In the end, next to its crudeness and the negative imagery of Colom-bian society corrupted by the narco aesthetics, *Sin tetas* touches on a se-ries of social ills where some respond to regional problems while others mirror global anxieties spurred by rampant consumerism. Violence, new clandestine forms of prostitution, an obsession with vanity, global human trafficking, and the decline of traditional values substituted by an econ-omy of instant gratification are just a few narco by-products decried to a degree in Bolívar's story. Having drawn its inspiration from sensational-ist, lowbrow material that traditionally pertained to the realm of gossip columns and popular hearsay, *Sin tetas* tantalized the masses by offering its own melodramatic interpretation of the nation's moral collapse under Escobar's evil sway. The fact that it opted for an ironic and at times campy mode, intertwining melodrama with satire and comedy, does not chip away at its cultural merit; *Sin tetas* opened a Pandora's box, corroborat-ing, intentionally or not, the urgency of confronting society's ills via the telenovela, its most popular form of entertainment.

6

Colombian *Sicariato* and Rosario Tijeras

Here always we have in mind that a motorcycle with a male passenger is synonymous with *sicarios* and danger.

Eduardo Rojas León, Medellín's secretary of security (Robbins)

Rosario Tijeras for President, Pablo Escobar for Vice President.

Franco Ramos, *Rosario Tijeras*, 73

The *sicario* surfaced in the public eye in the 1980s with the assassinations of such high-profile figures as the antidrug crusader and minister of justice Rodrigo Lara Bonilla.[1] On April 30, 1984, Iván Darío Guisado Álvarez and sixteen-year-old Bayron Albert Velásquez alias Quesito pulled up next to their victim's guarded Mercedes E-Class. They attacked using the trademark *sicario* method in which riding in tandem, the gunman, in this case Guisado, seated behind the driver opened fire, mortally wounding the unsuspecting minister. Lara Bonilla's assassin was killed in the ensuing shoot-out, but the other perpetrator survived. The Colombian public was stunned to see that Quesito, this enemy of the state, was childlike in appearance, and the threat of the adolescent *sicario* entered the public eye. The press began to write about the new social plague spread by Pablo Escobar and the Medellín Cartel, quoting the shocking number of three thousand pubescent mercenaries in the city of Medellín alone, more than 120 gangs roaming the hills surrounding the valley, and the existence of so-called *sicario* schools, where teenage killers were trained in the art of assassination ("Fábrica"). Their victims included presidential candidates and members of rival drug organizations, leftist party and union leaders, politicians, judges, police officers, prominent figures in the media, and ordinary people who happened to be in the wrong place at the wrong time. Devoid of political or ideological agendas yet acutely aware of the economic powerlessness of their social class, *sicarios* would throw themselves into almost suicidal missions in exchange for fleeting moments of money-fueled amusement. Quesito's comment, made many years after the assassination, exemplifies the overall ignorance and indifference with which young mercenaries risked their lives, eliminating others for a vague cause or for purely financial benefit:

> I was just a kid looking for money. . . . At the time, there was no way I could know the extent of the scandal we had started. Now I know what I didn't know then. I don't think even the people who wanted this done thought that it would explode as it did. All I knew was that he [Lara Bonilla] was fucking with El Patrón and if he was fucking with El Patrón then he was fucking with us. (Mollison 74)

Disaffected and trapped in the *comunas* clinging precariously to the hillsides that surround the valley in which the more affluent lived, these teenagers before the narco bonanza could only dream of accessing the economic and social opportunities of others. Thus, as Roldán put it, "when Escobar and Ochoa began to recruit troops for the narcotics trade, they found a ready pool of unemployed and alienated youths in the *comunas*" ("Colombia" 172–73).

Quesito, who served fourteen of his twenty-seven-year sentence for the assassination of Lara Bonilla, received a "salary" from the Medellín Cartel for the first six years while in jail, an amount that roughly equaled the promised five million pesos (U.S. $41,000) for a job well done (Mollison 74). He survived, unlike the great majority of teenage assassins from Escobar's army, largely because he did not rat anyone out and because he was locked up. Others died before reaching adulthood, inspiring drastically contrasting reactions of pity and fear.

Escobar's conflict with the state produced countless targets of his wrath and, with them, plenty of jobs for the violent poor. In 1985, Medellín became the murder capital of the world, with nearly 1,700 homicides, and the next year the rate more than doubled. If motorcycles were a rare sight in Medellín prior to 1970—with only one company, Lambretta, manufacturing an Italian-style scooter—by the end of the 1970s, Kawasakis and later Yamahas had filled the streets of Colombia, proverbially putting Colombia on wheels with an affordable and reliable product. The least expensive and most convenient mode of transportation, motorcycles became ubiquitous in Medellín, providing needed mobility for the poor. Simultaneously, they became stigmatized almost from the start as the preferred vehicle for hitmen (Robbins).

The halcyon days for Escobar's *sicarios* did not last long. The death of El Mexicano, the war between the Medellín and the Cali Cartel, and finally the demise of Pablo Escobar himself not only decimated the legions of adolescent hitmen but also led to the temporary decline of "assignments" and, with that, the subsequent unemployment of the violent youth. This caused hordes of trained assassins to turn to extortion, assaulting local businesses and attacking their competition. The disorder spawned another form of violence, the vigilante squads who set out to "clean up" neighborhoods overrun by young criminals. The death toll grew, sweeping the streets of adolescent gangsters and accidental victims who happened to be hanging out on the street corners of the *comunas*.[2] Robbins claims that the trend of motorcycle killings in fact worsened after Escobar's death, where *sicarios* began to charge as little as $200 per murder. He quotes Hugo Acero, a security consultant employed in the Bogotá mayor's office, who stated that the *sicarios'* assignments went beyond mafia deals, and "people used them to recover debts, to avenge an unfaithful lover. . . . *Sicarios* were used to punish." Present-day smaller, more fragmented, and more anonymous cartels in various cities still employ *sicarios* and even the so-called baby *sicarios*, whose incursion into the world of crime seems to occur at ever younger ages.[3] *La gorra*, a 2007 short film produced and performed by the residents of Dosquebradas, a municipality in the Risaralda Department and part of the Paisa region, shows the vicious cycle of violence and its effects on the youngest members of the community. Similarly, the 2010 Spanish documentary by David Beriain, *Baby Sicarios*, provides chilling testimonies of children from the Pereira slums willing to kill for a pittance. Beriain's film brought to light that one in every three homicides in the city is committed by a minor and that children are habitually employed by gangs because no one under the age of fourteen can be incarcerated for murder. The documentary sparked protests in Pereira, wherein journalists and the mayor's office accused the Spanish channel of conveniently stretching the truth to enhance the program's morbid allure. They questioned the production's veracity, in which underage interviewees claimed to have witnessed executions of policemen from the 1980s through the early 1990s, that is, prior to Escobar's death.

Pereiran detractors also accused the Spanish station of bribing the boys interned in the Center of Reeducation Marceliano Ossa with employment abroad in exchange for a juicy story. No protest however can erase the pandemonium of state and family neglect. Even with its commentator's far-fetched allegations—such that the telenovela *Sin tetas no hay paraíso* should be blamed for Pereira's social decline—the documentary substantiates a crisis in society, where children as young as six substitute toys for real guns, which they tote around with a chilling nonchalance.

Sicarios can be traced back to the so-called *pájaros*, spontaneous illegal gunmen of La Violencia period, who conducted massacres in rural communities across the nation, forcing survivors to seek shelter in the cities (Jácome 25–26; Ortiz Sarmiento). This onslaught transformed the Colombian landscape irrevocably by contributing to the rapid growth of hillside city slums. In *Our Lady of the Assassins*, Fernando Vallejo describes this decades-long legacy of murder:

> Humble folk who brought their customs with them from the countryside, customs like telling the rosary, drinking *aguardiente*, stealing from the guy next door and fighting to the death with machetes over peanuts. What could be born of such human splendor? More of the same. And more and more and more. And they've gone on killing each other over peanuts: after the machete came the knife and after the knife the bullet. (27)

Early marijuana capos from the Guajira region also employed private armies of killers called *gatilleros o pistolocos*, assassins on motorcycles whose job was to protect their bosses from competitors and traitors (Serrano Cadena 105). In the 1980s, *pistolocos* evolved into neighborhood groups of *sicarios*, whose job it was to eliminate public officials who dared challenge cocaine drug lords. Salazar, whose 1990 *Born to Die in Medellín* became an acclaimed study of their subculture, understood *sicario* violence as a revolt of the poor and the "only possibility of fulfilling their wishes and playing an active part in a society which has closed its doors to them" (J. Salazar, *Born to Die* 111). In his mind, *sicarios* were "simply the open sore, the external symptoms of an illness which afflicts the whole body of society. . . . They only become of interest when they strike at the nerve centers of power. If their violence is simply directed at each other, if it can be dismissed as a war within the poor neighborhoods, then the state and most sectors of society remain unconcerned" (Salazar, *Born to Die* 126–27).

This sympathetic perspective appeared in Víctor Gaviria's *Rodrigo D: No futuro*, his 1991 *El pelaíto que no duró nada*, and to some extent in Fernando Vallejo's *Our Lady* and Jorge Franco Ramos's *Rosario Tijeras*. Gaviria would explain to journalist Alma Guillermoprieto that for these youths, "who in their lives have never known the slightest power, delinquency is a way of looking for power" and that his interaction with them was "a dialogue that in reality was between the two cities that coexist in Medellín" (*The Heart That Bleeds* 104 and 103, respectively). In other words, Gaviria and Salazar reasoned that violent youth were the product of an unjust society and that their murderousness, which went hand in hand with vulnerability, resulting from a lack of opportunities. As Salazar commented to Guillermoprieto, "They all wanted so badly to find a place in the world" (*The Heart That Bleeds* 97). Like the older generations of *sicarios*, the newer ones seem to share what Salazar summed up as the myth "of war, of spectacular action and super-heroes that many of these youths have adopted as their ideal" (J. Salazar, *Born to Die* 120). Salazar attributed this attitude to the impact of global visual culture and particularly to Hollywood cinema, which provided the gullible dispossessed with make-believe combat imagery. It does not matter how soon you die; what matters is that you instill fear and become a legend. After all, heroes die young for their cause, even if that cause is as petty as a quick buck. Salazar's example, in *Born to Die in Medellín*, of a twelve-year-old boy's aspirations substantiates the sacrificial quality that shaped the fates of the youth from the Medellín slums:

> I'd like to be a killer, but I want me and my family to be respected. Just like Ratón, who has been shot now, but who was a guy who said nothing but killed anyone that stepped out of line. He would stand there with his 9mm pistol and if anyone stared at him he'd say: What are you staring at? And if they got cheeky he'd kill them, spit on them, and walk off laughing. That's how I'd like to be. (126)

Of course, these stories from Antioquia were not the only ones written on the subject of *sicarios*, but they were certainly the most disseminated, thereby becoming the standard for subsequent academic research.[4] The intellectual elite perpetuated the image of *sicarios* as yet another victim of a brutal, unforgiving environment and of indifferent state institutions. In fact, a significant gulf formed from the start between newspaper reports covering the real-life thugs and the sociological or literary take on them; fictional hitmen would bear noble if not redemptive characteristics that in turn converted them into a popular cultural referent among the readers and viewers of narco production.[5] Even more so, the existential vertigo that underscored their brief yet exhilarating lives granted them a cult status that is evident in how the portrait of Rosario Tijeras was later drawn and substantiated. Aside from depicting their hyperbolic violence, writers infused fictional *sicarios* with lives full of breathtaking passion, and the dance between Eros and Thanatos—so natural to their circumstances—has bestowed upon them the aura of the romantic sublime.

Medellín has come a long way since the 1980s, emerging as a showcase of successful urban planning and beautification projects that connected the neighborhoods perched on the hillsides with the rest of the city. The Metrocable of Santo Domingo, Park Arvi, and Biblioteca España increased Medellín's underprivileged dwellers' mobility and participation in city life.[6] Yet the *sicariato* as a phenomenon did not disappear, just as social inequality, which provided fertile ground for their emergence, remained in place. The battle between the two warring factions of the infamous Office of Envigado for control over Medellín's drug trafficking caused murders in the city to jump by 100 percent between 2008 and 2009 (Drost),[7] and in 2010 Medellín was again the deadliest city in Colombia, with a per capita murder rate double that of any other municipality. Again, the great majority of the victims were young men from the slums. In response to the unremitting violence, authorities attempted to stem motorcycle assassinations by requiring all motorcyclists to wear reflective vests and helmets displaying their license numbers. Then, in 2012, Medellín Mayor Aníbal Gaviria Correa signed a pilot law that forbade men (including male children) from riding as motorcycle passengers between 8 am and 10 pm (Robbins).[8] This prohibition was revoked in 2015 as a violation of the freedom of mobility of law-abiding citizens ("Prohibe"), but many cities or their parts imposed such laws (*restricción de parrillero*) as a response to persistent crime waves ("Ocho"). According to the Medellín police, since the law went into effect, "holdups of bank tellers diminished from 36 cases in November to four in December," and thefts and robberies decreased as well (Robbins). Yet the great majority of homicides committed in 2017 were carried out by killers on motorcycles, and *sicario* schools still exist in discreet fincas outside of the urban zones (V. Restrepo).

What the law does not prevent, however, is women's greater participation in crimes, spurred by gendered restrictions implemented by the state. Yet there seems to remain pervasive reluctance to accept female belligerence. The very title of Luis Noé Ochoa's 2004 article in *El Tiempo* says it all: "What's up with these women?" [¿Qué les pasa a las mujeres?]. Even though Ochoa cited the drastically rising number of women incarcerated for violent crimes—skyrocketing from 19,993 in 2002 to 28,913 in 2003—he still eroticized female aggression by stating humorously that "in 2003, the numbers rose like a miniskirt" [En 2003, la cifra subió como la minifalda] and that "now it can turn out deadly to say to a girl, rip my heart out" [ahora puede ser mortal decirle a una arráncame la vida]. These plays on words would never be applied to male offenders, and not just because of the miniskirts. What they corroborate is the persistent belief in women's innate docility, despite data to the contrary.

Violent Femmes—The Birth of Rosario Tijeras

Jorge Franco Ramos's second novel, *Rosario Tijeras*, winner of the 2000 Dashiell Hammett Award, catapulted the young author's literary career and made him and his eponymous heroine a household name in Colombia. It also initiated the myth of a female assassin from the hills of Medellín whose beauty, toughness, and vulnerability shed new light on the *sicario* subculture previously associated with men. Franco's fictional love story captivated the critics and the public, becoming another franchise in the panoply of narco best sellers with a telenovela and a feature film—Colombia's biggest box office success of 2005. The novel also became obligatory reading in Colombian high schools. Even Mario Vargas Llosa and Gabriel García Márquez, the two literary giants of the Boom era, applauded the book; García Márquez went as far as proclaiming Franco one of his literary successors. While the book and the film drew enormous attention, the 2010 telenovela experienced a somewhat different fate, in part owing to script changes and in part because by then, Colombian television had become significantly saturated with narco programs. What is certain is that Rosario Tijeras grew into an important element of the local folklore, powerful enough to overshadow both her creator and the actresses that stepped in to incarnate her.[9]

From the Colombian slums and the transnational culture of rough-and-tumble action films, Jorge Franco's Rosario Tijeras was born. She came to mesmerize the public with her body "full of vice, sex, bullets, pleasure, and pain," as Juanes sang in his 2005 hit that accompanied the cinematographic version of the story. One could deduce that she has proven more captivating than any real or fictional account of a male *sicario*, in part because her gender and her beauty allowed the resuscitation of female myths straight from Hollywood. A mixture of traditional femme fatale and modern "action chick," Rosario joins, irresistibly, global cultural mythology with local circumstances. She echoed the expanding pool of violent women in the global mass media while being tailored to the specific world of the *sicariato*; through her belligerence to a degree she subverted existing gender stereotypes and paved the road for the emergence of tough female literary characters.

The images of fierce heroines on television reflect the fact that women are defying the male monopoly on power and aggression, a shift that has significant ramifications for how gender is constructed. Such a transformation of gender roles is somewhat mitigated in stories involving revenge, for a desire to retaliate to some degree explains—if not justifies—the acts typically attributable to men. It also combines the two types of Hollywood dames in one explosive package: the femme fatale, who taunts men to their perdition, and the almost unwilling action heroine, who must resort to combat to do away with her oppressor. Classic rape-and-revenge movies, the subgenre of exploitation films most popular in the United States in the late 1970s, rework the structure of woman being raped, surviving the ordeal, and finally taking revenge on their male assailant(s). U.S. films such as *Lipstick* (1976), *The House by the Lake* (1976), *I Spit on Your Grave* (1978), *I Spit on Your Corpse, I Piss on Your Grave* (2001), or *Peppermint* (2018), for example, celebrate female fury over terrible abuses inflicted by men and the deadly revenge that the victims eventually unleash upon their wrongdoers. In the same vein, *¡Dispara!* (Spain, 1993) and *Baise-moi* (France, 2000) exalt female vigilantism, blurring the frontiers between seduction, coitus, and a deadly violence executed on aroused and unsuspecting males. The social avenger figure is also central to *Lola la trailera*, the 1983 Mexploitation film, which transformed the buxom actress Rosa

Gloria Chagoyán into an action film icon. In fact, despite its manifest kitsch, which made Lola hardly believable as an action heroine, the idea of an avenging warrior clad in campy tight suits was a precursor to Franco's Rosario.

Very different in its subject matter yet foregrounding female violence just the same was the highly popular television series *Mujeres asesinas* (Murderous Women), based on the 2000 best-selling trilogy by the Argentine criminologist Marisa Grinstein. Composed of real-life cases of women whose experiences or mental instability caused violence and the death drive to take over their minds, the book, converted into a television series, became a transnational franchise, garnering adaptations in Argentina, Mexico, Colombia, Ecuador, Spain, and Italy. Even though the message of the program underscores some form of victimization suffered by women—the primary condition for their release of fury—it simultaneously stylizes and trumpets female violence, exercised in the intimacy of their home. The success of the program and of the trilogy underscored the public fascination with dangerous femmes. The fact that they were somehow culturally "unnatural," even though criminal chronicles would tell a different story, added to the morbidity and sensationalism.

Crime narratives of the likes of *Mujeres asesinas* show that reality is often more brutal than fiction. Likewise, the violence that led to Colombia's sociopolitical decomposition bore gendered abuse, resistance, and transgression that in many cases superseded the gory fantasy of Hollywood exploitation films. Rape as a factor in domestic violence, as a weapon used to intimidate community members and exert control in gang confrontations, and finally as a practice of war employed by all armed groups and documented by human rights organizations has taught women that a tough demeanor is a necessary survival skill.[10] This refers to female *sicarias* as well. In preparation for her leading role in Emilio Maillé's 2005 film *Rosario Tijeras*, Flora Martínez visited the Buen Pastor prison in Bogotá, where she met with female assassins who shared with her their stories of domestic violence and repeated incidents of incest. One confessed that domestic abuse is precisely what allowed her to stomach the act of killing, in that it brought back rage and the subsequent desire to strike back at the ghosts of her past: "You psych yourself up to do it, you think of things that have hurt you" ("Rosario, cámara"). ["Uno se mentaliza para hacerlo, piensa en cosas que le han dolido" (my translation)].

Violence against women only intensified in Colombian barrios where drug trafficking made aggression and death an even more common occurrence. The 2016 testimonial novel *La cuadra*, by Gilmer Mesa, builds its entire premise around a rape-and-revenge scenario in a chilling first-hand account of growing up in the 1980s in the Medellín neighborhood of Aranjuez, ruled by Escobar's gang Los Priscos. Mesa describes the practice of "revolión," in which a presumably gentle boy seduces a pretty girl with the sole purpose of getting her alone and vulnerable. Naively counting on a romantic moment alone with her boyfriend, she would instead be raped and tortured by his entire gang while he stood by. Then she would be discarded like a used condom. Mesa's main story is that of the beautiful teenage Claudia, whose boyfriend, Denis, made her available to his entire gang in a vicious sexual attack that left her pregnant, broken, and shamed by all, including her family and neighbors. Fast-forward more than a decade, and it is Claudia's son, Denis, the product of that rape, who murders his own father at the age of thirteen. Before Denis's body is removed, the never-healed Claudia comes to whisper in the cadaver's ear, "See you in hell, my dear motherfucker" [nos vemos en el infierno, mi querido malparido 85], spilling out the hatred and resentment she had carried with her since the fateful attack. Unlike Rosario Tijeras, Claudia does not resort to violence in response to rape, but she brings up her son in a legacy of hatred that can only lead to annihilation—that of Denis, the father, and soon after, of her son himself.

In response to repeated questions about why *sicarios* and other gang members were so brutal to the neighborhood girls while adoring their mothers with an almost religious fervor, Mesa provides an insight that elucidates Escobar's relationship with his own mother and other women and such relationships among both real-life *sicarios* and fictional *sicarios* from novels and telenovelas. In his mind, one could blame some of the Medellín mothers for the ongoing violence, because they relentlessly stoked their sons' egos as they brought them up while simultaneously putting down women ["'pordebajean' a las demás mujeres," Jaramillo Zuluaga]. Thus, in this family dynamic, mothers turn a blind eye to their sons' patent criminality, and sons elevate their mothers to a status of sanctity. This mutual complicity allows both the outside dysfunction and the domestic affection to continue. This way, any and every woman outside the mother-son duo is an automatic intruder and, as such, ought to be destroyed (Caputo). One can only imagine the dangers facing girls from the *comunas* and the lack of support they receive, as was the case with the fictional Rosario Tijeras.

Unsurprisingly, the protagonist of Jorge Franco's story is by far the most volatile character, with the foundation of her fury—like that of Mesa's heroine, Claudia—deeply rooted in the sexual exploitation she suffered early in life. Now seemingly unconquerable, she handles both lipstick and bullets with equal ease. Antonio, the narrator (as well as Rosario's best friend and most fervent admirer), relates several episodes where his veneration intertwines with his simultaneous fear of Rosario's aggressiveness. Emilio, her wealthy boyfriend, and Rosario's delinquent friends from the Medellín slums are similarly apprehensive of her unpredictable outbursts of anger. Rosario works as a henchwoman for the drug mafia, readily carrying out orders to eliminate designated individuals. In her private time, she kills with equal effectiveness when she feels threatened, disrespected, or simply annoyed at the wrong moment.

Rosario's violence and her pervasiveness as an action heroine in the popular consciousness of Medellín would seem more characteristic of Hollywood productions and U.S. television series than of any real-life situations. Yet Franco's novel is presented in remarkably realistic settings, being the fruit of his research on women implicated in the Medellín *sicariato*.[11] Some critics argue that the novel moves away from the reality of male delinquency merely to articulate the perpetual masculine fantasy of the femme fatale, but Rosario has factual antecedents among the female population in Colombia, thereby calling attention to changing gender roles under volatile sociopolitical conditions. Documented female aggression not only complicates traditional Latin American gender dichotomies but also renders incomplete the practice of viewing women as unidimensionally passive.

Women in War/Gendered Violence

Following the insurrection sparked by the assassination of Jorge Eliécer Gaitán on April 9, 1948, violence has invaded all spheres of private and public life in Colombia. Epidemic criminality, social disarray, and impunity for those committing brutal acts forced both genders to confront the conflict. Some women took part in active combat, although most worked in support networks that sustained men in arms. During La Violencia, the confrontations were not limited to men producing principally masculine victims; sex crimes and murders of civilian women were a common practice, in part because "the combatants viewed women . . . as actual or potential procreators of the hated enemy" (Meertens 153). Since raping women would disrupt their function as the generator of life and bring shame to their men, perpetrators frequently sexually assaulted their victims in front of entire families for a bigger demoralizing effect (Roldán, *Blood and Fire* 12).

Moving ahead to the 1990s, while men continued to predominate as victims of violent acts, they held no monopoly on brutal deaths. Meertens notes the growing participation of young women in acts of violence; for instance, "in 1994, homicides of adolescent men (15–19 years old) represented 53 percent of the mortality of the age group, and homicides among adolescent women of the same age, where the increase was relatively more rapid, accounted for 19 percent of deaths, almost one-third the rate of men" (Meertens 156). Year after year, Amnesty International reports give chilling testimony of sexual violence against women and the impunity perpetrators enjoy, with incidents of gang rape and torture meted out as punishment for women's supposed collaboration with the guerrillas. The most egregious cases concern indigenous and Afro-descendant rural communities, which were forcibly displaced via sexual violence executed on both women and their children. The principal victims of the Revolutionary Armed Forces of Colombia (FARC) were girls between the ages of eleven and fifteen ("Las FARC"). Each front would recruit a number of female preteens destined for sex services to maintain the morale of guerrilla fighters. As punishment for perceived insubordination or attempts to flee, they were shot dead or raped by men infected with syphilis ("Las mujeres"). To prevent unwanted pregnancies, they were forced to abort each time or were ordered to use contraceptives at ages as young as ten. In other words, their initiation into sexual activity was early and violent, highlighting the ongoing instrumentalization of the female body in armed entities, even though women occupy their ranks nearly as often as men. Finally, scholars attribute the rise of femicide in Antioquia to women's growing role in illegal organizations. While their earlier involvement was sporadic, now they run the gamut of illicit businesses, arm in arm with their male counterparts (Arias).

To expose gender-specific violence and state-condoned impunity for perpetrators of sex crimes, women speak up, making the public aware of their suffering in contested regions of the country. Patricia Lara's collection of testimonies *Las mujeres en la guerra* (*Women in War*), winner of the 2000 *Premio Editorial Planeta* and adapted for the theater in 2001, recovered the voices of women widowed by war or implicated in armed conflict, as ex-combatants either for ELN, M-19, or FARC or for the various self-defense movements. Their confessions reveal that gender inequality persists even in circumstances where the male monopoly on physical strength and combat is threatened by equally capable women.

Liliana López, a FARC commander alias Olga Lucía Marín, related that the movement mirrored patriarchal Colombia in general, even though women constituted 40 percent of its ranks (Lara 115). She quoted the Eighth Conference, which proclaimed woman's freedom and equal rights in the guerrilla, rules that look good on paper but are another matter in practice, as men are still entitled to most of the decision-making. Speaking from her own experience, López concludes that to be respected women had no choice but to show a tough front and to affirm their power via traditionally "male" tools of aggression. A similar message comes from the female subjects interviewed for Salazar's 1993 *Mujeres de fuego*. Its narratives overlap with Lara's in that they include M-19 partisans, but they also feature judges involved in the prosecutions of the Medellín Cartel leaders, together with young women mixed up in *sicario* gangs and female militia fighters dedicated to "cleansing" local neighborhoods of homicidal youth. The accounts collected by Salazar are as noteworthy as Patricia Lara's testimonies of women at war, because they allow us to observe firsthand the shifting power relationships in a place where harsh living conditions forced women to take up new social roles based on confronting or executing violence. Each step in the direction of traditionally male territory seemed to be perceived as a threat to men, who, despite an outward open-mindedness, could not entirely set aside their patriarchal dogmatism. Thus, for example, María Eugenia Vásquez fought as an equal side by side with her M-19 male copartisans, yet when she married one of them, he demanded that she leave her political aspirations at the altar. Her militant past threatened the husband's sense of virility to the point where he needed to humiliate her to boost his own ego.

More damaging than familial discord about changing gender roles were premeditated rapes executed to convert the female body into a symbol of the disputed territory. Érika, a young woman associated with the *sicarios*, recalls how in her own neighborhood, rapes at one point became the vogue, and women were susceptible to attacks in the least expected situations. She especially remembers one individual whose eventual death was celebrated by all because, aside from robbing and killing, he had a habit of raiding local discotheques to violate female customers at his whim, in public view, and under threat of even worse punishment if the assaulted victims did not cooperate. Women learned that extreme precaution and sometimes outright belligerence were the only ways to potentially fend off aggressors, because rape went unpunished and was silenced, suppressed, and even normalized, thereby perpetuating the terrorizing and patriarchal oppression of women's bodies.[12]

Showcasing the lesson that the best defense is offence, Sandra, a member of the *sicariato*, did not shy away from acknowledging her volatile temper ("Whatever pops into my head I just do it; I don't care what people say," [Salazar, *Mujeres de fuego* 108]; my translation), proudly affirming her aggressive nature: "I have always been a fighter for whatever that's worth" (159). She admired an equally bellicose female companion, Gloria, who had taken up the killing business with a naturalness unfathomed by most women and who, eventually, died a brutal death herself: "She even killed her daughter's father because he acted like he was such a hot shit. You never knew what to expect from her; if anyone got in her way on the road, she'd take out her pistol and bam bam" (122). Salazar's testimonies are symptomatic of Colombia's evolving gender roles and confirm that women are gaining visibility in public and political spheres and that they express themselves through the "masculine" language of defiance and toughness. In fact, even ordinary housewives from the hills of Medellín often adopt aggression as a mechanism of survival. Doña Azucena, the mother of a *sicario* interviewed by Salazar, recalled her own penchant for open conflict, which emerged when she was a teenager and brutally attacked a teacher for having punished her unfairly in class. Accustomed since childhood to securing her turf by sheer force, she has lived by the sword and has inculcated the same attitude in all her sons, thus legitimizing further violence by aligning fear alongside respect. Like Patricia Lara's subjects, she learned that men's esteem can be gained exclusively by outshooting and out-brutalizing them, in other words, by beating the enemy at his own game. In fact, this lesson seems to have influenced all the women interviewed by Salazar. They portray toughness as a quality woven into the fabric of their everyday lives, borrowing the cockiness and emotional cool of the traditional macho man.

In the same vein, there emerged a curious model of female leadership,

exemplified by the Echeverry sisters from the Medellín slums. Characterized as emotionally tough and lacking fear (hence possessing a so-called
berraquera), the sisters were esteemed in their neighborhood as community leaders, even though they symbolized belligerence (the nickname
"butchers" was given to them for the pleasure they took in inflicting pain)
and were involved in drug-related violence as mules, drug-carriers, and
distributors. Riaño-Alcalá situates them in the category of "Amazon culture," a position that breaks gender stereotypes and invests women with
"masculine" notions of bravery (142). Not only does this construct prob-
lematize the old-fashioned dichotomy of hypervirility (machismo) and
female passivity and submissiveness (marianismo) associated with gender
roles in Latin America, but it also brings to the table the complexity of the
relationships between agency, gender, and violence, where victims and
victimizers could not be neatly divided along gender lines.

Scissors, Bullets, and Sexy Clothes: The Making of Rosario Tijeras

Like Salazar's female interlocutors hardened by their misogynistic surroundings, Jorge Franco's Rosario was forced to learn quickly the laws of
the urban jungle. She was raped repeatedly by one of her mother's transitory boyfriends at the tender age of eight and again, five years later, by a
member of a neighborhood gang. The 2005 film *Rosario Tijeras* shows her
early abuse in a veiled yet disturbing fashion. Seated at the kitchen table
with little Rosario, her stepfather is fingering the yoke of a fried egg, all
the while looking at her lasciviously. His body language is so sinister that
it leaves no room for doubts: Little Rosario is confronted with the other's
desire while her mother looks the other way.

While her negligent mother never accepted the girl's heartbreaking testimony, her *sicario* brother, Johnefe, avenged her by eliminating the first
rapist. He did not have to vindicate his little sister the second time around
because, by then, Rosario had learned to take matters into her own hands.
The heroine lured the next offender to her mother's house, stripped him
naked, then caressed and fondled him to relax him before her ultimate
revenge, attacking the unsuspecting aggressor with her mother's scissors
and cutting off his testicles. This shockingly brutal and sanguinary act
projects Rosario's future, marking the first time the heroine uses the double-edged sword of lethal seduction, in which succumbing to her charms
can (and usually does) result in the man's death. Her brutality remains

consistent with the previously discussed formulaic narrative of the rape-revenge genre, where women can be tough and manly only by having been previously broken by men.[13]

Exchanging her mother's scissors for a more lethal pistol, Rosario quite literally becomes the proverbial castrating bitch. She either cuts off men's testicles, shoots them in the chest while placing a final passionate kiss on their lips, or otherwise turns them into emasculated shadows of their former selves as they strive to gain some power in their relationship.

Socialized in crime and initiated in satanic rituals, Rosario does not hold a high opinion of institutions and regulations. Viewing all authority with utter disdain from her very early years, Rosario viciously attacks her teacher and is forever barred from school. Later on, she allegedly kills a man in one of her satanic gatherings for trying to force himself on her. She echoes the typical tough-minded and callous heroine who, as described by Jeffrey Brown, kills everyone who dares to objectify and act upon her sexual vulnerability. One such incident from the novel involves a male acquaintance who affronts her in a crowded bar. Rosario settles the matter then and there, by insisting on him kissing her while she mercilessly pumps a whole clip into his chest. This killing, the first one witnessed and described by the narrator Antonio, suggests a far greater scope of victims: males who remain anonymous in the text, cataloged rather than dwelled upon in the heroine's post-murder attacks of guilt.

This string of violent acts—committed, at least in Rosario's mind, for all the right reasons—depicts a heroine who is an outlaw, a renegade, and a menace to society. She seems to have risen above the law, since, historically, her only conceivable method of settling troubling issues, getting her message across, gaining respect, or avenging herself has always been murder. She simultaneously shocks and attracts both Antonio and Emilio, who come from the sheltered upbringings of well-to-do families. In fact, Emilio's amorous relationship with the *sicaria* is an act of temporary rebellion against his family's pampered lifestyle and their intention to groom him in their image. Rosario's ghetto background and her criminal occupation make her a terrifying pariah in the families' eyes, an intruder whose lack of pedigree cannot be hidden behind expensive clothes and a class-appropriate hairstyle. Ostracized by her boyfriend's family during a social event, Rosario lets off some steam by wishing she had gotten Emilio's mother's attention by chopping off her tongue with a meat cleaver. On a larger scale, her reaction can be interpreted as the wrath of the dispossessed, tired of invisible social class barriers that have locked them *ad perpetuam* on the fringes of society. To be sure, as the natural product of her peculiar surroundings, the heroine mirrors the Colombian women interviewed by Salazar; her pains, failures, and resulting inner resolve and fearlessness reflect the extraordinary *education sentimentale* of the tough ghetto women from Medellín. Rosario could be one and any of them, but her uniqueness ultimately lies in her sex appeal and in the extremes to which she has taken love and death in her entirely uncompromising way of dealing with the opposite sex.

In the course of Franco's novel, it becomes evident that Rosario is the one who "wears the pants" in each of her relationships with men, regardless of their status and character. She attracts men from all social classes and leads them on an exhilarating roller-coaster ride of danger and sublime pleasure, a challenge reserved for the most resilient: "We all liked Rosario, but Emilio was the only one who had the courage, because you've to admit, it wasn't just a matter of luck. It took guts to get involved with Rosario" (7). Her beloved brother Johnefe protects her from a distance, never interfering with her choices in personal relationships; her gang friend and former lover, Ferney, cannot but acquiesce with angry resignation when Rosario begins a long-term relationship with the former playboy Emilio; and finally Emilio and the narrator can weep and throw temper tantrums but ultimately have to accept Rosario's escapades with the powerful drug lords who come to finance her fancy new lifestyle.

Jorge Franco, who confirmed his fascination with formidable female characters in a number of interviews, argues that women *sicarias* turn out to be far more violent than their male counterparts. While hitmen can lean back on their mothers—the symbol of hope frequently conflated by them with the adored Virgin Mary—the dysfunctional family pattern of the *comunas* deprives girls of a father figure and, by extension, of God. This in turn alienates them even more, causing their wrath against society to be disconnected from consumerist drive, which has characterized male *sicarios*.

Gendering Toughness

Rosario crosses over into the traditionally masculine terrain of toughness with her explosive personality and penchant for immediate and brutal resolutions. Yet physically, she presents an ultrafeminine and highly eroticized physique. Though the author never provides a detailed physical description beyond her darker skin and provocative sexuality, it is easy to infer that Rosario forms part of the iconography of powerful and scantily clad babes packing weapons and giving orders. Antonio comments that "anybody could go crazy over Rosario" (Franco Ramos 16), and the novel itself is a tribute to her charisma but above all to her beauty.

Despite the economy of words, Rosario emerges as a modern woman whose body type and clothing respond to the modern standards of sultry "action chicks." She is athletic and toned, dressed in tight clothes that highlight her fit body, flat stomach, and perky breasts. Likewise, her fleshy lips mirror the ideal popularized by the Hollywood beauty standards of the 1990s:

> Out of smoke and the flashing lights . . . Rosario emerged like a futuristic Venus, with her knee-high black platform boots that raised her even higher than her dancer's pedestal, and her silvery miniskirt and neon green midriff top with tight sleeves. She had cinnamon skin, dark hair, white teeth, full lips, and as her eyes were closed, I imagined that it was her way of not being distracted from the music. (Franco Ramos 78)

Quintessentially womanly, her body overrides all the masculine connotations. She is rumored to be surgically enhanced, which in turn implies that her looks comply with the narco aesthetics of superbly voluptuous female beauty. Her complex and contradictory disposition emphasizes that she is remarkably expressive of emotions, a quality that only bolsters her status as a popular referent outside of the novel. Her fears, drives, insecurities, and desires seem to boil right beneath the surface of her skin, as if threatening to break through at any given moment. This passion and inner turmoil humanize Rosario, converting what could at first be perceived as a masculine fantasy of the ultimate femme fatale into an impressive reproduction of woman's complex nature in the very real circumstances of endemic violence. This very fusion of power and fragility and her emotional potential conflate the image of Rosario as a victimizer and a victim of her own circumstances, thereby mitigating if not exonerating her criminal actions.

Rosario demonstrates the same rich array of impulses that underwrite the hero genre's most characteristic men—simultaneously rational and reckless, decent and scandalous, vulnerable and callous. She thrives on open conflict, treating war as an essential component of life: "For Rosario the war was ecstasy, the realization of a dream, the detonation of her instincts. 'It really makes it worth living here, she said'" (Franco Ramos 67). Rosario exercises power and manipulates circumstances to her advantage, yet remains pronouncedly tortured and self-medicating to appease her inner demons. This inconsistency might echo Franco's research on *sicarias*, in which he discovered that, unlike the men who join gangs for fame or financial gain, women tend to get involved in crime to release their accumulated anger over witnessed violence and unhappy childhoods: "Whereas men decide to work in the drug business to get luxuries and excess, women do it to release their hatred, to get revenge, because of a growing rage which makes them kill" (Haw).

Though resolute and utterly unsentimental on the surface, Rosario does not shy away from exhibiting maudlin tastes typical of adolescent girls: "What I like is different, nice songs, love songs where you can understand what they're saying and where they say cool things" (Franco Ramos 72). Her iconic body exudes a superb femininity ("never before or after have I touched anything more real, more of the flesh, more beautiful," [72]), yet her daring and hard-as-nails character reveals her to be a domineering kingpin: "She always did what she wanted," because "nothing was tying Rosario down, not even the tough guys" (84). There is a degree of confusion between the two polarities of the typically feminine and masculine character traits in the novel, not only within the heroine but also in her relationships with others. At times, it seems that each gender adopts attributes of the other: masculinity (represented by Antonio, Emilio, and Rosario's old friends) comes to signal a greater vulnerability, whereas femininity (exemplified principally by the heroine) exhibits a greater emotional control. By conflating the notions of what is commonly perceived as the essential traits of manliness and womanliness, the novel creates characterizations that project an alternative image of both genders and their interrelation, rewriting the rules behind the gender-marked power plays. Rosario exposes with vivid clarity the complex uncertainties and the blurry instability of contemporary perceptions of gender and sexuality, and, as an embodiment of Jeffrey Brown's tough woman, "she personifies a unity of disparate traits in a single figure. She refutes any assumed belief in appropriate gender roles via an exaggerated use of those very roles" (49).

Sicario Culture, or Life Imitates Popular Art

Studying *Rosario Tijeras* through the prism of predominantly U.S. theory on action heroes in the mass media constitutes a cross-cultural and cross-media approach, yet though there exists an undeniably large gulf between Colombian reality and American pop culture, these two do meet in the global markets of neoliberalism. Young Colombians who enter a life of delinquency, for example, adopt the patterns of their volatile *modus vivendi* as much via Hollywood movies as through their daily experiences. Nowadays different aspects of culture intertwine and coalesce, demonstrating that global consumer society is a melting pot for both "high" and "popular" art. As Fredric Jameson notes, "aesthetic production today has become integrated into commodity production generally" (*Postmodernism* 4), where high literature, newspaper tabloids, independent movies, and above all formula-driven blockbusters are all grouped under a common denominator. Likewise, there is a considerable relationship between Rosario's persona and the North American mass culture industry, which has influenced the most remote regions of Latin America. This cross-cultural contact has been mutual of course, for the United States to a degree has internalized certain Hispanic standards, such as curvier female beauty promoted famously by Jennifer Lopez or Sofía Vergara.

Contemporary popular culture has had an integrating effect on its recipients from disparate parts of the globe and it has appealed to people's unfulfilled desires, seducing with what has never before been within their immediate reach. The concept of the popular, which, as Canclini argues, runs opposite to the phenomenon of folklore, arises not from what people are or have but from what originates elsewhere and becomes accessible via the global circulation of information (*Hybrid* 188). Yet Rosario Tijeras, an amalgam of changing standards of femininity à la Hollywood and of the idiosyncratic juvenile subculture of Medellín, has become almost immediately a part of Colombian folklore, thereby either erasing the bridge between Canclini's popular and folkloric, or indicating that Rosario has had enough real-life antecedents in Colombia to become such a powerful symbol of female combativeness within her nation.

Regarding the power of the media, the lack of constructive authority figures within the *sicario* community, a high level of illiteracy that has consecrated visual acculturation force-fed by television, and above all, the chance to possess through crime what global society deems desirable, have created an explosive concoction of consumerism and urban violence for reasons ever more trivial. For example, Wílmar from Fernando Vallejo's novel frames his consumer-driven dreams within a list of brand-name products: Reebok sneakers, Paco Rabanne jeans, a Honda motorcycle, a Mazda SUV, Calvin Klein underwear, and a Whirlpool refrigerator for his mother (F. Vallejo, *Our Lady* 99). This same refrigerator becomes his death sentence, as he falls victim to an ambush when trying to deliver the bulky present to his mother. The protagonist of *La gorra* loses his older brother in a brawl inspired by the main character's baseball cap, which is coveted by another thug. Likewise, an Xbox gaming system, a must-have among U.S. youth, becomes a pretext for a real-life murder among Pereiran slum children in Beriain's *Baby Sicarios*. What can be inferred from these senseless deaths is not only that products have grown to be the only conceivable signifier of happiness for *sicarios* but also that human lives themselves—both *sicarios*' lives and those of their victims—evolved into objects of economic transactions (J. Salazar, *Born to Die* 200).

In recent decades, visual images of tough action heroines have become a common reference point around the globe. Stepping down from the pedestal of Western-based comics and science fiction productions, they have become household names, making the lethal combination of physical attractiveness and danger a more readily palatable product. Rosario Tijeras belongs to the genre of tough chicks, yet at the same time, Franco's visceral presentation of a complex woman forced to fight bad luck and her own demons in the very specific circumstances of Escobar's war on the state and the chaos it unleashed on the *comunas*, and soon enough the rest of society, rescues the character from the dangers of cartoonish one-dimensionality. References to pop culture nonetheless stand out; in an interview for the movie, Flora Martínez, a Canadian actress of Colombian origin, assured readers that *her* Rosario Tijeras would possess "the ruthlessness of Hitler, the seduction of Marilyn Monroe, and the feistiness, the true Colombian-ness and authenticity of the Vendedora de Rosas" [la sin piedad de Hitler, la seducción de Marilyn Monroe y lo guerrero, lo colombiano y lo verdadero de la "Vendedora de rosas," (Moreno)]. She thus draws from an entire toolbox of transnational cultural references that conflate world evil, Hollywood sex appeal, and a sympathetic look at Colombia's social margins. María Fernanda Yepes found inspiration for the telenovela Rosario Tijeras in "the role of Marion Cotillard in *La Môme*, Jodie Foster in *Taxi Driver*, and Mallory Knox in *Natural Born Killers*, an

exquisite and seductive trio" ("María Fernanda"). For her part, Flora Martínez in a conversation with Freddy Canchón recurred to the language
of pop culture when denying the unidimensionality of her character: "I
won't be a Rosario Tijeras who resembles Nikita or Terminator . . . it's
more about utter sensitivity" [No seré una Rosario Tijeras que parezca
Nikita ni una Terminator . . . es más cuestión de sensibilidad pura (my
translation)]. The actress pinpointed the core qualities of her role through
the prism of popularly recognized action characters from U.S. mass culture. This motif returns once more when, in an article for *El País*, Ignacio
Echevarría portrays the novel's protagonist as a cross between Holly Go-
lightly (*Breakfast at Tiffany's*) and Bonnie Parker (*Bonnie and Clyde*), thus
emphasizing her conflicting fragility and belligerence. Evident in these
recurrent pop-cultural associations is the fact that Rosario Tijeras is a
markedly intertextual persona; she incarnates many things for many people, tapping into myriad cultural references and popular myths. Her rapid
entrance into the collective realm of what is popular makes her a perfect
representative of postmodern consumer culture, someone who, per Jameson's description, is almost impossible to understand "without the prior
interception of already acquired knowledge or doxa—something which
lends the text an extraordinary sense of déjà vu and a peculiar familiarity"
(*Postmodernism* 24).

Different Versions of Rosario

Of course, just like any successful literary character, Jorge Franco's textual
Rosario leaves a lot to the imagination, whereas televised renditions of his
heroine impose on the viewer a person of flesh and blood. The constraints
of each media, as well as the timing of each project, also affected the reception of the two versions. The 2005 film by the Mexican director Emilio
Maillé—a multinational production written by the Argentine Marcelo
Figueras, who also did the script for the 2000 blockbuster *Plata Quemada*,
and featuring the actors Flora Martínez, Spaniard Unax Ugalde (as Antonio), and Colombian Manolo Cardona (as Emilio)—was the first to put a
face on the iconic protagonist. It attracted enthusiastic reviews and record
audiences for a Colombian production, prompting the press to announce
that it was the first time Hollywood productions failed to overshadow a
local film. This event in turn gave a boost to the nation's self-esteem when
it comes to its cinematography, allowing a pair of films, the 2006 *Soñar no*

cuesta nada and the 2008 *Paraíso Travel* to garner an equally large audience, arguably on *Rosario Tijeras*'s coattails. But the trend was short-lived: by 2009, the national box office receipts were not even half of what they had been in 2006. Both the 2009 *El arriero* and 2009 *La pasión de Gabriel* attracted a meager two hundred thousand viewers each, just one-fifth of what Colombian blockbusters had managed a couple of years earlier. In contrast, Hollywood productions brought record numbers, more than two million in 2009, corroborating the low selling power of national films despite greater hype and investment.

Maillé built his version of the story around the actress Flora Martínez, whom he had imagined for the role even before casting the film. As the director recounted in interviews, Martínez channeled the "broken" quality of his heroine, making sexuality combined with a death wish both believable and heart-wrenching. Yet his fascination with the actress can be blamed for his one-sided interpretation of the *sicaria*, in which Martínez's trumpeted physical attributes and overplayed sex appeal froze Franco's multifaceted protagonist within the frame of a diluted femme fatale. Rather than displaying the complexities of Rosario's personality—a Colombian *berraquera* that allowed the reader to identify with her spunk in the first place—the film overplayed Rosario's generous curves, thereby objectifying the protagonist. Even though the actress received *La Biznaga de Plata* Award (Silver Cactus Flower) in the category of Best Actress at the 2006 Festival of Málaga, the box office success of the film and the critics' approval cannot hide the fact that Flora Martínez's Rosario for the most part strutted her sexuality at the expense of everything else. Whereas Franco's literary *sicaria* posed challenges to the masculine domain of violence, Maillé's heroine did little other than excite and sow discord among her men. Sure, she whacked a few of them in the process, but her fury and the barrage of incidents that made up her violent bildungsroman came through only as secondary themes, and hard-to-follow ones at that.

Maillé admits to focusing for the most part on the love triangle presented in Franco's book, but this triangulated desire spills beyond the three main characters in the story, converting the film into a display of erotic spectacle among the director, the male gaze of the camera, and the audience. The narrative's first scene takes place at a discotheque, where Emilio introduces Antonio to his new squeeze, and foregrounds the web of gazes while celebrating Rosario as a fetishistic male fantasy. Clad in a skimpy red dress, Flora Martínez sways sensually amid a backdrop of

Figure 13. Scene from Maillé's film, wherein Emilio and Antonio see Rosario for the first time.

nondescript youth, caressing her hair and sashaying for both the two men and the viewers. Her dance is more of a striptease, with the slow feline motions of a woman who knows that all eyes are on her.

Next comes a sexual encounter between Rosario and Emilio in the bathroom—the logical culmination of her enticing seduction on the dance floor. Rosario barely says anything but rather instinctively acts upon her sexual desires, thereby subscribing to the pornographic fantasy of a libidinous and available seductress who wastes no time on small talk. Minutes later, she kills a man in the same (busy) bathroom, placing a passionate kiss on his mouth before shooting him point-blank, an act provoked by the victim's disdainful remarks about her promiscuity. This is how her portrait as a sex-driven vixen is established and how it is consolidated later in the film: oscillating incessantly between sex and death, between nudity and murder, but always with the greater emphasis on the erotic.

Even critics who praised the film note the curious transformation of the protagonist, wherein Rosario's image becomes equated with an incessant bodily display, conveniently underdressed and staged before the ogling camera. One critic quips, "Rosario's extreme sexuality is so over-the-top—like a Latina Jessica Rabbit—that it threatens to topple the narrative into soft-core irrelevance" (Mack). Glen S. Close refers to Maillé's "shamelessly voyeuristic exploitation" of the actress's body (311), where "especially in

FLORA MARTÍNEZ   UNAX UGALDE   MANOLO CARDONA

ROSARIO TIJERAS

UNA MUJER QUE CIERRA LOS OJOS ANTES DE AMAR
Y LOS ABRE ANTES DE MATAR.

DVD

Figure 14. Racy box cover for the 2005 Emilio Maillé film *Rosario Tijeras*.

her cinematographic incarnation [Rosario] . . . is a *'sexual performance'* and bodily display for a male-operated camera and for an implicitly male spectatorial gaze" (312). Indeed, for no apparent reason, Martínez remains semi-dressed or straight-out naked through many scenes designed to un-veil the harsh realities of her life, thereby distracting the viewer from the serious content and veering attention to her voluptuousness.

This dissonance between the novel's plot and the film is fleshed out in the promotional poster that accompanied the film in Mexico, which seemed to promise soft-core pornography rather than insight into Colom-bian narco violence. Rosario's and Emilio's naked and somewhat blurry silhouettes are locked in an amorous embrace and spread out on a bed. He is reaching for her genitals while she holds on to him with an equally desirous gesture. As in the previous shot from the scene in the club, Rosa-rio's eyes are closed and her mouth sensuously semi open, thereby erasing any sign of her agenda beyond the erotic. The poster provoked criticism, and Flora Martínez felt obliged to publicly underscore the nation's double morality, where crime and corruption are found to be far less outrageous than skin. This being true, one may wonder why a story of love, rage, and murder, but, above all, action, has somehow been reduced to a murky semi-pornographic drama founded on one actress's seductive curves. A promotional film poster entices the audience with a single image that conveys the gist of the story. In this case, it is simply sex.

Nonetheless, gratuitous sex and nudity aside, the film reveals some interesting local color reflective of Medellín's drug culture during the 1980s. Viewers enter an exotic world of unpredictability alongside Antonio, a wealthy outsider allowed into the *comunas* through his relationship with Rosario. Noteworthy scenes include a morbid celebration surrounding the mourning of Johnefe and his burial, a ritual evocative of classic *sicario* funerals. Johnefe's body is taken to a bar where his buddies pour drinks straight into his mouth, fixed half-open owing to rigor mortis. Accompanying the booze and music, a stripper performs a final lap dance on the corpse, grinding her buttocks into his unfeeling private parts. Finally they drive the cadaver through the hilly barrios, blasting music from gigantic stereo equipment. He is sent off in style, like many others in the narco life who lived fast and died young.

At first glance, it would be tempting to conclude that with the exception of Johnefe's death, Medellín is de-emphasized in Maillé's film at the expense of rather generic interiors that take second stage to Martínez's physique. Yet some settings in the story prove the contrary. As the British actor Alex Cox recalls, in a number of scenes Maillé used a complex of four interconnected luxury apartments, which originally had belonged to a powerful Colombian drug lord now incarcerated in the United States. Playing the role of Donovan, a gringo capo, Cox had the opportunity to relax in the real-life kingpin's rooftop pools. He could also admire the priceless collection of modern art still hanging on the walls of the compound. Cox further explained that the staging for the film included a replica of a famous discotheque from the 1980s, *El Acuario*, where Maillé re-created a typical narco fiesta. Its particular touch was a requirement that everyone wear white, in tribute to the drug that made their hedonism possible. Finally, Medellín shantytowns were incorporated into various sections of the film, though some critics pointed out that the film treated the real-life *comunas* and its inhabitants as mere props (Jácome 183–84). Overall, the film enjoyed great popularity in Colombia, perhaps because the story of Rosario Tijeras was still new and perhaps because the nation was inspired knowing that this local/national topic attracted international interest.

The telenovela version of Franco's best seller drew criticism from a number of sources, illustrating the dangerous effects of overexposing the franchise ("La cruz"). In the media world, timing is everything, and the arrival of the 2010 *Rosario Tijeras* coincided with the market's saturation with narco productions. Both Caracol and RCN had been competing for greater audiences by releasing narco telenovelas; *El Capo, Sin tetas, La viuda de la mafia, Las muñecas de la mafia,* and *El cartel* (I and II) had assured a continuous supply of narco-themed entertainment, while the 2011 *Correo de inocentes* and 2012 *Escobar, el patrón del mal* were already in production. Another problem was the promotional slogan "It's easier to kill than love" [Matar es más fácil que amar], attached to the Rosario's name and plastered on billboards around the Medellín metro. Slogans or taglines serve to sum up and strengthen brand positioning (Gronlund 140), and in the case of Rosario Tijeras, they captured the essence of the narco brand with the female audience in mind. By juxtaposing murder and love, the catchy tagline worked through the shock value in that while rejecting "love," it nevertheless positioned love as the central dilemma. It proved to be a successful marketing move by generating criticism, thereby drawing attention to the product. Public outrage caused the Metro administration not only to remove the billboards and cancel its advertising contract with RCN but even to disallow filming the show on its premises. Even though the newspaper *El Colombiano* published scathing commentary seconded by hundreds of followers, the same department of Antioquia generated a 44.6 percent viewership (with 61 percent of its residents attending the premiere).

The 2010 telenovela by Carlos Gaviria and Rodrigo Lalinde took a different angle from those of the book and the film, focusing instead on Rosario's formative years as an assassin-to-be. In this sense, it became a prequel to Franco's original, even though its time span included Rosario's dramatic end. If the film—which, in its defense, suffered time constraints—focused on the three friends, with the marginal introduction of Rosario's neighborhood, the telenovela developed simultaneous worlds divided by social class and different geographical spaces within Medellín. The sweeping panoramic views of the city shift from *comunas* to the central Plaza Botero, visually marking the transition from the poor to the privileged. Yepes promised that her portrayal would be different from Flora Martínez's, and her Rosario was a girl-next-door, a *parcera* (buddy), whose life circumstances transformed her cheerful personality for the worse.

Dressed in a schoolgirl uniform for the greater part of the series (another fetish, but this time of a sexualized adolescent à la Lolita), Yepes's Rosario nevertheless captivated with her youthful innocence and later with her rage resulting from abuse and neglect. Of eight nominations for the 2011 Premios TVyNovelas, Yepes's Rosario won three, and similarly, the show collected four awards (of nine nominations) for the 2011 Premios India Catalina.

In the end, attention focused on the heroine's sexuality and her vulnerability may distract from the power she puts on display, but it cannot negate it. Nor can her underprivileged social status and untimely death pigeonhole Rosario as an overall victim of her circumstances and of Franco's story in particular.[14] True, she is a product of poverty and narco violence, a symbol of violent youth tainted and exploited by the cocaine cartels. And despite her sudden enrichment, she does not and cannot blend in with the traditional elite, failing, for example, to form a lasting bond with Emilio. Rosario also dies young, her bullet-ridden body exposed in its morbid near-death condition throughout most of the story, fulfilling the fate of a short-lived *sicaria* while her wealthy boy toys go on with their lives with varied degrees of success.[15] Finally, the glaring absence of a last name, compensated by her infamous nickname "Tijeras," suggests that the heroine is just another faceless, bastard child of a nation where the poor live and die in anonymity. Yet, defying all these truths, Rosario is anything but anonymous, having become instead a myth, a celebrity in her own right. She has proven so captivating that both the real-life residents of Medellín and tourists who know her story seek traces of her in the interstices of the hillside *barrios*, at times conflating her fictional character with a human of flesh and blood.

After all, cultural and literary protagonism has seldom been measured by a character's longevity or social status, underwriting instead the enormous impact they exert on their surroundings or the legacy they leave behind. In fact, heroes of Western civilization have principally been martyrs, destined for death in their prime to be useful in some ideological sense to their community. First, Rosario's incursion into the public sphere disrupted men's monopoly on aggression and visibility in the narco environment, all the while drawing attention to the female sector, whose fate was marked by the violence that has swept the nation. Constructed in the likeness of many real cases, Rosario has given a face to women who rebelled against their condition and fought like men's equals, either next to them or against them. Her fierceness became a paragon of Latin American "girl power," thereby expanding the traditional representation of womanhood in Colombian mass media. Her toughness and resolve have converted her into a curious if not contradictory role model among women, whose interest in naming their daughters after Rosario confirms the *sicaria's* allure. Additionally, Rosario's common origin made her an accessible, democratic heroine, the type more in tune with contemporary sensibilities trained on reality television, which privileges the proverbial everyman. In the same vein, her vulnerability and flawed personality have "humanized" her for the masses, who identify better with imperfect characters plagued by adversities. Uncommonly violent and beautiful, yet all the same the fruit of Medellín's *comunas*, she has become a popular referent in public discussions on Colombian drug trafficking, violence, and feminism. In this sense, Rosario has come to represent a powerful, easily recognizable symbol in Colombia's contemporary cultural referentiality.

The novel itself foregrounds Rosario's mythical status from the start by applying legend-building mechanisms both in the heroine's intimate relations and in broader images involving the entire community. Antonio, as well as Emilio, consider her superhuman in that she delivers death and yet herself is seemingly immune to danger, as if she wore a bullet-proof vest under her skin (Franco Ramos 6–7). Made of different stuff than the rest of humanity, Rosario's blood courses through her veins full of venom that entices men and leads to their perdition (7). In fact, everything associated with Rosario is enhanced, extraordinary, and hyperbolic, setting her apart from other women and putting her on a pedestal. Antonio recounts how she showed him the suicidal side of love, taught him that the greatest passion turned daily existence mundane, made him lose his mind, and made him live hanging on her every whim (88). This veneration is not limited to her close circle of admirers, for even simple people from the *comunas* murmur that she, rather than Pablo Escobar, should become the leader of the Medellín Cartel. She is the talk of the town and a living legend augmented via countless rumors that perpetuate her extraordinary status:

Rosario Tijeras has become an idol in the neighborhoods of Medellín. On walls you'd see "Rosario Tijeras, Sweet Mama," "Castrate me
with your kisses, Rosario T.," . . . Girls wanted to be like her, and
we heard of several who were baptized María del Rosario, Claudia
Rosario, Leidy Rosario, and one day our Rosario told us about an
Amparo Tijeras. Her story took on the same proportion of reality
and fiction as that of her bosses. (73)

In the original story, she leaves an everlasting impression on anyone who
crosses her path. She stands her ground and knows how to speak for herself. She goes head to head with the toughest of men and beats them at their
game while retaining the most salient female qualities, such as physical
beauty and extraordinary vulnerability. She rejects the customary codes
that contain female deviance and potential criminality by being as tough
as any man and by executing her own justice with the brutal effectiveness
of the most cold-blooded gangster. She revels in warfare and open conflict, proving with her actions that women can be callous, resolved, inured
to hardship, and profoundly feminine at the same time. Temperamental
and uninhibited, Rosario disturbs entrenched ideas about women's traditional passivity and composure, simultaneously corroborating a shift in
gender roles as she crosses over into the traditionally masculine terrain of
toughness. The literal embodiment of male castration anxieties, Rosario
responds to decades of all-encompassing terror and disorder in Colombia
with an outburst of formidable female fury. It is in this sense that María
Fernanda Yepes sees Rosario as a true female heroine "not because she
kills, but because in some way she has affirmed her rights and what she
has wanted in life, not allowing any obstacles deter her from her goals"
("Debemos"; my translation).

"Girl power" governs yet another version of Rosario Tijeras, but this
time in a 2016 Mexican telenovela that transports the story to the rough
neighborhoods of Mexico City. Played by Bárbara de Regil, this Rosario is a "strong, very confident, and hardened woman" (Barrera) who, as
El Tiempo claims, "has no need to be validated by the rich or to escape
her world" ("Estrenarán"; my translation). The Mexican soap, it affirms,
"does not instigate impoverished women to move to a princely mansion,"
and thus it advocates for "female empowerment" and "women's inner
strength" ("Estrenarán"). Issues of social class and female toughness are
at play in this version of Rosario's life, wherein being from the "hood" is a

virtue in itself, as it affords the female warrior cachet. Curiously, this Colombian transplant on Mexican soil promises to deliver "a more human" Rosario who, unlike her Colombian version, "does not have a beef with her mother." It appears that de Regil promotes her version by appealing to Mexican family values (presumably more upstanding than Colombian?) when she states that "Mexico is different and she [original Rosario] had something ugly going on with her mom, and our country is not like that" (Barrera). Thus, overall toughness translates well from one country to the next, but, curiously, motherhood seems more sacred to bourgeois Mexican audiences.

Returning to the Colombian context, Rosario is definitely not just a product of Franco's imagination or childhood memories of the narco boom of the 1980s, disconnected from contemporary Colombian womanhood. Yepes sees Rosario as a symbol of all women who suffered the consequences of the war and the drug trafficking violence in Colombia. "Her" Rosario stands for the woman of a *narcotraficante*, his daughter, his mother, anyone whose life crossed paths with drug trafficking ("Debemos"). So irreducibly human, she increasingly distances herself from the category of the merely fictional, beginning to exist outside of the realm allotted to her in the first place, and this goes beyond Mexican TV.

In a curious way, Franco's fiction has crossed over into reality. This phenomenon reflects Baudrillard's third order of simulacra, when no longer is the simulacrum a counterfeit or a series infinitely reproducible but, instead, the postmodern simulacrum becomes reality itself. It is here where the very concept of the true copy is dispensed with. In an interview with Luz María Rivera, Franco talks about the effect his fictional character has had on the public, therein substantiating Rosario's transition to the world of the real: "As a result of [the novel's] publication, the Colombian media uses the label Rosario Tijeras when referring to girls who, like the protagonist, live from day to day, killing for hire and surviving in a world which buries them in drugs." Young women evoke Rosario's name to either pledge their allegiance to the violent femmes or, conversely, to proclaim their nonviolent stance despite adverse conditions that could have pushed them over the edge. Some references to the volatile heroine are aimed at intriguing and enticing the public. The publicity folder for the 2009 *La Fiesta del Libro y la Cultura* in Medellín promised its visitors a spontaneous encounter with various Rosarios Tijeras who would surely frequent the event. Of course, this promotional trick exploited Rosario's charm as a high school girl, a Lolita with an edge who hides a barrage of experiences beneath her youthful appearance.

On the whole, Rosario's fictional origins become less and less apparent as tourists insist on seeking out her tomb in the old San Pedro Cemetery, hoping to prove that the *sicaria* did exist (Mora Meléndez). Even Rosario's childhood home, created for the purposes of the 2010 telenovela, has become an object of pilgrimages. The inhabitants of the *comuna* Manrique, which served as Rosario's home, observed with excitement how the street where Doña Rubi's house was erected filled with a continuous stream of visitors. The owner of a small store featured in the series decided to change its name to Rosario Tijeras ("El nuevo"). Jameson has spoken about postmodern fascination with the surface as one of its main constituents. Likewise, these replicas or traces of Rosario created for the purpose of the series yet quickly adopted into the living experience of the community supersede ontological hierarchies that privilege originals over replicas. Then again, what is the original here if not just a figment of Franco's imagination, a figment that found a fertile ground among the consumers of narco narratives and grew to be so pervasive that it became real? Postmodern experience is a simulated one, the real is dead (says Baudrillard), and the Death of the Real inspires a proliferation of myths of origin that create a mere model of what "an original" story of Rosario should look like. In light of such nostalgic attempts to resurrect the real in the present-day hyperreality, looking for Rosario's tomb, even if she never existed in the first place, seems to make perfect sense to the seekers of Rosario's imprint on Medellín.

EPILOGUE

Escobar's Global Brand

Pablo Escobar es el Hamlet de los actores hispanos.
[Pablo Escobar is the Hamlet of Hispanic actors.]

Benicio Del Toro (Ayuso)

What makes one story more captivating than another, and why are some so effective in branding techniques? Studies in business and marketing remind us that our brains are hardwired for narrative and that we interpret every aspect of our lives through stories. Frequently, a good story determines whether the brand will flourish or flop, and character-driven storytelling peaks the public's interest instantly, as it entices people to go the extra mile to build a genuine connection with the brand. This is because consumers of both products and entertainment tend to connect emotionally to certain narratives as a way to interpret their own lives. In the process of transforming stories into products of economic value, "crime and violence have become objectified and commodified and, as such, much desired whilst being distributed through various forms of media to be pleasurably consumed" (Presdee 59). In the same vein, Escobar's multiple transgressions as a bona fide Outlaw resonate in the collective subconscious of the audience.

A two-year content analysis of the most effective Super Bowl commercials conducted by a Johns Hopkins researcher proves that, rather than sex and humor, it is the dramatic plotlines that draw the largest crowds: plots with the same story arcs Shakespeare used and characterized by clear exposition, rising action, climax, falling action, and denouement (Rosen). As for the content, aside from a familiar dramatic arc, a good story for a brand needs to be unique, personal, emotional, simple, and authentic. There is thus a direct correlation between the copious raw material for entertainment available in Escobar's life trajectory and how his brand story has been successfully incorporated into the lives of new generations of consumers worldwide, from elements as basic as his moustache and floppy hairdo to aspects of human nature as complex as desire and transgression. The cultural wealth of Escobar-themed products projects the zeitgeist of the narco universe: high on adrenaline, consumer-oriented, capitalist, amoral, and hedonistic. Of course, it is barely real; it is re-created and thus imagined, spawning many different Escobars. It features gaudy fashions, busty trophy women, *sicarios* and *sicarias*, youths willing to die or prostitute themselves for brief moments of consumer *jouissance,* and, above all, plenty of action. The variety of Escobar-as-a-cultural-product provides fodder for a cornucopia of stimulating tales. Either earnest or laced with humor, they all manifest the dark side of humanity (e.g., pride, rebellion, greed, audacity, and wrath) played out either on a personal or a (trans)national scale. Each and every fragment of his life, his relationships, and the mayhem he caused constitute potential stories unto themselves. Escobar casts an ever-longer shadow, not only bringing together the slew of characters and practices from Colombia's terrifying collision with the narco that I have discussed here but also, more surprisingly perhaps, inspiring bizarre emulations and commodities, from bars, burger joints, and ice-cream shops to Escobar-themed bathroom rugs and kids' apparel.

On the subject of stories vis-à-vis Escobar, Rincón sarcastically notes that there is more dignity and truth to the narcos than to Colombia's politicians and that the capo embodies the dark side of the national character; audiences enjoy narco soaps like *Escobar, el patrón del mal,* because they can identify with so many issues they raise. While Colombians have a conflicted relationship with narcocultural production, it is no wonder that for other nations Escobar's life story enthralls with its concentration of action and exoticism : "It is awesome to watch this narco world, and it's fun to be scandalized with their lifestyle where anything goes, their silicone women, their abusive men, their aesthetics, slang, and popular music" (Rincón, "Amamos a Pablo" 100). [Es una gozada mirar ese mundo de los narcos y es divertido escandalizarse con su ética del todo vale, sus mujeres silicona, sus hombres abusadores, sus estéticas, lenguajes y músicas populares (my translation)]. The popularity of *Escobar, el patrón del mal* has brought new cultural tendencies to Colombian society, from music (the narcocorridos of Jorge Santa Cruz or the Hermanos Ariza) to "narco philosophy." Some of the capo's sayings in the version popularized by Andrés Parra have become part of the popular lexicon in Colombia, and the ones I provide here are but a fraction of it: "Think like you're poor and you will remain poor" [Piensa como pobre y vivirás como pobre]; "A dog with money is Mister Dog for you" [Al perro que tiene dinero se le dice 'Señor Perro']; "It makes no sense to make the rich richer" [No tiene sentido seguir haciendo a los ricos más ricos]; "Everything dangerous turns into money" [Todo lo peligroso se convierte en plata]; or "There are three ways of getting things done, well, badly, or the way I do them" [Hay tres maneras de hacer las cosas: bien, mal y como las hago yo] (Rincón, "Amamos a Pablo" 98). Whereas Rincón uses the word "brand" only in the more traditional context of the Escobar-themed T-shirts sold by Marroquín, what he points to is a far larger phenomenon with the well-defined footprint I have explored in this book.

Escobar, el patrón del mal was just the beginning of the capo's mediatic exposure, for his brand eventually reached a transnational audience with the 2014 film *Escobar: Paradise Lost*, directed by Andrea Di Stefano; the 2015 *Narcos*; and the 2017 *Loving Pablo*, by Fernando León de Aranoa. The first two productions by non-Colombians apply an unmistakably Anglo perspective to the stories, with Escobar—and Colombia by extension— portrayed as the exotic Other. Directed by the Brazilian José Padilha, *Narcos* came with a focus familiar to U.S. viewers: that of U.S. intervention abroad, where idealistic agents of the law battle an unfamiliar evil in an oversize gangster tale. The voice-over of DEA agent Steve Murphy (Boyd Holbrook) guides the viewer through shadowy albeit alluring forces that create a captivating backdrop. Although the very first scenes address Washington's covert ties to Augusto Pinochet's brutal dictatorship in Chile and its involvement in overthrowing the nation's socialist president Salvador Allende, this nuanced angle promptly morphs into the cultural imperialism that permeates the series—an imperialism undeterred by the liberal use of subtitled Spanish. The bumbling bureaucratic system that backed up Pinochet from within the U.S. government is now blind to the growing narco problem in the Americas, focusing instead stubbornly on the threat of Communism spreading through the guerrilla movements. In contrast, Murphy—a greenhorn DEA agent more accustomed to chasing Miami marijuana dealers in flip-flops than diehard narcos in Colombia—quickly cuts through all the bureaucratic nonsense to impart justice, even if it means playing by his own rules. He learns the ins and outs from his bilingual DEA partner Javier Peña, who himself is too iconoclastic to play the good guy. Though bent on destroying the narcos, Peña inhabits the underworld with too much ease, bedding attractive informants and hanging out with lowlifes. Isolated from such influences (largely due to his shaky Spanish skills), Murphy begins his own crusade, sidestepping the inept U.S. bureaucrats, who throw infinite resources down the proverbial rat hole. Thus, Murphy smugly interprets Colombian reality to the audiences with a narrative arch caught between exoticism and moralizing rhetoric, an approach that reifies the cultural differences between the Global South and North. He evolves into the "Dirty Harry" of the story, progressively becoming a law unto himself. Yet his own eventual "Colombianization" has far more to do with embracing violence than acclimatizing to a new culture.

A superimposed text at the beginning of each *Narcos* episode announces how magical realism is the natural consequence of the Colombian condition, yet one suspects this has less to do with García Márquez than with a "stranger than fiction" Anglo viewpoint. Weaving together the historical footage of a docudrama with the bravado of an action film, *Narcos* provides a somewhat false sense of cultural accuracy for a public with little exposure to Latin America. Its simplistic take on Colombian reality paints the country as enchanting yet corrupt beyond repair—the savage South seen through the eyes of the uncompromising and principled North. The reassuringly monolingual agent Murphy somehow finds himself present wherever the "real" action takes place: He rescues prostitutes, eliminates Escobar's *sicarios*, and even takes home an orphaned Colombian baby whose young parents are liquidated by Escobar's thugs. This is how the series confirms the U.S. hegemony in the Americas. Free from the restrictions imposed on common citizens, the maverick Murphy channels the Hollywood trope of the lone gunman: America's celebration of exceptionalism, individualism, and a big, powerful pistol. It approves of the U.S. foreign policy, its powers of surveillance, and its ascendance in global drug policy. Thus, its conceptual lesson confirms Gootenberg's preoccupation regarding today's ideologies of the North that stigmatize coca producers while whitewashing the buyers (314). The series reinforces the highly militarizing U.S.-led campaign against Colombian coca, validates the permanent U.S. antidrug bureaucracy, and justifies its full-scale eradication campaigns. Americans appear to be the crusaders of the right cause, but the fact that the cocaine consumer market is thriving in the United States, home to half its global clients, is not addressed.

But this book is about Pablo Escobar, as is the *Narcos* series. Seasons 1 and 2 would have little to offer if not for the Escobar brand. Like Satan in John Milton's *Paradise Lost*, Escobar is by far the most intriguing character. The show's theme song—a sensual Latin melody called "Tuyo" by Rodrigo Amarante—embeds in the minds of the viewers not only Escobar's centrality in the show but also the complexity of his character, wherein sentimentality and boundless ambition go hand in hand, thus creating a dramatic tension. The passionate lyrics subtly convey the Story Universe that *this* Escobar will deliver. With lyrics like: "I am the fire that burns your skin" [Soy el fuego que arde tu piel] and "I am the water that quenches your thirst" [Soy el agua que mata tu sed], or—when addressing his loved one—"And you say, what whims will you fulfill? My dear, just look at it, and it will be yours" [Y cuáles deseos me vas a dar, oh / Dices tú, mi tesoro basta con mirarlo / Y tuyo será, y tuyo será], the megalomaniac Escobar appears to be a romantic with longings of uncommon intensity. Amarante's approach when writing the captivating tune is the key to understanding his take on Escobar:

> [I sought] to humanize Pablo by writing a song that seemed like a view from the inside of the character, rather than a view from the outside. I had this idea to write a song that was his mother's favorite when he was a kid, something that would influence his idea of the man that he would like to be. . . . I wanted to deliver something romantic and deceivingly generous but if you listen to the lyrics you see that there's a narcissistic point of view. All of those men were all children at one point, so in my head the song gives the viewer a bit of context, rather than just saying, "Oh, these guys are animals." I think there's more to it. . . . The only reason to tell the story of a monster is to reveal the monsters that we ourselves have [within us]. (Romero)

Narcos's Escobar is an impassioned villain who was once innocent and well-intentioned—read: like the rest of us. Played by the Brazilian Wagner Moura, he is more nuanced and charismatic than his opponents on the "good" side of the law. His self-envisioned grandeur is buttressed by the very structure of the show, in that the visual opening sequences communicate the unbreakable bond between Escobar and Colombian history. Historical (genuine) footage of Hacienda Nápoles borrowed from

Escobar's home videos is intermixed with sweeping airplane shots of the rainforests that housed his drug labs and images of Escobar's terrorist acts against the state. They position the capo as a culturally pervasive entity, a one-man force strong enough to challenge entire nations—the United States as well as Colombia. In America, "heroes often have a slightly rebellious quality to them, and Outlaws—at least the ones people like—carry on the wilder, more rambunctious qualities of American life without actually undermining the society" (Mark and Pearson 103). Escobar is not an American outlaw, nor was he complacent with the state, of course, but his extreme individualism and nuanced morality can appeal to a U.S. audience accustomed to imperfect nonconformists on the screen. In some twisted way, his brazen attitude and business acumen reflect a darker side of the American Dream.

The second season of *Narcos*, and in particular its final episodes leading to Escobar's death, center on the precipitous decline of a man who fell from the summit to the proverbial rock bottom. Impassive and distant, the now powerless capo delves into the deepest human emotions, such as loneliness and despair. This human dimension of the monster reveals itself predominantly in his body language: heavy shoulders, a disheveled appearance, and desperation in his eyes. Betrayed by his former partners-in-crime and cornered by countless enemies, Escobar becomes introspective and much more vulnerable, even exhibiting gestures of tenderness. He obsessively calls his wife only to hear her voice and tell her how much he loves her. When he must abandon one of his safe houses in the countryside, he releases his pet rabbit to its natural environment, knowing that the animal can no longer be protected. As he watches the animal hop away, the audience knows that he wishes he himself could just disappear. Moura's capo always reveals more through his sighs than in words: It is evident that he regrets many decisions that deprived him of the simplest pleasures in life, most of all the freedom of anonymity.

There are two scenes in particular that illustrate Escobar's state of mind and his awareness that the game is up. The final episodes forgo action-driven scenes for prolonged moments of stillness, underscoring the mood that the capo is tired of running and instead is waiting for his doom. Yet he still has brief illusions of undoing everything and doing it right this time, either by living the simple life of a *campesino* (the proverbial *beatus ille*) or by vanishing into Medellín's urban anonymity. At one point, he visits the father he barely knows and whose farmer lifestyle had never appealed to him. In one of their few conversations (since the father is even more circumspect than the son), Escobar lays out his plan of buying a ranch next door and bringing the family to live happily ever after. Yet the father refuses to play into his son's fantasy, and the two remain uncomfortably silent for a while, until Escobar confronts the man and they end up in an argument. This failed attempt to reconnect with his impassible progenitor and their final goodbye devoid of any affection provoke the viewers' sympathy for the wayward son.

Soon after, when on his final birthday Escobar can no longer stand the enclosure and isolation of his Medellín safe house, he walks outside, takes off his sunglasses, and sits in a busy square to enjoy what others take for granted: the ruckus of street life. Through the slow-motion lens, we see what the smiling capo is looking at: children playing, fathers teaching their kids to ride a bicycle, and old men chatting. In contrast, Escobar is already a dead man, a ghost of his former self. Stripped of power and abandoned by friends, he is savoring what his boundless ambition had irrevocably taken away. The emphasis the series puts on Escobar's prolonged goodbye to his family and beloved city romanticizes and humanizes him, thereby weakening the Yanqui ideology that is so pronounced in the first season. Despite his obvious monstrosity, Escobar is an endearing character, perhaps the most touching of the entire series.

If Escobar's arrogance in *Narcos* is a significant part of his persona, it becomes a quality of biblical proportions in Di Stefano's *Escobar: Paradise Lost*, a narco-fueled retelling of Milton's epic. Here, the lush Colombia of beautiful beaches and equally attractive women first emerges as Eden, attained by two Canadian brothers, of whom one (Nick, played by Josh Hutcherson) is the protagonist. Escobar, played by the iconic Benicio Del Toro, predictably channels Satan, the principal crusader against God and humanity. Full of overweening self-confidence and pride, this Adversary of God is an ominous presence lurking behind the facade of patriarch, caudillo, and public do-gooder. He enslaves his followers with a seductive pitch of social equality and charity, yet his real, utterly self-serving and malevolent intentions eventually come to the surface, dragging everyone involved to their damnation and death. Arguably, this was the first time Escobar has been played by an A-list actor, whose Hollywood stardom is a brand in itself. The audience will not wonder how authentic his Escobar may appear but whether Del Toro will shine or fail in the role. The actor delivers a convincing portrayal of a deeply nefarious man whose presence on the screen makes the audience feel uneasy, even (or especially) when he shows his occasional avuncular side. Del Toro's Escobar is the most sinister rendition to date, evidenced by how he destroys the two brothers' mellow surfer-dude existence and, in the process, his own adoring niece's happiness, just to accomplish his nefarious plans. There is a historical mark contextualizing Di Stefano's tale somewhere between the public unearthing of Escobar's true sources of wealth (and thus his expulsion from politics) and the capo's decision to turn himself in to the state (the Catedral incident). While the tragic love story between Nick and Escobar's niece María is fictitious, its denouement serves as a canvas for Escobar's bottomless monstrosity. He has no loyalties, morals, or empathy, and he adjusts his codes of human conduct to his own narcissistic universe alone. Unrepentant and obsessed with power to the very end, he makes threats to God before accepting his incarceration, warning that he will be watching the Maker from his new tower in the hills of Medellín. As the delusional creator of his own reality, he—like Milton's Satan—consciously chooses to reign in Hell rather than bequeath his power to Heaven. This Escobar is the ultimate evil, tantalizing and terrifying at the same time.

Javier Bardem's rendition of the capo in *Loving Pablo* hypnotizes with a similar, seemingly incongruent mixture of affection (for his daughter in particular) and terror (for all others). The storyline follows Virginia Vallejo's memoir, her encounter with Escobar, their romance, the fallout, and the terrible consequences of a love affair that destroyed her career and put her life in danger. Yet even though the film is narrated by the heroine in an English-language voiceover, Penélope Cruz's Vallejo has little to perform other than to parade her perennial beauty and 1980s fashion. The title promises love, suggesting a focus on their romance, but the disjointed scenes of their interactions only punctuate what ends up being a conventional biopic centered on the public Escobar, with the usual rise-and-fall narrative arc. What could have been a glimpse into the private Escobar as seen through the eyes of his lover is, in the end, swept under the carpet by a panoramic run-of-the-mill approach.

Nonetheless, Bardem's Escobar appears magnetic, consciously drawn by the actor from what he observed as a dichotomy of energies in the documentary footage. Bardem focused principally on the capo's "notoriously quiet but deadly demeanor" (Castillo), that is, his overwhelmingly static body language (the protagonist barely moves, speaks quietly and never excitedly, and remains impassive physically and emotionally), juxtaposed against his quick and unpredictable acts of violence. Bardem frequently speaks of how he visualized Escobar as one of his pet hippopotamuses, slow-paced and heavy on the surface but cold-blooded and aggressive beyond belief. These characteristics liken the capo to a predator who lies low only to conserve his energy and strike when needed. Indeed, Bardem's Escobar puts the viewer ill at ease with his bulky physical essence, a seemingly delayed way of reacting to all circumstances, and a permanently broody disposition. There is one scene in particular wherein Bardem's Escobar appears no different from the hippos, as he slowly emerges from under the water in his pool to take a puff off a doobie, his massive frame taking over the screen space, his eyes barely blinking: a force of nature to be reckoned with. Both Bardem and Del Toro speak with enthusiasm about playing Escobar, whose life circumstances and range of evil are an ideal canvas for any actor's virtuosity, in a story as unique as it is memorable.

There are a couple of unforgettable scenes in *Loving Pablo*, which, for some critics only highlight the film's problematic focus on form over content, on delivering disjointed episodes that fail to form a cohesive entirety. Early in the movie, a steady flow of traffic on a 1982 Miami highway is abruptly brought to a halt when two semis suddenly park sideways to convert the road in front of them into a landing strip for a cocaine delivery. People try to protest, but gun-waving Colombian thugs force everyone into obedience. Dumbfounded drivers (cops included) look in disbelief as a massive plane almost brushes against the tops of their cars before it lands. Cocaine is unloaded in a matter of minutes right onto the pavement, and buyers rush into oncoming traffic to quickly pick up the goods. Some die, hit by cars, and some packages are ripped open, coating the oncoming traffic in white powder, but in a matter of minutes the traffic resumes as if nothing has happened. This is a metaphor for Miami's Wild West era: the most bizarre and outlandish occurrences that brought cocaine cowboys to America's attention. Overall, the film did not fare well; critics thought it clichéd, confused, and contrived, with Escobar's frequently exposed gut doing most of the acting (D'Angelo). Some saw what this movie could have been, had the script actually focused on the lovers (Minow).[1] The very love story seemed unconvincing to many, who found Penélope Cruz's voiceover and her accent irritating and the two protagonists unlikeable. In the film's defense, the sheer volume of Escobar-themed productions has raised audience expectations for a more unique angle. Had this film come out a decade earlier, it might have been received with more enthusiasm.

Not all the renditions of Escobar have been earnest. As elsewhere in Latin America, the 2012 telenovela *Escobar, el patrón del mal* became a smash hit in Chile, so much so that the celebrated comedian Cristián Henríquez created a successful persona based on the capo for the variety show "Morandé con Compañía." Like today's Escobar-like taxi drivers in Medellín, Henríquez based his comic character not on the historical figure of Escobar but specifically on the Escobar played by Andrés Parra. In other words, he drew his humor from Parra's fictional creation, in a representational mise en abyme. Just as Parra attempted to emulate the real Escobar's mannerisms and voice by researching the available audio-visual material of the capo, Henríquez's capo is even more hyperbolic. Thus, when it comes to his body language and vocal/verbal mannerisms, Henríquez's Escobar is arguably more Escobar than Escobar himself.

If other versions of the capo draw substantially from the historical figure, the Chilean variety show utterly erases the signifier with Henríquez's act, opting instead for a postmodern double imitation. The second-degree replica does away with ontological hierarchies, offering instead a chubby, *supposedly* evil goofball surrounded by incompetent hitmen. He is a sucker for the buxom bimbos who abound on the show, but ultimately he's a softie of a husband who falls apart when his wife threatens to walk out on him. If we want to put a theoretical spin on this, the Chilean reconfiguration of Escobar-as-a-cultural-icon embodies Baudrillard's ecstasy of communication: In the universe of media interconnectivity, a pure screen, a surface, no longer mirrors reality. It is a hyperreal spectacle moving toward a vanishing point of reference—a nullification where the simulacrum becomes reality itself.[2]

This is the genesis of Paulo Emilio Escobar Gaviria, aka Patrón del Pan (a play on words that preserves the original rhyme while associating cocaine with flour, thereby suggesting more of a baker than a drug trafficker). Henríquez acknowledges his high regard for Parra's acting chops and for the supreme quality of the Colombian telenovela in general. He comments on how he noticed that Parra's Escobar walked like a penguin, with his chest pushed forward and arms either dangling disconnectedly or crossed on his stomach to give himself an air of authority. He talked slowly and loud, making pronouncements rather than conversing, often referring to himself grandiosely in the third person and by his full name

Figure 15. Cristián Henríquez as the parodic Paulo Emilio Escobar Gaviria, aka Patrón del Pan, for the Chilean variety show *Morandé con Compañía*. Notice the oversize cell phone for comedic purposes. YouTube, accessed May 5, 2015.

and double surname. He wears too-small polo shirts that stretch over his paunchy stomach or a heavy poncho that invariably makes him sweat. He obsessively slides his hand over his flop-sided hair and licks his lips before inhaling to make a pompous declaration. Every once in a while, he takes out a little notebook from his pocket to jot down the name of his next victim. His speech is full of Colombian slang that is exotic and unfamiliar to Chileans [*parcero, cómo así, berraco, mamao, culicagado, momentico, vueltica, peladita*]. With his affected *paisa* accent, he recycles the most memorable phrases from the telenovela, just like the fake Escobar from a *Dark Tourist* episode, threatening to murder his opponent du jour's wife, children, and parents, and, in case any of them are dead already, promising to dig them up and kill them again ("El otro"). It is overkill in both a literal and a metaphorical sense.

Henríquez's sketches are funny and ultimately good-natured, since this Escobar is devoid of any real malice. His body language channels Charlie Chaplin's Tramp character. El Patrón del Pan is a sympathetic fellow somewhat down on his luck who keeps failing at his little schemes and projects. Flirtatious and prone to sweetness, he is hopeful for romance and business opportunities. He is inept at billiards, he forgets about a wounded *sicario* the moment a scantily clad babe walks on the stage, and he tries to push a chubby woman up a striptease pole. One of his business enterprises is a cotton-candy pushcart, but when a plump and penniless customer offers sex in lieu of payment, he runs away in panic. Upon his wife's insistence, he does a happy dolphin dance (*delfín gozador*) or slithers like an iguana.

He even crosses the fourth wall to complain about Chilean politicians or hand out cash to the studio audience, at the same time warning them not to squander their windfall on vices. On one occasion, he has the opportunity to reunite with his beloved cousin Gonzalo Gaviria, who happens to be Christian Tappan, the same actor who played Gonzalo in the 2012 narco telenovela. Tappan, who could not appear in the character of Gonzalo due to Caracol's copyright, is at first not recognizable to the audience or Henríquez's Escobar. There is a prolonged moment of confusion, where Escobar keeps looking alternately at the screen image of the telenovela Gaviria and at Tappan, not knowing what to think. When finally Tappan explains who he supposedly is—a fake character from the same fictitious world the protagonist of the sketch has been emulating—they fall into each other's arms, and the full suspension of disbelief takes place.[3]

The character of Escobar-El Patrón del Pan was featured in a Kino Lotería commercial for Father's Day, where a lackluster road trip turns into success because Escobar's son happens to buy a winning ticket. A "cero kilómetros" Toyota FJ Cruiser will take them on a magical vacation. Read: family bliss, Escobar-style.[4] Unsurprisingly, Colombians residing in Chile could not fathom how their nation's biggest villain could become a lovable tout for lottery tickets. Yet what happened to the myth of Escobar is not an isolated case of misrepresentation. The cultural climate has changed significantly since Escobar's death, making the proliferation of his image more palatable—though definitely not in Colombia. Social occurrences—including crime and violence—are mediated into a world of immediacy, stripping them of their history and specificity. They become "popular ahistorical knowledge," where all that is left is excitement and desire, the heightened pursuit of pleasure that constitutes the necessary lubricant of consumer life. Violence, as processed by popular media nowadays, is simplified and reduced, offering no moral debate, no remorse, no meaning. Likewise, watching the Escobar brand on the screen, just as

Figure 16. Image from menu, Pablo Tacos Bar, France (http://pablo-tacosbar.fr/menu-pablo/).

watching real-crime shows on television, becomes comparable to consuming Coke or Godiva chocolates (Presdee 28–65).

If *Escobar, el patrón del mal* inspired comedy in Chile, much to Colombia's chagrin, *Narcos* turned the capo into a recipe for trendy business ventures on a global scale: from Africa, Asia, the Middle East, and Europe, to North and South America. This promotional success has relied on controversy or what some call morbid marketing, which in turn brought media attention and subsequent hype. Esco*bars*, ice-cream parlors, taco and burger joints, and strip clubs with the capo's image popped up in Pakistan, Kuwait, Lebanon, South Africa, Singapore, Bangkok, Malaysia, Philippines, Australia, Russia, Bulgaria, Germany, France, Czech Republic, Canada, Argentina, Brazil, and the United States. Some only insinuate the Escobar brand, like the Johannesburg (South Africa) breakfast spot whose "Pablo Eggs Go Bar" pays tribute to the capo through word play. Others principally exploit his name, such as "Pablo Tacos Bar" in France, which, aside from its unthreatening logo featuring Escobar's lopsided hairdo, has to offer but one Pablo-themed product to add to their make-your-own-taco shtick: Chili Pablo.

Other venues employ the Escobar brand in a more elaborate and blatant fashion. Their logos bear resemblance to Escobar's face or that of his filmic version (played by Wagner Moura), with the menu straight from Escobar's stock narrative, in the likes of "Agent Peña," "El Patrón," "PEPES,"

Figure 17. Escoburgers in Melbourne, Australia.

"Popeye," "Tata" (his wife), or the infamous "plata o plomo" intimidation (as is the case of a bar in Barcelona). Their décor also capitalizes on the Escobar's brand, most often with paintings that idolize the capo as a saint or a celebrated gangsta. The Pablo Escobar ice cream parlor in Kuwait serves a treat called "Silver or Lead," while its employees sport T-shirts featuring the police mug shot from Escobar's first arrest. In Brno, Czech Republic, a bar named after Escobar sells articles with his image, from baseball caps and lighters to Pablo Escobar coffee. And in Samara, Russia, the Pablo Escobar Generation strip club references one of his other infamous obsessions.

Even more crude clues for crime and notoriety are the hangman's nooses hanging from the ceiling of Pablo's B.Y.O.B (Build Your Own Burger) in Islamabad, Pakistan. For its part, Singapore's Escobar Bar features a wall-to-wall mural of the Last Supper with Escobar as one of the apostles, and another mural of the capo sitting on piles of cash, burning some of it in a nearby fireplace. The impressive size of the murals makes up for the accuracy and quality of the art. Pablo's Escoburgers in Melbourne, Australia, provides a more interactive clue, as it finalizes each transaction by handing customers a check with a line of white powder and a rolled-up dollar bill.

These visual cues backtrack to the Outlaw nature of the Escobar brand, as delineated by Mark and Pearson in their marketing manual. These venues all build on the hype of danger and excitement, as if the patrons automatically walk on the dark side once they step in. Escobar Aspen, a nightspot in America's toniest ski resort, alludes to illegality with a minimalistic web page done in black. Aside from the cheeky double entendre of the heading "Epic snow. Epic sound," it lures its patrons with mystique: "Descending into the sleek underworld of Escobar, guests should get ready to transform into their boldest, sexiest selves. The irony of a nightclub that stashes itself beneath the streets, but evokes the illusion of flight, charges the atmosphere with adventure. . . . Amber lights wash the expansive bar in a seductive glow. Neon lasers shiver and flash over bodies in motion, further invoking the magic. And black-and-white portraits of Pablo Escobar keep measured watch all over—pleased, maybe, with the evidence of a modern, cool crowd claiming their right to feel gratifyingly alive" (https://www.escobaraspen.com/).

The club's promotional narrative speaks to the consumer's fear of leading an inconsequential and trivialized existence, and it proposes Escobar as a cure for their ennui. Escobar as a fetishized commodity is thus not just monetized but also culturally flattened, as he now globally sows a meaning far different from what still makes Colombians shudder: that of rebellion and violence. His brand is cathartic in that it reinforces antisocial behaviors to pursue one's own self-interest and pleasure, to release pent-up emotions, and to enable a collective need for blowing off steam. By branding Escobar as cool and simply "on the disturbing side," venues such as Escobar Aspen invite customers to fashion an edgier identity. Of course, a business model based on the Escobar brand does not claim to be ethically palatable. Quite the contrary, cheekiness is its asset. People who rankle under the bureaucratized monotony of existence come to Escobar Aspen to find an antidote to their routine, to feel naughty without paying the price (except for drinks). Simulated danger is another hip high for consumers worldwide.[5] Like Che Guevara, albeit in a different context, Escobar, the criminal and the terrorist, has been redefined in popular culture as the daredevil, with associations of freedom, rebellion, guts, and individuality.

Escobar Aspen also predictably sells themed vodka and Escobar clothing apparel on its website, from T-shirts and sweatshirts for grown-ups to baby onesies featuring the patrón's face, conveniently available in black, gray, and pink. Even Walmart offers T-shirts with Escobar's image, and the artist bazaar *Society6* stocks a variety of Escobar-themed objects, from iPhone cases to bed comforters, wall tapestries, shower curtains, and bath mats. Then there are Escobar throw pillows, where the capo can resemble the real-life criminal, the *Narcos* rendition by Wagner Moura, or a satanic rendition with juxtaposed horns.

Sebastián Marroquín has been selling Escobar-themed apparel since 2012, when he succeeded at last in registering his clothing under the brand "Escobar Henao," his father's and mother's surnames. His multiple appeals to register a Pablo Escobar brand (going back to 2006) were exhausted and denied by Colombia's superintendent of industry and trade, who condemned such a business venture as "an attack against the morals and public order" [atentar contra la moral y el orden público] ("Niegan"). In that petition, "the Escobar family had argued that a Pablo Escobar brand would 'transmit messages that invite humanity to reflect in order to create a society that recovers and respects human rights'" (Malkin). Indeed, Marroquín's line of clothing carries messages that go against the narco lifestyle, all the while exhibiting Escobar's images and his original signature. Featuring the capo's student ID card, driver's license, credit card, and savings book, they carry messages such as "What does your future look like?" or "Nice pace, but wrong way." Despite their steep price (between sixty and one hundred dollars), they sell particularly well in Culiacán, the capital of Sinaloa state and the home of Joaquín "El Chapo" Guzmán, or in Guadalajara, which was also swept up in Mexico's drug violence (Diaz). To the critics who accuse Marroquín of reinforcing a fascination with the cartel culture and getting rich from his father's name in a cloaked, pseudo-apologetic fashion, he responds that instead, everyone else is milking his father's legacy.[6]

The commodification of the Escobar brand unsurprisingly has been met with protest in Colombia, and it has created the opposite trend, surely born out of frustration if not straight-out outrage over the recodification of crime into cash. By the wishes of local authorities and some local communities, the traces of Escobar's past are being systematically obliterated, starting with the safe house where Escobar was killed, through Hacienda Nápoles, down to the Mónaco building in El Poblado, Escobar's residence from 1986 to 1988. Since my 2010 visit, the Escobar-related spots have undergone rapid change. The building in Los Olivos where he met his end houses a Spanish language school for foreigners, bearing no sign of Escobar's past. Hacienda Nápoles has been populated with six hundred animals of fifty different species, some mercifully rescued from circuses and other forms of entrapment, others handed over by their former owners. The menagerie includes panthers, lions, tigers, pumas, elephants, rhinos, zebras, ostriches, Watusi cattle, and hundreds of species of birds who now cohabit with the many descendants of Escobar's original hippos. Atecsa, the company that owns the place, has remodeled the site to liken it even more to a safari/waterpark adventure, enhancing its African theme through new sculptures and other cultural displays, perhaps to accompany the animals typically associated with the African steppes that now roam the Magdalena Medio. Ostentatious new structures, such as a monumental octopus waterslide complex, serve hundreds of families who come to cool off on hot days. The artificial Victoria waterfalls opened in 2015—allegedly the world's biggest falls in a waterpark. The falls were created to mimic the African habitat from the border between Zambia and Zimbabwe. Equipped to host one thousand people a day, the site rivals the world's most sophisticated water parks.

The iconic Cessna perched atop the Nápoles entrance during the Escobar era was first repainted with zebra stripes and later removed altogether. Some Colombians considered its existence an unacceptable form of revictimization ("Encartados"). The entryway is to be replaced with a statue honoring Vanessa, the estate's most people-friendly female hippo. Escobar's private bullring in Hacienda Nápoles was converted into an Africa museum, five hotels were built on the property, and a large camping area was designated for budget-minded visitors. What clearly did not benefit from these renovations was Escobar's old hacienda, which I visited in 2010, a semi-ruined house that served as a Memorial Museum, with numerous posters featuring Escobar's acts of terrorism and victims plastered on every wall.

Allegedly, it collapsed on its own in 2015, weathered by time and neglect. This event was barely mentioned in the Colombian press and never followed up on by inquiry or discussion. Overall, today's Hacienda Nápoles has been almost entirely stripped of its original character in favor of wholesome entertainment, its past overwritten to mask disturbing memories. It has become successfully Disneyesque, sanitized, and culturally homogenized to show a new philosophy of having fun, not to reflect on traumas of yesteryear. Amnesia wins out over memory.

In contrast, the Mónaco building disappeared with exceptional fanfare. At stake, as usual, was the memory of Pablo Escobar, the undesired attention it received from narco tours, and Mayor Federico Gutiérrez's

Figure 18. The ruins of Escobar's former house in Hacienda Nápoles, 2010, with the kitchen to the left. Photo by author.

Figure 19. Victims' portraits on display in the now destroyed Escobar house, Hacienda Nápoles, 2010. Photo by author.

impassioned attempts to turn the page on Escobar by erasing his physical footprint. First, in response to ever-more frequent narco tourism near the building, its walls were covered with posters with messages such as: "It's not fiction, it's reality" [No es ficción, es realidad], or "Respect our pain, honor our victims" [Respeta nuestro dolor, honra nuestras víctimas] (Jiménez González). It took just three seconds to demolish the building in a televised event on February 22, 2019, yet the spectacle served as an opportunity to commemorate victims of drug trafficking. Approximately sixteen hundred people observed the demolition from the safe distance of Club Campestre; Colombia's president, Iván Duque, who came to Medellín for the implosion, sent a message of hope on Twitter that "the fall of Mónaco is the defeat of the culture of illegality" [la caída del Mónaco es la derrota de la cultura de la ilegalidad] ("'Caída del Mónaco'"). In turn, the mayor delivered a heartfelt address on peace. Various descendants of high-profile Escobar victims, such as Miguel Turbay (son of Diana Turbay) and the sons of Rodrigo Lara Bonilla and Luis Carlos Galán, saw the demolition as a message of hope and expressed their gratitude for this act of honoring Colombia's collective memory ("'Caída del Mónaco'"). Mónaco will be replaced by a park for the capo's victims, with the purpose of promoting commemoration instead of commodification—an allusion to a constant flow of narco tours. Proponents say it will bring symbolic remembrance, and it will paint the city in a different light, no longer as the narco cradle of yesteryear.

Not everyone agrees with obliterating the traces of Escobar. Detractors find these gestures hardly effective, calling for better, more open discussions on Escobar and ongoing narco corruption. Typical is the opinion of Luis Carlos Manjarrés, curator and museologist on the subject of memory, who laments that "Colombians and the institutions have not confronted the problem of constructing a memory of this drug lord that would combat his fetishization" [los colombianos y las instituciones no han afrontado el problema de construir una memoria de este narcotraficante que enfrente la del fetiche] ("Hacienda Nápoles"). The Mónaco demolition inspired a forum titled "What shall we do with Pablo Escobar?" [¿Qué hacemos con Pablo Escobar?] under an initiative called "Lunes de Ciudad," a space for debates on subjects of public interest, organized by the private sector, academia, and civic organizations. Marta Villa Martínez, a historian from the Universidad Nacional, calls the official silence on Escobar a form of hypocrisy that only conceals his connections with the church, the political class, and society as a whole. She inculpated Mayor Federico Gutiérrez for tearing down the building as a pet project whose rationale or funding decisions were never addressed collectively. Another participant, *La cuadra* author Gilmer Mesa, expressed his discomfort with replacing the Mónaco building with a memory park, as if that would deter narco tours from visiting. In the end, the discussion raised more questions than answers, such as why the demolition would happen thirty years after Escobar's death (Habib Calderón). Elsewhere, Mesa criticized Gutiérrez for cutting funds for music schools in the same Medellín neighborhoods that spawned many of the capo's *sicarios* and instead buying a helicopter, allegedly to help him catch the bad guys (Builes). Mesa's argument that youth prefer guitars over guns undermines the mayor's highly visible activism as a self-promotional stunt rather than a sincere effort to eradicate crime.

Mesa adds that Antioquian writers continue to address the subject of Escobar and his era because, despite the commotion accompanying the demolitions, the evil surrounding Escobar and Colombian drug trafficking has not been openly addressed, nor does the nation acknowledge its own faults, focusing all its criticism on the capo and thus turning a blind eye to the narco corruption still firmly embedded in politics and society: "This is the weight we haven't been able to get rid of, I believe, because we have tended to blame it all on Escobar. Here, we throw blame with frequency, but many times we do not own up to our own moral duties and obligations to others and to the city" [Ese es un peso que no nos hemos podido quitar de encima porque creo que hemos tendido a echarle culpa de todo a Escobar. Aquí echamos la culpa con mucha frecuencia, pero muchas veces no somos responsables de nuestros deberes morales y de nuestras obligaciones con el otro y con la ciudad (Murcia Valdés)].

There is no telling which direction the Escobar brand will take next, for popular culture has its own unpredictable ways to transform and perpetuate myths. The capo himself was PR-savvy and relished the myths he was generating—whether hamming it up in a Pancho Villa sombrero and bandoliers, building houses for the poor of Medellín, or riddling an old Ford with bullets to create a Bonnie and Clyde "souvenir" for Hacienda Nápoles. This is how he ritualized banditry across time and space, actively manufacturing the relationship between past desperados, himself, and his thugs. By imbuing transgression with flattering romantic characteristics, Escobar consciously attempted to perpetuate his own myth as a social bandit, as someone voicing popular discontent with the establishment rather than simply pursuing profit. In the end, such efforts to whitewash his image might not have been necessary after all, because sadly—especially for Colombians whose lives were irrevocably marked by his villainy—we live in an age where the public venerates some figures precisely because of their ability to unleash violence. But one thing is certain: Escobar is now firmly ensconced in the pantheon of folk outlaws alongside Robin Hood, Butch Cassidy, and Mario Puzo's Godfather, and his cultural legacy will continue to be exploited and consumed for years to come.

Notes

Introduction

1. The 2011 *Pablo's Hippos*, directed by Lawrence Elman and Antonio von Hildebrand, draws parallels between Escobar and the hippopotamus Pepe, starting with juxtaposed postmortem photos of Escobar and the animal all the way to the hippos' acclimatization and propagation, which like drug trafficking itself could not be contained. It is difficult to determine whether the narrator, a cartoon grandpa hippopotamus with heavily accented English, is endearing or annoying. Nor is the film supportive of animal-rights activism, because the hippo population is portrayed as an environmental hazard to be "dealt with."

2. Hugo Aguilar Naranjo, the retired lieutenant colonel who led the fifteen-month-long hunt of the Bloque de Búsqueda that put an end to Escobar, accuses the American DEA of falsely claiming to have killed the capo themselves. The "trophy" photos taken by the Americans became the so-called proof of the Americans' protagonism in liquidating the capo. This misconception was further reinforced by Mark Bowden's *Killing Pablo*; see Caycedo Castro 185–86. Naranjo has been accused of paramilitary ties and of conspiracy with the now-defunct paramilitary organization AUC. As a result, he was banned from holding public office for twenty years, and witnesses to his parapolitics are withdrawing their statements.

3. Benavides considers *narcocultura* a paradigmatic example of contemporary cultural hybridity, born out of a network of relationships between the Latin American postcolonial condition and the United States as a neocolonial empire (112).

4. Poor urban neighborhoods in Colombia. Plagued by pervasive poverty, the *comunas* frequently become breeding grounds for paramilitary, guerrilla, and gang activity. It is from such areas in Medellín that Escobar originally recruited his killers, bodyguards, and armies of followers.

5. The series produced by Canal Capital and Centro Atico de la Javeriana won in the category Best Television Work by CPB (Círculo de Periodistas de Bogotá) in 2012.

6. It also suggests that Bogotá can be the only savior of the people, since Medellín is corrupted beyond repair.

7. I refer to those narcos with high visibility and a penchant for grandiosity, who either sought out social protagonism (Carlos Lehder and Gonzalo Rodríguez Gacha), threw lavish parties for different social circles and sponsored beauty queens (Hugo

Hernán Valencia, alias Fierrito, or Wílber Varela, known as Jabón), or surrounded themselves with flashy objects of luxury that became the staples of narco aesthetics (a style
that goes back to marijuana drug traffickers in the 1960s, embraced enthusiastically by
most members of later cartels).

8. Not that they themselves did not cash in on the profits anyway. As Gootenberg
explains, Pinochet was accused of financing his anticommunist terror network Plan
Cóndor and of amplifying his own personal wealth by means of drug trafficking (304).

9. For more on the trajectory of narcocultural production, see Fonseca 151–71.

10. For a panoramic view of narco-themed literature in Colombia, see Óscar Osorio's
La novela.

Chapter 1. Pablo Escobar and Narco Nostalgia

1. For more on the Mexican crisis, see June S. Beittel's reports and Ioan Grillo, "Mexico's Drug-Related Violence," *CRS Report for Congress*, May 27, 2009, http://www.fas.org/
sgp/crs/row/R40582.pdf.

2. While the term "Colombianization of Mexico" reflects concern over the chaos
caused by drug trafficking violence in Mexico, it also reinforces the old stereotype of
Colombia as a drug cradle, where cartels were powerful enough to confront the state
openly. Ironically, the more recent outrage among Mexicans, caused by a commentary
from Pope Francis regarding his fears of the "Mexicanization" of Argentina (the third
largest exporter of cocaine after Colombia and Mexico), attests to the transnational aspect of the problem; see Martín Pérez. For an interpretation of the term "Colombianization of Mexico," see Campbell, *Drug War Zone* 7–8; and Perramond.

3. A Special Report on *Drug Violence in Mexico* through 2018 documents a sharp peak
in homicide rates under Felipe Calderón (2006–2012), with an average of more than
twenty thousand homicides per year (fifty-five per day). During Enrique Peña Nieto's
term (2012–2018), violence only grew, leading to an average of more than twenty-three
thousand homicides per year. A significant portion of Mexico's increase in violence between 2015 and 2017 had to do with the 2016 rearrest of Joaquín "El Chapo" Guzmán,
kingpin of the Sinaloa cartel, and subsequent organizational conflicts among drug traffickers (Calderón et al). In the 2017–2018 election period, 114 candidates and politicians
were assassinated, allegedly by crime bosses to intimidate public office holders (Beittel,
"Mexico's Drug-Related Violence").

4. The Mérida Initiative faced strong opposition from both sides of the border: its
U.S. detractors fear that the funding will benefit corrupt agencies in Mexico, whereas its
critics in Mexico suspect that the Initiative will signal the militarization of Mexico and
greater U.S. interference in Mexican politics. These opinions are based, in part, on the
effect that Plan Colombia has had so far on fighting narcotrafficking.

5. See "El Pablo Escobar mexicano" from *Semana*, July 5, 2009, on Joaquín "El Chapo"
Guzmán.

6. I am referring to the seizure, for example, of Diego Fernando Murillo Bejarano
alias Don Berna, leader of the United Self-Defense Forces of Colombia paramilitary
group and one of the main Pepes (People Persecuted by Pablo Escobar) who collaborated
with the police and the DEA on the capture of Escobar. With Escobar's death, Don Berna

became the head of a powerful narcotrafficking organization in the district of Envigado (Medellín), known as the "Office of Envigado," and was supported by a strong gang of hitmen called "La Terraza." Don Berna was extradited to the United States in 2008. Another, more recent boss from "The Office," sought by Interpol with a reward of five million dollars, is Maximiliano Bonilla Orozco alias Valenciano; see Guarnizo Álvarez, "En la mira de la Interpol." Elizabeth Yarce reports the existence of other post-Pablo key players in the narco business, which she argues did not disappear but gained new more discreet leaders, such as the boss of North Valley Cartel, Miguel Fernando Solano ("Don Miguelito"), or "El Señor de los Caballos" in Pereira ("Los carteles").

7. Similarly, albeit in the Mexican context, Diana Palaversich refers to the "normalization" of the narco subject, quoting as proof the growing number of widely accepted neologisms in Spanish such as narcoglamour, narcoaesthetics, narcopolitics, narcosaints, narcoviolence, or narcoliterature; see Palaversich, "The Politics of Drug Trafficking."

8. Dabove analyzes the inherent ambivalence contained in the very concept of banditry, which destabilizes the paradigms of citizen/outlaw, state violence versus outlaw aggression, power and its lack (7).

9. J. Alonso Salazar, *La parábola de Pablo* 161. Likewise, General Hugo Martínez, who eavesdropped on hundreds of hours of conversation between Escobar and his associates over a four-year period, stripped Escobar's myth of its luster: "He was just like any other bandit. . . . I have always put a lot of the blame on the Gringos—the agencies, the press that built him up on the world stage as a mafioso who was very important. . . . They fanned the flames"; see Mollison 26.

10. For instance, in *The Way We Never Were*, Coontz debunks the U.S. cultural myth of successful families of the past as a conservative political agenda that fosters historical amnesia and veers the nation away from the true reasons behind the present-day "crisis of the family." Rather than forgotten values from the past, Coontz contends that they are the effect of the general transformation of economic and political mechanisms of wealth and care distribution, changes that make life harder for both sexes (xxvii).

11. Sylvia Molloy and Mabel Moraña warn about the effects of the commercialization of Latin America in a prepackaged exotic version, spiced up by a magical realism that serves as nothing more than a reinforcement of hegemonic interpretive paradigms. See Molloy; and Moraña.

12. For an analysis of Libardo Porras's *Happy Birthday, Capo*, see my "Narco Caudillos."

13. His presence in literature is increasing, largely because the writers of today grew up during his reign of terror and they see his nefarious effect on countless aspects of their lives. See J. J. Junieles's short story "Mucho gusto, Pablo Escobar Gaviria (from *El amor también es una ciencia* (Cartagena de Indias: Ediciones Pluma de Mompox S. A., 2009); David Gil's *Colección de tragedias y una mujer* (Medellín: Cámara de Comercio de Medellín para Antioquia, 2017); Gilmer Mesa's *La cuadra* (Bogotá, Colombia: Literatura Random House, 2016), and Juan Gabriel Vásquez's *El ruido de las cosas al caer* (Madrid: Alfaguara, 2011).

14. For a postmodern reading of Escobar phenomenon, see my "¿Qué destino le espera a Pablo Escobar?"

15. On public exchanges among people from Escobar's intimate circle and discussions

regarding who exactly contributed to his notoriety, see my "Peddling Pablo"; Abramov-itch; Anderson; and my "Going Down Narco Memory Lane."

16. As Rashotte defiantly but so correctly notes, "We are all narcos in the range of our greed and indifference, and in our longing for a better world beyond" (20). Audiences watch narco television because they recognize themselves in the characters and their dramas.

17. Gardel died in Medellín in 1935, in an airplane crash.

18. Though the few essays that address Escobar tourism claim that the capo-themed tours existed before 2010, I saw no evidence of this. Nor did I see any tourists at the Esco-bar-related sites. Today's crowds showcase a dramatic change in how Escobar's memory is disseminated and how quickly these places became pilgrimage destinations.

19. Roberto's profit-making take on the memory of his brother does not sit well with Escobar's victims or even his wife and children, who accuse him of opportunism (see Juan Pablo Escobar's *Pablo Escobar, mi padre*). In *Cierra los ojos, princesa* Castaño pro-vides a novelized version of events as recounted by Escobar's widow and son, where Roberto is a money-grabbing traitor who secured his position in exchange for Escobar's life: "El Gatico knew how to set his price: stay outside of the purge which took the lives of so many others and receive the guarantee that he would never be extradited, not he nor his son, nor any other of his kin. . . . El Patrón died because his brother sold him out" (113–14, my translation).

20. For more information about Escobar tours, see Birgit Koolen's 2018 master's the-sis, "Persiguiendo a Pablo: un análisis discursivo de la oferta del turismo alrededor de la figura de Pablo Escobar en Medellín, Colombia," Radbout Universiteit, Netherlands.

21. By then Aníbal Gaviria was in the office and he recognized Fajardo's role in the city's international success.

22. Called by social media "tough and heartfelt" (duro y sentido), the video delivers the following statement: "If the world refuses to forget him, it is first and foremost his victims we should not forget" [Si el mundo se niega a olvidarlo, es primero a sus víctimas a quienes no debemos olvidar].

23. As for Hoyos, perhaps more significant than his article was a photograph he took of Santofimio, Escobar, and his entourage, as they all enjoyed aquatic sports at Hacienda Nápoles on that memorable 1983 weekend. The picture circulated among the press be-came the smoking gun in the case of *Santofimio v. The People of Colombia.*

24. I am referring to the admirable plans of creating a refuge for different endangered species such as elephants, rhinoceros, bison, and camels, or converting the grounds into a film studio and dinosaur park.

25. See, for instance, Cristina Gallego and Ciro Guerra's 2018 film *Birds of Passage,* which traces the origins of the Colombian drug trade through the eyes of an indigenous Wayuu family, people involved in the booming narco business before the Escobar era.

26. Pointing to transnational rather than local circumstances, Herlinghaus links Escobar's success with "intuitively understanding 'intoxication' as a fundamental force within the global system" (102) where "tapping the North's own need for 'magic,'" made him and others like him economic powerhouses.

27. Escobar's preference for simple, local cuisine is described in Vallejo's memoirs

and his brother's second book (140), together with his fantasies of leaving the business behind and settling down on his Hacienda Nápoles, surrounded by nature (27). He wore a brand-new shirt every day of the year, which he would donate the next day to one of his many admirers; see Escobar Gaviria, with David Fisher 140. Salazar notes that Escobar deemed consumerism superfluous and that he always favored an unpretentious, simple lifestyle (*La parábola de Pablo* 157). Likewise, Serrano Cadena argues that Escobar's ally, José Gonzalo Rodríguez Gacha, alias "el Mexicano," had landowner ambitions, enjoying land much more than he appreciated cocaine (107). In fact, he purchased extensive property on the left side of the River Magdalena (with Escobar owning the right side of the same river), thus becoming the proprietor of some of the best land in the country (Serrano, head of the National Police of Colombia responsible for dismantling the Cali Cartel, wrote his memoirs about Colombian narcos with writer Santiago Gamboa).

28. Serrano Cadena details the flashy narco lifestyle born of excess (*Jaque mate*, 50), while Escamilla (36) and V. Vallejo (43–44) describe the gadget-mobiles of the drug traffickers. See Escamilla; and V. Vallejo.

29. See Virginia Vallejo's commentary to this effect coming from her conversation with Escobar (*Amando a Pablo, Odiando a Escobar*, 69), Serrano Cadena (*Jaque mate*, 202).

30. Hence the "pay now and enjoy later" connotation associated with the *prepago* tag.

31. See Salazar's *La parábola de Pablo*, where he describes narco lavishness and the emergent silicone-enhanced blond beauty type (75).

32. See Abad Faciolince's testimony *El olvido que seremos*, where anecdotes about Uribe attest to his bawdy sense of humor (as quoted in Rincón's "Narco.estética." Another, more menacing image of Uribe surfaces in relation to his verbal attacks against Gonzalo Guillén, a journalist presently employed at the Miami-based *El Nuevo Herald*, accused by Uribe of ghostwriting Virginia Vallejo's book. The magazine's director reveals that death threats have been made against Guillén from Colombia and that he is presently under protective custody ("'The New York Times' vuelve a citar texto.'"

33. Morgan, in "Sex, Soap, and Society," points out how Rincón's analysis of the popularity of narco telenovelas goes hand in hand with his dismay over a Colombian electorate that blindly adores the populist Uribe: "For Rincón, *uribismo* as both political discourse and cultural style was a poisonous broth of neoliberalism, nationalism, patriarchal values, religious piety, and thuggery. It was associated with the triumphalism of an *arriviste* bourgeoisie, whose intolerance and chauvinism were only matched by its love affair with consumption" (57).

34. Taussig interprets narco spending through Georges Bataille's notion of expenditure, in which consumption and unproductive spending (*depense*) rather than production drives all economic systems and exhibits itself with great visibility in the narco lifestyle (8–34).

35. For Huggan, contrary to logic, "fetishistic representations of an exotic other tend to repress the very cultural differences they are designed to reaffirm" (17–18), causing the audience to eagerly identify with marginal cultural groups. See Huggan. Likewise, the transnational public internalizes the vicissitudes of the narco protagonists, despite little relevance between the subject and their observers.

Chapter 2. From Man's Man to Mama's Boy: *Escobar, el patrón del mal*

1. All the translations from J. Salazar's *La parábola de Pablo* are mine.

2. Salazar narrates the story differently, even though he never mentions the woman by her name, asserting that Popeye killed his lover in an act of jealousy (J. Salazar, *La parábola de Pablo*, 165).

3. Mark and Pearson quote the case of Tabasco sauce as a product sold with the suggestion that its "bite" is worthy of an outlaw (271).

4. Popeye applies the same technique of framing his face on the cover with Escobar's now iconic image in his third (!) autobiography, this one written with Maritza Neila Wills Fontecha; see Wills Fontecha.

5. For more information on Pinina, see Baquero 125–27 and Juan Pablo Escobar 247.

6. The nickname Pinina comes from the name of a character played by the Argentine child star Andrea del Boca in the Argentine soap titled *Papá Corazón*. The actress became popular in Colombia for her role in the soap *Un ángel llamado Andrea*. Because of his squeaky voice, John Jairo Arias Tascón was called either "Pinina" or "Andrea" (Baquero 55).

7. Known as the "Street-level Pablo Escobar," Chopo was most feared for his brutality regardless of his short stature and stutter. Prematurely bald and wearing a toupee, Chopo carried out many purges inside the organization, killing, for instance, the administrators of the Hacienda Nápoles and Escobar's former bodyguard, Rubén Londoño, "La Yuca" (Baquero 129). He was famous for carrying a tiny gun, which earned him the ironic name "El Chopo" (firestick, gun, or even cannon) (Baquero 128).

8. Brances Muños Mosquera, aka "Tyson," was another high-ranking hitman for Escobar and a brother of the infamous Dandenys Muñoz Mosquera "La Kika," who was captured by American authorities in Jackson Heights, Queens, while talking to his family member in Colombia from a public phone. "Tyson" and "La Kika" were in charge of an army of one hundred and forty shooters for the Medellín Cartel; see Pacho Escobar. Called Tyson for his physical resemblance to the U.S. boxer, the *sicario* was considered far more brutal than his brother for the efficacy with which he was eliminating Medellín policemen on Escobar's orders (Baquero 145).

9. For a study of narco masculinity, see Marco Alejandro Núñez-González, whose ethnographic examination of Mexican narcos from Sinaloa displays different facets and nuances of accomplished and failed manhood within the narco milieu (the accomplished "pesados" vis-à-vis wannabe "mangueras" and failed nobodies called "tacuaches"); see Núñez-González, "Masculinidades en la narcocultura," 109–26. For the Colombian context, see my "Narco Spectacle" 49–66, which explores the exigencies of narco masculinity in the 2008 series *El cartel* (depicting the workings of the Norte del Valle Cartel) and its two members: Wílber Varela alias "El Cabo" [The Corporal] and Luis Alfonso Ocampo Fómeque as "Guadaña" [Scythe], played by Robinson Díaz and Julián Arango, respectively.

10. In *La parábola de Pablo*, Salazar writes that Escobar attempted to infuse his own son with the code of virility, teaching him to appreciate guns and adrenaline: "You gotta be tough, you have to be a man" ("Usted tiene que ser un berraco, un hombre," 216),

while Chopo, his hitman, was of a different mindset, arguing that they needed to keep their children away from violence. Another *sicario*, El Arete (The Earring), understands Escobar to this day, questioning any other possible attitude Escobar could have offered: "What other legacy could Pablo have left him? He couldn't hide the truth" ("¿Qué otro patrimonio le podía dejar Pablo? No le podía ocultar la verdad").

11. While this is how the series *Escobar, el patrón del mal* and Salazar present Doña Hermilda's influence on her son, Escobar's sister denies both that her mother would advise Pablo to commit crimes or that she would have an occasional drink with his henchmen ("Hermana de").

12. In Victoria's account, Escobar attempted to convince his mother to stay by pleading that he had been preparing a room she would really like, to which, after some silence, she responded that she needed to visit Roberto in jail. When he countered that she could see Roberto any time, her answer was curt and final: "This is my wish and my decision" [Esa es mi decisión y mi deseo]; see Victoria Eugenia Henao chapter 1. Sebastián Marroquín, Escobar's son, goes even further, claiming that his paternal side (his grandmother and his uncle Roberto in particular) betrayed Escobar and his immediate family by making deals with other cartels around the time of the capo's death. Simultaneously, they agreed to having Sebastián killed, to preclude him from becoming a replacement or potential avenger for his violent father ("La fortuna de Pablo Escobar").

Chapter 3. Romancing Pablo Escobar: The Allure of the Narco Caudillo

1. Sibylla Brodzinsky examines Uribe's conflict with the Supreme Court, at the base of which lies Uribe's suspected involvement with right-wing paramilitaries.

2. See Collazos and MacSweeney. Simon Romero quotes Uribe's pronouncements on Vallejo's book and comments on the former president's ties to the narcos as confirmed, for example, by Michael L. Evans, the director of the Colombia Project at the National Security Archive in Washington.

3. Another woman who consciously adopted a female angle on Escobar is his wife, Victoria Eugenia Henao. In the prologue to her 2018 memoir, staged as a recovery story, Victoria appeals to her readers with the language of romance: "Only someone who has loved so blindly and unconditionally as I did, *as a devoted wife and mother*, can perhaps discern from my personal and intimate perspective how certain facts occurred that I painfully dare to reveal today. I beg with humility and respect to be heard as an individual *and as a woman*" (Kindle prologue). [Solo quien ha amado de la manera ciega e incondicional como yo lo hice, *como devota esposa y madre*, quizá pueda vislumbrar desde mi perspectiva personal e íntima cómo sucedieron unos hechos que hoy con desgarro me atrevo a revelar. Pido con humildad y respeto ser escuchada como individuo *y como mujer* (my translation and emphasis)]. Her Escobar is a Lover, not a criminal mastermind, a man eleven years her senior who starts a relationship with the then thirteen-year-old girl, impregnates her, and forces her to an abortion at a tender age of fourteen. She adopts the role of wife and mother and invokes the sanctity of patriarchal society, wherein the wife's proverbial passivity and suffering exonerate her of responsibility. Her other angle, that of a young girl forced into sex, exposes sexual abuse and gender in-

equality, thereby unifying her with other such victims and with today's social movements against gender abuse.

4. As Gallagher and Greenblatt put it: "We used anecdotes . . . to chip away at the familiar edifices and make plastered-over cracks appear. However, because we also hoped to learn something about the past, the cracks themselves were taken to be recovered matter . . . the anecdote could be conceived as a tool with which to rub literary texts against the grain of received notions about their determinants, revealing the fingerprints of the accidental, suppressed, defeated, uncanny, abjected, or exotic—in short, the nonsurviving—even if only fleetingly" (52).

5. Sections of this chapter appeared in my "In Bed with a Narco" 155–71.

6. Overall, more accounts on the female narco are available in the Mexican context than in the Colombian. See, for instance, Campbell, "Female Drug Smugglers" 233–67; Ramírez-Pimienta 327–52; Ramírez-Pimienta and Tabuenca Córdoba; Santamaría Gómez; Ronquillo; and Scherer García. For real-life accounts on the Colombian narco milieu, see Colorado Grisales; López López and Camilo Ferrand; my "In Bed with a Narco"; and two book-length testimonies from lovers of infamous capos: Javier León Herrera's *La bella y el narco*, on Yovanna Guzmán's traumatic love affair with Vílber Varela alias Jabón, of the North Valley Cartel; and Aura Rocío Restrepo's *Ya no quiero callar*, on her relationship with Gilberto Rodríguez Orejuela of the Cali Cartel. To these, we could add memoirs that combine the female and the narco worlds to a degree, where the wives of infamous drug lords reminisce about their private life alongside men who destroyed their marriage once they morphed into criminals. I refer to Henao's *Mi vida y mi cárcel con Pablo Escobar* and *El Rey de la* Cocaína, by Ayda Levy, whose husband, Roberto Suárez Gómez, was the leader of Bolivia's largest drug empire and a major supplier for the Medellín Cartel. Anecdotally, Levy remembers her first impressions of Escobar and El Mexicano as two young men who arrived for a summit meeting dressed inappropriately (in casual attire), and whom her husband called "El Dúo Dinámico: Pelícano y Mexicano" [The Dynamic Duo: Pelican and the Mexican].

7. Roberto Escobar Gaviria refers to Pablo's particular affection for the film characters Robin Hood and James Bond, whom Pablo intended to emulate; see Escobar Gaviria, *Mi hermano Pablo* 20. Apparently, according to Vallejo's account, he succeeded.

8. Not for nothing were the narcos referred to as the magicians (*mágicos*) in Colombia. After all, they achieved unheard-of material success, brought unprecedented profits to the rich who sold them property, and gave the poor access to a lifestyle they could only dream of previously; see Roldán, "Colombia" 177. As Paul Eddy et al. comments, "Very few of Medellín's two million inhabitants remain wholly untouched by the magic"; see Eddy, Sabogal, and Welden 31.

9. Waldmann elaborates on Maria Victoria Uribe's 2004 *Anthropologie de l'inhumanité*.

10. Waldmann, "Is There a Culture of Violence in Colombia?" (67), quoting Sánchez and Meertens.

11. This is the main premise of Alejandra de Vengoechea's "El misionero enviado de Dios y el finquero de Colombia."

12. Corner, quoted in Drake and Higgins (89), argues that the public image of po-

litical figures is central to contemporary mediated democracy and that politicians are required to perform a private self as a way of signaling their intentions.

13. Uribe threatens his former employee by shouting, "¡Le pego en la cara, marica!" (roughly translated as "I'll smack your face, you little faggot"). Antonio Caballero argues that Uribe's vulgarity is wrongly assessed as directness and that the ex-president recurs to obscenities when he lacks arguments; see Caballero, "Fonda paisa."

14. Popeye remembers: "El Patrón never lacked beautiful women between the ages of 16 and 30. He was a red-hot lover. Even in the time of the worst persecution we would always arrange to bring him one or two women, one of whom had to be a lesbian for his private show" [Al Patrón nunca le faltaron mujeres bellas entre 16 y 30 años. Era un fogoso amante. Aún en plena persecución, siempre nos las arreglábamos para traerle una o dos mujeres, de las cuales una debía ser lesbiana para su show privado; see Legarda 251.

15. Popeye allegedly quotes his patrón: "Poor Virginia is getting old already" [Ya está viejita la pobre (Legarda, El verdadero Pablo, 251)].

16. Alba Marina claims to have listened to Virginia's conversations intercepted by Escobar, wherein a famous singer, whose identity remains undisclosed, demanded a commission from Vallejo for having the two meet up upon the diva's request; see Alba Marina Escobar, with Catalina Guzmán, 191. Not only did Virginia arrange her encounter with Escobar, but she was equally unrelenting as a lover, leading Escobar to concoct plans to keep her away; financing her shopping sprees to the United States was one of them (El otro Pablo 190–91).

17. J. Alonso Salazar, in La parábola de Pablo, describes Escobar's outrage when the capo was denied membership in the prestigious Club Campestre of Medellín, even though he had more money than any of its members (113).

18. Hoyos Naranjo writes how his sponsored report on Escobar did not see daylight for twenty years because its preparation coincided with the abrupt disenchantment of the public with Escobar. An enthusiastic report in Semana titled "Un Robin Hood paisa" and released before Hoyos's intended publication stirred outrage elsewhere in the press, bringing censure to its author and marking the end of Escobar's mediatic career.

19. Serrano Cadena, in Jaque mate, talks about the honor code specific to the mafia, where female infidelity and other forms of female indiscretion led to many vendettas among the narcos (198). Popeye, too, describes how during one of many parties at Hacienda Nápoles, Carlos Lehder killed one of Escobar's sicarios because the man was continuously disrupting the drug lord's tryst with a prostitute just to get cocaine from her. Angry to lose one of his hitmen, Escobar eventually gave away Lehder's hideout; see Legarda 96. Salazar deems the last rumor questionable, arguing that it would have been hardly advantageous for Escobar to have Lehder talk to the police (La parábola de Pablo, 154).

20. Such a term appears, for instance, in "Monólogos."

21. See Sánchez.

22. Quoted from "Virginia Vallejo en Univisión II," footage available on YouTube.

23. This is John Fiske's argument as presented in Marshall 47.

24. It is here that Vallejo lists criminal complaints of defamation undertaken against Fernando Rodríguez Mondragón, who wrote that she had been romantically involved

with his father, and against numerous journalists from *El País* and *Semana* who, in her mind, have committed slander and promoted hateful anti-Vallejo attitudes.

Chapter 4. Who's the Real Boss? Griselda Blanco Refashioned

1. See Soto 187–211; and Guarnizo Álvarez, *La Patrona de Pablo Escobar* 72.

2. All translations from Guarnizo's biography are mine.

3. See "La tumba de la reina"; and John Saldarriaga, "La Reina."

4. Cuervo remembers her in the following way: "She was still arrogant, she didn't lose the appearance of a rich lady. To the very end she had that mafia look: her nails painted, pretty hair, the jewels. She was a short, pudgy-cheeked woman. She wasn't like in that prison photo where she looks like a macho man. No. Griselda was dolled up, with plastic surgeries, she had fixed her wrinkly face" [Todavía era creidita, no perdió el matiz de señora adinerada. Hasta el final tuvo este toque de mafiosa: sus uñas pintadas, peinado bonito, las joyas. Era cachetona, bajita. No estaba como en la foto que muestran de la cárcel, que ahí se parece más a un macho. No. Griselda estaba arregladita, con cirugías plásticas, se había corregido las arrugas de la cara" (Guarnizo, *La Patrona de Pablo Escobar*, 34)].

5. All translations from Soto, *La Viuda Negra*, are mine.

6. Penfold-Mounce notes that "celebrity and the media have enabled the development of a social structure that encourages a wound culture centered on trauma. . . . Atrocity exhibition has led to people wearing damage like badges of identification or a fashion accessory" (81). In case of women in the popular culture of drug trafficking, both Rosario Tijeras and Arturo Pérez-Reverte's La Reina del Sur rise from trauma into the criminal universe.

7. Mermelstein describes how Sepúlveda, sickened with Griselda's unrefined upbringing of their son, took the boy to Colombia to offer him proper schooling and a normal life, something that Griselda never planned for her children (167).

8. When it comes to television ratings, the 2012 *Escobar, el patrón del mal* beat all the narco productions, with the 2008 *El cartel* and the 2006 *Sin tetas* close behind. In comparison, the 2014 *La viuda negra* featuring Griselda Blanco scored a whole 8 points less, perhaps because of the markedly inferior quality of the script and acting ("Rating Colombia," http://archivo.ratingcolombia.com/p/producciones-mas-vistas.html).

9. Played by Mauricio Mejía, who, coincidentally, also plays Escobar in *La viuda negra*, in *American Made*, and in the 2017 *El Chapo*. Mejía thus made quite the career of portraying the young Pablo.

10. My correction of Guarnizo's quote: Mario Henao was not her brother-in-law but her brother.

11. "Prejudice against exploring the subject is widespread and unites otherwise opposed ideologies, each of which is invested in ignoring it. Traditionalists and some feminists are odd bedfellows in regarding women as beyond violence"; Hendin 8.

12. See Lavezzari. Question number 40 relates to Cosby's wardrobe philosophy. Lavezzari asks: "Its obvious you're a fly ass nigga when it comes to your wardrobe, as the west coast don it's only right for you to have a playa ass wardrobe and stay on top of ya game. Do you think it's important to stay looking sharp when it comes to being on top

of any game? And for the people that don't know, has looking fly always been a part of your attire?"

CC: "I've always been a sharp dresser. A hustler's wardrobe, whether he's a pimp or a dope dealer, has to be designer casual—the most expensive. I've always worn custom tailored white linen. Why? Because it allows me to stand out in any crowd, it reinforces my status as a boss and it's nothing more appealing to a woman than to see a handsome chocolate man dressed in white linen. A successful dope dealer's wardrobe is as unique to his character as his fleet of cars."

13. He does not mention Charles Cosby, who claims to be the one running Griselda's business (and taking care of her child) while she is in jail.

14. These include rappers such as Jacki-O, Game, Pusha-T, and 2 Turnt.

Chapter 5. Mad about Boobs: *Sin tetas no hay paraíso*

1. There seems to be an error of translation here, where "colegios" should have been rendered as "high schools" and not "colleges."

2. Bolívar affirms that his numerous jail interviews with real-life narcos have confirmed the existence of the common ideal of beauty within the drug-trafficking community, one derived from Hollywood-created and silicone-enhanced blond bombshells; Grillo Trubba.

3. As Popeye recalls, "It was a golden era of paisa women, when they still had original tits and all the rest with no surgery" [Fue la época de oro de las mujeres paisas, cuando aún tenían las tetas originales y el resto sin cirugías ("Ellas fueron")].

4. See Manuela Henao's photo gallery, which illustrates how the aesthetic transformation under the narcos changed the beauty ideal in Medellín; http://www.huffingtonpost.com/manuela-henao/powerful-photos-capture-impact-of-narco-aesthetic-in-medellin-colombia_b_7623998.html. Web.

5. On Bolivar's screenwriting trajectory, see Daniela Renjel Encinas.

6. For more information on the reception of the telenovela in Colombia, see "Full-Frontal Soap"; Martínez, "Colombia"; Goodman. Bolívar's interview with Itania María sheds light on the success of *Sin tetas* as an international franchise.

7. The war of words began with Abad Facioline's 2005 column "Los hampones literarios." It was seconded by Collazos's "Impuestos y derechos de autor." Álvarez defended Bolívar in his 2007 column "El miedo al mercado." William Díaz Villareal examines their exchange in "Sobre la crítica en general."

8. For insightful readings of the telenovela, see Cabañas; Fernández L'Hoeste; and Morello.

9. Fernández L'Hoeste, who notes that the message was prepared by Caracol for the export version of the soap as a concession to foreign sensibilities, sees the coda as the network's disingenuous and half-hearted claim to sincerity after glorifying superficiality during the entire series (175).

10. For Cabañas, *Sin tetas* "paradoxically both essentializes women's subordination and sometimes even empowers female viewers to find and celebrate agency" (1). For Fernández L'Hoeste, "At first glance, it poses a harsh critique of gender. . . . At times, though, it validates this construction of gender, rather than indicting it" (166).

11. For the topic of woman's position within the Lacanian interpretation of men's sexuality, see Rose's *Feminine Sexuality*.

12. See Morgan, "Ese oscuro objeto del deseo" 45–47.

13. Chloe Rutter-Jensen decries the imposition of the international beauty aesthetics on Colombia's beauty pageants in the introduction to *Pasarela paralela* 11. See also Ochoa Hoyos 115.

14. "The publicly avowed, preferred model," which "depends on the circulation of mass media ideologies and images for its survival of prosperity"; see Hatty 117.

15. Hatty notes the hierarchical character of masculinities, in that marginalized groups (such as African American or Hispanic youth in the United States) who resort to crime face a lack of other opportunities, whereas middle-class white men achieve the same more readily through careers (*Masculinities, Violence, and Culture*, 117–18). In Bolívar's Pereira, drug trafficking is portrayed as the only way to attain hegemonic manliness.

16. Bolívar's sequel to this story (*Sin senos sí hay paraíso*) dispels such hopes when Hilda's and Albeiro's daughter (named Catalina to honor the original namesake) falls into the clutches of the evil Yésica despite growing up innocent and uninterested in the narco blitz.

17. "Agujero quiero salir del agujero" ("I want to get out of this rat hole") was composed by José Ricardo Torres years before the telenovela. Its original male voice was substituted by a female lead at the request of Caracol to better match the story.

18. For a broader analysis of how Colombian fiction sells through its "crude realities" to international media conglomerates, see Herrero-Olaizola.

19. See A. López 262; and Martín-Barbero and Muñoz 63.

20. Part of this chapter was published as my article "Deleitar denunciando."

21. Bermúdez Pabelón, Gavina Gómez, and Fernández Vélez; Francisco Celis Albán; Badel; and "Las prepago."

22. *La prepago* is based on the real-life autobiography *Las memorias de Andrea: La prepago del Blog de Soho*, by Andrea Va De Frente.

23. Vega, a fashion photographer by trade, is better known as a double agent, in that he served as an intermediary between various Colombian *narcos* (particularly the North Valley Cartel) and the American government. His participation led to a number of plea agreements that allowed some narcos to serve brief sentences and keep some of their wealth in exchange for giving up drug trafficking and voluntary surrender. *El cartel de los sapos,* which recounts the rise and fall of the North Valley Cartel, features a (shady) character named David Paz, played by Armando Gutiérrez and modeled after Vega.

24. Except that, despite his extensive research on the topic of the Black Widow, Smitten misspells the name of the city as "Parera."

25. The original sayings in Spanish are: "Soy de Pereira pero no ejerzo," "Eso dicen que cargan la estera bajo el brazo," o "Yo soy pereirana de colchón de algodón." These anecdotes come from Chávez; "Lanzan campaña"; "Protestan contra"; "Los pereiranos"; and Hernández.

Chapter 6. Colombian *Sicariato* and Rosario Tijeras

1. To be sure, "motorcycle murders" did occur before the assassination of Lara Bonilla, but they did so with less frequency, according to Fernando Quijano, investigator and director of Corpades [Corporación para la Paz y el Desarrollo Social], the Medellín-based human rights group (Robbins). In 2018, Quijano resigned his position owing to constant threats that his family would be "sliced into bits" if he did not stop talking about the presence of three Mexican cartels in Medellín (Sinaloa, Los Zetas, and Jalisco Nueva Generación) ("Fernando Quijano").

2. On *sicarios* and other warring groups in the Medellín of the 1980s and 1990s, see J. Alonso Salazar's *Born to Die in Medellín* and Alma Guillermoprieto's *The Heart That Bleeds*, chapters "Medellín 1991" and "Bogotá 1993." For statistics on youth unemployment in Medellín in the post-Escobar era, see Roldán's "Colombia."

3. Of course, Medellín is not the only city plagued by *sicarios*. Pereira's two infamous *sicarios*, Caballo and Cara de Ángel, presumably murdered more than three hundred people between 1974 and 1984. At the same time, the ultra-right Los Guajiros gang engaged in the systematic elimination of the city's homeless, prostitutes, transvestites, and other marginal groups. Things only got worse in the first years of the 1990s, when the North Valley Cartel consolidated. Entire neighborhoods became overrun by teenage assassins employed by cartels, by urban militias belonging to the FARC and ELN, and by the new ultra-right groups. The most infamous were Gato Triste, the bloodthirsty Rambo, and his best student, Martín Bala, whose "work assignments" took him all over the country (Álvarez, "El asesinato"). Crimes committed by *sicarios* rose again around 2007, owing to a turf war between the successors of the grand capos of the North Valley Cartel. *Semana* reported that the Bishop Emeritus of Pereira, Tulio Duque Gutiérrez, lamented that his city was living a worse nightmare than Medellín during the Escobar era. For an in-depth study of Pereira's *sicariato*, see Osorio Cinfuentes's 2010 dissertation, "Una Aproximación."

4. Óscar Osorio argues that scholars mistakenly tend to view *sicarios* through the prism of the most popularized stories from Antioquia, all the while ignoring Colombian literary production from elsewhere. Other *sicario* literature (from Cali, for example) defies the well-trod assumptions associated with this type of criminal career, including young age or the youth's existential ennui. See Osorio, *La novela*.

5. This argument was presented by Erna von der Walde, Camila Segura Bonnet, and Villoria Nolla. For other insightful readings of fictional *sicarios*, see Cano; Jastrzebska; Laroussi; Lorenz; Skar; Temelli; and Vanden Berghe.

6. Forrest Hylton comments that even though the state's presence in the *comunas* might be no longer repressive, its pod-like libraries look like prisons or "military research installations" with "security functions built into design" (87).

7. The "Office of Envigado" was set up by Pablo Escobar. A network of hitmen for hire and a home office regulating all criminal activities in the region, it imposed fixed monthly taxes on *narcotraficantes* and *sicarios* who had to hand in a percentage of their take from kidnappings, bank robberies, and extortions. Run initially by brothers Gerardo "Kiko" Moncada and Fernando "El Negro" Galeano, close associates of Escobar

who were eventually killed by him in La Catedral, it was taken over by Diego Fernando Murillo Bejarano alias Don Berna once Escobar died. Don Berna aligned himself with ultra-right paramilitary groups and became a sort of arbiter of all the drug traffickers in Medellín. In exchange, he collected via the Office of Envigado 30 percent of the profit from each and every delinquent act that took place in Antioquia ("¿El fin?").

8. Robbins writes that in Honduras, "which has the world's highest murder rate, Congress in 2011 banned all motorcycle passengers."

9. These four sections constitute an updated version of my "Towards the Latin American Action Heroine."

10. According to Pilar Riaño-Alcalá, the "construction of rape as the physical overpowering of a woman is rooted in . . . patriarchal attitudes. Locally, rape has been deployed in territorial wars and victims constitute war booty"; Riaño-Alcalá 150. She quotes two human rights organizations, the Gender and Armed Conflict Working Group and Women's Pacifist Route, which encounter a wall of silence when trying to investigate cases of rape, abduction, and sexual slavery, which are widespread among all the armed groups in Colombia.

11. Aside from mentioning the now classic texts by F. Vallejo, Salazar, and Gaviria, Franco refers specifically to a thesis written by his cousin, María Luisa Correa, which includes testimonies of young ex-*sicarias*, women presently in the process of reintegrating into society; Ravello.

12. Riaño-Alcalá recalls a discussion with the inhabitants of Barrio Antioquia on the topic of what constitutes rape. For her interlocutors, only penetration forced by two or more male offenders constitutes rape, because only with more than one attacker can a woman be physically immobilized and hence exonerated as an unwilling participant. This peculiar reasoning attests to the standardization of gendered aggression in the community (144).

13. Clover argues in her discussion on rape-revenge films that "paradoxically, it is the experience of being brutally raped that makes a 'man' of a woman" (*Dwellers of Memory*, 159).

14. Critics tend to underplay the novel's flashbacks where Rosario's power is displayed, exalting instead her inert, mute, and nearly dead body from the narrative present. The shell of her previously exuberant self serves thence as proof of Rosario's ultimate passivity and defeat, thereby fixing her in the culturally condoned mold of feminized victimhood. Another vehicle for trumpeting Rosario's victimization is her low origins, set in contrast to her boyfriends' patrician lineage. Rosario, the martyr, is said to be the scapegoat of a society where poverty, corruption, and crime lock the poor in the vicious circle of violence.

15. That is, with the exception of the telenovela, where both men are shot to death because they accompanied her during the most volatile times.

Epilogue: Escobar's Global Brand

1. Yet the fact that a site of such importance as rogerebert.com publishes film reviews that spell the nation "Columbia" undermines the gravitas of their opinion.

2. A similar phenomenon occurs with the character of Cabo (the real-life Wílber Varela, played by Robinson Díaz) from the telenovela *Cartel de los sapos*. He becomes an audience favorite as a comic character and crosses over to TV commercials. See my "Narco Spectacle."

3. Christian Tappan explains: "I was asked to perform Gaviria but due to the rules of the TV channel, we cannot perform these characters anywhere. As Christian I'll be able to do something. It will be good" (Ananías). [Me habían pedido que fuera Gaviria, pero por estándares del canal, no podemos hacer esos personajes en ninguna parte. Como Christian podré hacer algo; quedará muy simpático (my translation)].

4. The ad can be seen at kienyke.com, "Pablo Escobar protagoniza comercial en Chile."

5. See Brigitte Adriaensen's article, which explores tours such as a simulated illegal border crossing from Mexico to the United States, offered by a Mexican town whose local river stands in for the Rio Grande and whose inhabitants play the roles of brutal and intimidating cops and coyotes.

6. Many other family members of prominent narcos have attempted, some successfully, to register their infamous relatives as brands. Between 2011 and 2014, the two wives and a daughter of Joaquín "El Chapo" Guzmán presented twenty-four petitions to register the narco's notorious nickname with the Instituto Mexicano de la Propiedad Industrial (IMPI), and four of them (only for the alias El Chapo) were accepted in favor of his daughter from his first marriage, Alejandrina Giselle Guzmán. She can sell toys, watches, suitcases, jewelry, leather apparel, and Christmas decorations with her father's alias. See Martínez Ahrens. Likewise, the corporativo Gruma sells foods such as mustard, coffee, and tapioca with a brand that carries the alias of Sandra Ávila Beltrán, "La Reina del Pacífico." See Rangel; and "Narcotraficantes."

Works Cited

"25 años de la muerte de Pablo Escobar: Especiales Semana." *semana.com.co.* 2 Dec. 2018. Web.

"#ElOtroPatrón: El escalofriante testimonio de 'Popeye', el sicario de Pablo Escobar." *tn.com.ar.* 28 Sept. 2015. Web.

Abad Faciolince, Héctor. *El olvido que seremos.* Bogotá: Editorial Planeta Colombiana S. A., 2006.

———. "Estética y narcotráfico." *Revista de Estudios Hispánicos* 42.3 (2008): 513–18.

———. "Los hampones literatos." *semana.com.co.* 4 Sept. 2005. https://www.semana.com/opinion/articulo/los-hampones-literatos/74603-3. Web.

Abramovitch, Seth. "Netflix and Escobar Family in Bitter Trademark Dispute over 'Narcos.'" *thehollywoodreporter.com.* 20 Sept. 2017. https://www.hollywoodreporter.com/thr-esq/netflix-escobar-family-bitter-trademark-dispute-narcos-1041614. Web.

Abueta, Harold, and María Elvira Arango. "Popeye. Perfil del último sicario de Pablo Escobar." *cosecharoja.com.* 28 June 2012. Web.

Adriaensen, Brigitte. "Turistas sin fronteras: Representaciones literarias de viajeros en el territorio narco." *Hispanic Journal* 36.2 (2015): 139–59.

Alarcón, Daniel. "Narcotours." Radio Ambulante. NPR. 22 May 2018. Web. 10 Jan. 2019.

Alias el Mexicano. Dir. Diego Mejía and Mónica Botero. Prod. Fox Telecolombia, 2013. DVD.

Alias J. J.: Lo que pasa tras las rejas. Dir. Luis Alberto Restrepo et al. Prod. Caracol Televisión and Netflix, 2017. DVD.

Álvarez, Juan Miguel. "Cocaine Cowboys: Juan Miguel Álvarez entrevista a Billy Corben." *malpensante.com.* http://www.elmalpensante.com/index.php? doc=display_contenido&id=2242&pag=1&size=n. Web.

———. "El asesinato como forma de vida." *elespectador.com.* 6 Mar. 2010. Web.

Álvarez, Sergio. "El miedo al mercado." *semana.com.co.* 22 Jan. 2007. Web.

American Made. Dir. Dough Liman. Prod. Cross Creek Pictures and Others, 2017. DVD.

Ananías, Nayive. "La increíble transformación del primo del 'Patrón del mal,' que llega a Chile." *lasegunda.com.* 9 Apr. 2013. http://www.lasegunda.com/Noticias/CulturaEspectaculos/2013/04/837059/la-increible-transformacion-del-primo-del-patron-del-mal-que-llega-a-chile. Web.

Anderson, John Lee. "The Afterlife of Pablo Escobar." *thenewyorker.com.* 5 Mar. 2018. Web.

Ángel, Luis. "Escobar no ha muerto: Alfredo Serrano." *elespectador.com.* 6 July 2012. Web.

Aranguren, Mauricio. "Confesiones de Pablo Escobar a 'Popeye.'" KienyKe. 21 Sept. 2011. http://www.kienyke.com/historias/confesiones-de-pablo-escobar-a-popeye/. Web.

Arbeláez Tobón, Octavio. "Medellín: Tales of Fear and Hope." In *Cultures and Globalization: Cities, Cultural Policy and Governance,* ed. Helmut Anheier and Yudhisthir Ray Isar, 227–34. London: Sage, 2012.

Arias, Walter. "Mujeres, en la mira." *elespectador.com.* 15 Jan. 2012. Web.

Ashworth, Gregory J., Mihalis Kavaratzis, and Gary Warnaby. "The Need to Rethink Place Branding." In *Rethinking Place Branding: Comprehensive Brand Development for Cities and Regions,* ed. Mihalis Kavaratzis, Gary Warnaby, and Gregory J. Ashworth, 1–11. Switzerland: Springer, 2015.

Assaf, Maria. "'Like a Brand Called Hitler': Drug Lord Pablo Escobar's Family Wants to Trademark His Name for Clothing Line." *nationalpost.com.* 23 Sept. 2013. Web.

Astorga Almaza, Luis Alejandro. *Mitología del "narcotraficante" en México.* México: Plaza y Valdes, 1995.

Avrahami, Einat. "Impacts of Truth(s): The Confessional Mode in Harold Brodkey's Illness Autobiography." *Literature and Medicine* 22.2 (Fall 2003): 164–87.

Ayuso, Rocío. "Benito del Toro: 'Pablo Escobar es el Hamlet de los actores hispanos.'" *elpaís.com.co.* 27 June 2018. Web.

Baby Sicarios. Dir. David Beriain. Docureality for *REC Reporteros Cuatro,* Channel Four, Spain. Aired on 23 Apr. 2010. DVD.

Badel, Luis José. "Las chicas prepago: Amantes y acompañantes." *eltiempo.com.co.* 5 Nov. 2004. Web.

Baillargeon, Taïka. "Interview with Dr. Philip Stone, Executive Director of the Institute for Dark Tourism Research." *Téoros* 35.1 (2016): no pagination. Web.

Baldoví Giraldo, José María. "El trabajo 'sucio' de escribir la realidad." *elpaís.com.co.* 4 Nov. 2007. Web.

Baquero, Petrit. *El ABC de la mafia: Radiografía del cartel de Medellín.* Bogotá: Planeta, 2012.

Barrera, Juliana. "Bárbara de Régil comparte qué hace la nueva version de *Rosario Tijeras* más auténtica." *mundohispanico.com.* 2017. Web.

Baudrillard, Jean. *For a Critique of the Political Economy of the Sign.* Trans. Charles Levin. Candor, N.Y.: Telos, 1981.

———. *Simulacra and Simulation.* Trans. Sheila Faria Glaser. Ann Arbor: U of Michigan P, 1994.

———. *The Consumer Society: Myths and Structures.* London: Sage, 2017.

Beittel, June S. "Mexico's Drug-Related Violence." *CRS Report for Congress.* 27 May 2009. http://www.fas.org/sgp/crs/row/R40582.pdf. Web.

———. "Mexico: Organized Crime and Drug-Trafficking Organizations." *CRS Report for Congress.* 3 July 2018. https://fas.org/sgp/crs/row/R41576.pdf. Web.

Bellman, Sarah. "'Dark Tourist' Introduces Us to People Who Want to Vacation in a War Zone." *vice.com*. 23 July 2018. Web.

Benavides, Hugo. *Drugs, Thugs and Divas: Telenovelas and Narco-Dramas en Latin America*. Austin: U of Texas P, 2008.

Bengtsson, A., and A. F. Firat. "Brand Literacy: Consumers' Sense-Making of Brand Management." *Advances in Consumer Research* 33 (2006): 375–80.

Bermúdez, Ronald. "Posiciones filosóficas en la literatura colombiana contemporánea." *Revista Logos* 11 (2007): 75–80.

Bermúdez Pabelón, Ángela, Ana Milena Gavina Gómez, and Hamilton Fernández Vélez. "Estilos psicológicos de personalidad en un grupo mujeres adultas jóvenes dedicadas a la prostitución 'prepago' en la Ciudad de Medellín." *Terapia Psicológica* 25.1 (2007): online version.

Bilbija, Ksenija, and Leigh A. Payne, eds. *Accounting for Violence: Marketing Memory in Latin America*. Durham, N.C.: Duke UP, 2011.

Bird, Geoffrey, Morgan Westcott, and Natalie Thiesen. "Marketing Dark Heritage: Building Brands, Myth-Making and Social Marketing." In *The Palgrave Handbook of Dark Tourism Studies*, ed. Philip R. Stone, Rudi Hartmann, Tony Seaton, Richard Sharpley, and Leanne White, 645–65. London: Palgrave Macmillan, 2018.

Birds of Passage. Dir. Cristina Gallego and Ciro Guerra. Prod. Snowglobe, Blond Indian Films, Ciudad Lunar Producciones, Pimienta Films, 2018. DVD.

Bloque de búsqueda. Dir. Israel Sánchez and Rodrigo Lalinde. Prod. Sony Pictures Televisión for RCN, 2016. DVD.

Bolívar Moreno, Gustavo. *Sin tetas no hay paraíso*. Bogota: Quintero Editores, 2005.

———. "'Sin tetas no hay paraíso': Interview with Itania María." *Palabras Libres* 2 Sept. 2009. http://enmacondo.wordpress.com/2009/04/30/gustavo-Bolívar-moreno-sin-tetas-no-hay-paraíso-esta-noche-en-el-teatro/. Web.

Bowden, Mark. *Killing Pablo: The Hunt for the World's Greatest Outlaw*. London: Penguin, 2002.

Boym, Svetlana. *The Future of Nostalgia*. New York: Basic, 2002.

Braudy, Leo. *The Frenzy of Renown: Fame and Its History*. New York: Vintage, 1997.

Brodzinsky, Sibylla. "What's Eating Colombia's President?" *time.com*. 15 Oct. 2007. Web.

Brown, Jeffrey. "Gender, Sexuality, and Toughness: The Bad Girls, of Action Film and Comic Books." In *Action Chicks: New Images of Tough Women in Popular Culture*, ed. Sherrie Inness, 47–74. New York: Palgrave, 2004.

Brown, Stephen, Robert V. Kozinets, and John F. Sherry Jr. "Teaching Old Brands New Tricks: Retro Branding and the Revival of Brand Meaning." *Journal of Marketing* 67.3 (2003): 19–33.

Builes, Mauricio. "Mano a mano: Dos escritores que se obsesionaron con el mal en Medellín." pacifista.tv. 1 Feb. 2018. https://pacifista.tv/notas/mano-a-mano-dos-escritores-que-se-obsesionaron-con-el-mal-de-medellin/. Web.

Caballero, Antonio. "Fonda paisa." *semana.com.co*. 20 Sept. 2008. Web.

———. "Las tetas de Virginia." *semana.com.co*. 9 Nov. 2007. Web.

Cabañas, Miguel. "Narcotelenovelas, Gender, and Globalization in *Sin tetas no hay paraíso*." *Latin American Perspectives* 39.3 (2012): 74–87.

"'Caída del Mónaco es la derrota de la cultura de la ilegalidad': Duque." *eltiempo.com.co*. 22 Feb. 2019. Web.

Calderón, Laura, Octavio Rodríguez Ferreira, and David A. Shirk. *Drug Violence in Mexico: Data and Analysis through 2017*. *Justice in Mexico Project*. San Diego: U of San Diego, Department of Political Science and International Relations, 2018. https:// justiceinmexico.org/2018-drug-violence-mexico-report/. Web.

Campbell, Howard. *Drug War Zone: Frontline Dispatches from the Streets of El Paso and Juárez*. Austin: U of Texas P, 2009.

———. "Female Drug Smugglers on the U.S.-Mexico Border: Gender, Crime, and Empowerment." *Anthropological Quarterly* 81.1 (2008): 233–67.

Canchón, Freddy N. "La transformación de Flora Martínez en Rosario Tijeras." *cromos. com*. 22 Sept. 2003. http://cromos.com.co/4467/ actualidad3.htm. Web.

Canclini, Néstor García. *Consumidores y ciudadanos: Conflictos multiculturales de la globalización*. México: Grijalbo, 1995.

———. *Hybrid Cultures: Strategies for Entering and Leaving Modernity*. Trans. Christopher L. Chiappan and Sylvia L. López. Minneapolis: U of Minnesota P, 1995.

Cano, Luis. "Feminización de la violencia en *Rosario Tijeras* de Jorge Ramos Franco." *Hispanófila* 172 (2014): 207–23.

Caputo, Giuseppe. "El mundo de la cuadra." *eltiempo.com.co*. 5 July 2018. Web.

Castaño, José Alejandro. *Cierra los ojos, princesa*. Bogotá: Ícono, 2012.

Castillo, Monica. "Javier Bardem Plays Pablo Escobar without 'Glamour' in New Movie, 'Loving Pablo.'" *nbcnews.com*. 4 Oct. 2018. Web.

Catano, James V. *Ragged Dicks: Masculinity, Steel, and the Rhetoric of the Self-Made Man*. Carbondale: Southern Illinois UP, 2001.

Catsoulis, Jeannette. "A Culture Built of Guns, Drugs and Blood." Movie Review of *Cocaine Cowboys*. *New York Times*. 27 Oct. 2006. Web.

Caycedo Castro, Germán. *Operación Pablo Escobar*. Bogotá: Planeta, 2012.

Celis Albán, Francisco. "El mundo de las prepago." *eltiempo.com.co*. 6 Sept. 2007. Web.

Cetina, Eccehomo. *Jaque a la reina: Mafia y corrupción en Cartagena*. Bogotá: Planeta, 1994.

Chávez, Marcela P. "No más fama 'perreirana.'" *El Diario del Otún*. 7 July 2009. http:// www.eldiario.com.co/seccion/LOCAL/no-m-s-fama-perreirana-090706.html?score =3&id=16249. Web.

Close, Glen S. "Rosario Tijeras: Femme Fatale in Thrall." *Revista de Estudios Hispánicos* 43.2 (2009): 301–19.

Clover, Carol J. *Men, Women, and Chain Saws: Gender in the Modern Horror Film*. Princeton, N.J.: Princeton UP, 1992.

Clum, John. *"He's All Man": Learning Masculinity, Gayness and Love from American Movies*. New York: Palgrave, 2002.

Cocaine Cowboys. Dir. Billy Corben. Prod. Rakontur, 2006. DVD.

Cocaine Cowboys II: Hustlin' with the Godmother. Dir. Billy Corben and Lisa M. Perry. Prod. Rakontur, 2008. DVD.

Cocaine Godmother: The Griselda Blanco Story. Dir. Guillermo Navarro. Prod. Lifetime, 2017. DVD.

Collazos, Óscar. "Impuestos y derechos de autor." *eltiempo.com.co*. 14 Sept. 2006. Web.

———. "La diva y el Capo." *eltiempo.com.co*. 11 Oct. 2007. Web.

———. "La vida ejemplar de una diva." *eltiempo.com.co*. 27 July 2006. Web.

Collazos, Óscar, and Christina MacSweeney. "War on Words." *Index on Censorship 2008* 37.10: http://ioc.sagepub.com/cgi/reprint/37/1/10.pdf. Web.

"Colombia Coca Production: US 'Deeply Concerned' by Rise." *bbc.com*. 3 Jan. 2019. Web.

"Colombia's Coca Production Soars to Highest Level in Two Decades, US Says." *guardian.com*. 14 Mar. 2017. Web.

Colorado Grisales, Gustavo. *"Besos como balas" y otras crónicas de la zona oscura*. Pereira: Intermedio Editores, 2007.

"¿Cómo le podés pedir a un hijo que no quiera a su padre?" *180.com.uy*. 30 July 2010. Web.

"¿Cómo los diamantes no lo van a descrestar a uno?" *semana.com.co*. 14 May 2011. Web.

Coontz, Stephanie. *The Way We Never Were: American Families and the Nostalgia Trap*. New York: Basic, 1992.

Corben, Billy. "Griselda Blanco: So Long and Thanks for All the Cocaine." *vice.com*. http://www.vice.com/read/griselda-blanco-so-long-and-thanks-for-all-the-cocaine. Web.

Correo de inocentes. Dir. Clara María Ochoa. Prod. RCN, 2011. DVD.

Cortés, Fernando. *A los 20 años de la cacería de El Mexicano*. Bogotá: Intermedio, 2009.

Cox, Alex. "Gringo Star." *Guardian*. 1 Oct. 2004. http://www.guardian.co.uk/film/2004/oct/01/2. Web.

"¿Cuál es el encanto que ejercen en las mujeres los hombres peligrosos?" *eltiempo.com.co*. 4 Aug. 2006. Web.

Dabove, Juan Pablo. *Nightmares of the Lettered City: Banditry and Literature in Latin America, 1816–1929*. Pittsburgh: U of Pittsburgh P, 2007.

D'Angelo, Mike. "Javier Bardem's Exposed Gut Stars as Pablo Escobar in the Hokey *Loving Pablo*." *avclub.com*. 2 Oct. 2018. https://film.avclub.com/javier-bardem-s-exposed-gut-stars-as-pablo-escobar-in-t-1829464431. Web.

Darling, Juanita. "Drug Lords Tainting Beauty of Pageants." *latimes.com*. 13 Jan. 1998. Web.

Davis, Fred. *Yearning for Yesterday: A Sociology of Nostalgia*. New York: Free Press, 1979.

"Debemos ser solidarias con nuestro género: Reflexiones de la actriz, María Fernanda Yepes, hoy, en el Día de la Mujer." *and*. 8 Mar. 2010. Section: Cultura y Ocio, 20. http://issuu.com. Web.

Debord, Guy. *The Society of Spectacle*. Trans. Donald Nicholson-Smith. New York: Zone, 1994.

De la Paz, Patricio. "Pablo es un tour." *El Semanal*. 15 Jan. 2012. http://diario.latercera.com/2012/01/15/01/contenido/la-tercera-el-semanal/34-97296-9-pablo-escobar-es-un-tour.shtml. Web.

Delgado, Claudia. "Los buenos parece que somos pocos." *viva.org.co*. 2009. http://www.viva.org.co/cajavirtual/svc0157/articulo00181.pdf. Web.

DeMott, Benjamin. *Killer Women Blues: Why Americans Can't Think Straight about Gender and Power*. Boston: Houghton Mifflin, 2000.

Diaz, Lisbeth. "Pablo Escobar T-shirts a Hit in Mexico Drug War States." *reuters.com*. 2 Oct. 2012. Web.

Díaz Villareal, William. "Sobre la crítica en general y sobre la crítica literaria." *Literatura: Teoría, Historia, Crítica* 9 (2007): 9–23. 31 Aug. 2009. http://www.revistas.unal.edu.co/index.php/lthc/article/view/7921/8565. Web.

Domínguez, Óscar G. "La VV que conocimos." *eltiempo.com.co*. July 21, 2006. Web.

Drake, Philip, and Michael Higgins. "'I'm a Celebrity, Get Me into Politics': The Political Celebrity and the Celebrity Politician." In *Framing Celebrity: New Directions in Celebrity Culture*, ed. Su Holmes and Sean Redmond, 87–100. London: Routledge, 2006.

Drost, Nadja. "Bloodshed Returns to Medellín." *pri.org*. 20 May 2010. http://www.globalpost.com/dispatch/colombia/100331/medellin-violence-part-1. Web.

Echevarría, Ignacio. "Un corrido colombiano." *El País España: Babelia*. 16 Oct. 2004. http://jorge-franco.com/babelia-diario-el-pais-espana/. Web.

Eddy, Paul, Hugo Sabogal, and Sara Welden. *The Cocaine Wars*. New York: W. W. Norton, 1988.

"El alcalde de Medellín no quiere a turistas interesados en Pablo Escobar." *efe.com*. 31 Aug. 2018. https://www.efe.com/efe/america/portada/el-alcalde-de-medellin-no-quiere-a-turistas-interesados-en-pablo-escobar/20000064-3735471. Web.

El arriero. Dir. Guillermo Calle and Julián Díaz. Prod. Colombia, Spain: Fundación Lumière, 2009.

El Capo. Dir. Riccardo Gabrielli R. Prod. Fox Telecolombia, 2009. DVD.

El cartel de los sapos. Dir. Luis Alberto Restrepo. Prod. Caracol, 2008. DVD.

El Chapo. (Mexican television series). Dir. Ernesto Contreras and José Manuel Cravioto. Prod. Netflix and Univisión Studios, 2017. DVD.

"¿El fin del terror de Don Berna?" *semana.com.co*. 13 June 2005. Web.

"El hijo de Pablo Escobar critica las series por 'glamourizar el narcotráfico.'" *diariojornada.com.ar*. 11 Nov. 2015. Web.

Elkin Ramírez, Mario. "Madre santa, hijo perverso." *eltiempo.com.co*. 12 Mar. 1995. Web.

"Ellas fueron las hermosas amantes de Pablo Escobar." *debate.com.mx*. 12 Mar. 2017. Web.

"El libro de ocasión." *Semana* no. 1453. 8 Mar. 2010. Sección: Cultura, 106.

"El nuevo sitio turístico de Medellín." Official Page of Rosario Tijeras on RCN. http://www.canalrcnmsn.com/node/8377. Web.

"El otro Pablo Escobar se encuentra en Chile." *lapatria.com*. 11 June 2013. https://www.lapatria.com/variedades/el-otro-pablo-escobar-se-encuentra-en-chile-35794. Web.

"El Pablo Escobar mexicano." *semana.com.co*. July 5, 2009. Web.

"Encartados con la memoria de Pablo Escobar." *semana.com.co*. 17 June 2017. Web.

Escamilla, Óscar. *Narcoextravagancia: Historias insólitas del narcotráfico*. Bogotá: Aguilar, 2002.

Escobar, Alba Marina, with Catalina Guzmán. *El otro Pablo*. Bogotá: Publicaciones Semana, S. A., 2010.

Escobar, el patrón del mal. Dir. Carlos Moreno and Laura Mora. Prot. Andrés Parra, Angie Cepeda, Vicky Hernández, Nicolas Montero, Germán Quintero. Colombia. Prod. Caracol TV, 2012. DVD.

Escobar, Juan Pablo. *Pablo Escobar, mi padre*. Bogotá: Planeta, 2014.

———. *Pablo Escobar in fragranti: Lo que mi padre nunca me contó*. Bogotá: Planeta, 2016.

Escobar, Pacho. "'La Kika' paga una condena de 160 años por la bomba del avión de Avianca, y no fue él." las2orillas.co. 28 Nov. 2015. https://www.las2orillas.co/la-kika-paga-una-condena-de-160-anos-por-la-bomba-del-avion-de-avianca-no-fue-el/. Web.

Escobar Gaviria, Roberto. *Mi hermano Pablo*. Bogotá: Quintero Ediciones, 2000.

Escobar Gaviria, Roberto, with David Fisher. *The Accountant's Story: Inside the Violent World of the Medellín Cartel*. New York: Grand Central, 2009.

Escobar: Paradise Lost. Dir. Andrea di Stefano. Prod. Chapter 2 and Nexus Factory, 2014. DVD.

"Estrenarán version mexicana de telenovela *Rosario Tijeras*." eltiempo.com.co. 21 June 2017. Web.

"Exreinas destapan nuevo escándalo por cirugías plásticas." elespectador.com. 12 Aug. 2012. Web.

Ewen, Stuart. *All Consuming Images*. New York: Basic, 1988.

"Fábrica de sicarios." semana.com.co. 25 May 1987. Web.

"Federico Gutiérrez responde al artículo que llama a Colombia 'patria de los narcos.'" elespectador.com. 11 Sept. 2017. Web.

Feiling, Tom. *The Candy Machine: How Cocaine Took Over the World*. London: Penguin, 2009.

Fernández L'Hoeste, Héctor. "Gender, Drugs, and the Global Telenovela: Pimping *Sin Tetas No Hay Paraíso*." In *Soap Operas and Telenovelas in the Digital Age*, ed. Diana I. Rios and Mari Castañeda, 165–82. New York: Peter Lang, 2011.

"Fernando Quijano se retiró de Corpades por amenazas y denunció que en Medellín hay carteles de México." rcnradio.com.co. 26 Jan. 2018.

"Fin de una tragedia que cambió al país." semana.com.co. 1 Mar. 1994. Web.

Finding Escobar's Millions. Prod. Blackfin with Geno McDermott and Doug Laux for Discovery Channel, 2017. DVD.

Fiske, John. "Popularity and the Politics of Information." In *Journalism and Popular Culture*, ed. Peter Dahlgren and Colin Sparks, 45–63. London: Sage, 1992.

Fonseca, Alberto. "Una cartografía de la narco-narrativa en Colombia y México 1990–2010." *Mitologías Hoy* 14 (2016): 151–71.

Franco, Jean. "Going Public: Reinhabiting the Private." In *On Edge: The Crisis of Contemporary Latin American Culture*. Cultural Politics Series vol. 4. ed. George Yúdice, Jean Franco, and Juan Flores, 65–83. Minneapolis: U of Minnesota P, 1992.

———. *The Decline and Fall of the Lettered City: Latin America in the Cold War*. Cambridge, Mass.: Harvard UP, 2002.

Franco Ramos, Jorge. *Rosario Tijeras*. Trans. Gregory Rabassa. New York: Seven Stories, 2004.

"Full-Frontal Soap Slated for NBC." *New York Post*. 16 June 2007. http://www.nypost.com/seven/06162007/tv/full_frontal_soap_slated_for_nbc_tv_.htm. Web.

Gallagher, Catherine, and Stephen Greenblatt. *Practicing New Historicism*. Chicago: U of Chicago P, 2000.

Gangsters: America's Most Evil. "*The Godmother: Griselda Blanco.*" Season 1, episode 3. Aired on 24 June 2012. Prod. Asylum Entertainment. DVD.

García Márquez, Gabriel. *News of a Kidnapping.* Trans. Edith Grossman. New York: Alfred A. Knopf, 1997.

García Suárez, Carlos Iván. "La prostitución en la segunda mitad del siglo XX." In *Placer, dinero, y pecado: Historia de la prostitución en Colombia,* ed. Aída Martínez and Pablo Rodríguez, 281–326. Colombia: Aguilar, 2002.

Gaviria, Víctor. *El pelaíto que no duró nada.* Bogotá: Planeta, 1991.

Gil, David. *Colección de tragedias y una mujer.* Medellín: Cámara de Comercio de Medellín para Antioquia, 2017.

Glynn, Kevin. *Tabloid Culture, Popular Power, and the Transformation of American Television.* Durham, N.C.: Duke UP, 2000.

Goldman, R., and S. Papson. "Advertising in the Age of Hypersignification." *Theory, Culture and Society* 11 (1994): 23–53.

"Golpe al sicariato." *semana.com.co.* 16 June 1990. Web.

Gómez Méndez, Alfonso. Quoted from a video "Virginia Vallejo denuncia a magnates y narcopresidentes." *Noticias RCN* with Clara Elvira Ospina, debate with Edgar Tellez, Poncho Rentería, Alfonso Gómez Méndez and Jorge Armando Otálora. 21 Dec. 2009. YouTube.

Goodman, Joshua. "Breasts-Obsessed TV Show a Colombian Hit." *San Francisco Chronicle.* 19 Sept. 2006. https://www.jerzeedevil.com/threads/breast-obsessed-tv-show-a-colombian-hit.11852/. Web.

Gootenberg, Paul. *Andean Cocaine: The Making of a Global Drug.* Chapel Hill: U of North Carolina P, 2008.

Grainge, Paul, ed. *Ephemeral Media: Transitory Screen Culture from Television to YouTube.* London: Palgrave Macmillan, 2011.

Greenblatt, Stephen. *Marvelous Possessions: The Wonder of the New World.* Chicago: U of Chicago P, 1991.

Grillo, Ioan. *El Narco: Inside Mexico's Criminal Insurgency.* New York: Bloomsbury, 2011.

———. "Mexico's Drug-Related Violence," *CRS Report for Congress,* 27 May 2009, http://www.fas.org/sgp/crs/row/R40582.pdf.

Grillo Trubba, Diego. "Narcos, siliconas y prostitutas." *perfil.com.* http://www.diarioperfil.com.ar. Web.

Gronlund, Jay. *Basics of Branding: A Practical Guide for Managers.* New York: Business Expert, 2013.

Guarnizo Álvarez, José. "En la mira de la Interpol." *elcolombiano.com.* 3 May 2010. Web.

———. *La Patrona de Pablo Escobar: Vida y muerte de Griselda Blanco.* Bogotá: Planeta, 2012.

Guillén Jiménez, Gonzalo. *Los confidentes de Pablo Escobar.* Colombia: Impresol Ediciones, 2007.

Guillermoprieto, Alma. *The Heart That Bleeds.* New York: Alfred A. Knopf, 1994.

———. "The Return of Macho Politics?" *New Yorker.* 24 Feb. 2010. Web.

Habib Calderón, Salomé. "La caída del Mónaco y las conversaciones pendientes." *Contexto: Periódico de los estudiantes de la Facultad de Comunicación Social-Periodismo.*

21 Feb. 2019. https://periodicocontexto.wixsite.com/contexto/single-post/2019/02/21/La-ca%C3%ADda-del-M%C3%B3naco-y-las-conversaciones-pendientes. Web.

"Hacienda Nápoles: ¿Qué hacer con Pablo Escobar?" *semana.com.co.* 2 Feb. 2019. Web.

Harper, Stephen. "Madly Famous: Narratives of Mental Illness in Celebrity Culture." In *Framing Celebrity: New Directions in Celebrity Culture*, ed. Su Holmes and Sean Redmond, 311–27. London: Routledge, 2006.

Harvey, David. *A Brief History of Neoliberalism.* New York: Oxford UP, 2007.

Hatty, Suzanne E. *Masculinities, Violence, and Culture.* Thousand Oaks, Calif.: Sage, 2000.

Haw, Dora Luz. "Rosario Tijeras es una niña adulta . . ." Reforma. 15 Dec. 2004. http://jorge-franco.com/reforma-mexico/. Web.

Hawthorne, Susan. "The Politics of the Exotic: The Paradox of Cultural Voyeurism." *NWSA Journal* 1.4 (1989): 617–29.

Henao, Manuela. "Powerful Photos Capture Impact of 'Narco Aesthetic' in Medellín, Colombia." *HuffPost Latino Voices*, 19 June 2015. http://www.huffingtonpost.com/manuela-henao/powerful-photos-capture-impact-of-narco-aesthetic-in-medellin-colombia_b_7623998.html. Web.

Henao, Victoria Eugenia. *Mi vida y mi cárcel con Pablo Escobar.* Colombia: Planeta, 2018. Kindle Book.

Hendin, Josephine G. *Heartbreakers: Women and Violence in Contemporary Culture and Literature.* New York: Palgrave, 2004.

Herlinghaus, Hermann. *Narcoepics: A Global Aesthetics of Sobriety.* New York: Bloomsbury, 2013.

"Hermana de Pablo Escobar afirma serie 'Escobar, el patrón del mal' fue hecha por sus enemigos." 19 Nov. 2015. http://clariotrd.blogspot.com/2015/11/hermana-de-pablo-escobar-afirma-serie.html. Web.

Hernández, Salud. "Prostitución: Chicas para España; Viaje a la cuna de las prostitutas." 24 Nov. 2002. http://elmundo.es/cronica/2002/271. Web.

Herrera, Javier León. *La bella y el narco: La historia de Yovanna Guzmán, la viuda de alias "Jabón."* Colombia: Grijalbo, 2011.

Herrero-Olaizola, Alejandro. "'Se vende Colombia, un país de delirio': El mercado literario global y la narrative colombiana reciente." *Symposium* 61.1 (2007): 43–56.

Hobsbawm, Eric. *Bandits.* New York: New York P, 2000.

Hoyos Naranjo, Juan José. "Un fin de semana con Pablo Escobar." *Periodismo narrativo en Latinoamérica.* 13 May 2009. http://cronicasperiodisticas.wordpress.com/2009/05/13/un-fin-de-semana-con-pablo-escobar/. Web.

Huggan, Graham. *The Postcolonial Exotic: Marketing the Margins.* London: Routledge, 2001.

Hylton, Forrest. "Medellín's Makeover." *New Left Review* 44 (2007): 71–89.

Intxausti, Aurora. "Aumentar sus tetas les abre el paraíso de los 'narcos': Entrevista; Gustavo Bolívar Moreno." elpaís.es. 14 Mar. 2008. Web.

Jácome, Margarita. *La novela sicaresca: Testimonio, sensacionalismo y ficción.* Medellín: Fondo Editorial Universidad EAFIT, 2009.

Jameson, Fredric. "Globalization and Political Strategy." *New Left Review* 4 July–Aug. 2000. newleftreview.org.

———. *Postmodernism, or the Cultural Logic of Late Capitalism.* Durham, N.C.: Duke UP, 1999.

Janer, Sandra. "Más vivo que nunca." *semana.com.co.* 15 Dec. 2007. Web.

Jaramillo Zuluaga, César Augusto. "'La cuadra': Una novela de barrio que es también una historia del país." *www.diariodepaz.com.* 8 Feb. 2019. Web.

Jastrzebska, Adriana Sara. "Novela criminal colombiana: Muerte como marca comerical." *Fragmentos: Revista de Lingua e Literatura* 22.1 (2011): 95–108.

Jiménez González, Daniela. "El otro relato del edificio Mónaco." *elcolombiano.com.* 30 Dec. 2018. Web.

Jiménez Leal, Germán. "Intimidades de la mafia: Divas del narcotráfico." *elpaís.com.co.* July 23, 2006. Web.

Junieles, J. J. *El amor también es una ciencia.* Cartagena de Indias: Ediciones Pluma de Mompox S. A., 2009.

Koolen, Birgit. *Persiguiendo a Pablo: Un análisis discursivo de la oferta del turismo alrededor de la figura de Pablo Escobar en Medellín, Colombia.* Master's thesis, Radbout Universiteit, Netherlands, 2018.

"La cruz de Rosario Tijeras." *cromos.com.co.* 28 Feb. 2010. Web.

"La fortuna de Pablo Escobar: La traición de su madre y su hermano." *uvideoplay.com.* 13 Feb. 2017. https://www.youtube.com/watch?reload=9&v=l-uRZHlnwwk. Web.

La gorra. Dir. Andrés Lozano Pineda. Prod. Colombia, 2008. DVD.

"La historia negra de 'la Reina de la coca.'" *eltiempo.com.co.* 8 Sept. 2012. Web.

"La mafia creó un nuevo país." *semana.com.co.* 21 Aug. 2010. Web.

"La nueva vida de la mamá de Pablo Escobar." (por redacción *Cromos.*) *elespectador.com.* 23 May 2012. Web.

"Lanzan campaña contra la mala fama de las mujeres de Pereira." Caracol Radio. 7 July 2009. www.caracol.com.co/nota.aspx?id=841444. Web.

La pasión de Gabriel. Dir. Luis Alberto Restrepo. Prod. Universidad Nacional de Colombia, 2009. DVD.

La prepago. Dir. Carlos Gaviria. Prod. Sony Pictures Televisión for RCN Televisión, 2013. DVD.

Lara, Patricia Salive. *Las mujeres en la guerra.* Bogotá: Planeta, 2000.

Laroussi, Sabrina. "Dicotomía grotesca de la mujer en la narconovela colombiana: ¿Virgen o puta?" *Forum: Universidad de Puerto Rico* 22 (2014–15): 65–84.

"Las cirugías plásticas están fuera de control." *eltiempo.com.co.* 7 Nov. 1997. Web.

"Las FARC y la violencia sexual." *elespectador.com.* 9 Apr. 2015. Web.

"Las mujeres de las FARC, abusadas y violadas." *infobae.com.* 16 June 2011. Web.

Las muñecas de la mafia. Dir. Luis Alberto Restrepo, BE-TV and Caracol, 2008. DVD.

"Las prepago: Diosas de la noche." *eltiempo.com.co.* 8 Oct. 2004. Web.

Las víctimas de Pablo Escobar. Documentary. Prod. Bogota, Canal Capital and Pontífica Universidad Javeriana, 2012.

"La tumba de la reina de coca quedó a 120 pasos de la de Pablo Escobar." *caracol.com.* 15 Sept. 2012. Web.

Lavelle, Ciara. "Griselda Blanco TV Movie *Cocaine Godmother* is Campy and Sexist." *miaminewtimes.com.* 19 Jan. 2018. Web.

Lavezzari, Jason. "Talking Cocaine with the West Coast Don." *Mids Magazine.* 6 Feb. 2009. *charlescosby.com.* Web.

La virgen de los sicarios. Dir. Barbet Schroeder. Colombia, Spain, France: Canal+, Les Films du Losange, Proyecto Tucan, 2000. DVD.

La viuda de la mafia. Dir. Sergio Osorio. Collestrellas for RCN, 2005. DVD.

La viuda negra. Dir. Carlos Cock, William González Zafra, Alejandro Lozando, and Alejandro García. RTI Producciones and Televisa for Univisión and for Caracol Television, 2014. DVD.

Legarda, Astrid. *El verdadero Pablo.* Bogotá: Ediciones Dipon, 2005.

Levy, Ayda. *El rey de la cocaína: Mi vida con Roberto Suárez Gómez y el nacimiento del primer narcoestado.* México, D.F.: Debate, 2012.

Loaiza, Marcela. *Atrapada por la mafia yakuza.* Bogotá: Planeta, 2009.

"Lo bueno, lo malo, lo feo y lo tenebroso de 'La viuda negra': La creatividad televisiva está de luto." *lafiscalía.com.* 2 Sept. 2014. https://www.lafiscalia.com/2014/09/02/lo-bueno-lo-malo-lo-feo-y-lo-tenebroso-de-la-viuda-negra-la-creatividad-televisiva-esta-de-luto/. Web.

Londoño Hoyos, Fernando. "Claro que sí: Era ella." *eltiempo.com.co.* 20 July 2006. Section: Opinión. Web.

López, Ana M. "Our Welcomed Guests: Telenovelas in Latin America." In *To Be Continued . . . Soap Operas Around the World,* ed. Robert C. Allen, 256–57. London: Routledge, 1995.

López, Claudia. *Y refundaron la patria . . . De cómo mafiosos y políticos reconfiguraron el estado colombiano.* España: Random House Mondadori, 2010.

López, Luisa Fernanda. "Pablo Escobar: Imbatible líder mediático." *hilodirecto.com.* 18 Aug. 2012. http://hilodirecto.com.mx/pablo-escobar-imbatible-lider-mediatico/. Web.

López López, Andrés. *El cartel de los sapos.* Bogotá: Planeta, 2008.

López López, Andrés, and Juan Camilo Ferrand. *Las fantásticas: Las mujeres de El Cartel.* Doral, Fla.: Aguilar, 2009.

Lorenz, Aaron. "Rosario's Fugitive Voice: Deciphering *Rosario Tijeras's* Ironic Challenge to the Notion of Literatura Sicaresca." *Symposium* 65.4 (2011): 237–52.

Los archivos privados de Pablo Escobar. Dir. Marc de Beaufort. Colombia. Prod. Divina Producciones-Sierralta Entertainment, 2004. DVD.

"Los pereiranos marcharán este miércoles para protestar por 'Sin tetas no hay paraíso.'" *eltiempo.com.co.* 29 Aug. 2006. Section: Nación. Web.

Los tiempos de Pablo Escobar. Dir. Alessandro Angulo and Carlos Julio Betancur. Colombia. Prod. Laberinto Producciones, 2012. DVD.

Loving Pablo. Dir. Fernando León de Aranoa. Prod. Spain. 2017. DVD.

Lyotard, Jean-Francois. *The Postmodern Condition: A Report on Knowledge.* Minneapolis: U of Minnesota P, 2002.

Mack, Andrew. "AFI Fest Report: Rosario Tijeras Review." *twich.com.* 13 Nov. 2005. https://screenanarchy.com/2005/11/afi-fest-report-rosario-tijeras-review.html. Web.

Malkin, Bonnie. "Family of Pablo Escobar Attempt to Register His Name as a Brand." telegraph.co.uk. 14 Sept. 2013. Web.

"María Fernanda Yepes cuenta de su personaje como Rosario Tijeras." *Estereofónica.* 4 Feb. 2010. http://www.estereofonica.com. Web.

Mark, Margaret, and Carol S. Pearson. *The Hero and the Outlaw: Building Extraordinary Brands Through the Power of Archetypes.* New York: McGraw-Hill, 2001.

Marshall, P. David. *Celebrity and Power: Fame in Contemporary Culture.* Minneapolis: U of Minnesota P, 1997.

Martín-Barbero, Jesús. *Communication, Culture and Hegemony: From the Media to Mediations.* Trans. Elizabeth Fox and Robert A. White. Thousand Oaks, Calif.: Sage, 1993.

———. "Cómo se comunican los presidentes." In *Los tele-presidentes: Cerca del pueblo, lejos de la democracia,* ed. Omar Rincón, 15–18. Bogotá: Centro de Competencia en Comunicación para América Latina, 2008.

———. "Comunicación: El descentramiento de la modernidad." *Análisis* 19 (1996): 79–94.

———. "Memory and Form in the Latin American Soap Opera." In *To Be Continued . . . Soap Operas Around the World,* ed. Robert C. Allen, 276–84. London: Routledge, 1995.

Martín-Barbero, Jesús, and Sonia Muñoz. *Televisión y melodrama: Géneros y lecturas de la telenovela en Colombia.* Bogotá, Colombia: Tercer Mundo, 1992.

Martínez, Helda. "Colombia: Measuring the Cost of Paradise by Cup Size." *IPS News.* 25 Sept. 2006. http://www.ipsnews.net/2006/09/colombia-measuring-the-cost-of-paradise-by-cup-size/. Web.

Martínez Ahrens, Jan. "Una hija del narcotraficante logra registrar la marca El Chapo." *elpaís.com.mx.* 27 Jan. 2016. Web.

Martín Pérez, Fredy. "Bishop Says That the 'Mexicanization' Term Should Not Be Misunderstood." *El Universal.* 1 Mar. 2015. http://www.eluniversal.com.mx/in-english/2015/mexico-argentina-mexicanization-pope-francis-felipe-arizmendi-colombianization-102289.html. Web.

Mastrodoménico, Hugo. "¿Qué le vio la diva al criminal?" *eltiempo.com.co.* 4 Aug. 2006. Web.

"Mató a su novia y a su mejor amigo por Pablo Escobar: Ahora cuenta su historia." *americaeconomia.com.* 27 Sept. 2013. http://www.americaeconomia.com/politica-sociedad/politica/mato-su-novia-y-su-mejor-amigo-por-pablo-escobar-ahora-cuenta-su-historia. Web.

Mayer, Virginia. "Soy una rata: Popeye." *Kienyke.com.* 21 Aug. 2012. https://www.kienyke.com/historias/soy-una-rata. Web.

McEnally, M. R., and L. de Chernatony. "The Evolving Nature of Branding: Consumer and Managerial Considerations." *Academy of Marketing Science Review* 2 (1999): no pagination. Web.

McGowan, Todd. *End of Dissatisfaction? Jacques Lacan and the Emerging Society of Enjoyment.* Albany: State U of New York P, 2004.

McNamara, Thomas E. "Déjà Vu in Mexico." *New York Times.* 12 Aug. 2009. Web.

"'Medellín no es la que muestra Netflix': Alcalde Federico Gutiérrez." *elespectador.com.* 30 Nov. 2017. Web.

Meertens, Donny. "Victims and Survivors of War in Colombia: Three Views of Gender Relations." In *Violence in Colombia 1990–2000: Waging War and Negotiating Peace*, ed. Charles Berquist, Ricardo Peñaranda, and Gonzalo G. Sánchez Wilmington, 151–71. Wilmington, Del.: Scholarly Resources, 2001.

Mermelstein, Max. *The Man Who Made It Snow.* New York: Simon & Schuster, 1990.

Mesa, Gilmer. *La cuadra.* Bogotá: Literatura Random House, 2016.

Minow, Nell. *Loving Pablo* (review). *rogerebert.com.* 5 Oct. 2018. Web.

Mollison, James, with Rainbow Nelson. *The Memory of Pablo Escobar.* London: Chris Boot, 2007.

Molloy, Silvia. "Latin America in the U.S. Imaginary: Postcolonialism, Translation, and the Magic Realist Imperative." In *Ideologies of Hispanism*, ed. Mabel Moraña, 189–201. Nashville: Vanderbilt UP, 2005.

"Monólogos de la vagina." *semana.com.co.* July 29, 2006. Web.

Mora Meléndez, Fernando. "Lapidario." universocentro.com 64 (April 2015) https://www.universocentro.com/NUMERO64/Lapidario.aspx.

Moraña, Mabel. "El boom del subaltern." In *Teorías sin disciplina: Latinoamericanismo, poscolonialidad y globalización en debate*, ed. Santiago Castro-Gómez and Eduardo Mendieta, 233–44. México: U of San Francisco, 1998.

Morello, Henry James. "Voiceless Victims in *Sin tetas no hay paraíso.*" *CLCWeb: Comparative Literature and Culture* 19.4 (2017): no pagination.

Moreno, Katherine S. "Rosario Tijeras es una mezcla de Hitler y Marilyn Monroe." *ya.com.* 10 Sept. 2004. http://noticias.ya.com. Web.

Morgan, Nick. "Ese oscuro objeto del deseo: Raza, clase, género y la ideología de lo bello en Colombia." In *Pasarela paralela: Scenarios de la estética y el poder en los reinados de belleza*, ed. Chloe Rutter-Jensen, 44–57. Bogotá: Editorial Pontificia Universidad Javeriana, 2005.

———. "Sex, Soap, and Society: *Telenovela noir* in Alvaro Uribe's Colombia." *Journal of Iberian and Latin American Studies* 19.1 (2013): 53–76.

Morin, R. G. "Telenovela Watch: Surprise Hit *La viuda negra.*" welovesoaps.net. 3 May 2014. https://www.welovesoaps.net/2014/05/surprise-hit-la-viuda-negra-final.html. Web.

Moss, Donald. *Thirteen Ways of Looking at a Man: Psychoanalysis and Masculinity.* London: Routledge, 2012.

Mujeres asesinas. (Argentina) Dir. Daniel Barone. Prod. Pol-ka Producciones, 2005.

Mulvey, Laura. *Fetishism and Curiosity (Perspectives).* Bloomington: Indiana UP, 1996.

Murcia Valdés, Valeria. "Recuerdos a la vuelta de la esquina." *elcolombiano.com.* 15 Sept. 2018. Web.

Naef, Patrick James. "Narco-heritage and the Touristification of the Drug Lord Pablo Escobar in Medellín, Colombia." *Journal of Anthropological Research* 74.4 (2018): 485–502.

Narcos. Dir. José Padilha. United States, Colombia. Prod. Gaumont International Television for Netflix, 2015. DVD.

"Narcotraficantes que son marca registrada." *heraldodemexico.com.mx*. 7 Nov. 2017. Web.

Natterer, Kathrin. "Research Note: Nostalgia as the Future for Branding Entertainment Media? The Consumption of Personal and Historical Nostalgic Films and Its Effects." In *Handbook of Media Branding*, ed. G. Siegert et al., 199–214. Switzerland: Springer International, 2015.

Nguyen, Hanh. "*Cocaine Godmother* Review: Brownface Casting is Just One of Many Insults in This Schlocky *Narcos* Knockoff." *indiewire.com*. 20 Jan. 2018. Web.

"Niegan 'Pablo Escobar' como marca." *telemundoareadelabahia.com*. 11 Aug. 2015. Web.

Nolasco, Stephanie. "Cocaine Godmother's Son Claims 'Cartel Crew' Doesn't Glorify Criminal Lifestyle: 'We're Trying to Move on with Our Lives.'" *foxnews.com*. 5 Jan. 2019. Web.

Nullvalue. "Muerto el Chopo, jefe military del cartel." *eltiempo.com.co*. 20 Mar. 1993. Web.

Núñez-González, Marco Alejandro. "Masculinidades en la narcocultura: El machismo, los buchones, y los mangueras." *Revista Conjeturas Sociológicas* 40.5 (2017): 109–26.

———. Masculinidades y condición de clase en la narcocultura: Los "pesados" y los "tacuaches." *Intersticios: Revista Sociológica de Pensamiento Crítico* 12.1 (2018): 81–96.

Ochoa, Luis Noé. "¿Qué les pasa a las mujeres?" *eltiempo.com.co*. 22 May 2004. Web.

Ochoa Hoyos, Ana María. "Body Image: Differences and Similarities between Colombian and Dutch Teenagers." *Perspectivas en nutrición humana* 9.2 (2007): 109–22.

"Ocho capitales ya prohíben el parrillero en moto para combatir delitos." *eltiempo.com.co*. 22 Sept. 2016. Web.

Ortiz, María Paulina. "Relación amorosa de Virginia Vallejo con Pablo Escobar acabó con su vida profesional." *eltiempo.com.co*. July 20, 2006. Web.

Ortiz Sarmiento, Carlos Miguel. "El sicariato en Medellín: Entre la violencia política y el crimen organizado." *Análisis Político* 14 (1991): 60–73.

Osorio, Óscar. *La novela del narcotráfico en Colombia*. Cali: Universidad del Valle, 2014.

———. *La Virgen de los sicarios y la novela del sicario en Colombia*. Cali: Secretaría de Cultura del Valle del Cauca, 2013.

Osorio Cinfuentes, Uber de Jesús. "Una Aproximación al fenómeno de los jóvenes en el Sicariato en la ciudad de Pereira." Ph.D. dissertation, Universidad Tecnológica de Pereira, 2010: http://repositorio.utp.edu.co/dspace/handle/11059/1931. Web.

Ospina, Clara Elvira. "Virginia Vallejo denuncia a magnates y narcopresidentes." *Noticias RCN* with Clara Elvira Ospina, Debate with Edgar Tellez, Poncho Rentería, Alfonso Gómez Méndez and Jorge Armando Otálora. Online video clip. YouTube. 21 Dec. 2009. Web. 12 Jan. 2012.

"Pablo Escobar protagoniza comercial en Chile." *kienyke.com*. 9 June 2013. http://www.kienyke.com/confidencias/el-patron-del-escandalo/. Web.

"Pablo Escobar Refuses to Go Away." *semana.com.co*. 3 Dec. 2008. Web.

Pablo's Hippos. Dir. Lawrence Elman and Antonio von Hildebrand. United Kingdom, Colombia. Prod. Amber Entertainment/Drive Thru Pictures, 2011. DVD.

Páez, Angel. "Ni triste ni cándida: La historia del Capo Escobar." LaRepública.pe. 10 Mar. 2013. https://larepublica.pe/archivo/696607-pablo-escobar-ni-triste-ni-candida-la-historia-del-capo/. Web.

Palaversich, Diana. "La seducción de las mafias: La figura del narcotraficante en la narcotelenovela colombiana." *Hispanófila* 173 (2015): 349–64.

———. "The Politics of Drug Trafficking in Mexican and Mexico-related Narconovelas." *Aztlán* 2 (2006): 85–110.

Paraíso travel. Dir. Simón Brand. Prod. Paraíso Producciones, 2008. DVD.

Pearson, Patricia. *When She Was Bad: Violent Women and the Myth of Innocence*. New York: Viking, 1997.

Pecados de mi padre. Dir. Nicolás Entel. Prod. Red Creek, 2009. DVD.

Penfold-Mounce, Ruth. *Celebrity Culture and Crime: The Joy of Transgression*. New York: Palgrave Macmillan, 2009.

Pérez-Reverte, Arturo. "Mi amigo el narco." Blog. 9 Sept. 2001. http://arturoperez-reverte.blogspot.com/2011/01/mi-amigo-el-narco.html. Web.

Perramond, Eric P. "Desert Traffic: The Dynamics of the Drug Trade in Northwestern Mexico." In *Dangerous Harvest: Drug Plants and the Transformation of Indigenous Landscapes*, ed. Michael K. Steinberg, Joseph J. Hobbs, Kent Mathewson, 209–17. New York: Oxford UP, 2004.

"Personajes del año: El camaleón." *elespectador.com*. 8 Dec. 2012. Web.

Pettergrew, John. *Brutes in Suits: Male Sensibility in America, 1890–1920*. Baltimore, Md.: Johns Hopkins UP, 2007.

"Plantean ajustar temática de telenovelas por el mensaje negativo que transmiten." *eltiempo.com.co*. 20 Nov. 2009. Web.

Pobutsky, Aldona Bialowas. "Deleitar denunciando: La narco telenovela de Gustavo Bolívar *Sin tetas no hay paraíso* marca el pulso de la sociedad colombiana." *Espéculo* (Nov. 2010): no pagination.

———. "Going Down Narco Memory Lane: Pablo Escobar in the Visual Media." In *Territories of Conflict: Traversing Cultural Studies in Colombia*, ed. Alejandro Herrero-Olaizola, Chloe Rutter-Jensen, and Andrea Fanta, 282–93. New York: Rochester UP, 2017.

———. "In Bed with a Narco: Pablo Escobar and Wílber Varela Through the Lens of 'Trophy Women.'" *Hispanófila* 180 (2017): 155–71.

———. "Narco Caudillos and Pablo Escobar in José Libardo Porras's *Happy Birthday, Capo*." *Revista Canadiense de los Estudios Hispánicos*. Volume on "Tráfico y Producción Cultural" 38.1 (2013): 167–92.

———. "Narco Spectacle: *El cartel de los sapos* and how TV Makes Bad Capos Fun." Special volume on Narcocultura *Hispanic Journal* 36.2 (2014): 49–66.

———. "Peddling Pablo: Escobar Is Back; Cultural Renaissance of the Capo." *Hispania* 96.4 (2013): 684–99.

———. "¿Qué destino le espera a Pablo Escobar? Un viaje posmoderno por la historia del Capo." *Letras Hispanas* 13 (2017): 51–65.

———. "Towards the Latin American Action Heroine: The Case of Jorge Franco Ramos's *Rosario Tijeras*." *Studies in Latin American Popular Culture* 24 (2005): 17–35.

"Popeye: Perfil de un sicario que mató con su mano a más de 250 personas." *revistadonjuan.com*. 16 Sept. 2009. Web.

"¡Popeye sale de la cárcel!" *semana.com.co*. 14 Sept. 2013. Web.

Posner, Gerald. *Miami Babylon: Crime, Wealth, and Power—A Dispatch from the Beach*. New York: Simon & Schuster, 2009.

Presdee, Mike. *Cultural Criminology and the Carnival of Crime*. London: Routledge, 2000.

"Prohibe Bogotá pasajero hombre en motocicletas." *diario.mx.internacional*. 25 Jan. 2018. Web.

"Protestan contra el 'Canal RCN' por pregunta sobre las pereiranas en programa de concurso." *eltiempo.com.co*. 23 Feb. 2008. Web.

Quevedo, Norbey H. "Cristina Palacio, productora de TV: La dama del 'rating.'" *elspectador.com*. 21 Nov. 2009. Web.

Rak, Julie. "Pop Life: An Introduction." *Canadian Review of American Studies* 38.3 (2008): 325–31.

Ramírez-Pimienta, Juan Carlos. "Sicarias, buchonas y jefas: Perfiles de la mujer en el narcocorrido." *Colorado Review of Hispanic Studies* 8.9 (2010): 327–52.

Ramírez-Pimienta, Juan Carlos, and María Socorro Tabuenca Córdoba. *Camelia la Texana y otras mujeres de la narcocultura*. Sinaloa: Universidad Autónoma de Sinaloa, 2016.

Rangel, Jesús. "El Señor de los cielos y Reina del Sur, otras solicitudes de marca." *milenio.com*. 28 Jan. 2016. Web.

Rashotte, Ryan. *Narco Cinema: Sex, Drugs and Banda Music in Mexico's B-Filography*. New York: Palgrave Macmillan, 2015.

Ravello, Renato. "Rosario Tijeras . . ." *lajornada.com*. 10 Sept. 2004. http://www.jorge-franco.com /lajornadademexico01.txt. Web.

Redmond, Sean. "Intimate Fame Everywhere." In *Framing Celebrity: New Directions in Celebrity Culture*, ed. Su Holmes and Sean Redmond, 27–43. London: Routledge, 2006.

Renjel Encinas, Daniela. "Gustavo Bolívar: El hombre de las narcotelenovelas." *Mitologías Hoy* 14 (2016): 93–111.

Restrepo, Aura Rocío. *Ya no quiero callar: Mi historia como testigo, amante y confidente de Gilberto Rodríguez Orejuela*. Bogotá: Planeta, 2014.

Restrepo, Vanesa. "Sicariato, un mal que sigue vivo en Medellín." *elcolombiano.com*. 25 Aug. 2017. Web.

Riaño-Alcalá, Pilar. *Dwellers of Memory: Youth and Violence in Medellín, Colombia*. New Brunswick: Transaction, 2006.

Rincón, Omar. "Amamos a Pablo, odiamos a los politicos: Las repercusiones de Escobar, el Patrón del mal." *Nueva Sociedad* 255 (Jan.–Feb. 2015): 94–105.

———. "El narco del 'rating': El otro lado." *eltiempo.com.co*. 28 Sept. 2014. Web.

———. "Narco.estética y narco.cultura en Narco.lombia." *Nueva sociedad* 222 (July–Aug. 2009): 147–63.

———. "Nuevas narrativas televisivas: Relajar, entretener, contar, ciudadanizar, experimentar." *Comunicar* 36.18 (2011): 43–50.

———. "Sin tetas no hay televisión." *eltiempo.com.co*. 26 Aug. 2006. Web.

Rivera, Luz Maria. "El Universal, México." *eluniversal.com*. 15 Dec. 2004. http://jorge-franco.com/el-universal-mexico/. Web.

Robbins, Seth. "Medellín Gets Tough with Deadly Colombian 'Sicarios' on Motorcycles." *diálogo-américas.com*. 21 Jan. 2013. https://dialogo-americas.com/en/articles/medellin-gets-tough-deadly-colombian-sicarios-motorcycles. Web.

Rochy, Madame. *¿Amores prepago? Nuevos relatos de reinas, modelos y de algunas prepago* . . . Bogota: Oveja Negra, 2009.

Rocío Restrepo, Aura. *Ya no quiero callar: Mi historia como testigo, amante y confidente de Gilberto Rodríguez Orejuela*. Bogotá: Editorial Planeta Colombiana S.A., 2014.

Rodrigo D: No futuro. Dir. Víctor Gaviria. Prod. Colombia: Compañía de Fomento Cinematográfico, Focine, 1990. DVD.

Rodríguez Dalvard, Dominique. "Alonso Salazar habla sobre el mito de Pablo Escobar." *eltiempo.com.co*. July 7, 2012. Web.

Roldán, Mary. *Blood and Fire: La Violencia in Antiquia, Colombia, 1946–1953*. Durham, N.C.: Duke UP, 2002.

———. "Colombia: Cocaine and the 'Miracle' of Modernity in Medellín." In *Cocaine, Global Histories*, ed. Paul Gootenberg, 165–82. London: Routledge, 1999.

Romero, Angie. "Meet the Musical Minds Behind 'Narcos,' Netflix's New Pablo Escobar Series." *billboard.com*. 11 Sept. 2015. https://www.billboard.com/articles/columns/latin/6693172/narcos-netflix-music-rodrigo-amarante-pedro-bromfman. Web.

Romero, Simon. "Colombian Leader Disputes Claim of Tie to Cocaine Kingpin." *New York Times*. 3 Oct. 2007. Web.

Romney, Lee. "Newsman at Risk in Colombia Gets Help." *Los Angeles Times*. 2 Oct. 2006. http://articles.latimes.com/2006/oct/02/local/me-colombian2. Web.

Ronquillo, Víctor. *La Reina del Pacífico y otras mujeres del narco*. Mexico, D.F.: Planeta, 2008.

"Rosario, cámara, acción." *semana.com.co*. 22 Feb. 2004. Web.

Rosario Tijeras. (television series) Dir. Carlos Gaviria. Prod. RCN TV, 2010. DVD.

Rosario Tijeras. Dir. Emilio Maillé. Prod. Colombia, Mexico, Spain, Brazil: Dulce Compañía, FIDECINE, 2005. DVD.

Rosario Tijeras (Mexican TV series). Dir. Chavas Cartas and Alejandro Lozano. Prod. Teleset for Sony Pictures and TV Azteca, 2016. DVD.

Rose, Jacqueline. *Feminine Sexuality: Jacques Lacan and the école freudienne*. New York: W. W. Norton, 1985.

———. *On Not Being Able to Sleep: Psychoanalysis and the Modern World*. Princeton, N.J.: Princeton UP, 2003.

Rosen, Jill. "Super Bowl Ads: Stories Beat Sex and Humor, Johns Hopkins Researcher Finds." In *The Hub: News Center for Johns Hopkins*. 31 Jan. 2014, https://hub.jhu.edu/2014/01/31/super-bowl-ads/. Web.

Rueda, María Isabela. "Cómo historiador de la vida de Escobar, ¿cree en la versión de Virginia Vallejo?" *semana.com.co*. 29 July 2006. Web.

Rutter-Jensen, Chloe. "Introduction." *Pasarela paralela: Scenarios de la estética y el poder en los reinados de belleza*, ed. Chloe Rutter-Jensen, 6–11. Bogotá: Editorial Pontificia Universidad Javeriana, 2005.

Salazar, Hernando. "Polémica por documental de hijo de Escobar." BBC Mundo. *bbc.com*. 15 Dec. 2009. Web.

Salazar, J. Alonso. *Born to Die in Medellín*. Trans. Nick Caistor. London: Latin America Bureau, 1990.

———. *La parábola de Pablo: Auge y caída de un gran capo del narcotráfico*. Bogotá: Planeta, 2001.

———. *Mujeres de fuego*. Medellín: Corporación Región, 1993.

———. *No nacimos pa' semilla: La cultura de las bandas juveniles de Medellín*. Bogotá: CINEP, 1990.

———. Interview. "Pablo Escobar fue producto de la sociedad, no se cayó del cielo." *elespectador.com*. 5 Mar. 2013. Web.

Salazar, J. Alonso, and Ana María Jaramillo. *Medellín: Las subculturas del narcotráfico*. Medellín: CINEP, 1992.

Saldarriaga, John. "La Reina de la Cocaina murió como vivió: A bala." *elpaís.com.co*. 10 Sept. 2012. Web.

———. "Obras donadas por Botero: 400." *elcolombiano.com*. 22 Nov. 2009. Web.

Saldarriaga, León Jairo. "Escobar, en terrenos del mito." *elcolombiano.com*. Serie: "Diez años de la fuga de la Catedral." 20 July 2007. http://www.elcolombiano.com/proyectos/ serieselcolombiano/textos/narcotrafico/julio20/carteles.htm. Web.

Sánchez, José F. "¿Quién le teme a Virginia Vallejo?" *La Nueva Cuba*. 5 Sept. 2006. http:// www.lanuevacuba.com/nuevacuba/notic-06-09-507.htm. Web.

Santamaría Gómez, Arturo, ed. *Las jefas del narco: El ascenso de las mujeres en el crimen organizado*. México, D.F.: Grijalbo, 2012.

Schager, Nick. "Cocaine Cowboys." *slantmagazine.com*. 13 Oct. 2006. http://www.slant-magazine.com/film/review/cocaine-cowboys. Web.

Scherer García, Julio. *La Reina del Pacífico*. México, D.F.: Grijalbo, 2008.

"Searching for the Godmother of Crime." *Maxim*. 23 June 2008. https://www.maxim. com/maxim-man/searching-godmother-crime. Web.

Segura Bonnet, Camila. "Kinismo y melodrama en *La virgen de los sicarios* y *Rosario Tijeras*." *Estudios Colombianos* 14 (2004): 111–36.

Serrano Cadena, Rosso José, with Santiago Gamboa. *Jaque mate: De cómo la policía le ganó la partida a "El Ajedrecista" y a los carteles del narcotráfico*. Bogotá: Norma, 1999.

Sin senos sí hay paraíso. (alternative title: *Sin tetas sí hay paraíso*). Dir. Diego Mejía et al. Prod. Fox Telecolombia and Telemundo Studios, 2016. DVD.

Sin tetas no hay paraíso. Dir. Luis Alberto Restrepo. Prod. Caracol TV, 2006. DVD.

Skar, Stacey Alba. "El narcotráfico y lo femenino en el cine colombiano internacional: *Rosario Tijeras y María llena eres de gracia*." *Alpha* 25 (2007): 115–31.

Smitten, Richard. *The Godmother: The True Story of the Hunt for the Most Bloodthirsty Female Criminal of Our Time*. New York: Pocket, 1990.

Solano Peña, Aldemar. *La fama de las pereiranas*. Pereira: Sans Editores, 2015.

Sontag, Susan. "Notes on 'Camp.'" http://www9.georgetown.edu/faculty/irvinem/theory/sontag-notesoncamp-1964.html. Web.

Soñar no cuesta nada. Dir. Rodrigo Triana. Prod. Colombia, Argentina, CMO Producciones, 2006.

Soto, Martha. *La Viuda Negra*. Bogotá: Intermedio, 2013.

Strong, Simon. *Whitewash: Pablo Escobar and the Cocaine Wars*. London: Pan, 1995.

Surovell, Hariette. "Queenpins of the Cali Cartel." *Exquisite Corpse* 4 (Apr./May 2000): http://www.corpse.org/archives/issue_4/broken_news/surovel.htm. Web.

Sutta, David. "El hombre que capturó a la reina de la cocaina de Miami." *elnuevoherald. com.* 5 Oct. 2012. Web.

Taussig, Michael. *Beauty and the Beast.* Chicago: U of Chicago P, 2012.

Temelli, Yasmin. "Vivir el momento, morir al instante: El sicario como figura efímera en la narrativa colombiana." *Romance Notes* 57.2 (2017): 245–54.

"'The New York Times' vuelve a citar texto que dice que Uribe era 'amigo cercano' de Pablo Escobar." *semana.com.co.* 3 Oct. 2007. Web.

Tomasulo, Frank P. "'I'll See It When I Believe It': Rodney King and the Prison-House of Video." In *The Persistence of History: Cinema, Television, and the Modern Event,* ed. Vivian Sobchack, 69–90. London: Routledge, 1996.

Valasco, Ximena. "Extravagancias mafiosas hechas polvo." *elcolombiano.com.* 20 Feb. 2010. Web.

Vallejo, Fernando. *La virgen de los sicarios.* Bogotá: Alfaguara, 1994.

———. *Our Lady of the Assassins.* Trans. Paul Hammond. London: Serpent's Tail, 2001.

Vallejo, Virginia. *Amando a Pablo, Odiando a Escobar.* México: Random House, 2007.

Vanden Berghe, K. "¿Quién mató a Rosario Tijeras? Narco y culpa." *Bulletin of Spanish Studies* 93.1 (2015): 133–52.

Vásquez, Juan Gabriel. *El ruido de las cosas al caer.* Madrid: Alfaguara, 2011.

Velásquez, Jhon Jairo. *Sobreviviendo a Pablo Escobar: "Popeye" el sicario, 23 años y 3 meses de cárcel.* Bogotá: Ediciones DIPON, 2015.

Vengoechea, Alejandra de. "El misionero enviado de Dios y el finquero de Colombia." In *Los tele-presidentes: Cerca del pueblo, lejos de la democracia,* ed. Omar Rincón, 135–48. Bogotá: Centro de Competencia en Comunicación para América Latina, 2008.

Villoria Nolla, Maite. "(Sub)culturas y narrativas: (Re)presentación del sicariato en *La virgen de los sicarios*." *Cuadernos de Literatura* 8.15 (2002): 106–14.

Von der Walde, Erna. "La novela de sicarios y la violencia en Colombia." *Iberoamericana* 1.3 (2001): 27–40.

Waldmann, Peter. "Is There a Culture of Violence in Colombia?" *International Journal of Conflict and Violence* 1.1 (2007): 61–75.

Wallace, Arturo. "La relación bipolar de Colombia con Pablo Escobar." *bbc.com.* 2 Dec. 2013. Web.

Wielde Heidelberg, Beth A. "Managing Ghosts: Exploring Local Government Involvement in Dark Tourism." *Journal of Heritage Tourism* 10.1 (2015): 74–90.

White, Hayden. "Postmodernism and Historiography." Special Public Opening Symposium. 12 Nov. 2009. http://www.ritsumei.ac.jp. Web.

Wills Fontecha, Maritza Neila. *Jhon Jairo Velásquez: Mi vida como sicario de Pablo Escobar.* Nashville: HarperCollins Español, 2016.

Wolf, Eric R., and Edward C. Hansen. "Caudillo Politics: A Structural Analysis." *Comparative Studies in Society and History* 9.2 (1967): 168–79.

Yagoub, Mimi. "Narco-Aesthetics: How Colombia's Drug Trade Constructed Female 'Beauty.'" *Colombia Reports.* 5 Feb. 2014. http://colombiareports.com/narco-aesthetics-colombias-drug-trade-constructed-female-beauty/. Web.

Yarce, Elizabeth. "Los carteles de la droga tienen nuevos 'señores.'" *elcolombiano.com*. Serie: "Diez años de la fuga de la Catedral." 3 Dec. 2003. Web.

———. "Pablo y otros cuentos de la Catedral." *elcolombiano.com*. Serie: "Diez años de la fuga de la Catedral." 3 Dec. 2003. Web.

Index

and violence, 29–30, 244, 252nn2,3,4
and women in narco, 226–27
Miami, 3, 76, 95, 123
and drug trafficking, 11, 13, 136, 144, 148,
152–57, 159–60, 237 (see also *Cocaine
Cowboys I and II*)
Minuto de Dios (television program). *See*
García Herreros, Rafael (Father)
Mónaco building (Escobar's property), 244,
245–47. *See also* Brand: and place (travel);
Gutiérrez, Federico
Moura, Wagner (as Pablo Escobar), 7, 233, 234,
241, 244. See also *Narcos*
Mugre (alias of Luis Carlos Aguilar Gallego),
76. *See also* Escobar, Pablo: and *sicarios*
Mujeres asesinas (series), 205
Mujeres de fuego (book), 209, 210. *See also*
Salazar, Alonso: and women in war
Muñoz Mosquera, Brances (alias Tyson), 74,
84, 91, 256n8. *See also* Escobar, Pablo: and
sicarios
Muñoz Mosquera, Dandenys (alias La Kika/La
Quica), 84, 256n8. *See also* Escobar, Pablo:
and *sicarios*

Narco
and aesthetics, 6, 33, 54–62, 212, 252n7 (*see
also* Plastic surgery)
and architecture, 3, 5, 14, 17, 56–57
and bildungsroman (*see* Bildungsroman)
and caudillismo (*see* Caudillo: and narco
caudillismo)
and consumerism (*see* Consumerism)
and excess (society of enjoyment), 55–57,
76, 230
and female body (alterations), 214, 58–60,
122, 126, 139, 142, *171*, 176, 179–81, 184, 186,
191–92, 214–15, 220 (*see also* Breasts)
and lifestyle, 17, 54–57, 59, 108, 155, 162, 164,
174, 177, 240, 244, 254n27
and memoirs, 4, 15, 17, 41, 84, 95–99, 124–29,
164, 236, 257n3, 258n6
and mythology (*see* Criminal (narco) mythology; Escobar, Pablo: and myth)
and nostalgia, 24, 29, 32–38, 67, 186
and philosophy (as in *Escobar, patron del
mal*), 230–31, 244

and tours (*see Dark Tourist*; Hacienda
Nápoles; La Catedral: and tourism;
Mónaco building (Escobar's property);
Popeye: and dark tourism in Medellín)
Narcos (series), 231–35
Neoliberalism, 53, 216, 255n33
New Historicism, 18, 97, 136, 170
North Valley Cartel, 4, 68, 253n6, 258n6,
262n23, 263n3
and Andrés López López, 13
Nostalgia. *See* Boym, Svetlana; Narco: and
nostalgia

Ochoa family, 89, 154, 159, 198
Oedipus complex (in Pablo Escobar), 78,
79, 82, 85, 93. *See also* Escobar, Pablo: and
mother
Office of Envigado, 202, 253n6, 263n7, 264n7.
See also Don Berna
*Our Lady of the Assassins (La Virgen de los
sicarios)*, 12, 200, 201, 217. See also *Sicario*
Outlaw. *See* Archetypes in branding

Pablo's Hippos (documentary), 251n1. *See
also* Escobar, Pablo: and nature
Paisa (of Antioquia), 154, 199, 239, 125
and mother figure, 34, 63
and stereotyping, 10, 35, 42, 261
Paraíso Travel (film), 219
Parody. *See* Chile: and Escobar parody;
Escobar, Pablo: and parody
Parra, Andrés (as Pablo Escobar), 43, 65,
231, 238
Pastrana, Andrés, 90
Patriarchy, 77, 103, 122, 177, 209, 210, 235,
255n33, 257n3, 264n10
Patrón del Pan (variety show with Cristián
Henríquez). *See* Chile: and Escobar
parody
Pecados de mi padre (documentary), 47–49.
See also Escobar, Juan Pablo
Pepes (Perseguidos por Pablo Escobar), 104,
241, 252n6
Pereira, 169, 182, 184, 193, 262n15
and *sicarios*, 154, 183, 199–200, 217, 263n3
and stereotyping women, 175, 178, 192–96
Pérez-Reverte, Arturo, 177, 260n6

ALDONA BIALOWAS POBUTSKY is professor of Spanish in the Department of Modern Languages and Literatures at Oakland University.

Telling Migrant Stories: Latin American Diaspora in Documentary Film, edited by Esteban E. Loustaunau and Lauren E. Shaw (2018; paperback edition, 2021)

Mestizo Modernity: Race, Technology, and the Body in Postrevolutionary Mexico, by David S. Dalton (2018; first paperback edition, 2021)

The Insubordination of Photography: Documentary Practices under Chile's Dictatorship, by Ángeles Donoso Macaya (2020; first paperback edition, 2023)

Digital Humanities in Latin America, edited by Héctor Fernández L'Hoeste and Juan Carlos Rodríguez (2020; first paperback edition, 2023)

Pablo Escobar and Colombian Narcoculture, by Aldona Bialowas Pobutsky (2020; first paperback edition, 2025)

The New Brazilian Mediascape: Television Production in the Digital Streaming Age, by Eli Lee Carter (2020; first paperback edition, 2025)

Univision, Telemundo, and the Rise of Spanish-Language Television in the United States, by Craig Allen (2020; first paperback edition, 2023)

Cuba's Digital Revolution: Citizen Innovation and State Policy, edited by Ted A. Henken and Sara Garcia Santamaria (2021; first paperback edition, 2022)

Afro-Latinx Digital Connections, edited by Eduard Arriaga and Andrés Villar (2021)

The Lost Cinema of Mexico: From Lucha Libre to Cine Familiar and Other Churros, edited by Olivia Cosentino and Brian Price (2022)

Neo-Authoritarian Masculinity in Brazilian Crime Film, by Jeremy Lehnen (2022)

The Rise of Central American Film in the Twenty-First Century, edited by Mauricio Espinoza and Jared List (2023)

Internet, Humor, and Nation in Latin America, edited by Héctor Fernández L'Hoeste and Juan Poblete (2024)

Tropical Time Machines: Science Fiction in the Contemporary Hispanic Caribbean, by Emily A. Maguire (2024)

Digital Satire in Latin America: Online Video Humor as Hybrid Alternative Media, by Paul Alonso (2024)

Periodicals in Latin America: Interdisciplinary Approaches to Serialized Print Culture, edited by Maria Chiara D'Argenio and Claire Lindsay (2025)

www.ingramcontent.com/pod-product-compliance
Lightning Source LLC
Chambersburg PA
CBHW020829270326
41928CB00006B/469